SUBVERSIVE ITINERARY

The Thought of Gad Horowitz

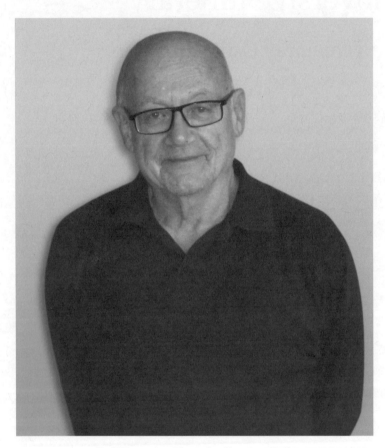
Gad Horowitz. Photo by Shannon Bell.

Subversive Itinerary

The Thought of Gad Horowitz

EDITED BY SHANNON BELL
AND peter kulchyski

UNIVERSITY OF TORONTO PRESS
Toronto Buffalo London

© University of Toronto Press 2013
Toronto Buffalo London
www.utppublishing.com
Printed in Canada

ISBN 978-1-4426-4532-5

Printed on acid-free, 100% post-consumer recycled paper with
vegetable-based inks.

Library and Archives Canada Cataloguing in Publication

Subversive itinerary : the thought of Gad Horowitz/edited by Shannon Bell
and Peter Kulchyski.

Includes bibliographical references.
ISBN 978-1-4426-4532-5

1. Horowitz, Gad, 1936–.   2. Canada – Politics and government.   3. Political
science – Canada.   I. Bell, Shannon, 1955–.   II. Kulchyski, Peter Keith, 1959–

JL65.S82 2013   320.971   C2013-900424-6

University of Toronto Press acknowledges the financial assistance to its
publishing program of the Canada Council for the Arts and the Ontario
Arts Council.

University of Toronto Press acknowledges the financial support of the
Government of Canada through the Canada Book Fund for its publishing
activities.

Contents

Introduction   ix
SHANNON BELL AND peter kulchyski

Part One: Life and Times

1 On Intellectual Life, Politics, and Psychoanalysis: A Conversation
   with Gad Horowitz (2003)   3
   COLIN J. CAMPBELL

2 The Life and Times of Horowitz the Canadianist   15
   NELSON WISEMAN

3 The Odd Couple of Canadian Intellectual History   42
   EDWARD G. ANDREW

4 Between Pause and Play: Conveying the Democratic Spirit   54
   JASON ROVITO

Part Two: Fragment Theory

5 The Political Culture of English Canada   73
   IAN ANGUS

6 Canada's Regional Fragments   92
   NELSON WISEMAN

7 Restoration, Not Renovation: A Fresh Start for Hartz-Horowitz   113
ROBERT MEYNELL

Part Three: Spirit and Power

8 Gad ben Rachel ve Aharon: *Parrhesiastes*   133
SHANNON BELL

9 What's Involved in Involution? A Psycho-Poetics of Regression: Freud–Horowitz–Celan   156
MICHAEL MARDER

10 The Sexed Body of the Woman-(M)Other: Irigaray and Marcuse on the Intersection of Gender and Ethical Intersubjectivity   174
VICTORIA TAHMASEBI

11 The Spark of Philosophy: Hartz-Horowitz and Theories of Religion   194
COLIN J. CAMPBELL

Part Four: Political Philosophy

12 Transcendental Liberalism and the Politics of Representation: Possessive Individualism Revisited   215
SEAN SARAKA

13 From the Narcissism of Small Differences to the Vertigo of Endless Possibilities: Horowitz among the Levinasians   237
OONA EISENSTADT

14 Adorno and Emptiness   256
ASHER HOROWITZ

15 horowitz dances with wolves: inquiries pursuant to the thought of gad horowitz   279
peter kulchyski

Part Five: Horowitz in His Own Words

emmanuel, Robert   293
GAD HOROWITZ

Bringing Bataille to Justice   303
GAD HOROWITZ

An Essay on the Altruism of Nature   316
GAD HOROWITZ

Bibliography   329
Contributors   351

Introduction

SHANNON BELL AND peter kulchyski

The process we label "self" is discontinuous. It renews itself from moment to moment. Almost non-metaphorically, you can say, and it has been said, that there is death every moment, that there is a gap or pause between this moment of life and the next, this moment of self and the next.

In this gap or pause one can appreciate the discontinuity of life and the possibility that this offers for liberation from the burden of insensate habit that ordinarily obfuscates the possibilities of fundamental change from one moment to the next. The speedier life gets, the more intense the illusion becomes of the continuity of self speeding through time.

Gad Horowitz[1]

Gad Horowitz has remained prominent among Canadian intellectuals and political theorists for close to fifty years. Horowitz, now in his mid-seventies, is most widely recognized for his early work – *Canadian Labour and Politics*, particularly his landmark essay "Conservatism, Liberalism, and Socialism in Canada: An Interpretation" (CLS), which planted intellectual dynamite under burgeoning Canadian political culture. What is perhaps less commonly known is Horowitz's subsequent work on Freud, Marcuse and psychoanalysis, modern political thought, Buddhism, general semantics, continental theory and post-structuralism.

Gad's intellectual trajectory reflects his Buddhist and post-structuralist understanding of self as set out above – that a self is discontinuous and never coming to rest. What cements Horowitz's diverse works together is that they are continuously and consistently subversive. Gad brings to political theory an incisiveness of critical thinking that originates not from a fixed position but rather from a series of shifting locations: Canadian political culture, psychoanalysis, post-structuralism, Buddhism, Judaic scholarship, and general semantics. Horowitz says "everything he has in mind"[2] with unnerving candour and undiluted courage. As Horowitz says in his interview with Colin Campbell in chapter 1, "My books, writing, and teaching make a statement about my attitude to academia, and that is the importance of eclecticism: the importance of being interested in and doing work in many fields, and not just one field."

The notion of itinerary is used to mark the movement that takes place through the course of an intellectual's lifespan: the itinerary marks stops, resting points that situate the inevitably fluid movement of thought. Within Horowitz's writings, the itinerary is a winding path that starts with an analysis of Canadian political culture and the hidden promise it bears to both left and right on the political spectrum, that apparently leaves these concerns or submerges them in a more philosophical concern with political problems related to repression and desire, and that twists again to deploy the analysis of a structure of power and thought to the ethical implications of contemporary continental theory.

What Horowitz unleashes on each of the fields or locations at which he stops is a radical critique of hegemonic liberalism and its inherent repressiveness. This critique begins with the "Hartz-Horowitz" view of the relation between toryism and socialism and the role of Canadian political culture as a (partial) escape from monolithic American liberalism. The second phase leaves the Canadian field, picks up Marcuse's distinction between basic (necessary) repression and surplus repression and carries it through the rest of the itinerary, beginning with the analysis of the market/hive in *Everywhere They Are in Chains* all the way to the discussion of Levinas/Derrida in *Difficult Justice*, where Kabbalah is enlisted in the service of the basic/surplus approach. Horowitz's present work on Korzybski produces a radical general semantics as one vehicle of a Marcuse-like emancipatory transformation of the human sensorium.

In marking Horowitz's itinerary with the notion that it is subversive, our hope is not to fall back into totalizing encapsulation but to point to the insistent detotalizing nature of Horowitz's intellectual projects. In the mid-fifties, to characterize Canadian political culture as potentially more emancipatory than that of the United States, and to show an affinity between a certain tendency on the Canadian political right and left, amounted to a deeply subversive reading of the political cultures of those places. In the mid-seventies, to probe the notion of repression in such a serious and systematic manner – giving in to neither the "repression is bad" zeitgeist nor the conservative "repression is good" reactions – in a reading that worked within but challenged Marcuse's use of Freud and Marx from an author whose work on Canada was already canonical, caught many by surprise and slowly has infiltrated intellectual work with its subversive spirit. Then, through the late eighties to the present, to engage with continental philosophy, from Rousseau to Foucault, with an elliptical yet intellectually forceful questioning of the ethical dimensions of social thought, to "discover" in the pores of a European intellectual history newly reconcerned with questions of language the striking work of the general semantics school, to puncture Levinas's balloons with Bataille's prick (and perhaps the reverse): these small challenges are submerged intellectual explosives whose effect will be felt in many years to come.

Horowitz is a subversive because he does overturn long-established canons of thought. Horowitz is a subversive because his thought does not stop, bounding between the philosophical, political, and anthropological, between the personal and the political, through the state and the body, suturing the laughter and the grammatical opening into the richly textured linguistic gap where meaning folds back over itself. Horowitz is a subversive because he retains a concern for the politics of social class: in his marrow he never forgets the indignities and the fundamental injustice of poverty that the established order rests upon and continually reinscribes. His work is magisterial in the command he brings to his fields of inquiry, but we refer to his "small challenges" because he belongs on the side of those who do not reap the rewards of the current world order. He is a subversive because he never forgets the destabilizing force and uncontainable pleasure of certain forms of laughter.

The words, pages, and chapters that follow engage with the subversive itinerary that has traced itself through the intellectual production – particularly writings and teachings – of Gad Horowitz. We want to separate or distinguish or problematize the relation between "Gad" and "Horowitz." By *Horowitz*, we in proper academic form call attention to the trace of a name that authors and authorizes a series of writings. Horowitz is cited, debated, "known" as a shifting set of critical interventions into public and scholarly life. Most, though not all, of the texts here are devoted to discussion of Horowitz and his signature contributions to the world of letters. Occasionally, in some of these writings and especially in Part One, "Life and Times," another figure puts in an appearance: Gad.

Gad, a man "of flesh and blood," as the existentialists used to say (and we are reminded of Gad's many reminders of the value of earlier traditions of critical thought, so often dismissed by the fashion-theory industry), is the Gad who once placed cigarette after cigarette on the lectern as he spoke, lighting each new one on the embers of the last; the Gad who pursues his transgressive pleasures to their inspiring ends; the sound of his voice; the way in which indignation at some or other stupidity moves his body; the Gad who shouts out in the cinema, who meditates, who pulls his body through one subcultural event after another, who sits on the witness stand and refuses to use any other word than *the pigs* to describe police officers. Horowitz does theorize the body in ways that challenge our conventional mind-body dualisms. But Gad is something more than the praxis associated with Horowitz's theory, just as Horowitz's theory is something more than a result of the body of Gad (though it is that, too). And there is the "body" of Horowitz's works, the ideas that emerge through the speaking of Gad at the lectern (or was that Horowitz who stood there?), the liberations and repressions carried by the words and the flesh in their entwined moments. Most of all, there is the childlike twinkle that emerges from eyes that have found a moment of critical playfulness.

We, Shannon and Peter, know of ourselves and suspect of most of our contributors a feeling of genuine privilege for having in the smallest of ways been touched by Gad, stung or encouraged by the sharpness of his words, by the gentleness or seriousness of his gaze, sharing food or travel or the endless series of wry black jokes and the deep friendship of shared laughter. Through his own writings and his mentorship of a diverse range of activists, intellectuals, and public intellectuals Gad Horowitz has had a significant influence upon Canadian scholarship and political discourse. This collection of essays pays tribute to Horowitz's ongoing work by either engaging his work directly or reflecting upon themes and issues inspired by his thought.

If a thinker's body of scholarship can be divided into early, middle, and later periods, then the early Horowitz would be the Canadianist whose work is engaged by Colin Campbell, Nelson Wiseman, Ed Andrew, Ian Angus, Robert Meynell, and peter kulchyski. His work on psychoanalysis, critical theory, and continental theory can be presented as constituting the middle period in Horowitz's scholarship. The contributors interacting with Horowitz's thought from this period are

Colin Campbell, Sean Saraka, Jason Rovito, Michael Marder, Shannon Bell, Asher Horowitz, and Victoria Tahmasebi. The later Horowitz encompasses Buddhism, post-structuralism, and general semantics, with the qualifier that always there is the defining presence of aspects of critical theory in the later work. These contributors concentrate on the later Horowitz: Oona Eisenstadt, Asher Horowitz, Shannon Bell, Jason Rovito, and peter kulchyski. Five contributors – Campbell, Rovito, Bell, Horowitz, and kulchyski – straddle these somewhat artificially designated periods in our engagement with Horowitz's work. *Subversive Itinerary* consists of five parts: "Life and Times," "Fragment Theory," "Spirit and Power," "Political Philosophy," and "Horowitz in His Own Words."

Part One, "Life and Times," involves critical biography and dialogic reflection on or with Gad. It begins with Colin Campbell's "On Intellectual Life, Politics and Psychoanalysis," in which Gad in discussion with Campbell sets out the content, context, and reverberations of his work from Canadian political culture to radical general semantics. The Campbell-Horowitz interview provides the frame for the fourteen essays in this collection, drawing out the overarching themes of red toryism, Canadian nationalism, socialism, basic (necessary) and surplus repression, radical general semantics, relation between self and other, Buddhism and Derridian deconstruction, Jewish philosophy, and Levinasian ethical obligation that are revisited by the contributors.

The interview is followed by Nelson Wiseman's elegant and meticulous history of Gad's engagements as a public intellectual through the defining crucible of the sixties. Wiseman interlinks Horowitz's academic and journalistic writings and his development as a public intellectual. He establishes Gad's role as a political activist and political scientist in defining the terrain of Canadian socialism and nationalism beginning in the mid-1960s. Wiseman credits Horowitz with raising "ideology to an unprecedented status in the study of Canadian politics."

Ed Andrew, in "The Odd Couple of Canadian Intellectual History," presents the intellectual friendship of two of Canada's defining thinkers: Gad Horowitz and George Grant. Andrew provides vignettes of the singularity and articulation of the two thinkers' philosophy. In Ed Andrew's view, Gad's Jewish identity, coupled with socialism, distinguished him from Grant and foreshadowed Horowitz's most recent work that brings together Herbert Marcuse, Jacques Derrida, and Emmanuel Levinas, linking these thinkers precisely through "the Jewish prophetic or messianic tradition." The Grant-Horowitz alliance is also discussed by Angus and Meynell, later in this collection, with Meynell deeming Horowitz-Grant's friendship "an odd marriage of ideologies."

Jason Rovito, in "Between Pause and Play," presents Horowitz as educator in the context of his current seminar, "The Spirit of Democratic Citizenship." Rovito posits "Horowitz as translator" between two very different discourses, that of Korzybski and that of Marcuse. According to Rovito, it is precisely Horowitz's schooling in and work on Marcuse that enables him to find the radicalism in Korzybski's General Semantics and produce a radical general semantics.

Part Two, "Fragment Theory," contains three chapters that set out the contemporary relevance of the famous Hartz-Horowitz thesis regarding the distinct political cultures of Canada and the United States. The chapters by Ian Angus, Nelson Wiseman, and Robert Meynell take up the fragment theory to investigate it at the national level (Angus), to extend it regionally (Wiseman), and to critically re-evaluate it in the face of its latest critics (Meynell).

Ian Angus, in "The Political Culture of English Canada," situates Horowitz's writing as itself political and not simply writing about politics. The focus is on Horowitz's socialist project and its legacy today. "In the absence of socialist transformation," Angus notes, "it is remarkable to see how many of Horowitz's dire 'predictions' have come into being: internal fragmentation, subsumption within the American identity, devolution of federal powers to the provinces due to the assertion of Quebec's claim to sovereignty within the current framework of Confederation."

Nelson Wiseman, in his second essay in the collection, "Canada's Regional Fragments," injects both a regional and a materialist analysis into the Hartz-Horowitz approach. He extends the Hartz-Horowitz fragment theory regionally, drawing out the differences and nuances in five Canadian regions: Atlantic Canada, Quebec, Ontario, the Midwest (Manitoba and Saskatchewan), and the Far West (Alberta and British Columbia). Wiseman adds as a further nuance to his analysis of Canada's disparate regional fragments: the differences in the five regions' economic structures.

Robert Meynell, in "Restoration, Not Renovation," responds to the latest critics – Ajzenstat and Smith – of the Hartz-Horowitz thesis. Meynell contends that the Ajzenstat-Smith attempted correction, which replaces Canada's organic-collectivism with Lockean republicanism, is a mythology that suppresses Canada's distinctive intellectual history in favour of cultural and political continentalism.

Part Three, "Spirit and Power," incorporates a set of theoretical chapters that engage with the psyche-body, libido, and repression and its limits. Here, the figures of Freud and Marcuse loom large in Horowitz's thought. The four chapters engage these thinkers with theoretical interlocutors of their own: Shannon Bell with Foucault, Michael Marder with Celan, Victoria Tahmasebi with Irigaray, and Colin Campbell with Girard and Bataille. Bell's essay begins this section and in fact introduces this and the next section with a discussion of the philosophical/ theoretical turn in Horowitz's work. Part Three explores the politics and power of pleasure and, if "fragment theory" and "red tory" were concepts developed in the earlier work, the critical distinctions between basic and surplus repression emerge here as central theoretical concepts developed by Horowitz, concepts that have a continuing urgent critical purchase.

Shannon Bell's "Gad ben Rachel ve Aharon" identifies Horowitz as a *parrhesiastic* thinker, "a thinker who speaks truth, new truths, and in speaking new truths opens horizons in knowledge terrains." Bell detects two forms of truth-telling in Horowitz's work: radical political truth-telling and pedagogical *parrhesia*. She examines truth-telling in Horowitz's writings on psychoanalysis, post-structuralism, Jewish mysticism, and Buddhism. Bell suggests that Buddhism gives way to Horowitz's "most extreme *parrhesiastic* moment." What she has in mind is Horowitz's use of what he sets forth as seven Buddhist truths "to construct a political groundlessness that will hold the radical in democracy." In the latter part of the chapter Bell sets out the pedagogical truth-telling developed by "Gad the Teacher" in his seminar "The Spirit of Democratic Citizenship: Sanity and Democracy" (1994–2011).[3]

Michael Marder, in "What's Involved in Involution? A Psycho-Poetics of Regression" "breathes of the secret," of the (un)common ground of poetic and psychoanalytic desires. Marder presents a Levinasian encounter in which each is brought into existence by the other, and what transpires is a singularity. The secret, Marder contends, when an asymmetrical encounter takes place between two singular others, such as poetry and psychoanalysis, is "that the relation to the other is forged as a teaching." What sutures Celan and Freud is the place Celan gives to breath in his poetry – "breath as breathlessness" – and the uncanniness in Freud's concept of regression that "undoes that which is said in the empirical systems of signification to uncover the saying that animates them in the first place." Marder is using the breathless breath of Celan's poem *"Lob der Ferne"* [Praise of Distance] and "the saying that animates" regression to situate the teaching of Gad Ḥorowitz.

Victoria Tahmasebi, in "The Sexed Body of the Woman-(M)Other," shows the necessity of the between in the encounter of Irigaray and Marcuse, which would, according to Michael Marder, be an "asymmetrical encounter" taking place "between two singular others." The teaching Tahmasebi is offering is a uniquely feminist encounter with Herbert Marcuse – the thinker whose work perhaps most influenced and whose work consistently has continued to influence Gad Horowitz. Tahmasebi holds a fidelity both to Horowitz's emphasis on Marcuse's concepts – basic and surplus repression – as core to Marcuse's thought and to his own thought.

Colin Campbell, in "The Spark of Philosophy," turns to the work of two very unlikely yet ideal continental philosophers – Rene Girard and Georges Bataille – to illuminate "the religious dimensions of the pre-liberal past," showing that "a religious perspective is already inherent in Hartz's earlier 'secular' social theory of political ideology." Campbell contends that Hartz's understanding of the political meaning of feudalism already contains the theory of religion. In addition, Campbell argues that "Bataille and Girard together provide an incomparable illumination of the highly contested identity of the red tory." It is precisely spiritual values alien to liberal morality, Campbell points out, that Gad Horowitz has always argued we have in our "tory touch."

The most recent phase of Horowitz's work, the latest stop on the itinerary, and Part Four of this book, is positioned under the title of "Political Philosophy." Part Four includes four philosophical encounters with Horowitz and/or the continental, Eastern, and Judaic philosophical thinkers and schools of thought that his work draws upon – Sean Saraka (Balibar, Marx, and Derrida), Asher Horowitz (Adorno and Nargarjuna), Eisenstadt (Levinas and Kabbalah) and peter kulchyski (Derrida and Levinas).

Sean Saraka, in "Transcendental Liberalism and the Politics of Representation," scrutinizes the defining market-hive framework of Gad and Asher Horowitz's *"Everywhere They Are in Chains": Political Theory from Rousseau to Marx*, a book that emerged out of Gad's lectures in modern political thought at University of Toronto's Department of Political Science. Saraka focuses on what he contends are the "silences and reversals" driving the Horowitz project: their strategic disordering of history and their collectivist/individualist subjectivation represented through developmental anthropology. Saraka relates the Horowitz work to the broader context of continental philosophy, referencing the work of Slavoj Žižek and Étienne Balibar, specifically in the areas of subjectivity and subjectivation. Saraka connects Balibar's critique of what he à la Balibar terms "Macpherson's unitary conception of possessive individualism" to Horowitz's more nuanced imaging of the modern subject.

Oona Eisenstadt, in "From the Narcissism of Small Differences to the Vertigo of Endless Possibilities" directs her attention to an intervention that Gad has made within Levinasian scholarship on the contested terrain of politics. Levinas supports an open regime, yet he provides no details, thus opening the political to both radical left liberation theology and classical liberal assimilation. Thinkers and activists supplement Levinasian ethics – that "owed to the other before self" – with their own politics. Eisenstadt contends that Horowitz "does suggest thinkers and positions that might supplement Levinas politically, he, however, does so only after a close reading of the passages in which Levinas points toward a politics, or declines to point toward a politics." Sections 6 and 7 of the chapter bring to Levinas scholarship what Eisenstadt identifies as "less sober strands in Judaism" – Isaac Luria and the Kabbalist Gikatilla. Isaac Luria, Isaiah Horowitz (the Shelah), along with Sabbatai Zevi are precisely the strains that Horowitz brings to bear in a radical Levinasian politics that incorporates "Marcuse's account of basic and surplus repression."

Asher Horowitz, "Adorno and Emptiness," engages a detailed discussion of the relation of Theodor Adorno's infamously difficult book *Negative Dialectics* to Buddhist thought. Influenced by Gad Horowitz's turning of continental philosophy towards Buddhism and Buddhism towards continental philosophy, Asher Horowitz turns the negative in Adorno's dialectic towards Madhyamika Buddhist philosophy, particularly the negative dialectic of Nargarjuna's thought. The impetus directing Asher's "Adorno and Emptiness" is the same as what directed Gad Horowitz's "emmanuel, Robert" – "Buddhism could benefit from a 'Western' insight into its own condition of possibility." Asher Horowitz suggests that "Buddhism might also be able to benefit from Adorno's transposition of negative dialectics into the realm of the natural-historical, the socio-individual reproduction of samsaric suffering."

Part Four and the collection conclude with peter kulchyski's "horowitz dances with wolves: inquiries pursuant to the thought of gad horowitz," an urgent call "to gad" to "join us in escalating the crises." Kulchyski says, "i speak not for him, as one who attempts to bear his legacy of critical thought in canada, but to him whose thinking in this moment/conjunction is more urgent to us than ever." Kulchyski calls "to gad" – "to you i have things to say" – reminding him of his ethical obligation to share his "thinking in this moment/conjuncture" with others. The call is urgent and imploring.

Kulchyski fulfils two main objectives. He supplements Gad's early work "Conservatism, Liberalism, and Socialism in Canada: An Interpretation," *Canadian Labour in Politics*, with indigenous rights – contending that red tory in its formation "was inflected with a certain kind of respect for aboriginal rights." Kulchyski also discloses the importance to gad of "thinking class issues" as a crucial link from his early work *Canadian Labour in Politics* (1968) to his later work "Aporiah and Messiah in Derrida and Levinas," *Difficult Justice* (2006).

Kulchyski provides an incisive concluding essay, one that returns Horowitz's late to early work and foregrounds the politics inherent in and driving it all. Kulchyski notes that Horowitz's early 1968 work "inaugurates and opens the space" for cultural politics; his middle 1977 work *Repression* proposes surplus repression as "the crucial question to ask of any particular culture and of cultural politics in general." Horowitz's later work on Derrida and Levinas warns how easily their work is co-optable by liberalism unless it is supplemented with a sociohistorical understanding of surplus repression and class politics.

Giving Gad the final say, the collection closes with Part Five, "Horowitz in His Own Words," which includes three of his later essays – "emmanuel, Robert" (2006), "Bringing Bataille to Justice" (2008), and "An Essay on the Altruism of Nature" (2012).

The essays of this volume demonstrate a range of concerns and nuance that defy our encapsulations, and in this they reflect Gad's rigour and lively curiosity: Gad the scholar constructing painstaking arguments as public intellectual and as our rabbi of high theory.

NOTES

1 Excerpt from Gad Horowitz, "Berlin Dharma: Motion, Thinking, Noise," a five-day interview-event, 14–19 February, 2007, interviewed by Shannon Bell. See "Berlin Dharma," YouTube, uploaded 1 June 2008, http://www.youtube.com/watch?v=4p9fHdjg_hQ.

2 Michel Foucault, *Fearless Speech*, ed. Joseph Pearson (New York: Semiotext[e], 2001), 12.

3 Gad's twenty-two lectures on radical general semantics are available at http://radicalgeneralsemantics.net.

PART ONE

Life and Times

1 On Intellectual Life, Politics, and Psychoanalysis: A Conversation with Gad Horowitz (2003)[1]

COLIN J. CAMPBELL

CAMPBELL: *Canadian Labour in Politics* remains a seminal text of Canadian political analysis and the history of Canadian socialism. In it you develop what has become known as the "Hartz-Horowitz thesis," a variant of Louis Hartz's "fragment theory" of political culture. Briefly, what was Hartz's theory and how did it change when your name was added to it?

HOROWITZ: "Seminal" – well, you know we don't like this word (*laughs*), but I guess, in fact, that's something like what it was. I had my fifteen minutes. It was and remained a seminal text because it spoke to real needs of the Canadian cultural, political elite, especially at that time.

Briefly, Hartz's theory is that the new societies that were established by immigrants were cultural fragments. In other words they represented, not the whole spectrum of political ideology in the mother country, but a fragment of that culture.

European political history has been marked by a dialectic of pre-liberal (feudal, monarchist, tory, etc.) and liberal (individualist, republican, etc.) ideologies, which eventually gives rise to post-liberal (socialist, communist, fascist, etc.) developments, which complicate the conversation further.

In the new societies founded by European settlers (New France, Colonial America, English Canada, Australia, New Zealand, South Africa) this dialectic is absent or very much attenuated because the settlers represent only a monochromatic "fragment" of the total, multicoloured ideological spectrum of the mother country.

Hartz's "fragment theory" begins with a close study of the founding of American society more than a hundred years prior to the

American Revolution. The first settlers left the feudal, aristocratic, organic-hierarchical conservatism of Britain behind. The American political conversation, exciting as it is, has taken place not between toryism, liberalism, and socialism, but entirely within liberalism, or what Hartz somewhat misleadingly calls "Lockeanism." Lacking the communitarian and class preoccupations of toryism, there is no possibility of a powerful, legitimate socialism developing as a synthesis of tory and liberal ideologies. The United States is "monolithically Lockean."

Whatever traces of toryism had persisted in the American fragment in the colonial period are expelled by the American Revolution. They are expelled to Canada, carried by counter-revolutionary refugees loyal to the British monarchy (loyalists who were actually called Tories).

Hartz and Kenneth McRae suggested that English Canada was another liberal fragment. Latin America and Quebec, on the other hand, were "feudal" fragments founded by emigrants from pre-liberal Spain, Portugal, and France. While the United States was an entirely liberal fragment, Quebec was a near-monolithic feudal or tory fragment until the upsurge of liberalism after the Second World War, culminating in the Quiet Revolution of the sixties. The persistence of the feudal past alongside the new liberalism helps to account for the strong influence of socialist/social democratic thinking in Quebec in recent times. Most interestingly, Hartz suggested that Australia was a radical fragment because Australia, being founded at the turn of the twentieth century by English and other British working-class people, privileged, as we might say, a very left-wing, close-to-socialist or social-democratic fragment in Australia.

People should read Hartz, especially *The Liberal Tradition in America*, and his second book called *The Founding of New Societies*, which he edited. *The Founding of New Societies* has pieces on all the fragment cultures. *The Liberal Tradition in America* was just about the United States. It's one of the most brilliant pieces of work that has ever been done, I think, in political science. It was very influential and much condemned and despised and debated in the United States, and it still is.

"How did it change when my name was added to it?" Well, I argued against McRae, who had contributed to Hartz's *The Founding of New Societies*, that in fact it was not correct to call English Canada a liberal fragment like the United States. I argued that there was a significant, let's say, "tory" or pre-liberal "remnant" in Canada, and that this is part of the reason that English Canada developed a vibrant and legitimate socialist tradition, in great contrast to the American scene. In the new

setting of the anglophone Canadian provinces this toryism, later reinforced by massive immigration from nineteenth-century Britain, becomes significant enough to enter into a conversation with British and
American liberalism, robust enough to produce an impressive though
never majoritarian socialism. English Canada is thus a liberal fragment
with significant tory and socialist touches.

Hartz didn't mind having his theory complicated. McRae was also
quite generous about it. Nelson Wiseman went on to develop an application of the fragment theory in an intra-Canadian way, so that, for
example, the prairie provinces, BC, the Maritimes, and Ontario are all
described in terms of fragment theory as having significant variations
from the pan-Canadian perspective.

CAMPBELL: *Canadian Labour in Politics* opens with the statement "In the
United States organized socialism is dead. In Canada socialism, though
far from national power, is a significant political force and the official
'political arm' of the labour movement."[2] And then you ask, "Why
these striking differences in the fortunes of socialism in two very similar
societies?"[3] Has your analysis of the Canadian political scene changed
since the 1960s?

HOROWITZ: My feelings have changed a lot more than my analysis. So I
suppose I won't work too hard at separating "feelings" from "the analysis." I think that the New Democratic Party has fallen on hard times;
its fortunes may improve, but I think party politics has become less important than it was, especially on the left. And that people, especially
young people, are more interested in non-parliamentary or extra-parlia-
mentary politics than they were before. I think that Canada has become
significantly more Americanized than it was when I wrote *Canadian Labour in Politics*, and that both toryism and socialism have been losing a
lot of their distinctiveness, have been blurring into liberalism at their
boundaries.

CAMPBELL: The "red tory" was a key figure in the Hartz-Horowitz analysis. What does this term mean?

HOROWITZ: Well that's what really became famous – this notion of the red
tory. First I should say that some people say I invented the term. I didn't
invent the term. I think that it probably is a term that was first used in
England, and anyone who wanted to do the research would figure that
out. There were Tories in England who were sufficiently anti-capitalist
– interested enough in what Disraeli called the "condition of the people" – to be called "red" Tories. So I defined, in the Canadian context,
a red tory as someone who – Eugene Forsey is a good example – was

a socialist who was sufficiently tory in many of his views – especially about the constitution, and the power of the Crown – to be called a red "tory." On the other hand there were tories who were sufficiently critical of capitalism to be called "red" tories – that would be George Grant, and others.

CAMPBELL: You have said in the past that the reason that George Grant lacked faith and hope in a socialist future was that he lacked faith and hope period. Where was the "red" in Grant's tory? Has your evaluation of Grant's evaluation of the possibility of socialism changed?

HOROWITZ: Well, he lacked faith and hope in English Canada – at least rhetorically. He would never have hoped for a socialist future. But he might have hoped for a future for an independent Canada, which put more importance, in his terms, on the "public good" than on private interests. Insofar as Grant recognized that both conservatism and socialism place the public good ahead of private interests, he would have been interested in socialism in that sense. He did contribute a chapter to the volume published by some founders of the New Democratic Party, called *Social Purpose for Canada*, edited by Michael Oliver, first president of the NDP. He had a very nice piece in there, which was as socialist as he ever got. I guess maybe I've said enough about where the "red" was in Grant's tory – he was very critical of capitalism and of the control of Canadian politics by indigenous and American-based capital. He thought that our business classes had sold out the country. I don't think he ever changed his mind about that. He had a genuine deep respect for ordinary people that was quite remarkable – which you might see shining through in that piece in *Social Purpose for Canada*. I think many of Grant's students and disciples like to underplay this side of Grant's thought. Certainly as a religious person he didn't lack faith and hope. As a deeply religious person, he was all about faith and hope. But it's a kind of faith and hope that transcends the political.

CAMPBELL: Joel Kovel dedicated his book *The Enemy of Nature: The End of Capitalism or the End of the World* to the anti-globalization protestors, in Seattle and in Quebec City. What did you think of the protest in Quebec City in 2001? Did it indicate for you that socialism remains "a significant political force" in Canada?

HOROWITZ: Well it was one of the most remarkable experiences of my life. I thought it was really marvellous. And I was furious about the tear gas. I don't think that it means that socialism remains a significant force in Canada. I think it means that the anti-globalization movement is a significant political force, and that political parties like the CCF-NDP, that people like NDP Leader Jack Layton have to negotiate some kind of re-lationship between old-style political structures and the new-style anti-globalization movement. The problem is that September 11 suddenly happened, and the anti-globalization movement, which for me was a kind of "big picture," ended up in a small corner on the right hand side.

CAMPBELL: You made a strong case for Canadian nationalism as a force allied with the emergence of socialism. Are you still, were you ever, "proud to be Canadian"?

HOROWITZ: I don't know if I would have ever used those words. I came to this country – I was born in Jerusalem – I came to Canada when I was two years old, and I grew up mostly in Calgary, Winnipeg, and Mon-treal. So I am a Canadian and I always felt myself to be a Canadian. But like so many other Canadians I really became conscious of this when I left the country to study abroad – abroad in this case being the United States. When I went to graduate school at Harvard, I felt my Canadianness very strongly, and other people felt it too. I would be singled out in seminars to express the "Canadian point of view." And, you know, my most glorious moment at Harvard was when I would jokingly suggest to my American friends that the American people should re-convene the Continental Congress, draw up articles of apol-ogy for the American Revolution, and petition to be brought back under the British Crown for their own good. And that we would find someone in Canada to go down there and act as governor general, you know, until they were ready for self-government. Americans didn't find that funny (*laughter*). They knew that I was joking but somehow weren't able to find it funny.

Well, you know, there's just not that much intensity in it anymore, but my view and my feelings actually haven't changed that much ei-ther. And I do love New York and San Francisco. Does that make me a good Canadian?

CAMPBELL: Do you have any particularly vivid memories of your early years at Harvard or McGill?

HOROWITZ: Harvard was a very interesting experience and that's where I met Louis Hartz and Sam Beer. Sam Beer is known to many people as the former president of the ADA, the Americans for Democratic Action. He wrote a book that was important to me, *British Politics in the Age of Collectivism*. As a graduate student I did some research for him, which contributed a bit to one of the chapters in that book. I did some research on Lord Randolph Churchill, who was actually the Tory democrat par excellence.

When I was at McGill doing my MA I wrote my master's thesis on
C. Wright Mills's *The Power Elite* and also on the Italian elite theorists
Mosca and Michels. As a matter of fact, years later someone sent me a
volume published by the Italian Ministry of Culture or something like
that, which pointed out that the only Canadian political scientist who
ever paid any attention to Italian political thought was the young theorist at McGill named Gad Horowitz, and it's too bad after doing that he
went on to other matters. I did a liberal critique of C. Wright Mills in
my master's thesis, but when I finished it I realized that I didn't agree
with my critique. I had actually been turned around by Mills, who was
of course one of the great names in American radicalism and still is or
ought to be. His books *The Power Elite* and *The Sociological Imagination*
and *The Causes of World War Three* are extremely relevant for today.

So I realized, you know, you come to criticize and you stay to sign
up. This is one of the great things about intellectual work, I think, for
people who are somehow not averse to this kind of thing. Whatever
you study, you become. The Talmud says, "From all my teachers I have
learned." So you can come to criticize something and learn from it, and
find yourself transformed in a way that maybe would have shocked or
appalled a previous self.

The other moment was during the Vietnam War. I was visiting Frankfurt, Germany, at the time and watching German television, and Lyndon
B. Johnson appeared on the screen in a military hospital in Frankfurt,
visiting the wounded American soldiers. Armless, legless, you know,
shipped from Vietnam to the military hospital in Frankfurt. So when I
saw Johnson shaking the arm, the one arm that was left, the one hand
that was left to one of these boys, you know it just hit me. In this recent war in Iraq, it kept hitting me again and again and again. That's
one thing that doesn't change for me – the anti-war position. And I've
learned lately, following some of the happenings on the web in connection with the Iraq war, that you can be ferociously anti-war as a right-
winger. It's not something that the left has any kind of monopoly on.
Some of the most ferocious opposition to war in the United States has
been coming from the followers of Pat Buchanan. So those were the moments of radicalization. Then, of course, when I was at Harvard, Marcuse hit.

CAMPBELL: Marcuse "hit"?

HOROWITZ: Marcuse hit me – Marcuse's book *Eros and Civilization*, which
wasn't yet widely known, but which was published in 1955. I went to
Harvard in 1959, and Marcuse's friend Barrington Moore, who was no

left-winger, was teaching a course at Harvard, and *Eros and Civilization* was on the course.

CAMPBELL: Your next major publication after *Canadian Labour in Politics* has been described by one sympathetic Canadian political scientist as a "tactical error." *Repression: Basic and Surplus* is an intensive introduction to psychoanalytic theory, to Freud, Reich, and Marcuse. What would you say is the relation between these books? Why would a political scientist write about psychotherapy?

HOROWITZ: After *Canadian Labour in Politics* I hung around in the area of Canadian politics for a while. And I did some stuff on TV, for example, with George Grant and others. At some point, however, I just stopped working in that field. It wasn't a tactical error, it was just a change in my priorities in terms of what I was interested in. *Canadian Labour in Politics* was my PhD thesis. I wrote it as a graduate student at Harvard. My supervisor was Sam Beer, and Louis Hartz had a lot to do with the first chapter.

And at the same time, as I just mentioned, Marcuse hit me. So this interest in psychoanalytic theory was there, from the start, and there was just a sort of natural swing towards developing that interest. But not so much psychotherapy as psychoanalytic theory, from a Marcusian, that is, a left-Freudian, point of view. *Repression* – it wasn't a tactical error, but it was a tactical failure, in the sense that the reason that I wrote it was to help make Marcuse's use of Freud more acceptable, more interesting to mainstream psychoanalytic theorists. And also to make psychoanalytic theory more interesting to people on the left. But it actually fell between the two camps and it's really a strange book in more ways than one. For one thing, as Joel Kovel pointed out to me, for a book about Eros, it was very unerotic, (*laughs*), which couldn't have been said about *Eros and Civilization* itself. *Repression* relied very heavily on a school of psychoanalytic thinkers known as the "ego psychologists," who were out of favour in terms of the politics of academia. It was a tactical error to base a lot of my terminology and theorizing on their work. I was naive, I didn't know that no one wanted to listen to the ego psychologists Hartmann and Rappaport. But it was fun, and a lot of people, you know, got something out of it. I actually had more fan mail for *Repression* than I did for *Canadian Labour in Politics*.

The relation between the books is that there is something left-wing happening in both. The fact that I published these two books makes a statement about my attitude to academia, and that is the importance to me of eclecticism – the importance of being interested in and doing work in many fields, and not just one field. I think people who find a field or a cause in graduate school and go on mining – mining it and mining it until they retire ... You know, we probably need people like that, but I don't think they should be considered the only legitimate or genuine scholars, while people who move around and study different things, as I have, are considered somehow less professional. Or, you know, maybe that's exactly what we are. Less professional would be a good thing. De-professionalization, in other words, might be exactly what is required.

CAMPBELL: So what is to be done?

HOROWITZ: A long time ago somebody interviewed me and I found myself describing myself as politically schizophrenic. I wouldn't use that term in the way I did then. But what I meant was that I had a split consciousness. In terms of my fundamental broad outlook, I was some kind of communist, and I'll tell you exactly what kind of communist I was: I was a Marcusian communist. But in terms of day-to-day politics, I was a sort of, you know, centre-left CCF-NDPer [Co-operative Commonwealth Federation–New Democratic Party]. I argued then and I would still argue that it's very important – it was very important for me and I recommend this to everyone, that they, as Marcuse himself was always saying, don't give up on broad, radical visions for fundamental, sweeping social change, just because it doesn't seem to be on the agenda, or indeed even because it never will be on the agenda. You still don't give up on it. "Don't give up" means don't give up. It doesn't mean "Don't give up as long as you think you have a chance." It means don't give up. Period.

CAMPBELL: You teach a course at the University of Toronto, "The Spirit of Democratic Citizenship," which included assignments with names, like "stepping out of worthlessness," and "writing in sensory grounded language." What are some of the things you hope to achieve in teaching it?

HOROWITZ: I feel this is one of the best things that I've ever done. And it's hard for me to talk about it – it's hard to describe what it is. But it's really a work of eclectic bricolage that I brought together out of many different disciplines. Korzybski's "general semantics," as you know, provides the frame, and actually the idea for doing this course came to me when I rediscovered his book *Science and Sanity*, published in 1933. I had read popular versions of general semantics, like Hayakawa's *Language in Action*, when I was a teenager, and then I forgot about it. In the late eighties I came upon *Science and Sanity* and rediscovered what I think is an idiosyncratic and flawed, but in some ways very powerful approach to getting across to people of all ages and descriptions, ways of dealing with the power of language, of discourses, of undermining the power of discourses, such as the discourse of "worthlessness" – undemocratic discourses – in their lives. I actually think that this sort of stuff is more important than therapy, and that if something like the general semantics movement could be revived that it would do more for people and for democracy than radical therapy approaches, or ordinary therapy approaches.

It didn't fit at all well with other courses in the University of Toronto's Political Science Department, but my department is a very "small c" catholic department, and we always have gotten along very well with one another. For example, our relations, or at least my relations with our Straussian comrades, are always generous and gentle. There was no objection to teaching a course like this.

It has three parts. The first part is about language, and about dehypnotization – understanding the power of the "consensus trance" – breaking the "consensus trance" that all sorts of received discourses have over our lives from a very early age.

The first part is called "No One Truth." "No One Truth" relies very · heavily on general semantics and deals with cognition. The second part, called "Evoking the Other," is about self-and-other. It has to do with understanding the relational process between self and others at both the interpersonal and inter-group levels.

CAMPBELL: "The Power of Not Understanding" is in Part Two.

HOROWITZ: "The Power of Not Understanding." This was an article by an Israeli social psychologist about discussions between Jews and Arabs in Israel/Palestine, which could only begin to make headway when both sides realized that they actually profoundly did not "understand" the other at all. Another angle: people can talk at the academic level about how the Israeli needs to take on the Arab's memories of oppression, and the Arab needs to take on the Jew's memories of oppression, but to say that is very different from actually going through a process in which you do that – actually do it. The whole course is about getting people to have experiences, rather than just learn academic formulae – no matter how profound and interesting and important these formulae might be.

Part Two is about evoking the other, listening to others, to *all* others, including the others within the self. There's a section on Gandhi in Part Two, because Gandhi is the best so far at transforming the traditional approach to the enemy, and entering into politics in a way in which you would understand the enemy and take the so-called enemy into account as much as possible.

The third part is called "The Spirit of Equality." Part Three takes it from the interpersonal to the more broadly social or political level. The part of it that I remember most vividly is called "Mapping Personal Problems in Public Space," which again, in an experience-based way, shows the connection between personal issues, personal problems, personal troubles, and the larger institutional and discursive forces that affect those problems. So that people who went through that would find it impossible any longer to focus most of their thinking about personal problems on the question of personal blame, personal guilt, personal responsibility – calling people to account, holding people responsible, and all that kind of thing. And they would be able to see the importance of action at a collective, rather than personal level.

Actually this goes back to C. Wright Mills too, because C. Wright Mills defined politics as, and I quote, "the translation of personal troubles into public issues" – so a large part of politics is keeping certain troubles personal, denying their political relevance.

CAMPBELL: How was general semantics different from a therapeutic movement?

HOROWITZ: The general semantics movement was a more general movement. Alfred Korzybski was interested in "sanity." I translated that more into "democracy." But Korzybski wasn't a therapist, he was a teacher. The general semantics movement brought people together to work together. It was more of a teaching, learning, a cooperative teaching and learning movement than a therapeutic movement. Korzybski thought that the whole culture, that the whole of civilization was unsane – not insane. The problem was not to treat neuroses and psychoses but to raise the level of civilization as a whole. He was almost megalomaniacally optimistic about the possibilities for personal, cultural change that could be brought about by something like the general semantics movement. Korzybski was no conventional leftist either. The general semantics movement brought people together in a non-political way – I'm sure they had all sorts of different political opinions, although, you know, extreme conservatives would have avoided it because of its "relativism." Imagine teaching "no one truth" at Leavenworth penitentiary, which was one of the places that had general semantics groups! And it was quite influential among university students also. At places like Berkeley, kids would be walking around carrying copies of *Etc.*, the general semantics journal, well into the sixties.

It fell apart because of the polarization of American society around the psychedelic revolution and around the Vietnam War. This split the general semantics movement because it proved to be impossible to keep people working together who had very different political views.

Gregory Bateson is also an important figure here. He became much better known than Korzybski. Bateson was one of the heroes of the American counterculture. Bateson had some association with general semantics. It was very important to Bateson, as a sort of polymath intellectual, especially in his famous work *Steps to an Ecology of Mind*, to undermine individualist presuppositions in life and in culture.

CAMPBELL: In "Groundless Democracy" you wrote, "It has been said many times: poststructuralist radicalism, having given up on Truth, is groundless in its opposition to the status quo: it is incapable of offering reasons for wishing to replace one 'regime of truth' with another."[4] What, if anything, do Marxists, or anyone else, have to learn from post-structuralism?

HOROWITZ: That was from a piece that I wrote that was actually a Buddhist critique of Ernesto Laclau and Chantal Mouffe. I wrote it before becoming a serious student of post-structuralist radicalism. So there I am offending one of my own rules, which is not to criticize anything without having worked really hard at trying to understand it from the inside. Because part of my eclectic position … it's a fanatic eclecticism. It's not a shallow eclecticism. I believe in many truths, and I think there's too much destruction of straw men in academia, and I think that too many people are familiar only with their own orientation and aren't capable of understanding different or opposing orientations from within. So it's always been my ambition, although I'm sure I've fallen short, to understand what I criticize from the inside. So after having written that, you know, I studied Derrida, especially, a lot more carefully, and then Levinas. It's quite clear to me now that there are strong possibilities in post-structuralism for rationalizing a desire to replace one regime of truth with another. I don't think that Derrida, or especially Levinas, wanted to be identified strongly with any identifiable political movement.

I think Marxists have a lot to learn, not only from post-structuralism, but from many other schools of the habitually ignored. And Buddhism – I maintain an interest in Buddhism, I am not a Buddhist. I'm a student of Buddhist philosophy and of certain Buddhist practices. There is a problem, you know, in Buddhism, in saying "I am a Buddhist." I know that Buddhists say "I am a Buddhist," but from my Buddhist point of view I don't think I want to say that. So I think you can already see a sort of connection between Buddhism and Derrida's deconstruction. One of the problems, one of the big problems in the world, is the West's failure to respect – and by *respect* I mean to really get to know and study closely – non-Western forms of thought. And for me that turned out to be primarily Buddhism. Buddhist theories of the self have been developed for two thousand years, in intricate detail and in many different forms, in ways that could only enrich post-structuralist approaches, if they wanted to pay any attention to them. I don't know if I would criticize Derrida himself for ignoring Buddhism, because I think Derrida is a very important figure in the history of thought. And in the history of thought, people sometimes choose to ignore certain things in order to be able to develop their own thought.

But my friend Robert Magliola, who started out as a Catholic teacher in English literature in the States and ended up at the University of Taiwan, studied Buddhism, and wrote a book called *Derrida on the Mend*, which seeks to bring together Derridean deconstruction and Madyamika Buddhism. His book was either trashed or ignored. My book *Repression* just fell between two schools, but Magliola's attempt to teach Derrida something from the Buddhist point of view, and teach Buddhists something from a Derridean point of view, was worse than ignored.

Then, when Levinas comes along, I write a short Levinasian critique of Buddhism, which is addressed to Magliola. Basically the notion there is that the Levinasian, or you might say Judaic, notion of the primacy of ethical obligation answers certain questions that Buddhism has always been accused of not dealing with effectively. I point out that when the Buddha arose from his seat under the bo tree, and was struggling with the temptation not to tell anyone about his Enlightenment because no one would understand, he came to the conclusion that he was obligated to teach – that he had an obligation to teach people how to achieve liberation, spiritual liberation, for themselves. So the question is, where does this obligation come from? Who theorizes this obligation? Levinas is the theorist of ethical obligation. I began to take this into Buddhism.

NOTES

1 A version of this interview was originally published on Ctheory.net, 29 October 2003, http://ctheory.net/articles.aspx?id=397.

2 Gad Horowitz, *Canadian Labour in Politics* (Toronto: University of Toronto Press, 1968), 3.

3 Ibid.

4 Gad Horowitz, "Groundless Democracy," *Shadow of Spirit: Postmodernism and Religion*, ed. Philippa Berry and Andrew Wernick (London: Routledge, 1992), 156.

2 The Life and Times of Horowitz the Canadianist

NELSON WISEMAN

In the mid-1960s, Gad Horowitz and his ideas became prominent in both the academic and real worlds of Canadian politics. He appeared in and then departed Canadiana like a shooting star: a luminous flash that leaves an indelible mark on the mind. This chapter traces Horowitz's career as a Canadianist and connects his academic and related popular writings with his personal development as a Canadian public intellectual. It looks at how the Canadianist corpus of his work came about and was received and how it fit with and fuelled Canadians' evolving identity and sense of their country's ideological heritage. It examines Horowitz as a political activist and political scientist.

When "Conservatism, Liberalism, and Socialism in Canada: An Interpretation"[1] was first presented at the 1965 annual meeting of the Canadian Political Science Association, it created an unusual stir. At twenty-nine, Horowitz was a newly minted Harvard PhD and his paper soon made its debut in print in the old *Canadian Journal of Economics and Political Science*.[2] Shortly thereafter, it was reproduced in the Canadian Political Science Association's exclusive reprint series. It was the first chapter of his dissertation, and a revised and extended version of it appeared in his *Canadian Labour in Politics*.[3] "CLS" challenged and exploded the staid conventional wisdom among political scientists such as R. MacGregor Dawson and J.A. Corry about the role of ideology (they discounted it) in Canadian politics. Under the influence of political analysts and historians like Frank Underhill – then the foremost scholar of Canadian political thought and parties – the Liberals and Conservatives, notwithstanding their origins and British namesakes, came to be depicted as having evolved into pale muted versions of America's Democrats and Republicans. Underhill had turned from

the social democratic CCF (whose *Regina Manifesto* he co-authored) to
the Liberals and embraced and vindicated an omnibus brokerage role
for Canada's parties. He saw them through the eyes of American political scientists.[4] As he wrote to Horowitz at the time, "Our two parties
in spite of their names – Liberal and Conservative – really remained
right down to the present typical American composite, non-ideological
parties."[5]

Horowitz's contrarian interpretation of Canadian politics contrasted
Canada's parties and party system with their American counterparts.
He raised ideology to an unprecedented status in the study of Canadian politics. The nub of his thesis was "that the relative strength of
socialism in Canada is related to the relative strength of toryism and
to the different position and character of liberalism" in Canada and the
United States. The very last sentence of "CLS" was no less notable for
its prescience: "The 'antagonistic symbiosis' of Canadian liberalism
and socialism probably cannot be ended even by the magic of a char-
ismatic leader."[6] Soon after, Pierre Trudeau ascended to the apex of the
Liberal party and Trudeaumania swept the land, but the social democratic NDP neither faded nor ended its mutually advantageous but hostile relationship with the Liberals. It propped them up in the early 1970s
on the heels of a campaign in which it had denounced them as agents of
"corporate welfare bums."

"CLS" was neither written nor received as an ideological or partisan piece, but it provided the theoretical infrastructure and a scholarly
platform for Horowitz's normative orientations. Those were expressed
in his closely connected polemical writings in *Canadian Dimension* magazine. They and "CLS" informed each other. "CLS" and its offshoots
came to be caught up in the politics of the time. In this sense, the story
of Horowitz the Canadianist is one of the relationship between one individual's stream of thought and the way it coincides with larger movements and streams of thought in various contexts. "CLS" "was written
by Canada, not by me. Had I written it at a different conjuncture, it
would have sunk like a stone."[7]

"CLS" did more than shake established verities; it took root and
proved enduring. It came to be cited in innumerable places but it was
also subjected to withering criticism. It proved pedagogically potent as
teachers used it in survey courses in Canadian government and politics as well as in more specialized courses on parties, political culture,
and ideas and ideologies in Canadian politics. Researchers across a
range of fields have deployed it in a host of ways, from throwing light

on the politics of Montreal's Ukrainian immigrants to accounting for differences in educational financing in Canada and the United States.[8] Among the virtues of "CLS" are that it is well written, is engaging, and addresses big ideas. It fuses political theory with the behaviour and policies of parties in a comparative context. References to it and its "red tory" formulation continue in standard textbooks in the field.[9] "CLS" has been reproduced in at least six anthologies.[10] It persists as a staple in Hugh Thorburn's long-running collection, *Party Politics in Canada*. Having first appeared there in 1968, it is still there in the eighth edition in the twenty-first century. The sweep, nuance, verve, and panache of "CLS" proved to be fertile and disputatious. One book came to be constructed around it and another around demolishing it.[11] Two decades after its appearance, "CLS" was subjected to an anniversary assessment, one hurling broadsides at it only after noting, "It is one of the few things in the field that practically everyone has read and remembers."[12]

In building on and extending the work of Louis Hartz and Kenneth McRae, "CLS" placed the Canadian experience in the context of the political culture of new societies. Compared to Hartz's brilliantly dense and elliptical style, "CLS" was relatively easy to follow. Its comparativist complexion offered something for those outside the field of Canadian politics and outside of Canada itself. A study of why socialist labour movements arose in some industrialized states and not in others, for example, drew on Horowitz's connection between Canada's "statist and collectivist tradition" and Britain's nineteenth-century "aristocratic ideology" and its Canadian representation by the Conservative party.[13]

Genesis

"CLS" contributed to looking at Canadian politics in a new way and it also contributed to the very language and conduct of Canadian politics with its introduction of the "red tory." Horowitz did not coin the term *red tory*, but he minted its Canadian usage in "CLS." No one in Canada had used the concept before or developed the idea. Its appeal lay in its appearance as a curious paradox, a truth standing on its head: he linked the "red" of the left and the "tory" of the right. "At the simplest level," he wrote, "a red tory is a Conservative or NDPer who preferred the other's party to the Liberals." "At a higher level, he is a conscious ideological Conservative with some 'odd' socialist notions (W.L. Morton) or a conscious ideological socialist with equally 'odd' tory notions (Eugene Forsey)." George Grant was presented as the quintessential

Canadian red tory, one preaching the protection of "the public good against private freedom."[14] For both Grant and Forsey, spiritual values impelled political engagement,[15] a dimension of their thinking that Horowitz appreciated but did not pursue (although a reviewer of his book in the organ of the Christian Labour Association divined "a sense of religious commitment" in it).[16] Grant's affinity for social democracy was demonstrated in his later contribution, in the reddest of his red tory moments, to Michael Oliver's *Social Purpose for Canada*.[17] That book was a conscious effort to replicate for the fledgling NDP what the CCF's brain trust, the League for Social Reconstruction, had done with its *Social Planning for Canada*[18] in the 1930s.

Since the appearance of "CLS," the "red tory" has become pervasive in the lexicon of Canadian politics. It is popularly used, misused, and abused by politicians, journalists, and the public as well as academics in various disciplines. John McMenemy catalogued the "red tory" and "red toryism" in *The Language of Canadian Politics: A Guide to Important Terms and Concepts* and attributed the idea to Horowitz.[19] The red tory has become an apparent permanent fixture in the day-to-day combat of Canadian politics. In every federal election and Conservative leadership race, journalists identify and differentiate red tories from their mirror image "blue tories" or classical free market liberals. "Blue tories" are not ideological tories at all because they are detached from the tory notion of noblesse oblige, the obligation of the privileged to provide for the welfare of the less fortunate classes. Toryism is anchored in the belief in an organic inherited intergenerational social order where class harmony prevails, bonding a community of hierarchically differentiated unequal classes. It is an order where priority is given to the public's collective welfare over the ambitions and aggrandizement of possessive individualism.

But where did the "red tory" come from and how did it find its way into Horowitz's political cosmology? He almost certainly first encountered the term in a graduate seminar at Harvard that provided the research infrastructure for *British Politics in the Collectivist Age*, authored by his PhD supervisor, Samuel H. Beer.[20] Horowitz is thanked in the acknowledgments, and the book is cited in "CLS."[21] Beer was no socialist, but he was a leftist – a one-time president of the Americans for Democratic Action, the progressive ideological yeast in the Democratic Party. Horowitz wrote a major research paper for Beer in 1960 on late nineteenth-century British conservatism titled "Tory Democracy." It dissected the thinking of Disraeli and Lord Randolph

Churchill. Red tories such as Disraeli accepted noblesse oblige and also championed the masses against bourgeois elites. He legalized trade unions, and his friend John A. Macdonald followed suit. Horowitz prominently cited Disraeli's *Sybil*[22] and noted that one of the novel's themes was that if forward-looking aristocrats failed to rally to the defence of the masses, then the masses' leaders would arise from within their own ranks. Britain's nineteenth-century liberals linked socialism with toryism by accusing anti-individualist socialists of wanting to regress to an older feudal order. Beer's book gives voice to the tory-socialist axis in highlighting the connections between British toryism, as exemplified by Disraelian Conservatism, class divisions, and social reform. J.R. Mallory, one of Horowitz's teachers, and later a colleague, may be the only one who connected Horowitz's thesis – both with respect to toryism's organic element and the Liberals' successful class-less centrist appeal that worked in Canada but not in Europe – with Beer's work.[23]

If red toryism helped to mould Britain as Beer demonstrated, then the leap Horowitz made to Canadian red toryism was fathomable. English Canadians in the nineteenth century were overwhelmingly of British stock – British subjects in British North America as their constitution proclaimed. Beer was less sanguine about Horowitz's assertion of "a stream of Tory democracy in Canada ... [but] You know far more about it than I do."[24] English Canadians looked to Britain as their ideological progenitor for political and cultural models; their imperialist minds saw the British Empire as a "providential agency."[25] They and their Loyalist forebears considered themselves Britain's pre-eminent colonists.[26] Ontario's provincial motto, *Ut incepit sic permanet fidelis* (As it began, so it remains, faithful), gives voice and symbolic testimony to the tory legacy.

As Horowitz was reading in British politics, Grant's *Lament for a Nation*, a national bestseller,[27] appeared. A Loyalist scion, Grant was pessimistic about Canada's prospects of maintaining some of its historically non-American values. Horowitz, as a socialist, was optimistic. He thought Canadian socialists could draw on their country's tory legacy to critique capitalist liberal America: "A tory past contains the seeds of a socialist future."[28] Where Grant looked kindly on socialists but saw them as hopelessly utopian, Horowitz considered socialism and Canadian nationalism as in need of each other if either had a future in North America. Horowitz parted with tories like Grant, Morton, Donald Creighton, and Roger Graham, whose analyses were even more anti-liberal and anti-pan–North American than his. He saw the Loyal-ists as primarily liberal with a tory touch; they saw them as primarily tory.

Horowitz's dialectical connection between the organic communitari-anism of classical conservatism and the radical collectivism of social-ism was novel in Canada but, of course, not novel per se, since it had been emphasized by Louis Hartz a decade earlier in *The Liberal Tradition in America*[29] and by others before him. Hartz, a member of Horowitz's PhD committee, was an exhilarating, passionate teacher with even-tual Toynbean aspirations in seeking to develop a synthetic holistic ap-proach to history.[30] Many American academics lumped him together with Richard Hofstadter and excoriated them as subscribing to the "consensus" rather than "conflict" interpretation of American history, one that emphasized ideological heritage rather than material condi-tions.[31] Hartz intentionally used "broad terms broadly"[32] so that terms like *feudalism* and *Lockean* were deployed to make a sweeping historical argument. His book won the highest awards in the American political science fraternity. Horowitz chose his thesis topic while reading Hartz's book, struck that he could use the same framework to study Canada. The contrast between Mackenzie King and Franklin Roosevelt occurred to him in relation to Hartz's analysis of what FDR would have been like if he had had to face a powerful socialist challenge in America. To Horowitz, this was precisely the situation King faced in Canada. From that moment, "CLS" developed.

Long before Hartz, Engels had made the connection between conser-vatism and socialism in writing of "feudal socialism." He contended, like Hartz, that "a durable reign of the bourgeoisie has been possible only in countries like America, where feudalism [i.e., classical conser-vatism or toryism] was unknown."[33] Horowitz incorporated the socio-logical findings of Seymour Martin Lipset's early Canadian-American comparative study[34] to demonstrate toryism in Canada's historical tra-ditions and society. Canadian political culture was more hierarchical, ascriptive, particularistic, orderly, and state-centred than the political culture of the United States, and Canadians were more deferential to authority and law abiding than Americans, who were more egalitarian, entrepreneurial, and lawless, grounded in mantras of individualistic achievement and freedom. Lipset, however, did not see the "red" in Canadian toryism until Horowitz made the point. Lipset, impressed by Horowitz's analysis, wrote to him and subsequently cited his applica-tion of the conservative-socialist dialectic to Canada.[35]

Horowitz stood on Hartz's shoulders, but it was McRae who served as the perfect foil for "CLS." The attention garnered by *The Liberal Tradition in America* led, a decade later, to Hartz's collaborative and comparative *The Founding of New Societies.*[36] Horowitz was nearing the completion of his dissertation when McRae's excellent and under-appreciated history of Canadian ideological development appeared. It painted a landscape of an English-Canadian political culture that was but a slight variation of the American liberal tradition: "As the central figure of the English-Canadian tradition we encounter once again the American liberal."[37] This could not explain, however, the relative vibrancy of social democratic politics in Canada in contrast to the United States, whose politics Horowitz was also studying at Harvard with Arthur Schlesinger Jr, John Kennedy's assistant and biographer of his administration. To McRae, the CCF-NDP appeared as Louis St Laurent once characterized the party: "Liberals in a hurry." Horowitz drew on McRae's history, highlighted the ideological differences between Canadian liberalism and socialism, and pushed Hartz's thesis further. He used its comparativist sensibility to elevate and illuminate the contribution of Canada's tories, beginning with the Loyalists. In this respect, Horowitz's "CLS" was a revisionist footnote to McRae, whose analysis of Canada as a dual fragment culture – spun off from Britain's American colonies and ancien régime France – he accepted.

Political Socialization

Was there something in Horowitz's personal upbringing that helps to explain his attraction to the red tory thesis and the dialectical dance between classical conservatism and socialism? An appreciation of his political learning requires giving attention to both the agents and processes of his political socialization. The process of learning is lifelong, but what swirls about in one's late teens and the temper of that era are pivotal in shaping where one stands politically, in informing one's world view. Those coming of age in the midst of the Depression, for example, did so in a crucible quite different from that of those coming of age during the war a decade later, or in the 1950s, as Horowitz did. It was a time when material prosperity and American economic and cultural prowess seemed unbounded.

It was a time in Canada when political life seemed grey, deadened, and apolitical, where bureaucracy and technology reigned. After more than two decades of uninterrupted rule, the Liberals "had truly become the Government Party – an instrument for the depoliticization and bureaucratization of Canadian political life."[38] This was also Horowitz's view: "The Liberals needed a rest. Canada being a one party state seemed too true."[39] This led him to rally in support of John Diefenbaker's Conservatives, slapping a "Follow John" bumper sticker on his car and working to defeat long-time CCF stalwart Stanley Knowles in the Winnipeg riding that he and party founder J.S. Woodsworth had held, uninterrupted, since 1921. For his efforts, Horowitz (like many others in Winnipeg North Centre) was thanked by the winning Conservative candidate and invited to meet him whenever he was in Ottawa.[40]

Horowitz, however, did not join the Conservative party: "It was all about Dief. To us in the West, he didn't seem like a stupid populist." Rather, "he appeared fresh, relatively young, and a progressive human rights lawyer with a sense of humour." Horowitz's support for Diefenbaker's Conservatives was "pretty much non-ideological, typical of young Westerners." So it was not toryism per se that attracted Horowitz to the Conservative banner. To him, as to others, the Conservatives in the late 1950s looked to be to the left of the Liberals, who appeared as a non-ideological, business-oriented, bureaucratic party. As an undergraduate, he favoured a two-party system, as in the United States, and he depicted the CCF and Social Credit as "superfluous, splinter groups – vestiges of the depression that should have disappeared years ago."[41] This led to an exchange with fellow student and future Manitoba premier Howard Pawley, who argued that Canada needed a two-party system along British lines – "one dedicated to the preservation of Free Enterprise and the other geared towards the establishment of Democratic socialism."[42] This became Horowitz's position a decade later in "Toward the Democratic Class Struggle,"[43] but at the time Horowitz thought it "sophistic" thinking.

Horowitz's family and peers, religious and educational exposure, the media, as well as his images of political leaders and parties played a role in his political socialization. As a nine-year-old in Calgary during the 1945 federal election and under the influence of his activist Labour-Zionist uncles, he saw himself as a CCFer. During his couple of years as a Diefenbaker acolyte, Horowitz was an undergraduate at Winnipeg's United College, the temple that had produced a generation of social gospel preachers earlier in the century, including Woodsworth, under the tutelage of Salem Bland.[44] For Horowitz, "there was an aura of Woodsworth about the place and the idea of a people's church." He saw himself as a "pro-American liberal," but subliminally he was influenced by his leftist teachers: Harry Crowe (the labour historian), Ken McNaught (Woodsworth's biographer), Michael Oliver (the NDP's first president), and Marxists J.H. Stewart-Reid and H.C. Pentland. Their impact on his thinking, however, was "delayed." The "seeds of socialism were planted" in him by his professors but he did not realize it at the time.

In later identifying red tories like Grant, Forsey, and Morton in "CLS," Horowitz was referring to long-established Anglo Canadians whose tory consciousness was consistent with their upbringing and environment. They were raised in an era when organizations like the Imperial Order of Daughters of the Empire were vibrant and enjoyed high status. Horowitz's red tory exemplars lived and studied Canada's British connection; Forsey was a keen student of the British parliamentary tradition and Morton of British conservatives Burke and Peel. To Grant, the defeat of Diefenbaker symbolized the very defeat of Canadian nationalism. For one of them to formulate a Canadian version of the tory-cum-socialist hypothesis would have fit with their backgrounds and the touchstones of their British Canadian society. (Indeed, Grant dedicated *Lament* to a columnist and public servant who, he said, "stood for 'A Tory Socialism.'")[45] Horowitz, in contrast, was born a half world away from theirs, in Palestine. He was descended from a long uninterrupted line of rabbinical scholars that came from central Europe and settled in the Holy Land in 1620.

At first brush, therefore, it might seem odd that Horowitz served as a messenger to expound on the distinctively non-American characteristics of Canadian conservatism. When Horowitz was born in 1936, Palestine was governed under a British mandate from the League of Nations, and his father, Aaron, had an intimate connection with the British authorities; he served as the Hebrew-English interpreter/translator in the Palestine Supreme Court in Jerusalem and, for a time, was the liaison between the British military authorities and the Israeli labour movement, the Histadrut. He admired the British system of government and law and carried that with him when he emigrated to Canada in 1938. (He believed Gad to be Canada's first modern Hebrew-speaking child immigrant.) Woodsworth, after hearing Aaron debate a leading Communist on the topic of "Capitalism, Socialism, and Communism – Which?," asked him to work for the CCF.[46] Unlike his father, however, Gad was no fan of socialism as an undergraduate.

The Horowitz family's emigration from Palestine was related to the grandfather having accepted an invitation to serve as the chief rabbi of

western Canada in the 1920s. A rabbinical sensibility infused Horowitz's family, and like his father he became a strong cultural Zionist. He
co-founded the Student Zionist Organization at the University of Manitoba in 1957. He brought soon-to-be premier Duff Roblin to speak on
"Israel Day."[47] In the 1960s, as he worked on "CLS," he served as the
director of western Canada's only Hebrew-speaking camp and sometimes sported a skullcap with the Hebraic acronym for NDP sewn on it.
Horowitz cited his Jewish identity in his review of John Porter's *Vertical Mosaic*.[48] He related English-speaking Canadians' ethnic particularisms – "the confusing mix that is English Canada" – to the unfortunate
weakness of English-Canadian nationalism. He did so before Canada
adopted an official multicultural policy, the first in the world, in 1971.
He noted that Canadian Jewry felt itself to be an extension of American
Jewry because unlike American Jews – who identified strongly with
the United States – there was little sense of a Canadian community to
identify with. His view was that multicultural discourse divided rather
than bonded English-speaking Canadians, because British Canadians
had come to see themselves as just another ethnic group in a poly-
ethnic kaleidoscope of equally valued cultures. He saw the celebration
of multiculturalism as some critics came to see it later: a case of selling
illusions, of mosaic madness.[49]

   In the 1940s and 1950s, Horowitz and his immediate family moved
back and forth between New York, Winnipeg, Calgary, Montreal, Baltimore, and Israel, as his father worked as an itinerant educator. In Israel,
during his stay there shortly after its independence, peers taunted him
as an "Americani."[50] Resentful of the negative attitude of certain leftist
Israeli circles to the United States in the early 1950s, and disillusioned
with Israel, he became nostalgic for North America. He became a vora-
cious reader of U.S. history and politics, and, as a fifteen-year-old, he
translated from English to Hebrew a whole series of articles lauding
America's way of life without giving much thought to the distinction
between Canada and the United States. The editor of the pro-American Israeli magazine that published them (*Ha Maarav* – "The West")
responded to him as "Doctor Horowitz." A year later, he wrote to *Time*
extolling Eisenhower, and the editor thanked him for his "thoughtful
comments on the American economic and political picture."[51] Within a
few years of his family's return to Canada in 1952, his negative Israeli
experience wore off.

   Horowitz began his elementary education and completed his high
schooling in Calgary, attending the school where Bible Bill Aberhart
had been the principal before his election as Alberta's premier. One

application of Horowitz's thesis notes that "CLS" is oblivious to the presence of Social Credit.[52] Horowitz was, however, acutely aware of it, exposed to some of what he took as the anti-Semitic intonations of some of Premier Ernest Manning's popular *Back to the Bible Hour* radio broadcasts. Although he did not write about it, Horowitz shared Donald Smiley's view of Social Credit as Canada's Poujadists,[53] an anti-finance capital, anti-establishment, anti-intellectual, and populist petit bourgeois force. He and some of his undergraduate colleagues expressed their antipathy to Social Credit in a satirical poem they circulated at a federal election rally in Winnipeg that featured British Columbia premier W.A.C. Bennett as the guest speaker. The commotion they created garnered front-page headlines in the local press and led to their questioning by police. Bennett shrugged and told the police to let them go, in the office of the theatre manager.[54]

When Horowitz moved on to McGill in 1958 he undertook in his master's thesis a liberal critique ("I would have been on Robert Dahl's bandwagon in that regard") of C. Wright Mills's *The Power Elite*.[55] However, that contributed to his own radicalization: "When I finished, I realized that he was right and I was not.... Mills began to reignite the long dormant childhood socialism in me." Two students of Canadian public administration later perceptively recognized Horowitz as an "adherent" of Mills.[56] In "Toward the Democratic Class Struggle," which appeared at the same time as "CLS," Horowitz pleaded for a creative politics centred on a fight between clearly distinguishable left and right parties in a polarized party system. He bewailed the fact that the most important decisions in Canadian political life were being made by bureaucratic, corporate, and privileged elites that operated outside the orbit of democratic politics. Horowitz saw Canada as a class-stratified society and Canadians as no less class conscious than citizens in other stratified polities. In his view, and under the influence of Porter's pathbreaking *Vertical Mosaic*, the failure of the Canadian political regime was that the self-styled brokerage Liberal and Conservative parties bamboozled the electorate by playing on issues such as biculturalism, national unity, federal–provincial relations, and regional economic disparities. That led the public away from a class-based discourse, one that would take national unity as a given.

Horowitz became a founding member of the NDP in 1961, having written his first published piece on the formation of the party. He favoured the CCF becoming more of a labour party. It fit with his dissertation and his sympathies for the labour movement, whose pro-CCF leadership was, like him, anti-communist. It appeared in *Root and*

Branch (a forerunner of the radical *Ramparts*), of which Cy Gonick, the founder of *Canadian Dimension*, was an editor. Gonick brought Horowitz, along with David Scheps, on as *Dimension* associate editors in 1965, and it was there that his most popularly accessible writings appeared. While at Harvard, Horowitz had been further radicalized by the Bay of Pigs invasion, the civil rights movement, the rise of the New Left, and the Vietnam War. It was in that context and under the intellectual mentorship of Beer and Hartz that "CLS" was written.

At Harvard, Horowitz became very conscious of being Canadian and strongly identified as one, "something which I had never done before." Just as he had identified positively with Israel as a child in Canada, and as he had identified as an American as an adolescent in Israel, he began identifying positively with Canada as a graduate student in the United States, a case of "delayed influences and delayed identifications." As he was becoming a socialist intellectual and Canadian nationalist, he began to have a new respect for Canada's toryism. Now he saw it and institutions like the monarchy as what made Canada distinctive and open to socialism, unlike the United States. Horowitz's dissertation "Canadian Labour in Politics" – which David Lewis assessed as "an excellent piece of work, accurate, objective and thoroughly readable"[57] – was thus consistent with his leftist sympathies. Those socialist sympathies coincided with and were reinforced by those of peers like his friend Martin Robin, a fellow Winnipegger who wrote *Radical Politics and Canadian Labour, 1880–1930.*[58]

With "CLS" completed and PhD in hand, Horowitz returned to McGill to teach. The Quiet Revolution was in full bloom. Quebec's rapid modernization and political radicalization proved to be a living demonstration of the Hartz-Horowitz hypothesis: that New World socialism is born out of the synthesis of conflicting classical conservative and liberal ideologies. At the very same time that Horowitz's "CLS" was gaining currency, Quebec sociologist Marcel Rioux – who apparently had never read Hartz or Horowitz – mapped Quebec's ideological evolution using the same conservative-liberal-socialist triad as they did.[59] Horowitz embraced Quebec's *indépendantist* project, writing of "Quebec collectivism," applauding René Lévesque ("English Canada needs a Lévesque"), and critiquing Trudeauism.[60]

Reception and Reaction

The reception for "CLS" and Horowitz's related ideas was "hot," "cold," and "cool." "CLS" was "hot" academically in that it came to be immediately and frequently cited by scholars. Eugene Forsey noted that he read it "with the greatest delight and admiration."[61] It was obviously filling a void in the constituencies that knew of it and quickly established itself as the new conventional wisdom on the nature of Canadian political culture. The reception was "cold" in that "CLS" provoked much sceptical criticism and served well as a whipping boy. Horowitz's ideas were "cool" in that his popular excursions – most of which appeared first as political tracts in *Canadian Dimension* – fed and fed off a new sense of English-Canadian identity and nationalism that united an older and out-of-fashion British and conservative sensibility with a contemporary agenda for nationalists and socialists.

It was this corpus of his work, rather than the detached and academic "CLS," that attracted elite political attention in English Canada and Quebec. "Tories, Socialists and the Demise of Canada," "Mosaics and Identity," and "On the Fear of Nationalism" were reproduced in more scholarly venues. All three appeared in a tome titled *Canadian Political Thought* as well as in other books.[62] The plea for moving "Toward the Democratic Class Struggle," probably the best written of the lot, resurfaced in one book looking at Canada's past and another setting its agenda for its future.[63] The critique, "Trudeau vs Trudeauism," was reproduced in a collection of the most notable pieces that had appeared in *Canadian Forum* over the span of a half-century.[64] On an academic level, Horowitz offered an explanation for why Canada had a socialist party. Conservative academics like William Christian, Morton, and Grant were attracted to Horowitz's thesis because it suggested that socialism was a transfiguration, a resurfacing, of some aspects of toryism. His position, however, was perhaps somewhat different from theirs in that it maintained that liberalism – as well as conservatism and other conditions such as large cities and a working class – were required for socialism to emerge. Horowitz, like Hartz, did not think of his ideological-cultural interpretation as a case of single-factor determinism.

Horowitz deals with French Canada only in passing in "CLS," but he was an unabashed enthusiast about Quebec's drive for autonomy. His ideas attracted the attention of *Le Devoir* editor Claude Ryan, who published his "Le statut particulier, formule libératrice pour les deux communautés" on the eve of Canada's centennial.[65] His critique of Trudeauism was hailed by eminent Québécois nationalist historian Michel Brunet as "excellent," one coinciding with his own view of Trudeau as "un fumiste."[66] Horowitz became the only English Canadian quoted by Lévesque in his *Option Québec*.[67] He supported Quebec's drive for sovereignty partly because he connected efforts to halt that drive with "the weakness of the will to nationhood in English Canada."[68] His pro-posals for three types of national institutions – Québécois, English Ca-nadian, and pan-Canadian – appear remarkably similar to the Parti Québécois's White Paper on Sovereignty-Association[69] published much later in the run-up to the 1980 referendum. He thought that English Canada could learn from Quebec's greater receptivity to socialist ideas and contrasted English Canada's "dominant American values of indi-vidualism" with "the collectivist terms of the organic community" of Quebec.[70] Ken McNaught observed that Horowitz's ideas had shifted the NDP's position on Quebec.[71] In retrospect, the call by Horowitz and others for a *statut particulier* or "special status" for Quebec ap-pear somewhat similar to its later designation as a "distinct society" in the failed Meech Lake and Charlottetown Accords – accords of which Horowitz was leery. He feared that they would strengthen not only Quebec but also Anglo provincialisms at English Canada's collective expense.

At the political level in English Canada, Horowitz offered a rallying point and strategic direction for socialists specifically and nationalists more broadly. Before then, being a Canadian liberal generally meant being pro-American. His popular writings on English-Canadian na-tionalism and identity drew a wide and receptive audience among to-ries, liberals, and socialists. As with "CLS" in the academic community, he was saying something that people wanted to hear. In this respect, academic critics of Horowitz like Rod Preece and H.D. Forbes are cor-rect that his thesis filled a nationalist need.[72]

The media offered a platform and evidence of the popularity of Horowitz's nationalist message. Immediately after his 1965 presenta-tion of "CLS," the *Vancouver Sun* cited him as an expert on the inability of American liberalism to cope with the world[73] (an idea he took from Hartz). He then wrote "Tories, Socialists and the Demise of Canada" for a debate with Trudeau and Laurier LaPierre at the founding confer-ence of a group co-chaired by Liberal MP Pauline Jewitt – Exchange for Political Ideas in Canada (EPIC) – that brought together NDP and Lib-eral party thinkers. Excerpts of the debate were broadcast on CBC TV's landmark public affairs series *This Hour Has Seven Days* (and rebroad-cast in 2003). The *Toronto Star* then embraced Horowitz's nationalist ideas editorially. In response to the publicity, he received unsolicited offers from people keen to contribute time and money to an indepen-dence movement.[74] The *Star* followed up by soliciting his co-authored (with Gonick and G. David Sheps) "Open Letter to Canadian National-ists," which appeared on *Dimension*'s cover as well as in the *Star* with much fanfare.[75] It appeared the same week as Canada's centennial, as Montreal was hosting Expo 67, and as national pride was being stoked with symbols like the new maple leaf flag. That it was three Canadian Jews who penned the "Open Letter" perhaps indicates, speculates Horowitz, that it was necessary that one of English Canada's marginal identities become precociously concerned with the issue of English Canadian nationalism. This was because English Canadians' nationality had been weakened over time by their revolt against the British father and British past, by a kind of Oedipal neurosis, compounded by a sense of guilt and embarrassment about their treatment of French Canadians and by the Americanization of English Canada's economy, culture, and political discourse.

Horowitz's writings complemented the changing temper of the times. The *Star*'s interest in Horowitz waned, however, after it commissioned, but rejected, a companion piece of his that stressed the need for socialism in addition to nationalism.[76] The *Star* ought not to have been surprised. Horowitz had harnessed the nationalist horse to a socialist cart and proclaimed that objective months earlier in the *Star*'s competitor, the *Globe and Mail*. He wrote of a "nationalism that values the independence of Canada not as an end in itself but as a means to the goals of social democracy."[77]

To declare oneself a nationalist in Canada in the 1950s had been rare, unpopular, and for the most part embarrassing. Nationalism, according to the prevailing line of thought, had precipitated two tragic and disastrous world wars. Attitudes towards nationalism in Canada changed in the 1960s against a backdrop of increased Americanization of Canada's economy and popular culture. With increasing rejection of America's Vietnam policy and a growing sense of a separate Canadian identity, Canadians began to express increasing pride in noting Canadian-American differences. The *Toronto Telegram*'s John Harbron weighed in that "CLS" was "brilliant," and Susan Swan, in the same newspaper, hailed him "as probably the most radical young professor around – according to some the most brilliant."[78] *Maclean's* featured a special report on "The Heartening Surge of a New Canadian Nationalism." Peter Newman quoted Horowitz at length and described his magazine's "ulterior motive … [to] fan the flames" of nationalism. Reverberations of the new nationalism were felt in the real world of politics: the Conservative Party as well as Liberal cabinet ministers proposed restrictions on the foreign ownership of Canadian industries, and Trudeau's office downplayed his anti-nationalism as "speaking only against chauvinism."[79]

Horowitz became a celebrity intellectual in the media and among red tory politicians. He co-hosted a TV series in 1965–6 with Grant – *Ideals of Democracy and Social Reality* – interviewing Charles Taylor, Ramsay Cook, and C.B. Macpherson, as well as engaging in conversational exchanges with Grant. He also hosted a half-hour CBC radio weekly commentary series, *In Canada This Week*. Periodically, he appeared on *Viewpoint*, a commentary that followed CBC TV's nightly flagship national news broadcast. Horowitz's entrée to the CBC was via an innovative producer who thought his review of Grant's *Lament for a Nation* was "brilliant, the best yet, certainly the most original and prescient." The producer, Roy Faibish, had served as a special assistant to Alvin Hamilton, the Diefenbaker minister Horowitz had interviewed for his thesis and identified as a "red tory."[80] Hamilton thought the review was the "most thoughtful and useful article of its kind he had read in the last 20 years."[81] Gonick reported from Winnipeg "that Duff Roblin is very attracted to your thesis and a great admirer of yours."[82] Red tories recognized themselves in "Tories, Socialists, and the Demise of Canada," although Horowitz the socialist was not himself a red tory. NDPers liked the piece too. Desmond Morton sought Horowitz's permission to reprint excerpts in a party publication.[83]

Academics were also quite taken with Horowitz's ideas. Denis Smith, writing in *Canadian Forum*, termed "Tories, Socialists, and the Demise of Canada" a "brilliant essay."[84] Donald Smiley lauded "CLS" soon after its appearance, describing himself as being "much enlightened" by it.[85] In assessing "Contributions to Canadian Political Science since the Second World War," he termed it "brilliant and provocative" and assessed it and Porter's *Vertical Mosaic* as the two most significant analyses "in the direction of generalized interpretations of the Canadian political system and the Canadian political experience."[86] He praised it for challenging the fundamental assumption among Canadian scholars that Canadian politics were devoid of ideological content and that brokerage politics was good for the country. Sociologist Mildred Schwartz, McNaught, and CCF historian Walter Young, among others, also weighed in on "CLS" as "brilliant."[87] Harry Crowe termed it an "excellent study, or more accurately [in reviewing *Canadian Labour in Politics*] two excellent studies," but he did not care for its Hartzian element.[88] Underhill, who had sat in the front row as Horowitz read his paper at the Learneds, described it as the best presentation he had heard in his decades of attending the Learned Societies meetings.[89] Charles Taylor aligned himself with Horowitz's call for a more class-polarized Canadian politics and cited "CLS" to help account for the relative strength of populism in the United States, as contrasted with the relative strength of socialism in Canada.[90]

Horowitz's thesis, however, was also summarily dismissed: Richard J. Van Loon and Michael S. Whittington, for example, in the first edition of their long-running textbook, judged it speculative and unverifiable.[91] Nevertheless, they kept citing it and devoted more attention to it in subsequent editions of their text. They also dampened and shifted their criticism of it, most recently pointing to its "failure to incorporate economic variables." They and many others, however, adopted Horowitz's idea of the red tory and associated it, as Horowitz did, with the ideological hybridization of Canadian liberalism, a product of Canada's "tory streak."[92] They, among many, saw Horowitz's thesis as lacking in attention to economic factors, but others, such as Ian Angus, astutely observed that Horowitz was well aware that the red tory thesis actually "buttressed the Innisian economic explanation for an interventionist state."[93]

"CLS" and its related pieces attracted positive response, but they also came to be derided. The critics ranged across the spectrum with a range of objections. Reg Whitaker labelled "CLS" "hopelessly idealist from a Marxist perspective."[94] Along this line, one academic criticism was that Canada's alleged toryism was the product, not the cause, of Canadian elites using the instrumentality of the state to control and develop the economy.[95] The Canadian Trotskyist press hurled the same charge at Horowitz's thesis and decried the presentation of Canadian ideologies as "products of importation" rather than as an outgrowth of indigenous development.[96] Critics across the spectrum were uneasy about speculative theory at the expense of detailed historical research. Survey researchers also entered the fray to test Horowitz's hypotheses. Some were sceptical, others supportive. One concluded that "Red Tories look like Liberals in disguise" and that Horowitz's conception of Canada's parties was unnecessarily "heroic."[97] Another deployed a "toryism-conservative scale," finding Canadian conservatism lacking in genuine toryism, and others used it as a touchstone for measuring attitudes towards equality in Canada and the United States among elites and the masses.[98] Still others discerned "striking empirical support" for the contention that Canada's Liberals, compared with American liberal Democrats, mitigated their class appeal.[99]

Preece wrote of "The Myth of the Red Tory."[100] From this perspective, David Bell, Elizabeth Mancke, and Elwood Jones also disputed the view that the Loyalists represented a "point of departure" for the divergence of Canadian and American political cultures.[101] Robert Brym felt that Horowitz was fixated with the tory and British roots of Canadian socialism, and that led him to underestimate the role of French, Scandinavian, Jewish, Italian, and Ukrainian workers.[102] He as well as McNaught and others like William Christian and Colin Campbell held no brief for the idea of a national culture congealing,[103] the key to Hartz's theory of ideological fragmentation in New World societies. To Raymond Bazowski, the Hartz-Horowitz formulation was "mechanistic" and "procrustean,"[104] a case of fitting history to theoretical design and ignoring facts. Janet Azjenstat and Peter J. Smith summed up this critique in faulting Horowitz with "Bad History, Poor Political Science" and, going a step further: "It cripples Canadians' understanding of Canada's identity, and precludes a debate about current issues."[105]

Ramsay Cook had great fun as Horowitz's nemesis. He poked disparagingly at both his philosophy and analytical framework, describing Horowitz's application of Hartz's model as a "Canadian subsidiary of a theory wholly owned" by an American. He mocked his nationalist call to arms and his proposals for special status for Quebec as "platitudinous arrogance." A trumpeter for Trudeau, Cook conceded that Horowitz was "one of the most brilliant theoreticians of the nationalist left," but he had only contempt for Horowitz's whipping up of nationalist fervour. He saw that as a "doctrine of the discontented" and a contradiction of what socialism was about, an abandonment of its internationalism. Encouraging socialists to become nationalists, as Horowitz did, was "bad tactically and disastrous philosophically," because the socialists would be out-jingoed by the other parties. Cook objected to the historical determinism he discerned in both Grant and Horowitz. He saw nationalism as the Achilles heel of reform and thought the organic view of society shared by tories and nationalists had little to do with socialism's communitarianism.[106]

Exit Canadiana

When he moved to the University of Toronto in 1967, Horowitz had the opportunity to pursue directly the issue of English-Canadian nationalism in its cultural capital. Praxis, however, was not to be. A shift in his thinking was evident in an interview with the student newspaper soon after his arrival. The reporter hailed him as "probably the most promising thinker in Canada today," but Horowitz described himself as "a political schizophrenic," a "frustrated radical" who supported the moderate social reform of the NDP but who really wanted a fundamental transformation of society. He refused to see the hippies as misdirected, escapist, or immature. He saw them as a heartening manifestation of true revolutionary fervour, although he did not expect them to trigger a social revolution. His vision of the United States was that it was "a chronically sick, frightfully insane society, tottering on the brink of total madness." Canada too is sick, he suggested in 1968, sharing many of America's symptoms of madness.[107] Thus, between the ages of fifteen and thirty, Horowitz went from admiring American ideology and its dominant forces to being repelled by them. In between, he became a leading Canadianist and Canadian public intellectual.

Horowitz's Canadianist phase faded by the late 1960s. Even earlier, in the mid-1960s, he declined an opportunity extended by Michael Oliver to work for the Royal Commission on Bilingualism and Biculturalism. When W.L. Morton asked him to write a paper on "The Monarchy and Socialism," he begged off.[108] Beyond the national question, Horowitz served fleetingly as vice-president of the Canadian Civil Liberties Association, out of concern that "we'll become a more oppressive society with social controls perfected,"[109] an echo of Herbert Marcuse's notion of repressive tolerance. As an academic, Horowitz focused on teaching political theory and largely exited the study of Canadian politics. He exited the field too as a political activist. The Movement for an Independent Socialist Canada, the Committee for an Independent Canada, and the Waffle, among other new nationalist formations, arose at the turn of the 1970s. Horowitz's writings in the *Forum* and *Dimension* had fed their socialist and nationalist agendas, and while sympathetic to them, he held aloof from joining them. When the NDP expelled the Waffle in 1972, he let his NDP membership lapse.

A decade after the appearance of "CLS," Horowitz briefly re-entered Canadiana by responding to an assortment of critiques.[110] Rejoinders, like sequels, however, do not capture the attention or convey the imaginative spark that originals do. They are not ventures onto the frontiers of new research or thinking, as "CLS" was. Some intra-Canadian extrapolations of the Hartz-Horowitz hypothesis by others appeared,[111] but Horowitz, influenced by counterculture figures like Allen Ginsberg, Timothy Leary, Abbie Hoffman, and Jerry Rubin, temporarily lost interest in the conventional academic world and left the national question to others. "I became an internal exile … much more interested in what was deep within me. I was too radical for organized politics." When the War Measures Act was imposed in 1970, "no day was colder" for him. His views of it, via a review of Gérard Pelletier's book about it, appeared simultaneously in *Canadian Forum* and *Le Devoir*.[112]

When Horowitz resumed writing academically, it was in the realm of psychoanalytic theory and, later, political philosophy. Marcuse's *Eros and Civilization*[113] had been slowly percolating in his mind ever since he had read it in the early 1960s. The eventual product, *Repression*, had a little joke embedded in it, however, that connected the two periods of his thought: the "tory Freudian" and the "red Freudian."[114] Horowitz used the former to describe psychoanalytic insights that reinforce a tory world view, a view that human nature is inherently faulty and problematic, a view of human existence as involving a high degree of unalterable pain.

In an era of increased academic specialization, most scholars devote themselves to establishing and extending their authority in a particular branch or field of their discipline. The remarkable diversity of Horowitz's intellectual engagement – from Canadian politics to modern political thought, psychoanalytic theory, sexuality, Buddhism, and general semantics – established him as much more than a mere eclectic. The depth and quality of his engagement within and beyond the conventional bounds of political science and its Canadian politics sub-field demonstrates breadth of ken, creativity, and profound insight.

NOTES

1 Hereafter "CLS."
2 Gad Horowitz, "Conservatism, Liberalism, and Socialism in Canada: An Interpretation," *Canadian Journal of Economics and Political Science* 32, no. 2 (1966): 143–71.
3 Gad Horowitz, *Canadian Labour in Politics* (Toronto: University of Toronto Press, 1968).
4 Carl Berger, *The Writing of Canadian History: Aspects of English-Canadian Historical Writing* (Toronto: Oxford University Press, 1976), 196.
5 Frank Underhill to Gad Horowitz, 18 February 1962. I am indebted to GH for access to his files.
6 Gad Horowitz, "CLS," in *Canadian Labour in Politics*, 3 and 57.
7 Interviews with Gad Horowitz, November 1987 and February–March 2006. I am grateful to GH for access to his files.

8 Yarema G. Kelebay, "Three Fragments of the Ukrainian Community in Montreal, 1899–1970: A Hartzian Approach," *Canadian Ethnic Studies* 12, no. 2 (1980): 74–87; and Stephen Lawton, "Political Values in Educational Finance in Canada and the United States," *Journal of Educational Finance* 5 (Summer 1979): 1–18.

9 For example: Stephen Brooks, *Canadian Democracy: An Introduction*, 4th ed. (Toronto: Oxford University Press, 2004), 37 and 503; Rand Dyck, *Canadian Politics: Critical Perspectives*, 4th ed. (Scarborough: Thomson Nelson, 2004), 317; James John Guy, *People, Politics and Government: A Canadian Perspective*, 6th ed. (Toronto: Pearson, 2006), 79 and 308; Robert J. Jackson and Doreen Jackson, *Politics in Canada: Culture, Institutions, Behaviour and Public Policy*, 6th ed. (Toronto: Pearson, 2006), 67; Heather McIvor, *Parameters of Power: Canada's Political Institutions*, 4th ed. (Toronto: Thomson Nelson, 2006), 38.

10 Janet Ajzenstat and Peter J. Smith, *Canada's Origins: Liberal, Tory, or Republican?* (Ottawa: Carleton University Press, 1995); Christopher Beattie and Stuart Crysdale, eds., *Sociology Canada: Readings* (Toronto: Butterworth, 1974); Mark O. Dickerson, Thomas Flanagan, and Neil Nevitte, eds., *Introductory Readings in Government and* Politics (Toronto: Methuen, 1983); Orest M. Kruhlak, Richard Schultz, and Sidney Pobihushchy, eds., *The Canadian Political Process* (Toronto: Holt, Rinehart and Winston, 1970); W.E. Mann, ed., *Canada: A Sociological Profile* (Toronto: Copp-Clark, 1971); J.T. McLeod and R.S. Blair, eds., *The Canadian Political Tradition* (Toronto: Methuen, 1987); H.G. Thorburn and Alan Whitehorn, eds., *Party Politics in Canada*, 8th ed. (Toronto: Prentice-Hall, 2001).

11 Ajzenstat and Smith, *Canada's Origins*; and William Christian and Colin Campbell, *Political Parties and Ideologies in Canada: Liberals, Conservatives, Socialists, Nationalists*, 2nd ed. (Toronto: McGraw-Hill Ryerson, 1983).

12 H.D. Forbes, "Hartz-Horowitz at Twenty: Nationalism, Toryism and Socialism in Canada and the United States," *Canadian Journal of Political Science* 20, no. 2 (June 1987): 287.

13 John H. Kautsky, *Social Democracy and Aristocracy* (New Brunswick, NJ: Transaction, 2002), 141–3.

14 "CLS," in *Canadian Labour in Politics*, 23.

15 William Christian, *George Grant: A Biography* (Toronto: University of Toronto Press, 1993); and Frank Milligan, *Eugene A. Forsey: An Intellectual Biography* (Calgary: University of Calgary Press, 2004).

16 Harry Antonides, *Guide* 18, no. 2 (February 1970): 18.

17 Michael Oliver, ed., *Social Purpose for Canada* (Toronto: University of Toronto Press, 1961).

18 League for Social Reconstruction, *Social Planning for Canada* (Toronto: Thomas Nelson, 1935).
19 John McMenemy, *The Language of Canadian Politics: A Guide to Important Terms and Concepts* (Toronto: John Wiley, 1980), 226–7.
20 Samuel H. Beer, *British Politics in the Collectivist Age* (New York: Alfred A. Knopf, 1965).
21 Horowitz, "CLS," in *Canadian Labour in Politics*, 19.
22 Benjamin Disraeli, *Sybil*, ed. Sheila M. Smith (1845; New York: Oxford University Press, 1981).
23 J.R. Mallory, *The Structure of Canadian Government*, rev. ed. (Toronto: Gage, 1984), 218 and 224.
24 Samuel H. Beer to GH, 6 June 1963.
25 Carl Berger, *The Sense of Power: Studies in the Ideas of Canadian Imperialism* (Toronto: University of Toronto Press, 1970), 217–18.
26 Sid Noel, "The Ontario Political Culture: An Interpretation," in *The Government and Politics of Ontario*, ed. Graham White, 5th ed. (Toronto: University of Toronto Press, 1997), 58.
27 George Grant, *Lament for a Nation: The Defeat of Canadian Nationalism* (Toronto: McClelland and Stewart, 1965).
28 Gad Horowitz, "Tories, Socialists and the Demise of Canada," in *Canadian Political Thought*, ed. H.D. Forbes (1965; Toronto: Oxford University Press, 1985), 359.
29 Louis Hartz, *The Liberal Tradition in America: An Interpretation of American Political Thought* (New York: Harcourt, Brace, 1955).
30 Paul Roazen, "Louis Hartz's Teaching," *Virginia Quarterly Review* 64, no. 1 (Winter 1988): 108–25.
31 Howard Zinn, "The New World: Fragments of the Old," *Nation*, 25 May 1965, 562–3.
32 Hartz, *Liberal Tradition in America*, 3.
33 Fredrick Engels, Introduction to *Socialism: Utopian and Scientific*, in *Selected Works in One Volume*, by Karl Marx and Fredrick Engels (New York: International Publishers, 1968), 394.
34 Seymour Martin Lipset, *The First New Nation* (New York: Basic Books, 1963), chap. 7.
35 Seymour Martin Lipset to GH, 28 February 1969, and 27 September 1983; and Lipset, "Historical Traditions and National Characteristics: A Comparative Analysis of Canada and the United States," *Canadian Journal of Sociology* 11, no. 2 (1986): 136.
36 Louis Hartz, ed., *The Founding of New Societies: Studies in the History of the United States, Latin America, South Africa, Canada, and Australia* (New York: Harcourt, Brace and World, 1964).

37 Kenneth McRae, "The Structure of Canadian History," in Hartz, *Founding of New Societies*, 219 or 234.

38 Reginald Whitaker, *The Government Party: Organizing and Financing the Liberal Party of Canada, 1930–58* (Toronto: University of Toronto Press, 1977), 420.

39 Gad Horowitz, interview by Nelson Wiseman, 25 February 2006.

40 Murray Smith to GH, 22 April 1958.

41 Gad Horowitz, "Our Cup Runneth Over," *Manitoban*, 20 September 1957.

42 H. Pawley, letter to the editor, "The Two Party System," *Manitoban*, 16 October 1957.

43 Gad Horowitz, "Toward the Democratic Class Struggle," *Journal of Canadian Studies* 1, no. 3 (November 1966): 3–10.

44 Salem Goldworth Bland, *The New Christianity* (1920; Toronto: University of Toronto Press, 1973).

45 George Grant, letter to the editor, *Canadian Dimension*, 2 June 1965.

46 Aron Horowitz, *Striking Roots: Reflecting on Five Decades of Jewish Life* (Oakville, ON: Mosaic, 1979), 7, 18–21, 50.

47 Duff Roblin to GH, 23 January 1958.

48 Gad Horowitz, "Mosaics and Identity," *Canadian Dimension* (January–February 1966; Forbes, *Canadian Political Thought*, 362.

49 Reginald Bibby, *Mosaic Madness* (Toronto: Stoddart, 1990); and Neil Bissoondath, *Selling Illusions: The Cult of Multiculturalism* (Toronto: Penguin, 2002).

50 Aron Horowitz, *Striking Roots*, 207.

51 Gwyneth Kahn to GH, 18 March 1952.

52 Hamish Telford, "The Reform Party / Canadian Alliance and Canada's Flirtation with Republicanism," in *Canada: The State of the Federation 2001; Canadian Political Culture(s) in Transition*, ed. Hamish Telford and Harvey Lazar (Montreal and Kingston: McGill-Queen's University Press, 2002), 132.

53 Donald Smiley, "Canada's Poujadists: A New Look at Social Credit," *Canadian Forum* (September 1962): 122.

54 "'Filthy Poem' Outrages West Coast Premier," and "Poetry, Politics, Police," undated clippings (likely March 1957), *Winnipeg Free Press* and *Winnipeg Tribune*, in GH's files.

55 C. Wright Mills, *The Power Elite* (New York: Oxford University Press, 1959).

56 Robert F. Adie and Paul G. Thomas, *Canadian Public Administration* (Scarborough, ON: Prentice-Hall, 1987), 564.

57 David Lewis to Frances G. Halpenny, 16 August. 16, 1966.

58 Martin Robin, *Radical Politics and Canadian Labour, 1880–1930* (Kingston: Industrial Relations Centre, Queen's University, 1968).

59 Marcel Rioux, *Quebec in Question*, trans. James Boake (1969; Toronto: James Lorimer, 1978).

60 Gad Horowitz, "Trudeau vs Trudeauism," *Canadian Forum* 48, no. 568 (May 1968): 29-30; and Horowitz, "Why René Lévesque Became a Separatist – Part III: A Symposium on René Lévesque," *Canadian Dimension* 5, nos. 2 and 3 (January–March 1968): 20–1.

61 Eugene Forsey to GH, 1 October 1964.

62 "Tories, Socialists and the Demise of Canada " is also in William Kilbourn, ed., *Canada: A Guide to the Peaceable Kingdom* (Toronto: Macmillan, 1970), 254–60. "Creative Politics, Mosaics and Identity" is also in James L. Heap, ed., *Everybody's Canada: The Vertical Mosaic Re-examined* (Toronto: Burns and MacEachern, 1970), 4–31; and "Mosaics and Identity" is in Bryan Finnigan and Cy Gonick, eds., *Making It: The Canadian Dream* (Toronto: McClelland and Stewart, 1972), 465–73. "On the Fear of Canadian Nationalisms: A Sermon to the Moderates" is also in John E. Kersell and Marshall W. Conley, eds., *Comparative Political Problems: Britain, United States, and Canada* (Scarborough, ON: Prentice-Hall, 1968): 255–9; and "On the Fear of Nationalism" is in Paul W. Fox, ed., *Politics: Canada*, 4th ed. (Toronto: McGraw-Hill Ryerson, 1977), 112–15.

63 Trevor Lloyd and Jack McLeod, eds., *Agenda 1970: Proposals for a Creative Politics* (Toronto: University of Toronto Press, 1968); and Bruce W. Hodgins and Robert J.D. Page, eds., *Canada since Confederation: Essays and Interpretations* (Georgetown, ON: Irwin-Dorsey, 1972).

64 J.L. Granatstein and Peter Stevens, eds., *Forum: Canadian Life and Letters, 1920–70* (Toronto: University of Toronto Press, 1972).

65 30 June 1967.

66 Michel Brunet to GH, 7 July 1968.

67 Rene Lévesque, *Option Québec* (Montreal: Les editions de l'homme, 1968), 49.

68 Gad Horowitz, "The Future of English Canada," *Canadian Dimension* 2 (July–August 1965): 12.

69 Quebec, *Québéc-Canada: A New Deal* (Quebec, 1979).

70 GH in conversation with George Grant, transcript of CBC TV program "Ideals of Democracy and Social Reality," 9 January 1966; and undated 1963 transcript of CBC TV program "Viewpoint."

71 Kenneth McNaught, "The NDP's Special Status Kick," *Saturday Night*, October 1967.

72 Rod Preece, "The Anglo-Saxon Conservative Tradition," *Canadian Journal of Political Science* 13, no. 1 (March 1980): 24; and Forbes, "Hartz-Horowitz at Twenty."

73 "U.S. Can't Cope in Other Politics," *Vancouver Sun*, 14 June 1965.
74 "A Voice for Canadian Independence," *Toronto Star*, 11 March 1967; and, for example, Ethel Nielson to GH, 13 March 1967; and Alan G. McKay to GH, 11 March 1967.
75 Mark Harrison to GH, 15 March 1967; and Gad Horowitz, Cy Gonick, and G. David Sheps, "An Open Letter to Canadian Nationalists," *Toronto Star*, 7 July 1967.
76 Gad Horowitz, "Canada in the Second Hundred Years" (unpublished paper, 1967).
77 Gad Horowitz, "21 Voices Call Out for Canada," *Globe and Mail*, 5 November 1966.
78 Susan Swan, "What's Wrong with the Political System?," 21 February 1968; and "Gad Horowitz Is a Resigned Revolutionary" (n.d., ca. 1968 or 1969), from the files of GH.
79 *Maclean's*, February 1970.
80 "CLS," in *Canadian Labour in Politics*, 22–3; and "Tories, Socialists and the Demise of Canada," in Forbes, *Canadian Political Thought*, 359.
81 Roy A. Faibish to GH, 15 July 1965.
82 Cy Gonick to GH, 12 May 1966.
83 Desmond Morton to GH, 21 April 1969.
84 Denis Smith, *Canadian Forum*, October 1969, 171.
85 Donald Smiley, *The Canadian Political Nationality* (Toronto: Methuen, 1967), 109n.
86 Donald Smiley, "Essay in Bibliography and Criticism: Contributions to Canadian Political Science since the Second World War," *Canadian Journal of Economics and Political Science* 33, no. 4 (November 1967): 575.
87 Kenneth McNaught, "Comment," in *Failure of a Dream? Essays in the History of American Socialism*, ed. John H. M. Laslett and Seymour Martin Lipset, 409–20 (New York: Doubleday, 1974); Mildred Schwartz, review of *Canadian Labour in Politics* by Gad Horowitz, *Political Science Quarterly* 85, no. 4 (December 1970): 692–4; and Walter Young, review of *Canadian Labour in Politics* by Gad Horowitz, *Canadian Historical Review* 50, no. 4 (1969): 86–7.
88 Harry Crowe, review of *Canadian Labour in Politics*, by Gad Horowitz. *Canadian Journal of Political Science* 2, no. 2 (June 1969): 270–1.
89 Interview with Ken McNaught, November 1987.
90 Charles Taylor, review of *Agenda 1970: Proposals for a Creative Politics* by Trevor Lloyd, *Canadian Journal of Political Science* 2, no. 3 (September 1969): 386; and Taylor, *The Pattern of Politics* (Toronto: McClelland and Stewart, 1970), 13.

91 Richard J. Van Loon and Michael S. Whittington, *The Canadian Political System: Environment, Structure and Process* (Toronto: McGraw-Hill, 1971), 275–6.
92 Michael S. Whittington and Richard J. Van Loon, *Canadian Government and Politics: Institutions and Processes* (Toronto: McGraw-Hill Ryerson, 1996), 94–5, and 101–3.
93 Ian Angus, "The Paradox of Cultural Identity in English Canada," in "Sociology in Anglophone Canada," special issue of *Les Cahiers de recherche sociologique* 39 (2003), http://www.ianangus.ca/paradox.htm.
94 Reg Whitaker, "Images of the State," in *The Canadian State: Political Economy and Political Power*, ed. Leo Panitch (Toronto: University of Toronto Press, 1977), 30.
95 R.T. Naylor, "The Rise and Fall of the Third Commercial Empire of the St Lawrence," in *Capitalism and the National Question in Canada*, ed. Gary Teeple (Toronto: University of Toronto Press, 1972), 18 and 39n57.
96 K. Holland, *Workers Vanguard* (Toronto), 16 December 1968.
97 Richard Johnston, "The Ideological Structure of Opinion on Policy," in *Party Democracy in Canada*, ed. George Perlin (Scarborough, ON: Prentice-Hall, 1988), 65.
98 Paul Sniderman, Joseph F. Fletcher, Peter Russell, and Philip E. Tetlock, *A Clash of Rights* (New Haven, CT: Yale University Press, 1996), 82–5; and Tom Truman, "A Scale for Measuring a Tory Streak in Canada and the United States," *Canadian Journal of Political Science* 10, no. 3 (1977): 597–614.
99 Allan Kornberg, Joel Smith, and David Bromley, "Some Differences in the Political Socialization Patterns of Canadian and American Party Officials: A Preliminary Report," *Canadian Journal of Political Science* 2, no. 1 (March 1969): 64–8.
100 Rod Preece, "The Myth of the Red Tory," *Canadian Journal of Social and Political Theory* 1, no. 2 (1977): 3–28.
101 David V.J. Bell, *The Roots of Disunity: A Study of Canadian Political Culture*, rev. ed. (Toronto: Oxford University Press, 1992), 39; Elwood Jones, "The Loyalists and Canadian History," *Journal of Canadian Studies* 20, no. 3 (1985): 149–56; and Elizabeth Mancke, "Early Modern Imperial Governance and the Origins of Canadian Political Culture," *Canadian Journal of Political Science* 32, no. 1 (March 1999): 3–20.
102 Robert Brym, *From Culture to Power: The Sociology of English Canada* (Toronto: Oxford University Press, 1989), 174.
103 Ibid., 30 and 63; and McNaught, "Comment."

104 Rymond Bazowski, "Contrasting Ideologies in Canada," in *Canadian Politics*, ed. James Bickerton and Alain-G. Gagnon, 3rd ed. (Peterborough, ON: Broadview, 1999), 92–3.
105 Janet Azjenstat and Peter J. Smith, "'The 'Tory Touch' Thesis: Bad History, Poor Political Science," in *Crosscurrents: Contemporary Political Issues*, ed. Mark Charlton and Paul Barker, 4th ed. (Toronto: Thomson Nelson, 2002), 68.
106 Ramsay Cook, letter, *Canadian Forum* 48, no. 570 (July 1968): 81–2; Cook, *The Maple Leaf Forever: Essays on Nationalism and Politics in Canada* (Toronto: Macmillan, 1971), 198–9; and Cook, "A Nationalist Intellectual behind Every Maple Tree," *Saturday Night*, April 1970, 21.
107 Stephen Bornstein, "Gad Horowitz versus Americrap," *Varsity*, 19 January 1968.
108 W.L. Morton to GH, 1 May 1972.
109 Susan Swan, "Gad Horowitz Is a Resigned Revolutionary."
110 Gad Horowitz, "The 'Myth' of the Red Tory?," *Canadian Journal of Political and Social Theory* 1, no. 3 (1977): 87–7; and Gad Horowitz, "Notes on 'Conservatism, Liberalism and Socialism in Canada,'" *Canadian Journal of Political Science* 11, no. 2 (June 1978): 383–99.
111 Gordon S. Galbraith, "British Columbia," in *The Provincial Political Systems: Comparative Essays*, ed. David Bellamy, 62–75 (Toronto: Methuen, 1976); Nelson Wiseman, "A Note on 'Hartz-Horowitz at Twenty': The Case of French Canada," *Canadian Journal of Political Science* 21, no. 4 (December 1988): 795–806; Wiseman, "The Pattern of Prairie Politics," *Queen's Quarterly* 88, no. 2 (1981): 298–315; and Wiseman, "Provincial Political Cultures," in *Provinces: Canadian Provincial Politics*, ed. Christopher Dunn, 21–62 (Peterborough, ON: Broadview, 1996).
112 Gad Horowitz, "The Perils of 'Complaisance.'" *Canadian Forum* 51, nos. 603–4 (April/May 1971): 39–41; and "Les *perils* de la *complaisance. Le Devoir*, 10 April 1971.
113 Herbert Marcuse, *Eros and Civilization* (1955; London: Abacus, 1972).
114 Gad Horowitz, *Repression: Basic and Surplus Repression in Psychoanalytic Theory; Freud, Reich and Marcuse* (Toronto: University of Toronto Press, 1977), 196–201.

3 The Odd Couple of Canadian Intellectual History

EDWARD G. ANDREW

My subject in this piece is not the couple designated for four years by *Frank Magazine* to be Canada's looniest academic couple, namely, one of the editors of this volume, Shannon Bell, and Gad Horowitz, but the latter's relationship with George Grant. Grant was Canada's leading conservative thinker, and Gad is our foremost socialist thinker. The friendly interaction between the conservative Grant and the socialist Horowitz produced the legend of the red tory tradition in Canadian intellectual history.

In *Typing*, Matt Cohen described his affection for George Grant as "an enormously overgrown and very mischievous schoolboy who had somehow escaped school for the afternoon." Cohen and Horowitz were drawn to Grant in the 1960s as the strongest voice in Canada against the Vietnam War, which they all saw as· the clearest manifestation of technological imperialism. Cohen and Horowitz were very successful, but not at home, in an academic world and seemed to admire Grant's playing hooky, while cocking a snoot at an academe serving the interests of international corporations. In a sense, Grant was "the other" for Cohen and Horowitz. He was, in Cohen's words, "part of what I saw as the British-Canadian ruling establishment, whose authoritarianism and anti-Semitism had frequently rung extremely sour notes in my life.... So, to begin with, Grant was clearly the enemy. On the other hand, Grant was also clearly a friend." Grant hired Cohen to teach at McMaster University, although he was unqualified to teach in a Department of Religion. Cohen described an intellectual impasse between himself and Grant towards the end of his stay at McMaster. Cohen told Grant that "as an egalitarian, he had to believe each person's essential worth was equal to any other person's, whereas as a Christian he

might be encouraged to believe that those who had accepted Christianity were in a different position, in terms of eternity, than others....
[Grant] held out his arms hopelessly. 'But I *am* a Christian,' he said. 'I *am*. I have to believe that Christianity has a higher truth than Judaism or anything else.'"[1] Grant thought religion should be taught from the inside, from the experience of faith, not as a research object correlating objective facts about religious behaviour, or, as Grant thought, religion taught from the outside. Grant thought every person's faith contained greater truth than other beliefs – why else hold that faith? – and when head of McMaster's Religion Department hired persons of many faiths, including Judaism, to articulate that experience.

Cohen's memoirs do not intimate that Grant was anti-Semitic but just that he needed to free himself of Grant's monumental presence and will to construct everyone in his own image.[2] Cohen was describing an unbridgeable difference between himself and Grant that was impeding his development of his identity as an author. Grant thought Christians had an inside lane on salvation, not a monopoly toll road to heaven. Cohen's objection is difficult for me to understand; firstly because he did not believe in eternity at the time of the confrontation, and secondly because his assumption that egalitarians have to be secularists and cultural relativists is questionable. Jews, Muslims, and Buddhists hold that their religion provides a better account of the way to be, or the manner of achieving virtue and happiness, than alternative religions, although decent religions do not insist that their way is the only true way. Further, decent individuals do not deprecate the religion of others. In his recently published lecture notes, Grant wrote, in the context of an account of Pythagoreanism and Orphism, the following offensively stupid and false remark: "Semitic religion or what Christians call the Old Testament seems to me in many ways a very dangerous and unspiritual and false religion."[3] Grant thought the Old Testament contained bloody militarism and seemed to be keen on uncoupling the historical link between Judaism and Christianity, and link Christianity with religions like Pythagoreanism, Buddhism, and Hinduism, which Grant thought offered access to eternity unmediated by the historical Judaeo-Christian tradition. He also thought the divine in the bare monotheisms (Judaism and Islam) too remote; Grant found Jesus and Krishna more approachable than William Blake's "Nobodaddy."

Despite his fidelity to the rabbinical tradition in which he was raised, Horowitz was and is attracted by Buddhism – perhaps because Buddhism has a more dialectical relationship to nothingness or is closer to atheism than other religions. Horowitz emphasized the historicity of our lives – that we are both creatures and creators of history – and emphasized the prophetic element in Judaism, the enunciation of the unprecedented. While the Grant–Cohen relationship suggests that there are (Christian, Jewish, atheist) philosophies (or ideologies) but no philosophy, the Grant–Horowitz relationship suggests that there is a common enterprise, namely, philosophy, in which both Grant and Horowitz participated.

It would be quite possible to interpret Grant as anti-Judaic, as he has been interpreted as anti-American. But those who have read "In Defense of North America" in *Technology and Empire* would know that Canada is part of North America as Christianity is part of the biblical tradition. Grant wished to distinguish the siblings from one another and indicate the grounds of his identification with Canada and Christianity.

Cohen objected not to Grant's Christianity but to his overpowering will to make over McMaster's Department of Religion in his image and likeness. Cohen had to wrest himself free of his overpowering friend to write his own life and eventually encounter his Jewish identity.

My theme is the relationship between two of Canada's leading thinkers, Gad Horowitz and George Grant. I have used Cohen's *Typing* because Horowitz's writings are not autobiographical as are Cohen's and Grant's. I was one of Gad's colleagues to wish that his study of psychoanalytic theory, *Repression*, included some of his diaries and dreams as he required from his students in his courses on psychoanalytic theory. The anti-Platonist Horowitz disappears into his subject matter as Plato did, whereas the anti-Nietzschean Grant approached the egoicity of *Ecce Homo* for self-revelation. For example, responding to Rodney Crook's "Modernization and Nostalgia: A Note on the Sociology of Pessimism," Grant wrote, "To take an example from myself, a sophisticated and lucid sociologist has asserted that I was saddened at the disappearance of the Canadian nation into the American empire, not because of my written reasons from political philosophy but because of my biographically determined situation. I belonged to an old class, which had its place in the old Canada and could find no place for itself in the new imperial structure. Or again, I know that my thinking about modern liberalism is touched by a certain animus arising from tortured instincts, because of the gynarchy in which I came to know that liberalism."[4] Despite almost forty years of warm collegiality with Gad at the University of Toronto, he has been much more guarded with me in his personal beliefs than Grant, although he equalled or bested Grant in the outrageousness of his political positions, such as his suggestion in the *Daily Telegram* that the lobby of the House of Commons would be a great venue for an acid party.

Gad has one of the best analytical and dialectical minds of people I have met. Harvard-educated, Horowitz often said that Grant's nationalism kept him from teaching at Harvard. In my view, Horowitz could have taught at Harvard and Grant could not, since Grant did not have as sharp and quick a mind as Horowitz has. Grant's strengths were, in Zdravko Planinc's felicitous phase, "tricks of the imagination," whereas the anti-Platonist Horowitz's strength was the coupling of ideas. In *Canadian Labour in Politics* and subsequent articles, Horowitz not only asserted that the conservative foundations in Quebec and western Canada produced its opposite – social (as distinct from liberal) democracy or democratic socialism – but also that socialism and conservatism shared some common features. Rather than a continuum from right to left, Horowitz developed a schema that suggested that socialism had similarities to as well as differences from conservatism and liberalism. The Tory idea of hierarchical cooperation is different from the socialist idea of egalitarian cooperation, but both differ even more from the liberal ideas of competition and possessive individualism, which ignore the reality of class differences in contemporary societies.

Horowitz invented "the red tory" tradition that allegedly distinguishes Canadian from American politics, and was based, in large part, on the writings of George Grant. The Canadian "red tory" tradition emphasizes cooperation and community, as distinct from liberal contractualism, which both Grant and Horowitz saw as a society of self-interested individuals who bargain with one another to maximize their interests, not a community that shares an identity and aspirations. Liberal reason, for Horowitz and Grant, is similar to Marcuse's instrumental or technical reason, not to Rawls's or Habermas's reasonableness or uncoerced consensus of individuals with differing values. Horowitz's socialism is libertarian, not authoritarian, based on free, reasonable individuals deliberating on common purposes. Socialism is more egalitarian than liberal equality of right and of opportunity but with social welfare provisions that minimize income inequalities with the eventual aim of eliminating class differences. While socialism shares with conservatism the priority of the community, it is not a hierarchical community, as in Plato's *Republic*, nor Aristotle's harmonious balance of masters and slaves, men and women, rich and poor, Greeks and barbarians, nor Burke's great chain of being. Nor, despite his Platonism, could

Grant conform to Horowitz's type of conservative – since he adhered
to St Paul's baptismal declaration (*Galatians* 3:23), "There is neither Jew
nor Greek, there is neither bond nor free, there is neither male nor female; for ye are all one in Christ Jesus." The redness of Horowitz's red
tory derived from Grant's Christianity, a point to which we shall return.

Horowitz's powerful analytical schema has had criticisms from Don
Forbes, Rod Preece, and Janet Ajzenstat but has had extremely fruitful
applications to Canadian politics in the writings of Nelson Wiseman
and others. Horowitz did not distinguish nationalism from conservatism, liberalism, and socialism as William Christian and Colin Campbell did in *Political Parties and Ideologies in Canada*. Gad told me that he
did not because there are conservative, liberal, and socialist forms of
nationalism. On this matter, I think he would differ from Grant, who
thought liberalism is inherently internationalist, and conservatism and
socialism lend themselves better to economic and cultural nationalism than liberalism. Also, Grant was a socialist for part of his life and
a nationalist for most of his life, while Gad was both a socialist and
a nationalist for most of his life. Grant saw some socialist ideas – nationalization of energy, transport, and communications – as means to
the preservation of national identity, while Gad may have shared the
Waffle Group's position that nationalism was a means to bring Canada
closer to socialist goals.

Although Horowitz did not think there was as close a link between
ideologies and parties, as appears in Christian and Campbell's book –
conservatism, liberalism and socialism are ideal types and have only a
mediated relationship to the Conservative Party, the Liberal Party, and
the New Democratic Party – he, like Grant, thought there is some link
between liberalism and Liberalism, and conservatism and Conservatism. Indeed, one of the reasons for the popularity of Grant's *Lament
for a Nation* was that it presented Canadian politics as principled; parties are not just honest or dishonest brokers trying to cobble together a
constituency to remain in power or to throw the others from power; it
was not just a story of the ins versus the outs but the story of the party
of technological homogeneity progressively getting the upper hand on
the party of national distinctiveness. In my view, there is a weaker link
between Conservatism and conservatism, of Liberalism and liberalism,
than Grant or Horowitz would allow. Walter Gordon and Marc Lalonde
were Liberals and economic nationalists. For me, the basic difficulty
in applying Horowitz's schema to Canadian politics is that since Wilfrid Laurier, the Liberal Party has been the political party favoured by

Catholics not only in Quebec but also in the rest of Canada. Laurier's "Political Liberalism" stated that the Liberal Party is not derived from French liberalism, which was anti-clerical, but from English Liberalism, which fostered Catholic emancipation in Britain.[5] The Catholic Church, while in practice split amongst conservative, liberal, and socialist elements, conforms to Horowitz's type of a conservative hierarchical community, emphasizing tradition and authority. I will note in passing those who see republicanism as an alternative to conservatism, liberalism, and socialism.[6]

In Canada's leading conservative thinker, we never encounter any contemporary slogans, such as "the brightest and the best," given such currency by the *Globe and Mail* and the *National Post*, to foster global competitiveness in our era of free trade and investment. Rather, Grant insisted, in *An Ethic of Community*, on human equality. Moral choices "matter absolutely," and "this act of choosing is the ultimate human act and is open to all. In this sense all persons are equal and differences of talent are of petty significance."[7] Grant maintained that it is spiritually bad for people to be either in a relationship of permanent subordination or unchecked superiority, and hence Canadians "must give economic content" to our professions of human equality. Grant never specified what industrial democracy entailed and never took seriously Simone Weil's detailed proposals for eliminating domination and restoring dignity in work. When Zdravko Planinc claims that Grant saw in Weil a gnostic refuge from our technological civilization, he has got Weil and Grant exactly wrong, although, to be sure, Grant did not emphasize Weil's immersion in factory labour and modern science, and her specific proposals to alleviate the conditions that deprive work of all dignity and challenge. Although Weil was Grant's supreme authority on things moral and spiritual, he accepted the view of Max Weber, Martin Heidegger, and Jacques Ellul that technological civilization requires hierarchical bureaucracies that block the promise of technological abundance and leisure. Since Grant did not attend to Weil or other thinkers who "gave economic content" to human equality, he did not provide concrete guidance to his principle that "the hierarchy of talents must always be subordinate ... to the basic equality of persons."[8]

Grant's socialism was that of a Christian social democrat. Human equality is gauged not on the basis of equal intelligence, equal power, or equal susceptibility to suffering but on the basis of our moral choices. Contemporary conservatives prize freedom of consumer choices, the right of the wealthy to purchase quick medical treatment, of parents to find the schools and the kind of child care they can afford. Grant was not a proponent of a free market of consumer choices, and he came to turn against Rousseauian-Kantian principles of equal freedom because the secularization of moral autonomy led to market consumerism. Grant thought egalitarians should attend to the truth of the doctrine of original sin – that the propensity to greed, self-centredness, and domination is a historical constant – and thus socialists should be wary of liberal notions of freedom that imperil both community and equality. To oversimplify, the uninhibited Platonist thought inhibitions a good thing, while the anti-Platonist Horowitz thought inhibitions (as surplus repression) a bad thing. By the mid-sixties, when Grant had published *Lament for a Nation* and *Technology and Empire*, he thought socialists unrealistic in espousing anarchic freedom and equality. His central teaching is that liberalism is the fitting doctrine of technological modernity because its defining notion – that the human essence is freedom and thus humans should be free to construct a world as they choose – facilitates technical advances in medical experimentation, bioengineering, reproduction, and warfare. Conservatives and socialists have ideas of order and justice that, according to Grant, should limit or qualify their espousal of technological progress (surrogate motherhood, harvesting Third World organs for transplant, napalm, enriched warheads). However, socialists of the 1960s, Grant thought, were so taken by Marcusean doctrines that civilized restraints had become technologically obsolete that they espoused the liberal view that human beings are free to make the world as they choose.

Gad Horowitz's egalitarianism had sources different from Grant's Christianity. Two Jewish atheists, Marx and Freud, synthesized in the Jewish left of the Frankfurt school, particularly the thought of Herbert Marcuse, were the central sources of Horowitz's thought. Although *Everywhere They Are in Chains: Political Theory from Rousseau to Marx* (1988), written with his brother Asher, celebrates a somewhat Marcusean Rousseau, Gad's *Repression* (1977) champions Marcuse for providing a more liberating psychoanalytic theory than Freud. In a recent chapter of *Difficult Justice* (2006), entitled "Aporia and Messiah in Derrida and Levinas," Horowitz indicates that these philosophers, who have brought ethics to the forefront of political theory and have made the face of others central to their reinterpretation of the Jewish tradition, could have learned from Marcuse's libertarianism, an argument he also used in his criticisms of Foucault in a *Political Theory* article (1987) entitled "The Foucaultian Impasse: No Sex, No Self, No Revolution." In *Difficult Justice*, Horowitz hints that the Nazis might have been right in calling psychoanalysis "Jewish science" or "a Godless Judaism."[9] Whether godless or godly, Horowitz's thought derives from the Jewish prophetic or messianic tradition, however heterodox it may appear to orthodox Jews. Horowitz's attachment to Levinas's *Totality and Infinity* stresses that humans are not subordinate to the totality of what is but are infinitely free to make the world anew. Grant might well have taken this aspect of Levinas's thought to be liberal, or a restatement of the Kantian disjuncture between *Sein* and *Sollen*, what is and what ought to be.

Horowitz thought Marcuse was the key thinker who had distinguished necessary repression – what constitutes human identity or distinguishes us from other animals – and surplus repression – what props up a civilization founded on patriarchal domination and the exploitation or alienation of labour. Marcuse borrowed this distinction from Marx's distinction between necessary and surplus labour, the former necessary to reproduce the socially determined needs of producers, and the latter, which is ripped off by the owners of the means of production. However, Horowitz finds all societies to be patriarchal, including the Mbuti pygmies,[10] who play a role in Gad's theory comparable to Marx's "primitive communism" or the social stage of Rousseau's state of nature. Perhaps Horowitz followed Marcuse in thinking that alienated labour would disappear with complete automation, but he did not clarify whether industrial democracy (Marx) or automation administered by technical experts (Marcuse) would lead the way to a free society. In short, there is no way to distinguish between basic and surplus repression until alienated labour is abolished and a non-patriarchal society is created. Expressed alternatively, the difference between basic and surplus repression is a historical project, rather than an analytical model for empirical application.

Perhaps one might say that the central difference between Grant and Horowitz is that the former based his thought on original sin, an unchanging human nature, while the latter based his thought on a Rousseauian repudiation of original sin, or on human history. However, I suspect that such a dichotomy is oversimplified. From reading *Repression* and extrapolating on Horowitz's account of the Mbuti, I find it possible that Gad thinks that human nature has its nasty side but it can be transfigured by play. It is not that he disagrees with Grant's view that greed, sexual exploitation, and the *libido dominandi* are not integral to human beings as such, but acting out the little Nazi in us all is a harmless way to give vent to passions of lust, domination, revenge, and greed (that Platonists think should be controlled by reason). Perhaps if the boring board games, such as *Monopoly* and *World Conquest*, were made part of the school curriculum, kids would be turned off by greed and war. Nevertheless, it is clear that Grant thought a just society requires more repression than Horowitz does, despite Grant's sympathy with Horowitz's view that much "civilized" sexual repression is unnecessary. Perhaps the difference between Grant and Horowitz is that the former held to the idea of an eternal order to which human beings are bound, while Horowitz thinks that subordination to a pre-existing order restricts human possibilities. Human nature, for Horowitz as for Marx, is "the ensemble of social relations," the totality of human practices and their transcendence in transformative practices.

Despite Grant's dismissal of Marcuse's theory as "orgiastic gnosticism,"[11] Horowitz and Grant had much in common in the 1960s. Grant's interviews with Horowitz and "Canadian Fate and Imperialism," which Grant wrote for *Canadian Dimension*, attest to this affinity.[12] Grant's attraction to the Canadian left in the 1960s arose from his spirited opposition to the Vietnam War, which he depicted as liberal imperialism and unlimited in its brutality. In Grant's view, the absence of moral limits was the hallmark of liberal modernity; the acceptance of nuclear weapons in Canada was the occasion for his attack on L/ liberalism in *Lament for a Nation*, and his insistence that the Vietnam War was initiated by the northern liberal establishment, rather than southern rednecks, made him a partisan foe of L/liberalism. Although he sometimes praised liberal adherence to human rights as informing protest to the Vietnam War and support for the civil rights movement, particularly when responding to Horowitz's assessment of American civil rights and anti-war protest, he often held the civil rights movement to be a front for liberal imperialism against the conservative political culture of the American south. Grant failed to foresee that the absence of unionization and welfare would place the American south as the dynamo of Walmart imperialism.

Grant and Horowitz are the odd couple of Canadian intellectual history. Horowitz shared Grant's emphasis on the role of the state in economic and cultural life. Grant's Tories who built Ontario Hydro, the CNR, the CBC, etc., have been replaced by "conservatives" who want to abolish Crown corporations, public broadcasting, or what Northrop

Frye and Robertson Davies called "aristocratic socialism." In response to Horowitz's question about how Canada is better than the United States, Grant replied, "A much greater use of the public good against private enterprise ... in other words, you have to move towards something like a socialist society in which the public good takes precedence over the individual right to use the resources they want to build the society they want."[13] Horowitz did not press him on the agents of a socialist nationalism; the civil servants Diefenbaker distrusted for their alliance with the Liberal Party but Grant insisted were essential to limit corporate power have been tremendously tarnished by their participation in the sponsorship scandal. If Grant's red toryism seems obsolete, Grant's suggestion to Horowitz that cities will replace nations as sources of identity and allegiance strikes a contemporary note.[14]

Grant was much less optimistic than Horowitz about a counterculture. While Grant found a religious dimension in the Beat generation and the Yippies, and he declared anti-war protest noble, he thought Freudian Marxism merged with drugs, sex, and rock music. Grant declared that the left was fooling itself by parasitically dropping out of the technological society on which they depend. The bond between Grant and the left was forged in opposition to the Vietnam War and was broken when Grant later came to denounce euthanasia and abortion. Grant objected to the Christian right's attempt to tie his right-to-life position, which he took to be consistent with his pacifism and opposition to capital punishment, with "family values" or opposition to gay rights and extramarital sex. Horowitz has recently spoken to me regarding our need for a Grantian voice to oppose American foreign policy and to distinguish our public policy and military involvements from the American empire. However, with the American left lining up solidly in favour of abortion and euthanasia, and opposing the evangelical dimension of the American right, it is by no means clear that Grant would be Horowitz's man. Horowitz's red tory has died, as has red toryism. Horowitz is left to lament the dying of social democracy in Canada as Grant lamented the death of the conservative half of North America four decades ago.

Did the friendship between Grant and Horowitz indicate their common pursuit of a philosophic way of life? Or did their relationship exhibit differences between "Christian philosophy" and "Jewish philosophy"? Talk of "Jewish science" or "Canadian science" is parochial at best and racist at worst. But is philosophy more a matter of culture than the natural sciences? Was Grant just trying to render lucid and coherent the presuppositions entailed in a Christian world view, as Horowitz elucidates the Jewish prophetic tradition? Horowitz is openly heterodox, while Grant's conservatism hid his heterodoxy. In my view, both contributed to a common enterprise.

NOTES

1 Matt Cohen, *Typing: A Life in Twenty-Six Keys* (Toronto: Random House, 2000), 38–9, 74.
2 Alan Mendelson, in *Exiles from Nowhere: The Jews and the Canadian Elite* (Montreal: R. Brass Studio, 2008), believes the growing difference was not due to Cohen's emerging awareness of himself as a Jew but to Grant's anti-Semitism. Mendelson was a protégé of Grant's rival, Edward Sanders, who thought of religion as a field of "objective" research as distinct from Grant's view that faith was "subjective" experience. Mendelson did not consult any of Grant's Jewish friends and colleagues of various faiths in arriving at this verdict. Michael Ignatieff's *True Patriot Love: Four Generations in Search of Canada* (Toronto: Viking, 2009) discusses Grant's forebears but ignores George Monro Grant's career as principal of Queen's University and (like Mendelson) his assistance in founding and funding a synagogue in Kingston. Both ignore Grant's other grandfather, Sir George Parkin, a racist, imperialist anglophile. If Parkin's biographer, William Christian, were right in thinking that Grant followed in the footsteps of Parkin, then Mendelson's views would have some support. See William Chrisitian, *Parkin: Canada's Most Famous Forgotten Man* (Toronto: Blue Butterfly, 2008).
3 *Collected Works of George Grant*, ed. Arthur Davis and Henry Roper (Toronto: University of Toronto Press, 2005), 3:724.
4 Ibid., 3:378–9.
5 Sir Wilfrid Laurier's "Political Liberalism" may be found in H.D. Forbes, ed., *Canadian Political Thought* (Toronto: Oxford University Press, 1987), 134–51.
6 I think republican discourse almost entirely spurious, however current it is with Philip Petit, Quentin Skinner, and Maurizio Viroli. J.G.A. Pocock's *The Machiavellian Moment: Florentine Political Thought and the Atlantic Republican Tradition* (Princeton: Princeton University Press, 1975) provided an alternative to Hartz's interpretation of American thought and Macpherson's interpretation of liberalism as possessive individualism but has been successfully challenged by Joyce Appleby and Paul Rahe (amongst others) who insist on the liberal character of America's foundation. Skinner combines

an insistence on historical context with a completely transhistorical understanding of republicanism (which serves as an alternative to Thatcher's right turn to the magic of the market and to the socialism of the pre-Blair Labour Party, without clearly espousing "the third way," as Anthony Giddens did). See Janet Ajzenstat and Peter J. Smith, *Canada's Origins: Liberal, Tory or Republican* (Ottawa: Carlton University Press, 1995), for the application of this fashionable doctrine to Canada.

7 *Collected Works of George Grant*, 3:41.
8 Ibid., 3:44.
9 Asher Horowitz and Gad Horowitz, eds., *Difficult Justice: Commentaries on Levinas and Politics* (Toronto: University of Toronto Press, 2006), 312.
10 Gad Horowitz, *Repression: Basic and Surplus Repression in Psychoanalytic Theory; Freud, Reich and Marcuse* (Toronto: University of Toronto Press, 1977), 118, 160–1.
11 *Collected Works of George Grant*, 3:495.
12 Ibid., 3:431–54, 519–32, 595–602.
13 Ibid., 3:442.
14 Ibid., 3:440.

4 Between Pause and Play: Conveying the Democratic Spirit

JASON ROVITO

Historians of science have to take ideas as facts. Epistemologists have to take facts as ideas, and place them within a system of thought.[1]

How does one – how can one – write about a teacher? In particular, about a teacher as a historical being, the supreme fact of biography? Even if we place the thorny question of transference aside – that is, if we ignore the interpretive distortions that issue from the perspective of the (or this) student – we must still acknowledge the resistance-to-being-written-about that accompanies the very figure of the teacher. For, in its constitutive act, this figure is always already made of writing, of words – the words, most often, of others. The teacher, in short, is allegorical (*allos*, "other" + *agoria*, "speaking"). Or, to be more dramatic, the teacher *is* Allegory, its action personified. And in what sense can one write factually – or biographically – about Allegory, when the nature of its being is always one step removed, or removing? Closer to the object level, how does one write about *this* teacher: "Horowitz"? About *Horowitz as educator*? And, particularly, about Horowitz in regards to his most lasting pedagogical venture: the enigmatically titled seminar "The Spirit of Democratic Citizenship: Sanity and Democracy"? Especially as it offers the elusive creed, "Whatever you may say about it, *it is not*"? Perhaps by introducing a third. Not Horowitz as educator, as teacher, but instead *Horowitz as translator*. Or Horowitz as educator via Horowitz as translator; the teacher as one who can be found – in order to be written about – residing only between the languages, the words, of others.

But, of course, if the teacher is a translator, she is not one of the literary sort. She sits not between already published text and expectant blank page. But instead, *before the class*: between the memory of the words that have been read and the breath that animates the words remaining to be spoken. Between these two words the teacher exists as intention-to-translate – which is also to say, *as tongue*. For the tongue (*lingua*) is not only language (*lingua*) embodied, the possibility and means of its expression, but also its remembering, its archive. The foreign word trips and twists and contorts the tongue, until it is remembered, archived, and no longer foreign. And the translator's tongue, the teacher's tongue, remembers not only language, but languages plural – their differences and similarities, their tastes and textures. More than encyclopedic, this tongue dreams harmony as it absorbs disparate fragments and speaks them as one.

Thus (perversely), to find Horowitz – the teacher via the translator – in his lettered tongue. In his tongue that speaks "Korzybski" – the first face of the General Semantics movement: that twentieth-century fusion of quantum physics, mathematics, brain science, etc., that history happened to forget. The very same tongue that speaks "Marcuse," with libidinal, mytho-poetic accent. And between and across those two words, interlinear – Horowitz's own words: *"conveying the democratic spirit."*

* * * * *

Walking into his office for the first time, one of Korzybski's new batch of students introduces herself. In plain voice, Korzybski, starkly bald, invites her to sit on the "chair" facing his desk. The student does so, only to discover – once deposited by gravity onto the floor – that the "chair" was missing an adjective: "broken." Korzybski had previously sawn one of its legs. Here, scare quotes find their calling – announcing the linguistic origin of this tragic, if lower-case, fall. In privileging the flexible generality of the noun (the *chair*) over the stubborn singularity of its article (*the* chair, *this* chair), the student, in effect, attempted to sit on a word. Her "expectation," in this instance, a perverse twist on the spontaneous nature of its etymological root – *ex-spectare*, to look out for (what has already been seen to look in).

When Korzybski would point with one hand towards an object, while pressing the index finger of his other hand tight against his lips, the meaning of his intention was clear: words are *not* the objects to which they refer; they are different. And yet, his gesture intended more. Words, as abstract entities, are different from objects, certainly, but they are also more than this difference: in similarity, for "the object" is always already an abstraction produced from what Korzybski refers to as "the unspeakable event." And thus the trinity of abstraction: event-object-label, and its corresponding doctrine. The apple that we can see, touch, taste, while more "physical" than the "apple" that we speak, is nonetheless abstract: a macroscopic representation of energetic processes that exist beyond our naked powers of perception. Given enough time, even a boulder will turn to dust. *Objects as verbs.* At the same time, this similarity extends in the opposite direction, as words become objects, either as material for the infinite processes of abstract thought, i.e., when we talk about talking (about talking), etc. Or, at the other pole, as effective hallucinations, i.e., when the invocation of "sin" elicits the all-too-queasy feeling of guilt, an individual is transformed into a credit rating, or "freedom" is exported to Iraq (Libya, etc.).

By positioning word, object, and event within the unified continuum of abstraction, Korzybski's "chair" promises a dynamic ontological revisioning: of *Homo sapiens sapiens* as the sole animal for which it is possible to speak of multiple orders of abstraction. Here, the term "multiple" is key, for abstraction is by no means an exclusively human capacity. If the bat hears more clearly, it is only on account of the fact that its perceptual apparatus is capable of producing abstractions more finely tuned to the unspeakable material of the event level – finer, yet nonetheless mediated. Even the bat doesn't hear everything. Thus, in the animal world – let us speak of neither plants nor gods – an initial, "objective" order of abstraction takes place. It "takes place," Korzybski stresses, within a very precise region of the animal brain: *the thalamus,* where energies emitted by external stimuli, having been gathered by various sense organs, accumulate and commingle as smells, sounds, sights, etc., thereafter subject to processes of transformation and synthesis that produce the sensual appearance of a navigable, material object-world. For the animal as form-of-life, this abstract – essentially fictional – reality is truly the only one possible, since it would be unable to act/survive if not protected from the paralyzing over-stimulation that would inevitably arise from an "immediate" perception of world-as-total-flux. Thus, with the rest of the animal kingdom we share the inability to exist without the subtle abstractions of the thalamus, without the intercession of "objects," without – as Nietzsche knew quite well –

the power to forget what's already been forgotten. If, however, we want to discover the uniquely human, it's in the cortex that we must search. Or, more precisely, within *the cortico-thalamic relation*.

For Korzybski, "the human" begins by chance, with the evolutionary whim of enlarged cortical mass. Neurological space is infinitesimal and our infamous "bigger brains" (by 2–4 mm) provide just enough duration for additional neural pathways to develop. Introducing an extended temporal delay between the (human) animal's reception of external stimuli and its consequent response, this quantitative increase in space holds qualitative weight, insofar as the lower-order abstractions of the object-world are subjected to a yet further process of abstraction and are thereby transformed – *refined* – into the virtual (or, "less material") objects of memory and language. On longer drives we're granted time to think. Thus, if the thalamus recognizes the nature of difference in constructing the object-world (i.e., *this* tree looks different from *that* one), then the cortex builds the virtual on the basis of the higher-order abstraction of similarity-between-differences (i.e., both trees are nonetheless "trees").

The significance of this cortico-thalamic vision of human being cannot be overemphasized. Confronted by an impassable river, on the other side of which lies abundance, the fox can perceive only difference: between the torrent of the water and the relative stability of the land, between the bareness of its present habitat and the plenty awaiting it, teasing it, on the other bank. Although this level of awareness is enough to ensure the survival of the fox – preventing it essentially from experiencing the impossible, death – it also consigns it to the temporality of fate, for before it can act on its desire to cross the river, the fox must await a miraculous transformation of the object-world (i.e., a dramatic drop in temperature). The human, however, equipped with the capacity for producing higher-order abstractions, interacts with the conditions of reality quite differently. Remaining by the shore for a moment longer, slightly longer than the fox, Smith recognizes not only that the rapidly moving water is different from the objects carried along its surface, but also that those objects themselves share certain essential properties. Most significantly, they float. This stable relationship of difference–similarity, which registers and resounds within the neurological space of Smith's extended neural pathways, inspires her to name this property "buoyancy." And it is from this particular sequence of reverie-to-name that the stage is set for the human voyage from necessity to freedom, as Smith,[2] the animal of multi-ordinal essence, transforms knowledge into action – felling the barren trees that surround her to build a raft with which to cross the river, in order to redeem that most primary thalamic desire, which she shares with the rest of the animal world: the reduction of suffering. Hence the essential relation that composes the precise title of Korzybski's opus (*Science and Sanity*): *science* as the ideal cortico-thalamic project of the human species, a collective, evolving system of virtual insights derived from object-level observations and experimentation, and *sanity* as that psycho-physiological disposition that contributes to, and results from, an active participation in the interrogative movement of the scientific spirit.

Or, at least, so the story goes; essence in no way securing actuality. That is why Korzybski is careful to discuss orders and not pluralities of abstraction, for "order" implies a definite, ideal trajectory – event > object > label – from which a diagnosis of *dis*order, regression, *un*sanity may be derived. If the species-being of the human is to be distinguished from that of the animal according to its capacity to transform event-level stimuli from lower to higher orders of abstraction, from objects to words, and then to employ this virtual intelligence to transform the otherwise unyielding conditions of existence, then the very category of "the human" *is purely operational.* That is, Smith exists only as Smith – as human, opposed to "as animal" – when, conscious of the powers/dangers of abstraction, *she abstracts well,* when she's able, in effect, to hold in mind the slippery insight that the map, as cortical product, is not the territory (which isn't even itself) – an insight most certainly positioned within the immediate grasp of Korzybski's fallen student who, by mistaking the useful, yet purely auxiliary virtuality of the word-memory "chair" for the lower-order (weight-bearing) abstraction that it resembles, fell victim to a confusion between different orders of abstraction.[3]

Of course each diagnosis promises remedy; no story of the Fall is complete without one of redemption. Searching for his in a world of "mild" unsanity (in 1933), Korzybski pursues the ambivalent fluidity of abstraction to its very pure limit: to the contentless language of mathematics. Or, more precisely, Korzybski, as engineer, adopts a mathematical attitude towards language. He elects to render words as variables in an effort to access that abstract – albeit material – space in which the potentiality of the human is betrayed: the neurolinguistic "mind."[4]

"The apple is red."
"The lemon is red."

Despite appearances, despite the fact that our eyes glide more seam-
lessly across one as opposed to the other of these two statements, neither
of them is correct. "Apple" is not red, but a five-letter word, a "spell-
mark," printed here in black type on white page. There is no red on this
paper. It only makes an appearance on the virtual level, where a trace
of redness continues to exist as memory of our past encounters with red
apples (whether "natural" or "artificial"). This familiarity allows for an
almost automatic associative chain. "'The-apple-is-red'-of-course-it-is" –
this is what Korzybski intends by his arch-enemy: *identification* – a
neurolinguistic phenomenon most apparent in the anecdote of that hy-
per-allergenic soul who, faced with the shadow of a rose fallen upon an
opaque screen, begins to sneeze violently. That the "rose" behind the
screen is merely made of paper is a wholly irrelevant fact for this animal of multi-ordinal essence. Her neural pathways are already engaged
in the psycho-physiological confusion of a semantic reaction, in which
the label and the object are identified as "same."

Meanwhile, most of us have never encountered a red lemon. Its sensory contours have never passed through our neural pathways as abstracted energy and we are far more hesitant, untrained to associate
these two words. The drive always seems longer on unfamiliar roads.
As occasioned by an explicitly novel experience, the character of this
confusion is of a sort different from the confusion-of-identification. This
is a confusion that *resists* identification, that slows everything down – a
kind of confusion within which we can spy that uncanny combination
of naivety and scepticism that Korzybski values virtuous in the figure
of the mathematician, or, more precisely, in the extensional nature of the
mathematical gaze through which "the mathematician," as scientific
figure, is actualized. To this gaze, "apple" contains no more (and nor
no less) meaning than the variable x. Committed in equal measure to
the banal and the exotic, to witnessing the very shimmering of the two
in one, this neurolinguistic habit transforms the imperceptibly loaded
sentence "the apple is red" into the more neutral formula "x is red" – a
transformation that elicits an almost irresistibly curious itch: eyes dart-
ing about, bodies pivoting in search of x: "*What*, exactly, is red? *To which
apple are you referring*?"

The presence of the mathematically induced question-mark-as-itch –
more than just an occasion for verbal inflection – heralds the total,
psycho-physiological mobilization of the human as language-inhering-
in-body-in-its-environment. It ushers in the body-mind of a scientist, a

reality-tester – a moment of presence that Korzybski dramatizes in the neurological scenography of *the cortico-thalamic pause*, in which the all-too-easy temptation is resisted to identify, on the grounds of similarity, the impression communicated to our thalamus by a present object (*this* chair, that *boulder*) with a word-memory that we've previously collected and stored in our cortex. This resistance to the absolute repetition of the past extends as invitation to participate in the creation of a future, for when the apple is transformed into a variable, when it becomes x, the word is freed from its gravity of meaning, from its nightmarish historical weight, and the speaking being becomes reacquainted with the pleasure of naming. If Korzybski's "identification" secularizes original sin by restaging it as an eternally present possibility within the profane relation between thalamus and cortex, then his valorization of "the pause" operates the reverse. It is a kind of weak messianism, similarly ever-possibly-present in the human's particularly proper experience (event-object-label) of this universe of abstraction: "Everything that man heard in the beginning, saw with his eyes, and felt with his hands was the living word.… With this word in his mouth and in his heart, the origin of language was as natural, as close and as easy as a child's game."[5]

And yet, there is no virgin birth; the word is always already social, so that before it even gets a chance to prove its worth as variable, as either red or not red, true or false, the word "apple" is first determined by the order to which it belongs. Despite its best efforts at consistency, the apple of "the apple is red" is most certainly not the same as its apparent double in the formulation "the red is apple." This second apple is inescapably determined by the nonsense of its social order. Thus, the insight to which Korzybski remained ever faithful: although it may appear counter-intuitive, we must stress that the interrogative task that actualizes the multi-ordinal essence of the human (as human) cannot truly begin on the ground, with the-things-themselves-as-sensed, but instead must first pass through the virtual reality, the bottom-up metaphysics, of *functional forms*.

In mathematical language, a "propositional function" qualifies as the most basic functional form: a being that determines the parameters of meaning for the singular variables residing within the virtual environment of a definite proposition. Thus the propositional function "x is red" allows for a large number of meaningful interpretations of the variable x (i.e., as apple, lemon, piano, etc.), which then – after having been tested – transform the otherwise neutral proposition-as-a-whole into one that is either correct or incorrect (an incorrect proposition nonetheless qualifying as "meaningful"). At the same time, "x is red," as a propositional function, excludes – that is, *represses* – a smaller range of possible interpretations of the variable x, so that when x is made to stand for "red" itself, the proposition becomes tautological (i.e., "red is red") and thus of no real (extra-rhetorical) significance. Similarly, the propositional function "x is a member of Parliament" does not allow for – that is, *represses* – the possibility that the variable x could stand for "Parliament."[6] And yet, just as words do not appear in isolation, neither do the propositions that order them. As subset, the possible sense of a proposition is subject to the structural presuppositions of the "doctrinal function" from which it is derived (i.e., the structural bias of our thesis). And again, this doctrinal form is itself subject, at the highest linguistic order, to the formal parameters established by the structure of the particular language in which it is expressed: *its system function*.

Thus, as his ultimate achievement, Korzybski undertook an analysis of the presuppositions informing the structure of (Indo-European) language itself, *as such*. At the base/apex of this monumental excavation project, Korzybski discovered Aristotelian logic as the supreme formal being that establishes the possible-impossible limits of what is to be considered meaningful and not. *A is A; A is not B; A cannot be both A and B.* While this law of mutual exclusivity may not appear on everyday lips, it nonetheless circulates within the most common of verbs, "to be," where an object is made identical to the judgment of its attribution. Thus, no matter how banal it may appear, everyday language regularly contributes to the (re)production of a very particular understanding of existence, one that, significantly, is based upon the false-to-facts logic of identification: "the boulder *is* solid; the apple = red." Korzybski thus updates Newton in discovering the neurolinguistic gravity that orders the (non)sensible world of the human: "Here we come across a tremendous fact; namely, that a language, any language, has at its bottom certain metaphysics, which ascribe, consciously or unconsciously, some sort of structure to this world."[7]

Of course, in considering the social relations of event-object-label, it would be foolish for us to blame a single individual identified as "Aristotle" for all of the ills of the human animal. And as a bio-epistemologist, this was hardly Korzybski's aim. Instead, the spell-mark "Aristotle" stands in for the being of "science" in its infancy, for a space-time in which observations of "nature" – whether natural or human – were still dependent on the limited, macro-perceptual powers of abstraction allowed by the human senses. To Aristotle's eyes, hands, etc., the boulder *really did* appear solid, a Thing. Since that time, however, the sense-gathering potential of "science" has become ever finer, the result largely of technological developments in observational instrumentation (as themselves concretizations of earlier higher-order abstractions, which were themselves based upon observations derived from cruder instruments, etc.). And at the most recent limits of scientific inquiry, at the threshold of what Korzybski refers to as *non-Aristotelian* thought, the discoveries of quantum physics reveal that, depending on the method of observation, a particular phenomenon may appear as *either* wave *or* particle; *x* can "be" *both* A *and* B. Nonetheless, this cortico-thalamic insight – which replaces "identity" with an alternative, *non-Aristotelian* system-function based on "relativity" – has not yet fully penetrated the deep structures of language. While our selves may thus be materially located in the space-time of the twenty-first century, our neurolinguistic habits continue to preserve the epistemological reality of 350 BCE.

This epochal time lag between "bodies" and "minds" proves to be not without political import, because "the apple" *is* red – or because "Canada" *is* a "democracy" (even, and especially, with its Parliament prorogued) – it most certainly can't be rotten. Nor even, more minimally, can it be considered the variable product of cortico-thalamic processes and thus subject to inquiry. Accordingly, when the WHO announces that we have now officially entered the pandemic of the swine, we are confronted most fully with the epistemology of Terror, legislated to identify the sense experience of an everyday label (a colour, an animal) with the "objective" presence of apocalyptic conditions. "And out of truth it must make our brains."[8] The corresponding identification (apocalypse = everyday), amplified exponentially by social media, produces a neurological storm of speed-of-light fear, effectively suspending the cortico-thalamic right to pause. Thus, as the statement is made, "Nine out of ten scientists agree: you should get the vaccine" – with no protest advanced by the corresponding "ninety out of ninety" lay people for being performatively constructed as mere consumers of truth – the scientific task of verifying the correspondence between event-object-label is outsourced, external to the individual's cortico-thalamic circuit, so that the intimate labour of translating orders of experience is excluded – that is, *surplus repressed* – by the silent proposition of perpetual war, and language is thus transformed into a set of circulating imperatives that we are "free" to either ignore or accept:

It should be realized that in the Aristotelian system of evaluation many individuals profit in various ways by what amounts to distracting the attention of mankind from actual life problems, which makes us forget or disregard actualities. They often supply us with phantom semantic structures, while they devote their attention to the control of actualities not seldom for their personal benefit. If one surveys the Aristotelian situation impartially, one occasionally feels hopeless. But, no matter how we conspire one against another, and thus, in the long run, against ourselves, the plain realization that the difficulty is found in the standards of evaluation establishes the necessary preliminary step to the escape.[9]

* * * * *

Here, Horowitz's tongue shifts registers, as "Korzybski" slips almost imperceptibly into "Marcuse" – the Marcuse from *Eros and Civilization*, and in particular, the Marcuse who there wrote, as epilogue, the "Critique of Neo-Freudian Revisionism." It was here that Marcuse took exception to Fromm's vision of a "humanistic psychoanalysis," purchased at the cost of eliminating the sense of depth crafted by Freud's mytho-poetic theory of the instincts. In doing so, Marcuse was preserving the possibility to dig parallel to Korzybski, concerned in his own fashion with exposing the social relations of language and, ultimately, the virtual sanction of the system-function as supreme formal being.

In excavating the myth of Ananke, Marcuse thus names the functional entity that "unconsciously" ensures the effective reproduction of capital as sovereign and, at the same time, allows for the falsely subversive values of the "green economy" and "office yoga," for, operating behind the Ananke myth, propping it up, we find not the Aristotelian proposition of identity per se, but its most intimate relation: scarcity. *A is identical to itself; its properties (food, shelter, money, vaccine) can be shared with no other – and certainly not with B; but, not to worry, even the rich can sleep under bridges.* As long as this myth, as a higher-order abstraction, reigns supreme as sense-making form, the meaningful range of the particular value "freedom" excludes one fundamental possibility: the freedom from toil. In order to build the bridge towards "enough," sacrifices must be made, for that future, just around the corner, one more push, no complaining … so that, in an age where "the available material and intellectual resources (the potential of liberation) have so much outgrown the established institutions that only the systematic increase in waste, destruction, and management keeps the system going,"[10] only the now-fictitious image of implacable Necessity could render the term "unemployment" objectively shameful. To "not work" is to be *without* work – only a "bum" could think otherwise; only a "thief" would take the money and run (or possibly "the bankers," but that's another story). With the dream of the dream thus sacrificed to the stubborn reason of the performance principle – according to which Smith performs today "just because" she is afraid of not being allowed to perform again to-morrow – we are confronted by a regulated psycho-moral economy, in which, via the "oppressive rule of the established language and images over the mind and body of man," individuals have "introjected the needs and values of their masters and managers and made them their own, thus reproducing the established system in their minds, their consciousness, their senses and instincts."[11]

And yet, far from an excuse for despair, Marcuse's one-dimensional vision suggests the mechanics for its reversal – specifically, via a radical intervention into the materially abstract realm of the "erotic mind," in which an interruption of Ananke's monopoly to sanction non-sense could release a surplus of erotic energies, thus available to be channelled into the sense-making potential of an alternative system-function. Thus, as he comes to sketch the image of the Great Refusal – as something of a translation of Korzybski's "cortico-thalamic pause" into a collective force – we find Marcuse documenting the necessary first stage of this potentially erotic movement in the emergence of a kind of system-function literacy within the student radicals of 1968: "They recognize the mark of social repression, even in the most sublime manifestations of traditional culture.... In one word: they have taken the idea of revolution out of the continuum of repression and placed it into its authentic dimension: that of liberation."[12] Torn from the semantic matrix that emanates from, and ex post facto rationalizes, the now-false-to-facts proposition of scarcity, the erotic matter of guilt – a force of production like any other – becomes unbound, free-floating, in search of another reason for its existence, another genealogy.[13] Potentially, it is not guilt of the primal crime – some mythical aborted revolution for which we are even today still being punished in carpeted, fluorescent labour camps – but instead, guilt of guilt, guilt of not knowing a pleasure needlessly deferred, guilt of an "innocence."

And yet, *contra* Marcuse, what if the rationality of scarcity – what gives it such sense and in turn authorizes it to produce the sensible – isn't but a dead letter enforced? What if it is still, or even just once again, "objectively" *and austerely* true? In offering the symbols of Orpheus and Narcissus as alternatives to Ananke, by depicting the existence of strange creatures who are allergic to domination, *without* advancing arguments to convince those who don't already agree, isn't Marcuse, far from being a "scientist," acting as demagogue, seducing the youth away from our actually existing democratic institutions, with nothing more than mere fantasy, *mere wordplay*? Nominally persuasive, this line of argument can maintain its force only through misrecognition of the communicative scene that informs the labour of Marcuse's "psychoanalytic philosopher." If we take the time to imagine ourselves behind Marcuse's words, behind his spell-marks, if we consider his poetics, how can we ignore the quite obvious fact that no appeal, demagogic or otherwise, is here being made. Seated at his typewriter, as he presses on keys that have themselves been cast and ordered elsewhere, Marcuse does so not with an image of an "us" in mind, an us who would need to be convinced by his words. If anything, his words are directed beyond the parameters that constitute this "us" as understood by the realism of common sense. He is not at all, like Fromm and the revisionists, attempting to engage in "inter-personal" communication. But instead, beyond and below, Marcuse attempts to speak for the *intra*-personal – concerned solely with acting as chronicler of some-thing known as "the historical vicissitudes of the instinctual dynamic." We must imagine, during the pause between each sentence, his eyes return to Freud's mytho-poetic motto hung above his typewriter: "The Oedipal wish is … the biological carrier of this archetype of freedom."[14] This is not to say that we should envision Marcuse as stark raving mad, attempting to cast off his human skin and entering into direct dialogue with Eros and Thanatos, but instead, by filtering his words, his values, through the depths created by a counter-factual system-function – that is, the pleasure principle, the logic of joy, rather than scarcity – Marcuse is able to *produce* a set of higher-order abstractions that cohere into a map of a territory that is strangely familiar but essentially different. And, perhaps most significantly, it is a territory that is suddenly more populous, for it is from this uncanny elsewhere that the "us," after being reduced from moral value to mere variable x – hardly an assault on "human dignity" – finally expands to incorporate its otherwise unconscious elements: not only the system-function that orders it under the illusion of necessity [$f(x)$ = Ananke], but the function of that function as historically contingent and potentially one day unnecessary – that is, the variable dream of history itself ($f[f(x)]$).

* * * * *

Thus, we return to the tongue, and to Horowitz's own words that speak in an interlinear way: "conveying the democratic spirit." And in returning to this fragment – to which he himself so often returns in the seminar, a neurolinguistic habit to be sure – how can we ignore that the tongue takes place in a body, which itself takes place in a social scenography? That is to say, the tongue speaks only within the context of its conveyance. And, in this case with Horowitz's tongue, the context-that-informs is that of the seminar room, or, more precisely, that of *a* seminar room, as authorized by the institutional seal of the Department of Political Science ("the Ministry of Truth").[15]

Under the semantic sway of this particular authority, this phrase – "conveying the democratic spirit" – sounds sensible, intelligible enough. Obviously, to be concerned with "conveying the democratic spirit," within the tradition of political science, is to be concerned with the spell-mark "democratic," with the idea of democracy. And since no one could take exception to the effort to convey *democracy*, not even its harshest critics – for they are but critics of "democracy" – we can all go home happy, satisfied with the day's work, the election procedures ruled sufficiently democratic, if only by the smallest of margins. Hence, on the epistemological plane, the democratic imperative, which occupies "political scientists" as some of its most loyal functionaries serving the strictest mathematical duty.

And yet, what about those, at the end of the day, without homes to which they may retire? Such a query is not to invoke the figure of the poor, of the homeless, whether sub-prime or just subhuman, for that appeal is but the other side of the "democratic" Möbius strip. But instead, as one who is also without home, and yet perhaps in a fashion significantly different from that of the homeless (who are always already imagined as having *lost* their homes), what about the rogue? Interestingly, the word "rogue," denoting an vagrant or beggar, first entered usage in the mid-sixteenth century, around the same time that Pope Pius IV decreed the construction of the monumental Archiginnasio in Bologne as the first centralized university complex, a propositional function in architectural form. Encouraging the identification of "the university" with a building, the Archiginnasio finally secured the autonomous institution of the *universitas* – until then, a linguistic relation between masters and students, letting rooms throughout the city – within the fold of the papacy/state. The word "rogue" comes from the Latin *rogare*, "to beg, to ask" – simultaneously the root, most curiously, of *interrogation*. And so, to gather the pieces together: without institutional affiliation, with neither tenure nor mortgage, "mobile" before the word became gadget, the rogue, whether officially a scholar or not, must – or, *chooses to* – make her living through her capacity to ask questions of others (both human and non-human), to enter into dialogue with the world as what-is-going-on-and-on, with little more than her curious tongue, autonomous, her operational state is inter-rogative – she is always, she survives, in between questions.

This is not to say to scholars of the world, "Be more roguish!," but instead to wonder: if the rogue's state offers us an alternative doctrinal function from which to transform our variables into values, where would the accent of "the political" fall in Horowitz's repeated phrase, "conveying the democratic spirit"? Perhaps, from here, unhinged from the democratic imperative of the Institution – for the rogue knows only the force of the question mark – the political might instead wander backwards, away from its stubborn identification with "democracy," and towards Horowitz's irregular choice of verbs: "convey." It is irregular insofar as it is an unabashedly material variant, seldom employed, of the common term "communication." Just as pipes are laid to convey water to a dwelling, or a taxi conveys passengers to their ultimate destination, one who communicates under the order of conveyance is obliged to acknowledge the structural, spatio-temporal parameters of her activity. In the act of conveyance – in "conveyative action" – the actor is never in possession, never the originator, but instead she is always only *with* what she is to accompany (*con-viare*, "together, on the way"). If she is to convey something, it is not with the privilege of the genius, but with the delicate *techne* of an escort, with the pretentiousness of the engineer, not the prophet. And one step more: if we are to identify the political in this context with the idea of conveyance, so that the "democratic" is but a derivative effect of this particular communicative ethos – that is, the dependent variable in the equation – what would happen to the x of "political science"? What reveries would be elicited by those words fresh on our tongues – for so long now informed by institutional values, almost as cues for an almost automatic associative chain that links corridors, bureaucrats, alumni, insignia, curricula, opinion polls, etc.? If "political science" were just an x, wholly operational, to be defined by the process of its definition, through the very acts of "political scientists," couldn't the accent shift here too? We could then speak of *a* "political science," which would occur – or would be occurring – only in the presence of scientists who consider themselves "political" precisely in the doing of their "science." They would comprise an order concerned not exclusively with asking questions, be they political or not, but also with questioning the historical conditions of possibility that determine the posing of questions as such. And further, they would be questioning in such a fashion that these historical conditions are made to appear to populate the everyday, so that the objects of the everyday, and the events to which they refer, are rendered foreign: not beyond, but precisely before, the judgment of recognition, to letter the tongue anew. They would be measuring the measures, positioned integrally between questions – Horowitz as political scientist of the most curious sort: "As keen and sweet as an engendering act: curiosity gives place to the hope of creating."[16]

NOTES

1 Gaston Bachelard, *The Formation of the Scientific Mind* (Manchester: Clinamen, 2002), 27.
2 Or, as a modification of Korzybski's convention of employing the variable "Smith" as representative of the human animal, it would be more accurate to here employ, as placeholder, "the Smiths" – given the inherently social nature of language. That is to say, it is truly doubtful that it would dawn on Smith, as an autonomous individual outside of society, to name anything for himself, without others with which to share this name (and/or to teach him how to use his vocal chords). And, moreover, even if Smith did manage to name "buoyancy" miraculously in isolation, it is undoubtedly certain that the consequent project of the raft – and, after that, the bridge – would be an impossible result of this higher-order abstraction without the help of other Smiths to appreciate the significance of his insight. (Of course, the collectivization of "Smith" as variable is only a first step – we still need to address "his" implicit gender, ethnicity, etc.)
3 "Experience and experiments show that the natural order was 'sensation' first, 'idea' next; the 'sensation' being an abstraction of some order, and the 'idea' already an abstraction from an abstraction, or an abstraction of a higher order…. Experience shows again that among humans, this order in manifestations is sometimes reversed; namely, some vestiges of memories [first], and 'sensations' next, without any external reason for the 'sensations.' Such individuals are considered 'mentally' ill; in legal terms, they are called 'insane.' … This reversal of order in its mild form is involved in

'identification,' or the confusion of orders of abstractions; namely, when we act as if an 'idea' were an 'experience' of our 'senses,' thus duplicating in a mild form the mechanism of the 'mentally ill.'" Alfred Korzybski, *Science and Sanity*, 5th ed. (Fort Worth, TX: Institute of General Semantics, 1994), 169–70.

4 Korzybski's neurolinguistic vision of a post-Newtonian physics – under the law of abstraction – incorporates all kinds of otherwise "spiritual" matter into the knowable (and actionable) cosmos. The implications of this new physics on some of the infamous taboos for historical materialists – i.e., morality, education, and will – are only gestured towards here. But we should note that it is this conduit between "the material" and "the spiritual" that qualifies General Semantics as such a potentially radical science.

5 Johann Georg Hamann in Walter Benjamin, "On Language as Such and on the Language of Man," *Selected Writings*, ed. Marcus Bullock and Michael W. Jennings (Cambridge, MA: Belknap, 1996), 1:70.

6 Indeed, anyone who would vigorously assert that "Parliament is a member of Parliament" would either be without logical capacity or, in utter disregard for the reality principle of language (which ensures survival through the basic repression of certain false-to-facts correspondences), fatally decadent. (Or perhaps a poet.)

7 Korzybski, *Science and Sanity*, 89.

8 Bachelard, *Formation of the Scientific Mind*, 21.

9 Korzybski, *Science and Sanity*, 199.

10 Herbert Marcuse, *An Essay on Liberation* (Boston: Beacon, 1969), 7.

11 Herbert Marcuse, *Counterrevolution and Revolt* (Boston: Beacon, 1972), 79–80.

12 Marcuse, *Essay on Liberation*, ix–x.

13 Korzybski considers an almost identical process: "In many instances serious maladjustments follow when 'hate' absorbs the whole of the affective energy of the given individual. In such extreme cases 'hate' exhausts the *limited* affective energy…. Thus an individual 'hates' a *generalization*: 'mother,' 'father,' etc. and so by identification 'hates' 'all mothers,' 'all fathers,' etc., in fact, hates the whole fabric of human society, and becomes a neurotic or even a psychotic. Obviously, it is useless to preach 'love' for those who have hurt and have done the harm. Just the opposite; as a preliminary step, by *indexing* we *allocate* or *limit* the 'hate' to the individual Smith, instead of a 'hate' for a generalization which spreads over the world…. The more they 'hate' the individual Smith, instead of a generalization, the more positive affective energy is liberated" (Korzybski, *Science and Sanity*, lxi).

14 Sigmund Freud in Herbert Marcuse, *Eros and Civilization* (Boston: Beacon, 1955), 270.
15 Gad's twenty-two lectures on radical general semantics are available at http://radicalgeneralsemantics.net.
16 Bachelard, *Formation of the Scientific Mind*, 18.

PART TWO

Fragment Theory

5 The Political Culture of English Canada

IAN ANGUS

In a series of short, intense articles written between the mid-1960s and the early 1970s Gad Horowitz made a remarkably pertinent and prescient contribution to the thinking of the political culture of English Canada in order to define the parameters of a socialist political will. That contribution was made in the context of the politics of the 1960s, which attempted to synthesize a socialist politics of class with a nationalist politics of community. Any similar attempt forty years later needs to both acknowledge his founding contribution and to measure our own distance from the theoretical discourse of the 1960s. It is one indication of that distance that many of Horowitz's essays were written in small journals, without footnotes, and in a definite first person. What was being said was the most important thing. The burying of substantive argument under mounds of scholarly apparatus – such as in this essay – that predominates today is an index to what extent form has submerged content. Writing is no longer political but *about* politics.

The impetus behind Gad Horowitz's theory of English-Canadian political culture is much more a matter of political will than a social scientific hypothesis. Political will pertains to the kind of life that one thinks humans should live and what approximation to that life one can attempt to live here and now. Social scientific investigations take on meaning only within the classic conception of politics as the definition and enactment of the good life. Thus, my interpretation of Horowitz's contribution is based in the socialist project that animated it and what that legacy should mean for us now. Both in the 1960s and today the socialist project is animated by the conviction that equality is the foundation of decent human relations.

I

The starting point of Horowitz's articles of the 1960s was the fragment theory of Louis Hartz, which analyzed the political cultures of New World societies in terms of their origins in European societies.[1]

Without rejecting the Hartzian theory of the dominance of the liberal fragment in Canada, it was substantively modified by Horowitz through his observation of Canadian politics.[2] Horowitz argued that the political value of the Hartzian approach was to show that the roots of socialism in Canada were in its non-liberal past. As he often repeated, the problem in English Canada was that we had not found our Lévesque.[3] While the analysis of the 1960s transformation in Quebec was conventional, Horowitz's argument for a parallel English-Canadian nationalism was not. It went so far as to claim that a partnership between these two nationalisms could transform Canada in a socialist direction and that the success of either would depend on that of the other.[4]

There was a fly in the ointment, though. English Canada didn't seem to be on the move in anything like the same way as Quebec. "We English Canadians are too pragmatic, too pudding headed, to undertake such a task."[5] Quebec had its own problems, too, in its colonial mentality, that might lead it to settle for an incremental increase in autonomy rather than a sudden break – though the existence of the forces represented by Lévesque might break through.[6] Well, politics never attains the clarity of logic, but that was not the main issue here. It could not be predicted with certainty, since it was a matter of political will, whether the necessary self-consciousness and break with the past would come. Quebec was further ahead in self-consciousness, certainly, but in neither case was the matter of political will clear – certainly not in the 1960s, probably no more so today.

Only with independent self-assertion of the two communities could the question of federalism, or living in proximity and perhaps in common, be clearly addressed. This possibility was, and is, seriously impeded by the asymmetrical structure of Canada's current federal system. While the French-speaking community had an effective base in the Quebec government, there wasn't, and still isn't, any representative of English Canada as such. The nine provinces do not do it and the Ottawa government does not either. The first because they represent too little – regional divisions within English Canada – the second because it represents too much: "From the English Canadian point of view, it

[Ottawa] has often been seen as so heavily influenced by the French, so much in need of making 'concessions' to them, that it cannot, in its symbols and policies, express English Canada."[7] The political solution had to be special status for Quebec, but the more basic problem was the absence of a political representative of English Canada who could negotiate the future of Canada with Quebec. Later constitutional debates tried without success to address this structural asymmetry through proposed reforms.[8] This failure has led to the current impasse where English Canadians see Ottawa as a representative of Quebec, or a too-deferential accommodation of Quebec, whereas French-speaking Quebeckers see it as an instrument of English Canada. No one sees Ottawa as the expression of its interests and views, though some accept the impasse itself as inevitable.

The problem was where to find the political will for the two nationalisms. Indeed. Well, history is not over and the future remains uncertain. But the past is clear enough. The political will was not there. And, in its absence, it has gone as Horowitz told us forty years ago. Greater power for Quebec, a necessity for its growing self-consciousness and confidence, has meant devolution of federal powers to the provinces, undermining any sense of national identity for English Canada.[9] Special status, coming slowly to Quebec rather than in a sudden show of autonomy, has meant that the provinces have been "assimilated into the surrounding North American homogeneity."[10] The failure to find English-Canadian nationalism has meant an unsatisfied but continuing identification with Ottawa – in short, a country that shunts aside its own best traditions and aspirations in order to fit more easily into the un-mixed liberal hegemony assaulting us from the south while meanwhile succumbing to internal fragmentation. What was needed? Horowitz said that too. "It is time to dignify French Canada's demands, to recognize them as normal human demands, by making the same demands for ourselves. Harmonious interpersonal relations can exist only among fully developed persons. The same applies, not metaphorically but strictly, to nations, whether they are within a single state or not."[11]

The authoritarian collectivist component of English-Canadian political culture, our distinctive thread, was our chance to build an egalitarian collectivist future – from toryism to socialism. The "between" here, the passage from–to, could be forged only by political will. In his confrontations with the work of sociologist John Porter and philosopher George Grant, Horowitz produced a distinctive version of the political will that might come to forge socialism in Canada. In an activist interpretation rather against the grain of Porter's sociological realism, and admitting that "Porter himself does not elaborate this argument sufficiently," he argued that the core of the classic *The Vertical Mosaic* is "the insistence that the undemocratic characteristics of Canadian society are perpetuated by uncreative politics, and that uncreative politics are perpetuated by ethnic and regional fragmentation."[12] A creative politics would be socialist insofar as it would be based on class difference. This difference would subsume other differences and create identification with an English-Canadian nationalist project. "When politics is not based on class, but on regional or ethnic divisions, the personal troubles of ordinary people are not readily transformed into issues."[13] Notice that this formulation shifts from the Marxist or quasi-Marxist category of "class" to a populist rhetoric of "ordinary people." While it is not drawn out here, this formulation suggests a Gramscian notion that the "people" (consisting, as it does, of different groups) can form a new hegemonic alliance, or unity, through a focus on class. Class is thus claimed to be the unifying element, so that the task of the Canadian left is "to encourage the translation of regional and ethnic conflicts into class terms,"[14] whereas other differences – notably region and ethnicity – have only divisive potential.

Aside from political-party affiliation, Horowitz also thought that "a class politics in Canada would take for granted that the nation exists and will not be dismembered."[15] The "nation" here is meant to be Canada – not really a nation but a collection of two or more nations – so that the translation into class terms of socialist political will aims both at unifying English Canada and, in a higher level dialogue, allowing a federal unity with a class-conscious, independent Quebec. "English Canadian intellectuals, like those of other under-developed nations plagued by tribalism, must become self-conscious nation builders, as 'survivance' conscious as the Quebecois."[16] The nation that they should struggle to build should focus its collective energy on addressing the question of class.

Horowitz thought that a class politics would be expressed through the New Democratic Party, even going so far as to suggest in 1965 that the NDP might achieve real gains in Quebec.[17] The NDP seems to have failed to live up to this possibility until very recently. Its fortunes in Quebec remain uncertain, whereas it has succeeded in English Canada only to the extent that it has left aside explicit class identification and aimed directly at the "national-popular" vote. Its high point, again until very recently, was in the 1980s when Ed Broadbent based his campaign on "ordinary Canadians." Horowitz appears to say in the last chapter of *Canadian Labour in Politics* that the formation of the NDP from the Co-operative Commonwealth Federation in 1960 was a retreat from class politics. On paper, this is certainly true, particularly if one remains focused on the Regina Manifesto. But the NDP was closer to the unions than the CCF, and the CCF's basis in agrarian socialism was undermined by the shift to an urban labour base. It seems clear that any sort of socialist alternative in Canada had to find a way to unify these, and other, tendencies. In Gramscian terms, the political task was to forge a national-popular bloc from the various critical and socialist tendencies rather than polarize them along class lines – which would lead to their disintegration and thereby to the marginalization of the socialist alternative.[18]

Horowitz defined a leftist by the "belief that, ultimately, inequality is the most noxious of social problems,"[19] but he did not seem to consider that problems of region and ethnicity were also problems of inequality. He might have replied, of course, that inequalities of region and ethnicity are thoroughly influenced by inequality of class – and this is indeed true. But inequalities of region and ethnicity, insofar as they are problems of inequality (and not racial prejudice, for example, unless one were to define this as a form of unequal treatment), are not *only* problems of inequality. Or to say it differently but to come to the same point, inequalities between regions and ethnicities are not only inequalities of class. The economic and political ruling class in Canada, especially in the 1960s but still today, is a class rooted in Central Canada with European roots and outlook. Critique of these non-class forms of inequality is surely not marginal to political polarization tending to highlight inequality. The same might be said of the inequality of women, an issue that didn't arise in these essays: while it might well be "merely bourgeois" to agitate for the equal treatment of women within the capitalist system, unequal treatment of women is genuine inequality all the same. It may well be *insufficient* for a leftist to argue for gender equality, but it is also inadequate to suggest that gender equality is either nothing or a disguised form of class inequality. Of course, a lot more has been said and done about these matters since Horowitz wrote these articles. But this retrospective reflection does allow one to pinpoint a key problem with his analysis: posing the question as *either* falling into regional and ethnic, and perhaps gender, particularism *or* unifying them all under a politics oriented to inequality is a false and misleading opposition. Beyond those aspects of ethnic, regional, and gender inequality that can be traced back to class inequality, there are also distinct forms of inequality manifested in these issues. It is no doubt true that politics since the 1960s has tended to accept this opposition in the terms inherited from the 1960s that Horowitz uses here, though in a mirror image: regional, ethnic, and gender politics have been articulated, at least in their dominant and successful forms, by pushing away the question of class inequality. One could well accept Horowitz's definition of a leftist but recognize that inequality takes various forms that need to be *hooked into* a universalist perspective rather than *opposed to* it.

The dialogue and confrontation with George Grant was more extended than that with Porter because, it would seem, Grant personified the collectivist tory legacy in Canada that Horowitz was seeking the political will to turn in a socialist direction.[20] During the mid-1960s, Grant based his political views on his analysis of European modernity as based in the domination of nature by technology. He saw the dominant form of technology as the imperialism of the United States, though he admitted the possibility of other forms – such as Communism. In such a society, "people think of the world as indifferent stuff which they are absolutely free to control in any way they want through technology.... The technological society is one in which men are bent on dominating and controlling human and non-human nature."[21] Drawn to Grant's compelling description of the contemporary world, and hearkened by Grant's willingness to call the dominant form of technological society capitalist, Horowitz – like many English-Canadian socialists at the time – found in Grant's work a deep source of historical continuity for the attempt to forge a popular socialist political will.[22] He coined the term *red tory* in this context. "Thus, at the very highest level, the red tory is a philosopher who combines elements of toryism and socialism so thoroughly in a single integrated *Weltanschauung* that it is impossible to say that he is a proponent of one as *against* the other."[23] In every one of his conversations and interviews with Grant he raised the question of whether the socialist alternative was really just another form of technological society, as Grant suggested or assumed. In every one of his writings on Grant, he criticized what he called Grant's pessimism and insisted that socialism was a genuine alternative to the society Grant analyzed. He claimed that Grant "*identifies* the inevitability of technological progress with the inevitable failure of any attempt to control and use it for human purposes. It *assumes* that progress is *entirely* incompatible with any ideology but liberalism because liberalism alone gives it complete freedom."[24] Stressing the continuity between the conception of an organic, hierarchically articulated whole that underlies toryism and an organic, egalitarian whole that motivates socialists, Horowitz argued that "a young new leftist would say that it is not the total overcoming of chance [by technology] that is involved, but rather the total overcoming of the human suffering which is necessitated by repression and by domination. So that chance and even strife will remain, but not the type of suffering that emerges precisely out of the distortion of the human organism and the human psyche to suit the requirements of the machine."[25] Against Grant's conservative equation of the technological control of nature with the technological domination of human nature, Horowitz attempted to keep open the possibility of a technological overcoming of human suffering without technological control of human beings. The problem, of course, is that this is the traditional promise of liberalism. Twentieth-century politics and philosophy have been defined largely by the recognition that the domination of nature cannot be held apart from the domination of humans as nature. Massive bureaucracies, armies, and corporations that dominate the individual seem to be the necessary price of modern technology. The power of Grant's philosophy consisted precisely in his capacity to capture this relationship. The articulation of a socialist alternative would have to do more than reassert a liberal possibility that was already historically surpassed and shown to be based in an inadequate understanding of the phenomenon of technology.

Despite Grant's willingness to see the validity of overcoming unnecessary repression, and unwillingness to say that suffering is in itself good, he held to "the ancient tradition that human greatness and nobility are not possible without the virtues of moderation and courage. And this in some sense must mean the overcoming of passion."[26] Like many socialists of the time, Horowitz wanted to take on board Grant's philosophical account of European modernity but to mute its rhetoric of lament with one of decision, will, and an orientation to the future.[27] He was looking for a socialism grounded in one's place within an organic whole, but without the repression of individual passion that such a conservative image has traditionally required. It is no wonder that such a search for an egalitarian and passionate socialism oriented to the overcoming of suffering would lead to his next book being heavily influenced by Herbert Marcuse.[28]

But instead of moving on, let us tarry with this signal moment in the demand for a political will for Canadian socialism. There is no doubt that in some sense it is a lost and forgotten moment, but in what sense?

Horowitz presented us with an alternative between fragmentation into particularisms – especially those of region and ethnicity, where "in the absence of a Canadian identity, we identify – all of us, though to varying degrees – with the American national community"[29] – and the forging of an English-Canadian identity that could match that of French-speaking Quebec and negotiate a new federalism. The latter alternative required the political will to polarize Canadian politics around the centrality of class, which could then unify the fragmenting forces of region and ethnicity. I have suggested, albeit quickly, that two threads of this analysis can be seen to be vulnerable: the argument for the centrality of class politics to socialism and the argument that technological society can be made to serve human purposes.[30] A contemporary socialist political theory would have to address these two issues in a different manner. Perhaps in this way what can be recovered from this forgotten moment can be infused with new life for the future.

II

Horowitz's essays of the 1960s brought together the two themes of nationalism and red tory political culture in order to contribute to the formation of a socialist political will. In the absence of socialist transformation, it is remarkable to see how many of Horowitz's dire "predictions" have come into being: internal fragmentation, subsumption within the American identity, devolution of federal powers to the provinces due to the assertion of Quebec's claim to sovereignty within the current framework of Confederation – loss of commonality in general. The context for this miasma has been provided by free trade agreements with the United States orchestrated by the capitalist class in Canada. The problem remains the same, though intensified, but the solution needs to be rethought.[31] Given where the abandonment of the socialist politics of the 1960s has led us, it is perhaps worthwhile to think within a contemporary framework about what of it retains relevance.

Whereas Horowitz claimed continuity with a certain strain of conservatism from the left, the ascendance of a purely right-wing, business conservatism in the 1980s led some conservatives to look for deeper foundations for their politics and to admit a certain commonality with the left. Charles Taylor's influential book *Radical Tories* (1982) attempted to revive a distinctive conservative Canadian tradition of political thought. He referred to the malaise of Canadian politics in the 1970s and early 1980s, which he laid directly at the feet of "the rhetoric

of a dominant liberal ideology which placed few limits on man's freedom to shape his future, and which envisaged unprecedented technological achievement and material abundance."[32] His list of Canadian
conservatives contained many expected names (Leacock, Creighton,
Morton, Grant) but also some surprises (Purdy, Forsey) that he wanted
to rescue from their inclusion in a liberal or socialist canon. From each
of these Taylor gathered central aspects of conservative thought: the
importance of history and tradition, national sovereignty, place and environment (this is how he roped in Purdy), a sense of wonder, and,
most important, a conception of society as an "organic whole." The
philosophical core of conservatism is an organic whole that goes even
beyond society to include humans within nature and to ultimately reconcile them with a transcendent God.

Taylor's book was given urgency by a persistent worry: is conservatism more than a defence of power and privilege? So successfully was
this worry put to rest that he claimed that conservatism is not bound
by ideology, citing its "socialist" use of public industry, and arguing
that it incorporates a defence of human rights normally associated with
liberalism.[33] His argument reached its apogee in the chapter on George
Grant, since the term *red tory* was coined by Gad Horowitz in his writing about Grant. Grant argued that technological society becomes more
centralized, homogeneous, and bureaucratic through the uprooting of
all premodern traditions and attachments to place and particularity. It
must be a tyranny, in this sense. Yet the core of conservatism is belonging within a larger "organic" whole in which this political moment is
an aspect of a longer history – a moment of the expression of a people,
a people rooted in a tradition of a particular place, and the tradition of
a particular place encompassed by a unity of nature and history called
God. The fragmenting and individualizing nature of modern society
must drive such a conception to the margins and underground.[34]

So how does it stand with contemporary conservatism? In an after-
word to the 2006 edition of *Radical Tories*, Rudyard Griffiths argued that
the contemporary relevance of Taylor's pilgrimage is minimal – after
all, free trade was ushered in by the Conservative Party. He asserted
that the "Radical Tory program of rooting-out 'un-Canadian' influences
in our culture" is finished (but neither Taylor, nor Grant, nor Horowitz ever defended such parochialism), that Canadian nationalism can
survive in the new globalizing age, and that the conservative idea of
participation in a larger whole "happens all the time in our day-to-day
lives."[35] In short, everything's fine. Clearly, there is no place for red

toryism in the current Conservative Party or anywhere else on the political spectrum. It only remains to wonder if this really should be cause
for jubilation.

The core of our response to this question depends on whether the
red tory assessment of the failure of liberalism is accurate. A thoroughgoing philosophical individualism must regard any rooted collective
identities as impositions, as a tyranny from a premodern past. If there is
anything valuable in it, there may be a relevance for philosophical conservatism, even if its political expression has disappeared or changed
radically. Michael Ignatieff's post-national cosmopolitanism provides
a contemporary litmus test for the contemporary viability of conservatism's critique of liberalism. The attempt to fuse state power with
human rights is the best face that can be put on contemporary liberalism, otherwise it too would represent only the rule of the business
class.[36] Denis Smith argues that Ignatieff "writes as a courtier in the
antechambers of power, periodically adjusting his pronouncements
to keep within hailing distance of Blair's Downing Street and Bush's
White House,"[37] and this indeed seems to be the crux of the matter: the
economic and military power of the modern state is clearly an apparatus required by modern technology in George Grant's sense. The story
of Ignatieff's retreat from human rights is the story of the divergence of
power and good in the modern state, which shatters the hopes of liberalism. But there is a dilemma here: Ignatieff has argued that "the function of human rights ... is to protect real men and women in all their
history, language, and culture, in all their incorrigible and irreducible
difference,"[38] but the function of "protecting" to be effective must, for
liberal internationalists, make peace with the power of the state and
technology, in particular, military technology. Thus it yields a slippery
slope towards the extension of power at the expense of rights. It seems
that one must either accept this dilemma as unsurpassable in our time
and attempt to keep one's footing on the slippery slope, or one must
look elsewhere for the defence of human rights.

But where is this elsewhere? All contemporary Canadian political
parties are liberal in this sense. The Conservative Party expresses the
raw interests of the business class; the Liberals try to dress this up with
human rights, but succumb to the tyranny of technology; NDP foreign
policy shows no evidence of being fundamentally different but wants
the international defence of human rights without the concession to
the mechanisms of coercive power that they entail.[39] The liberal ideology and power structure that corresponds to the homogenizing and

deracinating forces of technology certainly has preferred its free enterprise variant, but the repressed CCF-NDP has posed no philosophical
alternative comparable to red tory conservatism. Its socialism is not in
principle different than the "socialism" of government intervention
and ownership to which conservatives, not even "red" ones, have re-
sorted to provide the infrastructure of the capitalist system. Political
conservatism of the red tory type no more gained expression in the corridors of power than the CCF-NDP. Philosophical "conservatism" may
express something true about human beings, but it does so at the expense of having a voice in the public realm.

The conservative idea of participation in an organic whole, loosed
from its connection to a practical politics, is no longer necessarily conservative at all. The idea that individual humans form meaningful lives
through participation in larger unities is a philosophical idea meaningful apart from any political conclusions that might be drawn from it.
Indeed, what conclusions might be drawn is a matter for political debate and not logical inference. A thoroughgoing philosophical individualism must regard any rooted collective identities as impositions, as
a tyranny from a premodern past. Correlatively, if this motive of participation in a larger whole is washed out by the technological assumptions of conventional politics, it may still be able to motivate a politics
of place, sovereignty, and solidarity outside, and in opposition to, such
conventions.

III

How would such a politics express itself? In what sense would it trace
its lineage back to the socialist nationalism of the 1960s?

If the red tory cannot be found anywhere on the political spectrum
nowadays, no more than a radical left-wing alternative to capitalism, it
does not follow that it can be found nowhere in Canadian society. It may
well be that this sense of participation in a larger whole is what motivates many in their political participation, even though it is washed out
by institutions and procedures. Perhaps the new social movements of
environmentalism, feminism, anti-poverty activism, and so forth have
sprung forward because of a deep sense of individual participation in
the community and the world, combined with the perception that official politics is devoid of exactly such participation. I think that this is
what Bob Davis had in mind when he recently claimed to be not a red
tory but a tory red.[40] Perhaps the continuing capacity of humans, and

citizens, to care about the destiny of their place, their nation, and their world is based upon an involvement that liberal ontology cannot recognize. Maybe the red tory, or tory red, phenomenon is characteristic of a certain formation of Canadian society, stretched between modernity and tradition, that has had a formative influence on the character of Canadians. Its red part, as was Horowitz's definition of a leftist, must be focused on the question of inequality. Our question is, "How can a politics of community and place – which continues to animate Canadian politics far beyond what is institutionally acceptable – be combined with a rigorous focus on inequality?"

While the Hartzian form of analysis that Horowitz adopted as his starting point does not deny that new forces come into being in the historical *present*, its specific contribution is to focus on the past, on the *origin* of the class fragments. These fragments themselves are understood on a Marxist model: aristocracy, bourgeoisie, proletariat – perhaps including the peasantry. In this sense is likely true that Hartzian analysis is primarily a corrective to crude Marxism.[41] It may be this emphasis that led Horowitz in his essays of the 1960s simply to assume that the collectivist past of English Canada could be turned towards a socialist future through a polarizing class politics – in which "class" stands for the working class understood in a Marxist way. I suggested above that other forms of inequality in region, ethnicity, and gender should not be opposed to class in this way but that they should been seen as complementary forms of inequality to be overcome by socialist will. A stricter focus on Canadian history would suggest, I think, that these other forms of inequality have also brought forth forms of solidarity and that these new forms of community must not be negated but built upon by the socialist project. In general one could say, then, that particular communities should not be opposed to a universal, or potentially universal, one, so that in the absence of the universal they reassert themselves as destructive *particularisms*. Rather, particular solidarities are the ground for the growth of more universal ones. Insofar as the socialist political will is tied to a universal critique of inequality, it must infuse particular communities with its universality, without negating their particular forms. I would say that it is a faulty formulation of the relation between particularity and universality in the politics of the 1960s that we must leave behind now. It is this faulty counter-posing of particular and universal that led later movements, when dissatisfied with class, to turn against the universal socialist project – thereby they became *particularist*, that is to say, confined within their particularity rather than using it as a springboard to ever more inclusive forms of solidarity.[42] If we understand socialist politics as going *through*, not against, particularities towards the universal in this way, issues of region, ethnicity, gender, etc. become central to the formation of a socialist national-popular will. On this basis, these newer movements can be brought alongside a more traditional leftist politics of class.

If one would rewind the socialist thread of the 1960s socialist-nationalist synthesis in this way, how would one rewind the nationalist thread? It's not too much to say that nationalist is treated almost everywhere as a dead dog these days, not only because of the atrocities committed in its name in the last few decades, but also because of a greater awareness of the homogenizing and centralizing forces within Canada, expressed through the Canadian state, that de-legitimate it as a pole of identification. Here, again, we can take some direction from the plurality of particular communities straining towards some approximation to universality. The nation state – or in Canada, the nations state (English Canada, Quebec, First Nations) – is not the universal form of community (even within Canada, apart from outside). It is potentially, insofar as it enacts this solidarity in policy and practice, one form of social solidarity that to some extent coordinates others and to another extent deals only with a thin layer of identification. Contemporary neoliberal politics of course undermines even this thin layer of national solidarity. Still, to the extent that we defend social programs and a common civilized life, we are forced to articulate common perspectives and values oriented towards a national identification. The nations state is one form of the contemporary encounter with the question of the grounds of human solidarity.

It cannot be ignored, however, that English Canada has failed to assert itself as a nation over the last forty years. It still has no form of political expression and doesn't seem to want one – so much so that it has come to be accepted that one of the virtues of our "moderate" political system is its avoidance of issues of principle in favour of muddling through. Starkly drawn political principle, it would seem, courts the danger of radical and immoderate action. If there is some merit to this view, and I think there is, then the failure of English Canada to assert itself as a nation is not only a failure but is a thoroughly precedented one in the history of our political culture. Perhaps the invisibility of English Canada to itself is a significant part of its own identity. It is hard to know what to do with this thought but impossible to un-think, given our fortunes since the 1960s.

It would seem to me that English-Canadian intellectuals should continue to follow Gad Horowitz insofar as they should speak of, and think for, English Canada. Not only my suggestion above, but also Horowitz's analysis of the 1960s, shows that, even though we may imagine the contrary, we are not simply Canadians but English Canadians who are thereby Canadians. We owe this clarity to the other groups who comprise Canada to help create a space for their self-expression. We also owe it to ourselves because, even if our politics remains a muddle, intellectual life cannot be so. The relation between politics and intellectual expression has become less clear. English-Canadian intellectuals shouldn't any more think of themselves as nation-builders, but they should be builders of the self-expression of the fragment, and fragmented, identity of English Canada.

NOTES

1 It has been consequently assumed by many commentators that Horowitz's contribution to thinking the political culture of English Canada thus stands or falls with the validity of the Hartzian approach in general. This is not so, especially since there are other historical, political, and philosophical interpretations that corroborate Horowitz's contribution. There are his dialogues with the work of John Porter and George Grant noted in the text below, for example. See also Leslie Armour, *The Idea of Canada and the Crisis of Community* (Ottawa: Steel Rail, 1981), which argues on historical grounds for the predominance of pre-Enlightenment communitarian influences in Canada; and Leslie Armour and Elizabeth Trott, *The Faces of Reason: An Essay on Philosophy and Culture in English Canada, 1850–1950* (Waterloo, ON: Wilfrid Laurier University Press, 1981), which argues for the predominance of communitarian conceptions of political life in Canadian philosophy. The reduction of the Horowitz thesis to its Hartzian origin, rather than its consideration within the framework of interpretations of English-Canadian culture, depends in large part on a disciplinary blindness deriving from the canons of political science as institutionalized in Canadian universities.

2 Whether the Hartzian approach is valid, of course, depends in large part upon what one takes it to be. I will not engage in a general evaluation of the Hartzian approach here but rather sublimate it into a consideration of Horowitz. Hartzian fragment theory is, in my view, a mid-level theory, that is to say, its usefulness consists in specifying questions for empirical research and in concretizing political theory on specific, mainly national,

cultural contexts. Therefore, it cannot be simply refuted by empirical research, nor can it achieve the purity of political theory. In general, I agree with H.D. Forbes that most of the critiques are quibbles and that Horowitz's work is an interpretive attempt to account for a real difference in political culture. See Forbes, "Hartz-Horowitz at Twenty: Nationalism, Toryism and Socialism in Canada and the United States," *Canadian Journal of Political Science* 20, no. 2 (June 1987): 305. (Forbes's article usefully refers to most of the critical literature on the so-called Hartz-Horowitz theory.) This does not mean, however, that such an interpretation cannot be subject to conceptual refinement or supplanted by a better interpretation. Forbes's general point that greater clarification of the notion of "corporate-collectivist-organic ideas" is needed – which Horowitz uses to point to similarities between toryism and socialism when compared to the individualist-contract character of liberalism – is well taken. This is a matter of historical interpretation and hermeneutic matters do not admit of right or wrong answers but of better or worse interpretation. One key aspect of a productive interpretation is that it selects a relevant axis of comparison. The difference between Canadian and American political cultures and the difference between the dominant liberal-contract theory and collectivist alternatives remain relevant differences for a politics that regards liberalism as an inadequate view of the good life and is situated in English Canada. This evaluation itself, of course, rests on "higher" or more universal grounds.

3 Gad Horowitz, "Why Has René Lévesque Become a Separatist? – Part III: A Symposium on René Lévesque," *Canadian Dimension* 5, nos. 2 and 3 (January–March 1968): 21; Horowitz, "Tories, Socialists and the Demise of Canada," *Canadian Dimension* 2, no. 4 (May–June 1965): 15; and Horowitz, "Quebec and Canadian Nationalism: Two Views," *Canadian Forum* 50 (January 1971): 357.

4 Gad Horowitz, "The Future of English Canada," *Canadian Dimension* 2 (July–August 1965): 2; and Horowitz, "Le statut particulier, formule libératrice pour les deux communautés," *Le Devoir*, 30 June 1967. This argument by Horowitz was quoted by René Lévesque in *Option Québec* (Ottawa: Les editions de l'homme, 1928), 49. The attempt to put together French and English nationalism under a progressive left-wing agenda has had a continued, though minor, effect in Canadian intellectual life. See, for example, Susan Crean and Marcel Rioux, *Two Nations* (Toronto: Lorimer, 1983), which was published in both English and French.

5 Horowitz, "Why Has René Lévesque Become a Separatist?," 20.

6 Ibid.

7 Horowitz, "Future of English Canada," 25.

8 For example, Philip Resnick, *Toward a Canada-Quebec Union* (Montreal and Kingston: McGill-Queen's University Press, 1991).
9 Horowitz, "Trudeau vs Trudeauism," *Canadian Forum* 48, no. 568 (May 1968): 30.
10 Horowitz, "Why Has René Lévesque Become a Separatist?," 20.
11 Horowitz, "Future of English Canada," 25.
12 Gad Horowitz, "Creative Politics," *Canadian Dimension* 3 (November–December 1965): 14. This article, together with its continuation "Mosaics and Identity," *Canadian Dimension* 3 (January–February 1966): 17–19, constitutes Horowitz's dialogue with John Porter.
13 Horowitz, "Creative Politics," 15.
14 Ibid.
15 Ibid.
16 Horowitz, "Mosaics and Identity," 19.
17 Gad Horowitz, "Nouveau Partie Democratique," *Canadian Dimension* 2 (July–August 1965): 16–17.
18 Gad Horowitz, *Canadian Labour in Politics* (Toronto: University of Toronto Press, 1968), especially 261.
19 Gad Horowitz, "Toward the Democratic Class Struggle," *Journal of Canadian Studies* 1, no. 3 (1966): 7.
20 Horowitz had two televised conversations with Grant (CBC, 7 and 14 February 1966) and interviewed Grant in "A Conversation on Technology and Man," *Journal of Canadian Studies* 4, no. 3 (August 1969): 3–20, later republished as "Horowitz and Grant Talk," *Canadian Dimension* 6, no. 6 (November/December 1969–January 1970): 18–20. These conversations and the interview are now republished in George Grant, *Collected Works of George Grant*, ed. Arthur Davis and Henry Roper, vol. 3, *1960–1969* (Toronto: University of Toronto Press, 2005). In addition, Horowitz published the article (which is mainly a review of Grant's *Lament for a Nation*) "Tories, Socialists and the Demise of Canada," *Canadian Dimension* 2, no. 4 (May–June 1965): 12–15; and "Conservatism, Liberalism and Socialism in Canada: An Interpretation," *Canadian Journal of Economics and Political Science* 32, no. 2 (May 1966): 143–71, which was revised to form the first chapter of *Canadian Labour in Politics*.
21 Grant, "Technology and Man," in *Collected Works*, 3:595.
22 See my own account of one such encounter in "For a Canadian Philosophy: George Grant," *Canadian Journal of Political and Social Theory* 13, nos. 1–2 (1989): 140–3.
23 Horowitz, *Canadian Labour in Politics*, 23.
24 Horowitz, "Tories, Socialists and the Demise of Canada," 15.

25 Gad Horowitz in "Technology and Man," in Grant, *Collected Works*, 3:598.

26 Horowitz in ibid., 3:598–9.

27 See my *A Border Within: National Identity, Cultural Plurality and Wilderness* (Montreal and Kingston: McGill-Queen's University Press, 1997), 30–5.

28 Gad Horowitz, *Repression: Basic and Surplus Repression in Psychoanalytic Theory; Freud, Reich and Marcuse* (Toronto: University of Toronto Press, 1977).

29 Horowitz, "Mosaics and Identity," 19.

30 I will leave out of consideration the interesting historical question of whether these two points of vulnerability become visible only in retrospect or whether they were available alternatives at the time. Note, however, that the centrality of class was a key point of the national liberation politics that predominated in the 1960s (and which Horowitz tried to adapt to English Canada). The second point was made by Grant in his conversations with Horowitz. Socialists tried to deny the necessity of the technological control of human beings, even while it was the descriptive power of exactly this in corporate capitalism that attracted them to Grant. If a socialist alternative is to be opened up here, it cannot be by accepting a Grant-like analysis of the present and then simply denying it to the future by asserting a political will.

31 Horowitz himself has suggested that his 1960s rejection of Grant's pessimism needs to be retracted in the light of subsequent experience. See Cara Spittal, "Interview of Gad Horowitz," 6 August 2007 (private circulation, copy provided by Gad Horowitz): "And for the socialist in Horowitz it's really disturbing to think that whatever prospects there are of anything less than a monolithically liberal society in English Canada are going to disappear.... Back then I accused Grant of being too pessimistic. But now, I don't think so." The common accusation of pessimism against Grant is superficial, however. The bigger issue is whether his analysis of technology was accurate. Horowitz doesn't indicate in this interview the grounds for his re-evaluation.

32 Charles Taylor, *Radical Tories* (1982; Toronto: House of Anansi, 2006), 7.

33 Ibid., 113, 71, 189. It is tempting to wonder what Taylor would have made of John Boyko's careful documentation of the relentless distortion of the NDP as Communist totalitarians by the Conservative Party and the deployment of illegal police surveillance by Conservative Ontario Premier Drew. John Boyko, *Into the Hurricane: Attacking Socialism and the NDP* (Winnipeg: Shillingford, 2006), chap. 4 and p. 101.

34 Though Grant's *Lament for a Nation* oriented itself to the loss of national sovereignty signified in the defeat of Diefenbaker's government, it is more

deeply about the necessity of that loss. Thus, argues Grant, conservatism in practice becomes exactly the justification of "the continuing rule of the business man and the right of the greedy" from which Taylor looked to the red tory to rescue conservative politics. Taylor quotes this phrase of Grant's from *Lament for a Nation* in *Radical Tories*, 144.

35 Ibid., 221–2.

36 Denis Smith follows rigorously Ignatieff's evolution from post-Yugoslav ethnic conflict, through the "war on terror," to the invasion of Iraq in *Ignatieff's World* (Toronto: James Lorimer, 2006). Smith documents Ignatieff's progressive retreat from the priority of human rights to the recognition that international defence of human rights presupposes that "a great power must have vital interests in the region" (55), to defence of the new American empire (92), targeted assassinations (113), a worry that the modern state system may disintegrate (123), and finally "letting torture in by the back door" (118). Perhaps most irritating for Canadians are his willingness to speak as an American while in the United States (73, 148) and his notion that the core of Canadian political thought is that "the state creates the nation" (Ignatieff, quoted in Smith, 134). Grant was Ignatieff's uncle, in a powerful political family with deep roots in Upper Canada. Smith ends by wondering what Grant would have thought of Ignatieff's assigning of Canada to a subordinate role in the American empire (147). Indeed.

37 Ibid., 145.

38 Michael Ignatieff, *The Rights Revolution* (Toronto: Anansi, 2000), 43.

39 This is the irony of John Boyko's history in *Into the Hurricane*: he documents effectively that the failure of CCF-NDP politics to enter the corridors of power was dependent less on their own failures and more on the concerted attack and misrepresentation that all other parties, the business class, and much of organized religion made on it. But, while the founding ideas of the CCF were certainly anti-capitalist and "based on an ideological premise that was outside the Canadian mainstream" (155), Boyko does not contest that it progressively abandoned this premise (13–14). So the CCF-NDP seems to have suffered the repression often visited on a radical alternative, without enjoying the difference from liberal ideology to which such an alternative pretends.

40 Bob Davis, "The Death of Isaiah Berlin," *Friend* 3, no. 2 (2001): 20.

41 H.D. Forbes, "Hartz-Horowitz at Twenty"; and Gad Horowitz, "Notes on 'Conservatism, Liberalism and Socialism in Canada,'" *Canadian Journal of Political Science* 11, no. 2 (June 1978): 383–99.

42 This explains why, as H.D. Forbes points out in "Hartz-Horowitz at Twenty," the category of collectivism is unclear in Horowitz, even though it is true that there is such a thing when considered in comparison to liberalism. The problem of collectivism is here understood to be the question of the origin of human solidarity in its many forms, only one of which is the nation.

6 Canada's Regional Fragments

NELSON WISEMAN

In the United States, Louis Hartz's "fragment theory" as presented in *The Liberal Tradition in America*[1] (*LTA*) commanded attention and respect if not embrace. It was quickly eclipsed there and, by the 1980s, was deemed "practically dead."[2] Hartz's message challenged Americans' positive view of the United States – that its polity and discourse had benefitted only from having left the Old World behind. He argued that Americans unreflectively embraced an exalted version of seventeenth-century Lockeanism, severing them from further Western intellectual development. Hartz's thesis undermined what his contemporary colleague, radical sociologist C. Wright Mills, described as American intellectuals' "celebration of America." Americans were loath to compare their country to others except when comparative analysis cast the United States as superior.

What especially captured scholarly imaginations was Horowitz's creative use of Hartz.[3] Hartz's method was in the best traditions of both political theory and comparative politics. He took thinkers and movements from one national setting and placed them in another, asking, for example, how an Alexander Hamilton would have fared in Australia, or how Roosevelt's New Deal would have been greeted in Europe.[4] Hartz's comparative method insists on such unlikely transpositions. Horowitz deployed Hartz's method by placing Mackenzie King and his Liberals comparatively. He depicted them as triumphant centrist forces with powerful adversaries to their left and right unlike the liberal and decidedly leftist reform movements and parties of both America and Europe.[5] He similarly compared and contrasted Canadian conservatism and socialism with their American counterparts and showed how British they were.

Canadian developments are more likely compared with those in the United States than in France and Britain, despite the British and French roots of Canadian identity.[6] Seymour Martin Lipset's classic sociological study, *Agrarian Socialism*, of the Saskatchewan CCF serves as a telling example. His first chapter, setting the stage, is titled "The Background of Agrarian Radicalism."[7] Of the sixty-four footnotes it offers, not one is from a British (or for that matter Canadian) source. Yet Saskatchewan's agrarian and socialist leaders, as the balance of his book attests, drew disproportionately on British immigrants and British Labour's policies. All of Lipset's references in that introductory chapter are to non-Canadian literatures, especially ones on the American agrarian experience, including the *Iowa Journal of History and Politics* and the *Mississippi Valley Historical Review*.

To be sure, in many respects the United States showed the future for Canada: America's agrarian revolt of the late nineteenth century and its Progressives had their Canadian versions in the early twentieth century; the West's demand for an elected Senate in late twentieth-century Canada had its forerunner earlier in the century in the United States; the designation of "affirmative action programs" in the Charter of Rights and many of its provisions such as those regarding "cruel and unusual punishment" and "self-incrimination" mimic phrases coined by American policymakers and courts to address similar issues. But Saskatchewan's socialism and its agrarian radicalism had much more to do with Britain and Britons – like Tommy Douglas, Old World Fabian M.J. Coldwell, and chocolate family scion George Cadbury – than with American socialism. And, I would contend, it had much to do with cities and unions too – Douglas, Coldwell, and Cadbury were not farmers. Coldwell led his province's Farmer-Labour Party, and Douglas fought for a New Party to merge with organized labour and became its leader. That was something few American agrarian or labour leaders cared for during the Cold War. That Lipset's American frame of reference for Saskatchewan's agrarian radicalism went unnoticed reflected Canada's intellectual environment at the time. Agrarian politics on the Canadian prairies were assumed to be variants of American prototypes, yet Saskatchewan's farmers called for "free trade with the mother country" and debated land nationalization. They organized a wheat pool that some of them depicted as a stepping stone to socialism, and they insisted on a government monopoly to market that wheat.

Geography and Technology

The fragment theory serves as a backdrop against which other developments may be situated. The pursuit of a regional dimension of Hartz's thesis, however, would likely have struck him as a waste of time and beside the point he was making. He was explicitly dealing with *national*, not sub-national or regional, political cultures. A dual-fragment analysis of Canada fit with his thesis, because French Canadians constituted a *nation* with a different language, ethnicity, history, religion, culture, and ideology. In this respect, *The Founding of New Societies* (FNS) went beyond *LTA*'s analytical frame of the American nation state. Hartz was intentionally pursuing a single-factor thesis in *LTA* and *FNS* to see how far one could push the interaction of ideologies in a national setting as an explanatory device. He demonstrated in *FNS*, however, that he was not a dogmatist who insisted that all new societies' political cultures were cut from the same ideological cloth.

Horowitz's "Conservatism, Liberalism, and Socialism in Canada: An Interpretation" ("CLS"), like Hartz's *LTA*, focuses on the ideological superstructure of a *national* political culture, that of English Canada. It refers in passing to socialism's strength in certain regions such as Saskatchewan and British Columbia,[8] but this is incidental to its national fragment framework. "CLS" refers to Michigan and New York, but Manitoba and Nova Scotia are ignored, beyond a footnote relaying voting data. Horowitz accepted and followed the cultural duality pointed to by McRae and other students and practitioners of Canadian politics. The English-French divide runs from the Quebec Act of the 1770s, to the Durham Report and the Baldwin-Lafontaine joint ministry in the Province of Canada in the 1840s, to André Siegfried's observations as a foreigner in the early twentieth century.[9] It continued with the Conservative party's *deux nations* proposal of the 1960s, the "distinct society" clauses in the Meech Lake and Charlottetown Accords in the 1980s and 1990s, to the House of Commons voting overwhelmingly to recognize the Québécois as a "nation" in 2006.

Horowitz observed that, from a global perspective, the differences between the liberal political cultures of English Canada and the United States appear marginal but that from a North American perspective they are significant. Similarly, one may observe that within a North American context the differences in the cultural traditions of Nova Scotia and Saskatchewan are less salient than those between English Canada and

French Canada or those between English Canada and the United States. Within Canada, however, they are conspicuously striking.

A fundamental difference between Kenneth McRae and Hartz is that McRae deployed an approach informed by the frontier to develop his historical account. His analysis refers to developments ranging from the Maritimes to the prairies' Metis. Ironically, Hartz's thesis was formulated as, among other things, an assault on the regional emphasis of Frederick Jackson Turner's frontier thesis.[10] For Hartz, "Turner, like the average American, 'cannot see' Europe. He is, however, able to see the open land on which the European drama is enacted."[11] McRae adopted something of a frontier thesis in noting regional variations in English Canada's origins and peoples, although he "was entirely unconscious" of it. At the time, Hartz conveyed reservations to him about the very use of the term *frontier*.[12]

If one looks for a national political culture, one will discern it; if one pursues regional cultures within a country, one will discern those too. It is a matter of perspective, of the design driving the analysis. Regionalism is one of the fault lines or axes of Canadian politics but not in the same way that it is in the United States. If one thinks of the frontier experience as critical in the North American case, then a vital distinction arises between Canada and the United States. The latter had a "soft" frontier: settlement proceeded steadily from east to west, across the Midwest and Great Plains, onto the inter-mountain states and the Pacific. In Canada, in contrast, a "hard" frontier – the Canadian Shield and the more northerly Rockies – meant that people and their cultures did not so much ooze across the land as effectively leapfrog it with the extension of a more advanced technology. The railway was a prerequisite for western Canadian settlement. Without it, Canada could not have colonized the prairies. Settlement was more sudden and decidedly more dominated by immigrants than in the United States. Those born abroad outnumbered Canadians in much of western Canada.

The railroad played a powerful role in Canada's creation in a way that it did not in the United States: without the promise of the Intercolonial Railway, New Brunswick and Nova Scotia would have remained aloof from the Confederation project. It was precisely the irrelevance of such a project to the economic prospects of PEI and Newfoundland, both islands, that initially kept them out of Canada. And it was its relevance that induced British Columbia to join. Before the railroad, Manitoba's orientation to older societies was northerly through Hudson Bay and the Nelson River system – as the route of the pioneering Selkirk settlers demonstrated. Without the CPR, Manitoba's orientation would have proceeded southerly, through the Red River basin and, eventually, the Minneapolis grain market. In Canada, a large proportion of the labour force powering railroad growth was imperial – imported British labour – and foreign – Continental European and Chinese. Even after an overbuilt rail network was in place, the railroad companies in the 1920s continued to lobby aggressively for more immigration because there were 34 million acres of unoccupied land within fifteen miles of rail tracks.[13]

Canada had no distinctive founding myth. Notwithstanding assertions by some like Georges-Étienne Cartier that Canadians represented a "new nationality," there was no formative national ethic to spread across the new state, beyond the truism that Canadians were British subjects and, in that, consciously un-American. There is a dearth of mythical deities or indigenous fantasies to worship in a satellite, colonial state. Canada did not spread from east to west with surveyors like the Americans Lewis and Clarke acting on behalf of a central government imbued with the sense of a manifest destiny. Canada's 1867 foundation was a business deal supplemented by bicultural and military considerations. English-Canadian political culture was cobbled together over time and space. It was not a country forged in crisis or war like the United States, the Soviet Union, West Germany, or Bangladesh. Nor was it a product of imperial fabrication like Iraq or Chad. The very idea of a federal state sat ill with Anglo-Canadians keen on "a Constitution similar in Principle to that of the United Kingdom."[14] The Province of Canada's dualism and the deadlocks engendered by its dual ministries and double majority principle, however, made the American federal model rather than British unitary one necessary. The experience of ten separate, unstable governments between 1854 and 1864 and seventeen such governments in total between 1841 and 1867 in the Province of Canada demonstrated that.

As the twentieth century unfolded, roads and highways complemented railroads whose deployment consolidated the Canadian state in the nineteenth century. An alternative to the overbuilt rail networks appeared with the rise of a newer technology, the motor vehicle. Railroads physically separated Canada from the United States in ways that waterways – from the St Lawrence, to the Great Lakes, Lake of the Woods, and the Red, Missouri, and Columbia River systems – did not. If one examines North American rail lines, one notices how many of their spurs come within sight of the border, yet how few actually cross it. In contrast, if one looks for the highways traversing the forty-ninth parallel, one notices how many – fifty-two – run north-south across the border.[15] Highways fostered continental integration, whereas the railroads nourished national separation. By the time roads overtook rails, America's nineteenth-century threat to the North-West and Canada's very survival had passed.

What was less definitively fixed than the border was Canada's identity, its ideological and cultural underpinnings. It was no paradox that as Canada's British connections began to fray in the 1920s, the Americanization of its political culture accelerated. This was occasioned by the rise of new technologies and communications networks, from the telephone at the turn of the century to radio in the 1920s, to television in the 1950s, to the widespread continental circulation of magazines like *Time*, *Life*, and *Reader's Digest*. The growth of air travel and eventually the Internet continued to make the border more culturally permeable. An example of an American practice replacing a British one was the way Canadian political parties began to select their leaders: between 1919 and 1927, the Liberals and Conservatives opted for delegated leadership conventions and broke with the British model of selection by Parliamentary caucus. The 1920s was also the decade in which American capitalists replaced British ones as Canada's principal financiers.[16]

A difference between the Canadian and U.S. frontiers that became evident as the twentieth century unfolded was that Canada's shifted from the West to the North. Tory nationalist John Diefenbaker campaigned on a "northern" vision of the country, and his enfranchisement of what were then legally known as status Indians – located largely in the territories and northern reaches of the provinces – was followed by their being granted heightened constitutional status in the 1980s. The devolution to the territories of province-like powers by Ottawa and the creation of Nunavut in the 1990s – the only jurisdiction where Aboriginal peoples are in the majority – led some to redefine Canada as a trilateral relationship among English-speaking, French-speaking, and Indigenous nations.[17] Americans speak of their country stretching "from sea to sea"; Canadians have come to speak of theirs "from sea to sea to sea."

Immigration

Hartz floated the idea that the political culture of a new society founded by Europeans congeals. It becomes blind to ideological currents foreign to its formative founding ideology. Historians have lambasted this notion.[18] It also sits uncomfortably with political scientists, because it suggests, as Hartz put it, "immobilism" and the inability of a society to change fundamental ideological course. Canada's dramatic changes in its social composition, economic structures, and technological environment, like those of the United States, speak to movement, not stasis, within the unchallenged framework of liberalism, whether pure or tory-touched. What is striking from a party politics perspective, however, is the constancy and stability of the regional party systems and the relative positioning of those parties on a political spectrum. Compared to the United States, with its two national parties competing in every region and state, Canada sports a multiplicity of provincial party systems. There are striking variations in support for federal and provincial parties of the same stripe in many provinces, and the parties vary across provinces.

Since Confederation, only Conservatives and Liberals have ever governed in the Atlantic provinces. Only in 1998 did a third party, the NDP, rise to official opposition status in one of those provinces, Nova Scotia, where they were elected to govern ten years later. In Quebec, the pattern since the 1930s has been the presence of a distinctive nationalist party and the absence of Canada's original party, the Conservatives. In Ontario, the provincial mould has appeared as a smaller replica of the English-Canadian federal norm – a three-party system, with the CCF-NDP as the chronically weak third sister. The West has featured populist parties, with the eastern prairies (Manitoba and Saskatchewan) electing social democratic governments that have ruled those provinces in every decade since the 1940s and 1960s respectively. Alberta, in further contrast, has had a quasi-party tradition with an astounding lack of regime changes (only three: in 1921, 1935, and 1971) since the province's creation over a century ago. British Columbia has had self-avowed labour-socialists in its legislature since the 1890s and has a fiercely ideological bipolar party system – the only province where, for most of the last half of the twentieth century, neither of the leading federal parties, the Liberals and Conservatives, was a serious player. The key to explaining these variations lies in tracing the initial ideological orientations of the charter settlers of the regions and connecting them with the parties.

It is critical from the fragment-theory perspective to appreciate the time of founding settlers' departure from the older to the newer society. The idea that Canada has a single formative group, however, is not viable. The Hartz-Horowitz hypothesis focuses on Canada's two founding peoples, *les habitants* and the Loyalists, both royally sanctioned. One may contend as a counterpoint to this dualist model that, since disparate Canadian regions were settled at such different times by peoples of quite different societies, then the regions have disparate dominant ideological dispositions too.

If I were pressed to pick a point of congealment for Canadian political culture, it would be the 1926–31 period in which the King-Byng affair and the Statute of Westminster effectively restricted the British Crown's discretionary powers and formalized Canada's appearance as an independent actor on the world stage. From a Hartzian perspective, a good reason to select the late 1920s as pivotal is the peopling of the country. Canada's formative ideological infusions had taken root. By that decade the multicultural, if not multiracial, character of the country was determined. Relatively few entered the country between the early 1930s and the mid-1940s.[19] Those who arrived after the Second World War, moreover, were not pioneers and homesteaders like so many of those who had preceded them before the First World War. Nevertheless, the British imprint on Canada lingered: a distinct Canadian citizenship was introduced only in 1947, and Canadians remained British subjects until 1977.

Canada, to use a cliché, is a country of immigrants. The United States also sees itself as a country of immigrants. The difference in the volume and composition of the two countries' immigrants is striking, however, yet rarely noted and even less appreciated. In the twentieth century's year of greatest immigration to the United States, 1907, for example, one immigrant arrived for every eighty Americans. In Canada, in its equivalent year of greatest immigration, 1913, an immigrant arrived for every eighteen Canadians.[20] This renders a quantitative demographic difference a qualitative one, especially when considered in the context of the Canadian West, where most of these immigrants settled. There they created and sustained political parties in a way that did not occur in the United States, where immigrant populations were more easily absorbed into established parties and third parties withered.

An instructive extension of the Hartz-Horowitz hypothesis is to look at Canada's distinct waves of immigration in their regional settings. Such an analysis connects ideological currents in time and space. One brushstroke approach is to fix more or less arbitrarily on five regions – Atlantic Canada, Quebec, Ontario, the Midwest (Manitoba and Saskatchewan), and the Far West (Alberta and British Columbia) – and five historical immigrant waves: the pre-Conquest French; the Loyalists; a

British group in the first half of the nineteenth century; a mix of Britons, Americans, and Continental Europeans at the turn of the twentieth century; and the varied new Canadians that have landed since the Second World War.

The historical pattern of Canadian politics, seen from the regional ground up, is thus understood by looking broadly at these five distinct immigrant waves since their appearance in their "new societies." The first wave, the seventeenth-century "feudal" or classically conservative French fragment had its *ancien* traditions reinforced by a more *ancien* hierarchy, the Catholic clergy. Horowitz prominently elevated the second wave, the Loyalists, to highlight Canadian-American ideological distinctions. The third wave, composed largely of Britons arriving after the Napoleonic Wars, also included post-revolutionary Americans in search of land as well as the culturally distinct Old World Irish fleeing their famine. The fourth wave – that stew of modern Britons, Americans, and Continental Europeans came from dramatically different societies – one industrial, the other agrarian, and the third – as in the case of Ukrainians and Russians – not far removed from the vestiges of serfdom. The fifth and last wave, that veritable farrago of peoples, races, and cultures, have appeared since the Second World War. Placing these waves in the regions that received them, and paying attention to the ideological outlooks that differentiated them, helps to disentangle the question of why some political parties arose and gained traction in some regions and why others did not. The interaction of different ripples in the immigrant waves explains the socio-ideological character of regional politics.

Quebec is the oldest part of Canada. Once its most conservative region, since the Quiet Revolution it has been a leader in progressive social legislation, province-building, public administration, and democratic reform. Atlantic Canadians live in the oldest, most tory and rural English-Canadian region. They are the least mobile of English Canadians, ideologically and geographically. Ontario expresses archetypal English-Canadian culture. Values that have historically characterized Old Ontario's politics, such as "ascriptive, elitist, hierarchical, stable, cautious, and restrained," have been assigned to the whole of English Canada.[21] The Midwest is the bastion of Canadian social democracy, established and initially sustained there by transplanted British labour-socialists. The Far West features a parvenu political culture. Despite the continental divide between them, Alberta and BC are both upstart provinces. This region has beckoned migrants from other parts of Canada with a promise of entry to a charmed circle, and it now accounts for more than four of five westerners. There are, of course, dramatic ideological-cultural variations within as well as between provinces. Northern Ontario – disaffected, sparsely settled, passive, alienated, and remote from the levers of political and economic power – has more in common with northern Saskatchewan or Labrador than with urbanized, industrialized, and dominant southern Ontario. Within the immigrant waves too there are variations and more and less prominent ideological ripples. There are also important differences in how they distributed themselves regionally.

The French fragment, cut off and isolated from the mother country, was like Bourbon France in that both were overthrown in the second half of the eighteenth century. This exclusively Catholic society – Huguenots could settle in New England but not in New France – went from thinking of itself as French Canadian to comporting itself as *la nation québécoise* by embracing the idea of a common civic culture, a *culture publique commune.*[22] This entails accepting diversity, integrating cultural minorities, and embodying the values of democracy, free expression, and equality. Today's Quebecers maintain the *ancien idée* of social solidarity but are required to abandon their exclusive focus on a distinctive ethno-religious history. The Maritimes, an early northerly extension of pre-revolutionary New England, came to absorb three times as many Loyalists as Upper Canada, but one would not glean this from *the* Ontario-centric account of "CLS." New Brunswick was created for them, with St John – dubbed the Loyalist city – granted a royal charter. In Nova Scotia, Loyalists blended with a pre-Loyalist fragment that held much in common with New England. In both the Maritimes and Upper Canada, the Loyalist wave represented North America's counter-revolution, while Quebec was bypassed by it except for traces in the Gaspé, the Eastern Townships, and in Montreal's anglo merchant-industrial class.

The post-Napoleonic immigrant wave to which both McRae and Horowitz draw attention – what is now Ontario exploded from 77,000 souls in 1811 to 952,000 in 1851[23] – was composed largely of early reform or tory-touched British liberals. The land-hungry Americans among them headed for the then Canadian frontier, western Ontario. It was there that the 1837 rebels rallied sympathy and support. The Irish ripple was imported to build Canada's canals and railroads. They arrived after the Loyalists had gravitated to eastern Ontario and had put their stamp on what became tory Toronto. The Britons were carriers of

British reform liberalism, but the Americans were more radical liberals still. The titles of some of the region's newspapers convey the ideological orientations of their day: the Galt *Reformer*, the St Thomas *Liberal*, and, in a city that also became a refuge for former American slaves, the *Chatham Freeman*. The appearance of a British labour-socialist class in turn-of-the-twentieth-century Ontario was not as pronounced as in the West because Ontario had long been settled. Its earlier ideological and partisan traditions were set by then. Nevertheless, the gravitation of this new immigrant group to Ontario's cities and the province's ascendant manufacturing sector helped to throw up press titles like *Industrial Banner*, the *Palladiums of Labour*, the *Ontario Workman*, *Labor News*, and *Trade Unions Advocate*.

The Midwest, Canada's "New West" at the turn of the twentieth century, was the "breadbasket of the British Empire." It drove the national economy when wheat was king. As Canada grew by a record 34 per cent in the century's first decade, Saskatchewan's population exploded by a phenomenal 439 per cent and became the third-largest province in short order. Alberta, similarly, expanded by 413 per cent. Manitoba, where the CPR and pioneering Ontarians appeared earlier, grew by 145 per cent in the 1880s when national growth was but 12 per cent. Ontarians brought to Manitoba their eastern "tory" and "grit" loyalties and parties, the Conservatives and Liberals, and served as their leaders and backbone. The province also had enough of the prairies in it to produce a farmers' government and to provide the leadership for the national Progressives, Parliament's second-largest party in the 1920s. Manitoba also had in it enough of modern, urban, industrial Britain to supply the leadership for the General Strike – every strike leader but one was born there and arrived in Winnipeg between the 1890s and the strike's outbreak. Saskatchewan's demographic mix included Ontarians, Britons, and Americans but also the country's largest percentage of Continental Europeans. This group, initially deferential to the Liberals and maligned by the province's 125 Ku Klux Klan locals in the 1920s, became sufficiently established and secure by the 1940s to vote for the CCF.

The Far West then became Canada's new "New West" – a magnet for Canadians from other regions – as the century wore on. BC is the only province whose share of the national population has never declined. Once the smallest province, it will likely overtake Quebec as the second-largest in this century. BC Social Credit was no more than a convenient nameplate for a coalition of Liberals and Conservatives bent on keeping the CCF-NDP from office. In Alberta, agrarian radicalism gave way to agribusiness, and horse wranglers gave way to oil wranglers. Alberta Social Credit, once critical of the banks, transformed itself into a purposefully fierce anti-socialist force at peace with the financial establishment. Ernest Manning went from being Social Credit's finance minister and premier to serving as a director of the Canadian Imperial Bank of Commerce.

Differences between the Midwest and Far West as well as the differences within them reveal the interaction of immigration, ideology, and political destiny. Manitoba, formed in the nineteenth century, came under the sway of Ontarians – every premier in the twentieth century but one until the late 1980s was either born in Ontario or was the son of Ontarians. One of them, Hugh John Macdonald, was John A.'s son. Saskatchewan, formed in the early twentieth century, had an unusually high proportion of British labour-socialists who took up farming. Saskatchewan also had a higher percentage of non-Anglo-Saxons, mostly Continental Europeans, than any other English-Canadian province. Initially politically deferential to the Liberals, they became a critical component of the winning coalition that catapulted the CCF to power as acculturation, intermarriage, and the appearance of a more self-confident second generation of non-Anglo-Saxons appeared in the 1940s. Alberta represented the Canadian equivalent of America's "Last Best West," which had been staked by the 1890s. The province was a repository for an unusually large number of American farmers steeped in populist radicalism. Where in the world have Americans ever constituted between a fifth and a quarter of a foreign jurisdiction's population as Alberta's Americans did in 1911?[24] BC's radical political culture was like Australia's: both represented Great Britain on the Pacific and both featured a mix of modern Britons, labour-socialists, and enterprising adventurers clashing in a setting of natural resource wealth. The somewhat older Australian fragment, however, exhibited a trace of an older Old World influence, Chartism,[25] that had no resonance in Canada.

The American impact on Alberta's agrarian politics was evident in the composition of the United Farmers of Alberta. Eight of its nineteen executive members were American-born, outnumbering its British or Canadian-born members.[26] The *Calgary Herald* recognized the UFA as "the bosses of the situation in the province"[27] even before its election to office. Its leader from 1916 to 1931, and the chairman of the Alberta Wheat Pool through most of the 1920s and 1930s, was Henry Wise Wood, who emigrated to the province as a forty-five-year-old veteran Missouri populist. He had participated in the formation of both the

Farmers' Alliance and the Populist Party in the United States. As a political thinker, Wood "can be explained," as tory historian W.L. Morton, pointed out, "only by reference to his American background," being a person "who had toiled and died within the simple and narrow limits of an unreflecting individualism and of Jacksonian democracy."[28]

Dominant in the politically over-represented rural areas and in the leadership of the UFA, Americans influenced Alberta in a radical liberal direction. Their liberalism, quite unlike that of Ontario and the Maritimes, was devoid of any hint of toryism. Alberta produced an ideologically consensual quasi-party system while Ontario and the Maritimes produced colonial equivalents of the British Conservative and Liberal parties. British Columbia, in contrast to Alberta, has featured pronounced ideological polarization throughout the twentieth century and beyond. It has been depicted as an "Edwardian fragment,"[29] for during Edward VII's reign in the twentieth century's first decade the province expanded by 120 per cent, from fewer than 180,000 to nearly 400,000. Newly arriving Britons in the fourth wave of immigration flocked into BC's cities and work camps. As elsewhere – from Cape Breton's coal miners to Calgary's working class represented by socialist MP William Irvine – many of the Britons were sympathetic to labour-socialism. In BC, they joined forces with radical labour leaders and workers who hailed from the American Pacific Northwest, where similar frontier mining and timber industries operated.

After the American agrarian influx at the turn of the twentieth century, the proportion of Americans among Alberta's immigrants declined steadily. Americans comprised 30 per cent of Alberta's immigrants between 1900 and 1920.[30] By 1921, there were more British-born Albertans than American-born ones, but the Americans outnumbered the Britons in all fifteen of the province's rural census divisions.[31] They constituted approximately half the farmers in southern Alberta. The presence of both fewer British farmers and fewer European Americans in Alberta than in Saskatchewan helped tilt Alberta in a right-wing direction.

Even in a context of relatively few American-born Albertans in the twenty-first century, their influence and ideas continued to far exceed their numbers. They were prominent, for example, as executives and senior managers in the provincial oil industry. Conspicuous too were the Americans in the conservative and very un-tory "Calgary school" that emerged at the University of Calgary. One, Tom Flanagan – raised in a Republican household and a fellow of the right-wing Fraser Institute – served as Stephen Harper's professor and his campaign manager in the 2002 Canadian Alliance leadership race, and he directed the

Conservative campaign in the 2004 federal election. He and Harper were among the six intellectuals who authored a "firewall" letter calling on Alberta's government to insulate itself from federal intrusions.[32] Flanagan also taught Ezra Levant, who established the Alberta-based *Western Standard*, the Canadian equivalent of the archconservative U.S. *Weekly Standard*. Another "Calgary school" American, F.L. (Ted) Morton, was elected by Albertans as a senator-in-waiting and then as an MLA. In 2007, he contested the Conservative party leadership and the premiership. A telling link between past and present was that Morton performed best in that contest in the very same rural southern Albertan districts where the American demographic imprint had been most profound a century earlier.[33]

The foregoing suggests that regional immigration patterns are the key to accounting for the disparate pattern of partisan and ideological politics across the country. The Maritimes' parties, the Conservatives and Liberals, reflect the political heritage of late eighteenth-century British and American politics. Anglo Maritimers represented an extension of both Britain and New England when the Maritimes were part of British North America. The French fragment is of an even earlier European era. Detached from Europe by the Conquest, Quebec eventually took on a twentieth-century "world ethic" after its Quiet Revolution unfolded "in a setting that embraces Asia and Africa as well [as Europe]." What Hartz termed "bombardment" generated ideological diversity as "the French Canadian exchanges a partial 'Frenchness' for a partial place in a culture wider even than that of the Canadian dualism."[34] This fragment's founding ideology imploded. It was forced to confront wider worldly currents of thought as the contradictions between Quebec's inherited ideology and its material conditions proved unsustainable. This impelled a new form of political management. In Quebec, following the Hartz-Horowitz model, social democratic formulations appeared as they had in Europe – emerging from an admixture of older feudal and modern liberal ideas. Socialist thinking surfaced in the 1960s only because liberalism, finally, had made a significant mark in the province. As evidence of its socialism, the Parti Québécois applied to join the Socialist International, and, reciprocally, the SI's president attended René Lévesque's funeral.[35]

Economic Structures

Although Hartz focused on national ideological underpinnings, he was acutely conscious of economic and regional factors. The title of his first book, *Economic Policy and Democratic Thought: Pennsylvania, 1776–1860*[36] revealed as much. The connection between economic structures and ideology is pivotal to students of Canadian political culture working in the Innisian tradition and to Marxists. Marxists criticized Hartz for dwelling on the superstructure of politics and neglecting its material base.[37] The notion of false consciousness – explaining why the subordinate labouring classes embrace the values of the dominant capitalist classes – certainly helps to account for the differences in farmers' politics in different Canadian regions. To the question "Why have Atlantic Canadian farmers always rallied behind their traditional ideologically indistinguishable parties, the Liberals and Conservatives, while western farmers have a pronounced history of protest parties and governments?" there is a Hartzian rejoinder consistent with a materialist analysis. It lies in the conditions of farmers and the nature of agriculture. They differed regionally, and the differences are connected to patterns of political engagement. Atlantic Canadian agriculture developed on comparatively small lots, with mixed crops tended to, in many cases, by subsistence farmers. Surplus yields were exchanged locally with neighbours. West of Quebec and especially on the prairies, agricultural production was more specialized, mechanized, and exported to distant and volatile international commodity markets. Indeed, one of the appeals of Confederation to Upper Canadian wheat farmers and the financiers backing railroad expansion was that their wheat would have a year-round outlet via the Maritimes' ice-free ports, which Montreal and the Great Lakes lacked.

In western Canada, in contrast to Atlantic Canada and Quebec, agriculture began and has always been driven by commercial, not subsistence, factors. This meant that western farmers were more dependent on grain merchants, elevator companies, banks, insurance firms, transportation networks, and governments for their welfare. Western farm labour was always subordinated, while most Atlantic and Quebec farm labour was not. That is why westerners supported cooperatives and collectivist solutions, like wheat pools and the monopoly Canadian Wheat Board, to address their woes.[38] For many Atlantic Canadians, farming was part-time, one activity among others – fishing, lumbering, working in town, and later, relying on government income support payments. A strategy of "occupational pluralism" could provide a living.[39] In the West, farming has always been a business where size, crop insurance, capital, input and output prices, and transport issues have been vital. Western Canada's farmers could point to exploiters of farm labour; Atlantic Canada's could not. The West's conditions made for the radicalization of farmers; the East's did not. Thus, western farmers attacked the established "old line" parties and partyism itself; easterners had less reason to do so. They embraced partyism for the spoils it offered.

Differences in economic structures in combination with geography contributed to variations in the same ideology's shading. The BC case is instructive. Socialism in BC was on the whole more radical than on the prairies, because BC's hinterland economy featured more hard-rock mining, coal, and lumbering, and less farming. Isolated and remote one-company towns with concentrations of single men, rough living conditions, many industrial accidents, and few families fed militant class consciousness and syndicalist sympathies. In contrast, workers' outlooks were moderated, their socialism more tempered, reformist, and less revolutionary in urban settings like Vancouver and Victoria. There, labour's conditions were better, the social composition less homogenous with the presence of non-British immigrant ghettos, and urbane intellectual Fabian socialists preached an evolutionary road to socialism.[40]

Such a "materialist" analysis is consistent with Hartz's approach if one considers the "point of departure," as Hartz put it, from old to new society. Atlantic Canada was settled more than a century earlier than the prairies, at a time when toryism still carried some ballast, socialism was an unknown, and liberalism was more elitist and less populist, democratic, welfarist, and state-oriented, than it came to be. The West's immigrants from more economically developed old societies combined with the region's more rugged climate, its severe droughts and flooding to make for both a more rugged individualism and more cooperative, socialist, and collectivist endeavours than in the East.

The differences in the prairies' individualist and collectivist agrarian impulses become apparent when settlement patterns and ideological heritages are contrasted among farmers and workers in Saskatchewan and Alberta. British labourists streamed into all three prairie provinces at the height of the wheat economy, but those in Manitoba and Alberta gravitated to cities, explaining Winnipeg and early Calgary's radicalism. In Saskatchewan there were fewer Britons than in either of its neighbouring provinces, but it had as many British-born farm operators as the other two combined.[41] Americans led the United Farmers of Alberta and Ontarians led the United Farmers of Manitoba, but British socialists were in the vanguard of the United Farmers of Canada (Saskatchewan Section) and its predecessor, Farmers Union of Canada.

These differences were reflected in the struggle over the wheat pool in the 1920s. The Albertans, led by veteran Missouri populist Wood, insisted on a voluntary scheme; the Saskatchewanians wanted a compulsory one. The legacy of this battle lived on, expressed at the end of the century when Saskatchewan's farmers voted to maintain the Wheat Board's monopoly on barley sales and Alberta's farmers voted against it.[42] Into the new century, the battle continued, with Manitoba and Saskatchewan's NDP premiers fighting on one side and Alberta's Conservatives on the other.[43] The early American influence in Alberta's agricultural politics had its counterpart in the later American influence in its oil and gas sectors. Of the fifteen presidents of Calgary's exclusive Petroleum Club between 1955 and 1970, nine were Americans.[44]

Economic theories and models of older societies were looked upon favourably in Canadian regions settled by their emigrants. In Alberta, the rural American late nineteenth-century agrarian radicalism, as manifested in the Free Silver movement and Greenbackism, came to be expressed in the mania for Social Credit's inflationary monetary theories. Saskatchewan's British-born CCFers looked to British Labour's platform as a social policy blueprint in the 1940s. In Manitoba, where an "ethnic revolt" brought the NDP and the province's first premier of Continental European descent to power in the 1960s, his model was the Scandinavian social democratic state, and his party invited both the Swedish prime minister and German Social Democratic chancellor to address its annual conventions.[45] In Newfoundland, an ideological fragment of Ireland and West Country England,[46] economic planners came to cite Ireland's "Celtic Tiger" economy of the 1990s as a model.[47] Into the twenty-first century, Albertans like American-born Conservatives Ted Morton and Tom Flanagan touted the virtues of American neo-conservative public choice models and market solutions while simultaneously attacking the group rights of Aboriginal peoples[48] and others.

In the last quarter of the twentieth century, identity politics supplemented the Old World ideological triad of conservatism, liberalism, and socialism. Specifically, the influx since the 1970s from continents and countries whose peoples had formerly been excluded from Canada transformed Metro Canada. Visible minorities, ethno-religious fraternal organizations, Aboriginal peoples, and organizations representing women, gays, lesbians, and the disabled, however, did not redefine ideological politics as Canadians' faces literally changed after the Second World War with the fifth wave of immigration. This wave's incorporation into the existing political parties and its failure to launch any new parties confirms it as not being a formative ideological influence as the other waves had been.

The foregoing analysis presents political parties and movements as the ideological exoskeletons of formative waves of immigrants. Politics in Canada's regions continues to reflect different inherited traditions. This speaks to different regional settlement patterns and the distinct ideological baggage of settlers. One may look at the leaders of the political parties in the 2006 federal election to see the flesh-and-bone imprint of the formative immigrant waves in the regions. Bloc Québécois former leader Gilles Duceppe is a descendant of the first wave in the seventeenth century that established New France. Forebears of Paul Martin, Stephen Harper, and Jack Layton run back to between the late 1600s and 1774. Harper's English paternal ancestral home is in eighteenth-century Nova Scotia, and his English maternal ancestors appeared in Upper Canada with the third immigrant wave in the 1830s. Martin's mixed French-Irish family is descended on the maternal side from the pre-Conquest era and on the paternal side from the 1840s third wave. Layton's great-great-uncle was a Father of Confederation, and his grandfather and father were, respectively, Union Nationale and federal Conservative Cabinet ministers. All four leaders were born in Ontario and Quebec where their ancestors' waves settled. Harper's move from Ontario to the Far West and Layton's from Quebec to Ontario point to Canada's regional demographic shifts. Finally, Canadian society, once oriented exclusively to Europe and always sensitive to its powerful southern neighbour, is increasingly influenced by the peoples, if not the ideologies, of the Far East and Asia.

NOTES

1 Louis Hartz, *The Liberal Tradition in America: An Interpretation of American Political Thought since the Revolution* (New York: Harcourt Brace, 1955). Hereafter *LTA*.
2 H.D. Forbes, "Hartz-Horowitz at Twenty: Nationalism, Toryism, and Socialism in Canada and the United States," *Canadian Journal of Political Science* 20, no. 2 (1987): 289.
3 See Gad Horowitz's summary of the Hartz-Horowitz thesis set out in Colin Campbell's interview with him, "On Intellectual Life, Politics and Psychoanalysis: A Conversation with Gad Horowitz," in this volume.

4 Louis Hartz, "United States History in a New Perspective," chap. 4 in *The Founding of New Societies: Studies in the History of the United States, Latin America, South Africa, Canada, and Australia*, ed. Louis Hartz (New York: Harcourt, Brace & World, 1964), 89 and 111. Hereafter *FNS*.

5 Horowitz, *CLS*, 29.

6 Philip Resnick, *The European Roots of Canadian Identity* (Peterborough, ON: Broadview, 2005).

7 Seymour Martin Lipset, *Agrarian Socialism: The Cooperative Commonwealth Federation in Saskatchewan; A Study in Political Sociology*, updated ed. (1950; Garden City, NY: Doubleday, 1968).

8 Horowitz, *CLS*, 8–9.

9 André Siegfried, *The Race Question in Canada*, ed. Frank Underhill (Toronto: McClelland & Stewart, 1966). Originally published in French, 1906.

10 Frederick Jackson Turner, *The Significance of Sections in American History* (New York: Henry Holt, 1932).

11 Hartz, *FNS*, 10n.

12 Kenneth D. McRae, "Louis Hartz's Impact on Political Thought in Canada," prepared for the Symposium on Louis Hartz, Harvard University, 23 January 1987, 26.

13 Myron G.G. Gulka-Tiechko, "Inter-War Ukrainian Immigration to Canada, 1919–1939" (master's thesis, University of Manitoba, 1983), 21 and 138.

14 Preamble to the Constitution Act (British North America Act), 1867.

15 American Automobile Association, Manitoba/Saskatchewan and Alberta/ British Columbia, maps (2004–6 editions).

16 A.E. Safarian, *Foreign Ownership of Canadian Industry* (Toronto: University of Toronto Press, 1973), 7 and table 1, 10.

17 John Ralston Saul, *Reflections of a Siamese Twin: Canada at the End of the Twentieth Century* (Toronto: Penguin, 1998).

18 Kenneth McNaught, "Comment," in *Failure of a Dream? Essays in the History of American Socialism*, ed. J.H.M. Laslett, and S.M. Lipset, rev. ed. (Berkeley: University of California Press, 1984), 355.

19 *Canada Year Book*, 1948–49, table 1, 175.

20 *Canada Year Book*, 1921, table 20, 126.

21 John Wilson, "The Red Tory Province: Reflections on the Character of Ontario Political Culture," in *The Government and Politics of Ontario*, ed. Donald C. MacDonald, 2nd ed. (Toronto: Van Nostrand Reinhold, 1980), 214.

22 Daniel Salée, "Quebec's Changing Political Culture and the Future of Federal–Provincial Relations in Canada," in *Canada: The State of the Federation 2001; Canadian Political Culture(s) in Transition*, ed. Hamish Telford and

Harvey Lazar (Montreal and Kingston: McGill-Queen's University Press, 2002), chap. 7.

23 Frederick H. Armstrong, *Handbook of Upper Canadian Chronology* (Toronto: Dundurn, 1985), 272.

24 Canada, Dominion Bureau of Statistics, *Origin, Birthplace, Nationality and Language of the Canadian People* (Ottawa: 1929), table 46, 99.

25 Richard N. Rosencrance, "The Radical Culture of Australia," *FNS*, 300.

26 W.L. Morton, *The Progressive Party in Canada* (Toronto: University of Toronto Press, 1950), 39.

27 *Calgary Herald*, quoted in L.G. Thomas, *The Liberal Party in Alberta, 1905–1921* (Toronto: University of Toronto Press, 1959), 177.

28 Morton, *Progressive Party in Canada*, 38–9; and Morton, "The Social Philosophy of Henry Wise Wood, the Canadian Agrarian Leader," *Agricultural History* 22, no. 2 (April 1948), 115.

29 Gordon S. Galbraith, "British Columbia," in *The Provincial Political Systems: Comparative Essays*, ed. David J. Bellamy, Jon H. Pammett, and Donald C. Rowat (Toronto: Methuen, 1976), chap. 5.

30 Howard Palmer, *Patterns of Prejudice: A History of Nativism in Alberta* (Toronto: McClelland and Stewart, 1982), 67.

31 Census of Canada, 1921, vol. 2, table 50, 298–330; table 53, 334–40; and table 71, 480–2.

32 Jill Mahoney, "No 'Firewall' Needed around Alberta, Says Klein," *Globe and Mail*, 8 February 2001.

33 See illustration, Dawn Walton and Katherine Harding, "Can Alberta's Moderate Tories Take to 'Premier Ted Morton'?," *Globe and Mail*, 27 November 2006, A.

34 Louis Hartz, "Fragmentation Patterns: Feudal, Liberal, and Radical," in *FNS*, 64–5.

35 *Globe and Mail*, 6 November 1987.

36 Louis Hartz, *Economic Policy and Democratic Thought: Pennsylvania, 1776–1860* (Cambridge, MA: Harvard University Press, 1948).

37 Howard Zinn, "The New World: Fragments of the Old," *Nation*, 25 May 1965, 562–3.

38 Robert J. Brym, "Political Conservatism in Atlantic Canada," in *Underdevelopment and Social Movements in Atlantic Canada*, ed. Robert J. Brym and R. James Sacouman (Toronto: New Hogtown, 1979), 65–6.

39 Phillip J. Wood, "Nova Scotia: Social Structure and Politics," in *The Provincial State: Politics in Canada's Provinces and Territories*, ed. Keith Brownsey and Michael Howlett (Mississauga, ON: Copp Clark Pitman, 1992), 65–71.

40 A. Ross McCormick, *Reformers, Rebels, and Revolutionaries: The Western Ca-nadian Radical Movement, 1899–1919* (Toronto: University of Toronto Press, 1977); and Martin Robin, *The Rush for Spoils: The Company Province, 1871–1933* (Toronto: McClelland and Stewart, 1972); and Robin, *Pillars of Profit, 1934–72* (Toronto: McClelland and Stewart, 1973).
41 Census of Canada, 1921, vol. 1, table 16, 312–37.
42 "Producer Vote Supports Single-Desk Sale of Barley," Agrivision (April 1997): 3; "One Vote Could Decide Barley Marketing," *Agriweek*, 11 November 1997, 1.
43 Joe Friesen, "Let Farmers Decide about Wheat Board, Tory MP Says," *Globe and Mail*, 11 November 2006.
44 Howard Palmer and Tamara Palmer, *Alberta: A New History* (Edmonton: Hurtig, 1990), 306.
45 Donald Swainson, "Ethnic Revolt: Manitoba's Election," *Canadian Forum* 49 (August 1969), 98–9; Ed Schreyer, "Interview," *Winnipeg Tribune*, 5 July 1969; and Nelson Wiseman, *Social Democracy in Manitoba: A History of the CCF-NDP* (Winnipeg: University of Manitoba Press, 1983), 136.
46 S.J.R. Noel, *Politics in Newfoundland* (Toronto: University of Toronto Press, 1971), 4–5.
47 J.D. House, *Against the Tide: Battling for Economic Renewal in Newfoundland and Labrador* (Toronto: University of Toronto Press, 1999).
48 Thomas Flanagan, *First Nations? Second Thoughts* (Montreal and Kingston: McGill-Queen's University Press, 1999).

7 Restoration, Not Renovation: A Fresh Start for Hartz-Horowitz

ROBERT MEYNELL

Introduction

In the 1770s, the inhabitants of the British North American colonies had to decide whether or not to support the British Crown, and their decisions were to set the course for the national character of their descendants. The choice of independence or duty, whether to be revolutionaries or loyalists, marked a coming of age for the United States and gave a new sense of purpose for the rest of British North America that would later be Canada. Little wonder, therefore, that Canadians should so often define their country in relief against the United States. It is not that Canada has little distinctly its own. The enormous impact of the American Revolution could not help but lead to a political culture significantly different from that of the colonies that chose to remain a part of the British Empire. Canadian political culture is not just the outcome of passivity and neutrality, an absence of the revolutionary spirit; it is the result of an action that was filled with intent, the commitment to a set of ideals that were threatened by that revolution.

This essay is an effort to identify some of the broader implications of this historical parting of the ways, emphasizing their diverging conceptions of freedom. Of particular interest is the relative success of Hegelian idealism during its revival in the late nineteenth century. The British parliamentary system, with its unique constitutional and ideological history, is the trunk from which both Canada and the United States branch off, hence at their base they have everything in common and cannot be portrayed as radically different political species. However, this does not mean that the differences are minor. Their respective allegiances in the 1770s set them on different paths involving distinctive government policies and social environments, and despite some notable areas of convergence,[1] they seem to continue towards different ends. In the United States, Lockean liberalism and its attendant commitment to negative liberty still takes precedence when defining the "American way," while "compassionate," collectivist Canada tenuously holds onto positive freedom, which in the late nineteenth century came to be understood in idealist terms.

The purpose of this essay is twofold: to reaffirm this traditional account of a Lockean America versus a liberal Canada with a significant "tory touch," thus curbing the efforts of revisionists to treat both countries as indistinguishable variants of Locke's brand of republicanism; and to show that by accepting the Hartz-Horowitz fragment theory we are better positioned to recognize and understand the importance of certain intellectual traditions in Canadian political culture, such as idealism as an ideological resolution to the Canadian tensions between Toryism, liberalism, and socialism.

Hartz's Thesis: The Origin of Americanism

The most famous account of Lockean political culture in the United States is Louis Hartz's groundbreaking *The Liberal Tradition in America*, and it is by no means intended to be an unqualified celebration of American freedom. Rather, it is largely a response to the restraints on freedom exhibited during the red scare hysteria of the McCarthy hearings. Hartz seeks to explain America's intolerance of socialism and how the ostensible defence of freedom can mutate into an oppressive, intolerant cultural absolutism. However, he seeks not only causes, but also cures. At the heart of American conformism there is an individualism that he hopes will flourish once it blends with the wider ideological spectrum that is introduced with the emergence of a more integrated global community. Thus, his criticism is also a call for an intellectual renewal in the United States, a call to replace liberal homogeneity with ideological diversity.

Feudalism and *liberalism* are terms Hartz uses as "symbols for a brand of political thought."[2] They are generalizations that intentionally overlook those particularities that do not seriously challenge the hegemonic character of a given society.

According to Hartz, the American Revolution was not revolutionary. It was a political self-realization rather than a redefinition.[3] American nationalism combines the traditional contractualism of the Puritans

with Lockean liberalism and establishes itself as a national identity
with a universal and absolute world view. Independence for the colonies thus transformed Puritanism from a mere fragmentary colonial
ideology, which carried with it a certain humiliation of being somehow incomplete, to a new nationalism. Through the revolution, what
was once a minority group in Britain is reborn as "American."[4] Meanwhile the competing ideologies in Europe are too deeply intertwined
to mature. Ideologies must be "fragments" in order to fulfil their potential as a national identity. Hartz explains that in new societies, "a
part detaches itself from the whole, the whole fails to renew itself, and
the part develops without inhibition."[5] Ideological fragments congeal
in the new societies because they no longer compete with other widely
accepted ideologies, such as toryism, whiggery, and socialism. Because
there were no significant competing ideologies or traditions, Lockean
liberalism became universalized as Americanism, and the bourgeois
class became members of a classless society, regardless of the degrees
of economic disparity.

   With the assumption that there are no classes, combined with the
confidence that with hard work everyone can improve their material
condition, socialism is unable to get any purchase in the United States.
Hartz argues that in order to thrive, socialism must play off feudalism.
Not only does feudalism provide a healthy antagonist to give socialism meaning, but feudalism, unlike liberalism, accepts the view that
society is currently class structured, corporate, and collectivist. Without
the class identification that comes with the feudal ethos, and without a
tradition of ideological revolutions, socialism cannot gain a foothold.[6]

   Hartz points out the irony that instead of socio-economic disparity
in the United States turning peoples' minds to revolution, the Hora-
tio Alger spirit drives the average American more hotly in pursuit of
wealth, oblivious to a new hierarchy that is being created by this hard-
nosed individualism. He wishes to remind Americans that their individualism includes an implicit collectivism, and with it comes a high
degree of ideological and cultural uniformity.[7] Hartz tries to make this
collectivism more explicit, pointing out that it revolves around the
sense that they are participants in a common way of life that upholds
the principles of individual freedom and egalitarianism. American nationalism is grounded in the conviction that Lockean liberalism is a
universal truth that has been realized in American institutions, as well
as American hearts, and foreign countries and ideologies are sadly be-
nighted. The cultural absolutism of the pure liberal fragment is closed

to debate about its fundamental principles. It is also characteristically cheerful and rather indifferent to criticism, except on those rare occasions when it is threatened, at which point it suddenly gives rise to a great national hysteria, and civil liberties begin to collapse.[8]

This is the sort of hysteria that drove Senator McCarthy's grim campaign.[9] America was confronted with an ideological challenge that threatened its conviction of universalism by exposing it as a mere fragment. "The fragment reactionary exhausts himself in a thousand Treason Trials, clerical excommunications, and congressional investigations. But after all of his effort the Martian remains. Indeed, as in a horror tale, he keeps coming closer all the time."[10] As stated above, it is ultimately Hartz's hope that America's individualism will lash back against the tyrannical conformism and choose to relinquish its own strict national identification with Lockean liberalism and invite a variety of views into the American pantheon.

The Case of Canada: Hartz-Horowitz and the Canadian Revision

Hartz compares the United States to Canada and finds that Canada is markedly different and less prone to liberal absolutism. For the purposes of this paper, we are interested primarily in his conception of the political culture in English-speaking Canada.[11] Hartz finds that although Canada is also a liberal fragment, it is not so unadulterated. It is infused with a tory touch, which means that there is a slightly feudal conception of society. Just as it is the absence of feudalism in the United States that keeps Americans from developing a class consciousness and therefore any major socialist movement, so can it be said that the tory touch in Canada brings with it sufficient class consciousness to inspire a mild socialism as found in the Cooperative Commonwealth Federation (now the New Democratic Party). However, it seems the degree of socialism is proportionate to the degree of toryism, therefore its strength is not sufficient to threaten a socialist revolution as experienced in Europe.[12]

Gad Horowitz's landmark essay, "Conservatism, Liberalism, and Socialism in Canada: An Interpretation," expands upon Hartz's thesis to give a more complete picture of the characteristics that distinguish Canada from the United States and how these characteristics play out in contemporary political parties.[13] Where Hartz seeks to explain the failure of the United States to develop a mainstream socialism, Horowitz explains why Canadian socialism has been so much stronger than

U.S. socialism, though weaker than European socialism. Our interest is not in the political parties but in his account of Canada's character, which he attributes to there being a "tory touch" in Canada prior to the American Revolution that was further enhanced by the immigration of United Empire Loyalists as a consequence of the revolution, and again by the proportionally substantial immigration of Britons who were "infected with non-liberal ideas" in the first half of the nineteenth century.[14] The established "imperfection" of the Canadian bourgeois liberal fragment meant that new arrivals from Europe were not compelled to give up their tory or socialist ideas; they are not dismissed as un-Canadian. Whereas in the United States the liberal democracy of Jefferson and Jackson had thoroughly imposed a one-myth ideological absolutism, in Canada ideological diversity was legitimate, and aside from the dominant bourgeois liberalism it included most prominently the right-wing, elitist liberalism of the whigs, as attested to by the Family Compacts, and socialism.

The tory touch engendered in Canada a greater deference to authority, less praise for achievement and egalitarianism, preference for choosing law over individual liberty, and a "far greater willingness of English Canadian political and business elites to use the power of the state for the purpose of developing and controlling the economy."[15] Consequently, the conception of community is more organic and collectivist than one might find in a purely liberal political culture that takes a contractualist view of society as an "agglomeration of competing individuals."[16] And this organic component enables socialism to thrive. When the tory or feudal society struggles for equality, it leans more heavily towards equality of condition rather than equality of opportunity. There is a greater emphasis on cooperation and community over competition and a laissez-faire self-serving pursuit of happiness. In effect, when a tory society hears the call for equality, it is natural that it turns to socialism or a combination of the two, as found in a red tory like George Grant.

In response to those liberals who resent this toryism for its appeal to Britishness and its seemingly stodgy deference to traditional mores, Horowitz points out that they fail to appreciate the value of the diversity it brings. "The secret dream of the Canadian liberal is the removal of English Canada's 'imperfections' – in other words, the total assimilation of English Canada into the larger North America culture."[17] Such assimilation efforts persist, as we find in a collection of essays by a group of Canadian thinkers influenced by Bernard Bailyn and J.A. Pocock.[18]

These authors challenge the Hartz-Horowitz account of Canada and either redefine and disparage the characteristics that comprise the tory touch or deny there is any notable distinction at all between the two political cultures. They claim, "The challenge to nineteenth-century liberalism arose from a republican ideology on the political left, rather than Toryism on the right. The formative influence in Canada's past was not solely liberalism, or the combination of liberalism and Tory conservatism, but a lively opposition between liberalism and a civic republican philosophy with a progressive agenda."[19]

Their scholarly historical study has an explicit practical purpose. They hope that in reviving the overlooked republican tradition they will dispel the "culture of distrust" that has enveloped Canadian politics and invite a greater will to political participation.[20] Unfortunately, in their haste to rescue Canada's civic participation, these new contextualists have borrowed a mythology that erases the distinction between Canada and the United States. Just as Bailyn and Pocock erased the Lockeanism that distinguished the United States and replaced it with an amorphous republicanism,[21] Ajzenstat and Smith are taking Canadian history in the same direction. The implicit practical significance of this argument is that there is little or no difference between Canada's political tradition and that of the United States, other than the names. If accepted as the authoritative reading of Canada's political culture and its history, there will be no defence against the loaded questions, "Why does Canada have policies on taxation, health care, welfare, employment, and culture that are different from those of its wealthy and powerful soul mate to the south?" And, ultimately, "Do we need a border separating the two countries?"

These new Canadian republicans overlook the works of many others and build their case on a refutation of Horowitz's contention that Canada's organic-collectivism is inherited from its toryism.[22] In contrast, they claim that the struggle between republicans and Lockeans has defined the character of emerging liberal democracies in the eighteenth and nineteenth centuries. "When the searchlight of this new outlook is turned on Canadian political history it indeed finds little evidence of Tory conservatism in Canada's past or in Canadian political culture today. Toryism is being read out of the ideological temple."[23] Whereas Hartz's success at revealing general ideological themes that distinguish different political cultures rested on his comparative method, the republican thesis is built upon a miscellaneous collection of data that, by force of imported ideas and creative thinking, are made to conform to

a republican framework. The results of these efforts range from the unlikely to the monstrous.[24] They pick up Bailyn and Pocock's republican
tinted spectacles and look for republican traces in Canada's intellectual
history. The trouble is that republicanism is and has been present in European political thought for over two thousand years and even more so
since the Renaissance. It has been a basic element of the political atmo-
sphere and can hardly be regarded as a distinguishing factor, unless it is
intentionally isolated from all other influences. Whether or not republicanism is present in modern political discourse ought not to be a question.[25] The question is whether other ideological influences are in play
and to what extent. Must whigs, tories, and socialists really be read out
of the history books?[26]

Janet Ajzenstat and Peter J. Smith spearhead the group, refuting
Horowitz's claim that feudal toryism has had a formative impact on
Canadian culture, by dubbing those who have constituted Canada's
elite "capitalist robber barons."[27] The Christian morality and sense of
noblesse oblige that historians understood to be the elite's ideological
foundation are replaced with the self-interest of capitalism, thus recast-
ing them all as Canadian J.P. Morgans. Horowitz's effort to salvage the
worthwhile facets of Canadian conservatism is dismissed as clinging
to an impotent myth. While Ajzenstat and Smith share the view that
toryism is insignificant to Canada, they disagree on whether liberalism
or civic republicanism is the dominant or most valuable strain in Canadian political culture. Ajzenstat argues that Canada was founded on the
competing vision of populist democrats, constitutionalists, and Lockean liberals. Smith argues that the primary strains included civic humanism, natural jurisprudence, and commercialism. Central to Smith's
argument is the notion that John Locke was not the fountainhead for
North American liberalism.

Smith contends that there was a competition between commercialism
and civic humanism, which he describes as the "dialectic of wealth and
virtu." This dialectic repeated itself in Canada and the United States. In
Canada, the capitalist elite were known as "tories," though they held
no similarities to Britain's pre-capitalist toryism.[28] Canada's tories may
have valued order, authority, and hierarchy, as Horowitz maintains, but
only to support their position of privilege and their principal interests –
trade, commerce, and empire. In other words, these were whigs for
whom liberty meant "social liberty, the freedom to add to one's economic
and cultural resources."[29] Political participation was reserved for the
wealthy elite. Smith believes that Canada's republican civic humanists

were reformers who valued democracy and responsible government. These were Canada's republicans who advocated civic virtue and universal education, but they were not history's winners. Smith contends that the major force behind Canadian Confederation of 1867 was the desire of the "robber barons" to have a strong central government that would better facilitate trade and commerce while maintaining political stability. For him, tories were mere statists keeping government beyond the reach of the people. Nevertheless, despite their contrary views, over time the republicans and the robber barons began to overlap in a peculiar melange that foils any effort to isolate identifiable groups today.[30] Ajzenstat agrees with Smith that civic republicanism has played a role in the formation of Canada, but she argues that it is not as important as the role of liberalism or liberal constitutionalism.[31] She believes Smith is "wrong to see Upper Canada's conservatism as little more than a justification of patronage and privilege."[32] She presents Lord Durham and John Beverly Robinson as notable exceptions whose conservatism was informed by strong and cherished liberal values. They sought solutions to Canada's political divisiveness. They were not tories promoting a feudalist notion of an organic-collective society; they were liberals concerned with protecting social stability and individual rights and freedoms through the establishment of a democratic political system that would rein in the destabilizing influence of populist parties. According to Ajzenstat, Durham and Robinson criticized populist leaders for deceiving and exploiting their followers to further their own ambition. To curtail them, Durham and Robinson proposed to institute a popular house while ensuring moderation would prevail. For Robinson this meant restricting the power of the popular house to voting on money bills. For Durham, this meant a mixed constitution wherein the political executive is distinct from the popular house, thus curtailing a tyranny of the majority.

In another contribution, Ajzenstat examines the ideologies of Étienne Parent and Joseph Howe. She argues that they represent an important strain of constitutionalism that struggled against the populist democratic movements of Papineau and Mackenzie. In their efforts, Parent and Howe sought a responsible government within a parliamentary system rather than the Jacksonian democracy of the United States.[33] Ajzenstat's constitutionalism is a synthesis of Locke's individual equality and a mixed constitution. Her argument ends with the disconcerting conclusion – at least from a Canadian nationalist's point of view – that

Canada did not have "a cultural or national character markedly different from that of the US."[34]

Refuting the Canadian Republican Thesis

Jeremy Rayner accuses Smith and Ajzenstat of distorting the past to fit the present.[35] He argues that the basis for their historical methodology is sound, but they fail to stick to it. The method involves studying the history of ideas by considering them in light of "the rules and conditions that made them meaningful to those to whom they were directed."[36] Rayner argues that Ajzenstat and Smith, among others, use this method up to a point, then corrupt any good work they might have done by discussing their discoveries in terms of "a grand atemporal context masquerading as an historical context, the great tradition of western political thought, thereby contributing to a gigantic anachronism."[37] They subordinate the past to fit the present by imposing contemporary categories on the people they study, such as the liberal-communitarian debate.[38] This present-centredness results in one or all of three major distortions. It creates a past in the image of the present, discusses occurrences in terms of present categories that were absent, or allows preconceptions to determine what parts of the past are important, thus putting the cart before the horse, the conclusion before the evidence. The sources are thus transformed by the assumptions that were "smuggled into the process of sifting and assembling the 'evidence.'"[39] Historical figures and their works are rescued from history and tailored to fit a given thesis within a contemporary debate, such as the presence of a civic republican tradition in Canada, in an effort to reconcile the conflict between liberalism and communitarianism.

Blinded by their efforts to impose the present on the past, Ajzenstat and Smith overlook the importance of Hegelian and British idealism to Canada's intellectual history. Idealism played a far larger role in promoting a holistic conception of society than the form of republicanism Bailyn attributes to the United States. Ajzenstat and Smith obscure the existence of Canada's idealist tradition by following Bailyn and Pocock's misreading of American political culture and adapting it to dismiss Hartz-Horowitz. Though Horowitz's article has been criticized before, until now, even Horowitz's critics appreciated that he was onto something.[40] Consequently, Ajzenstat and Smith are left seeking what is not there and blind to what is. Had they followed Horowitz's tory

touch argument, they might have been open to the philosophical transformation this toryism took in the late nineteenth century.

The idealists were enormously influential both in universities and
in public affairs.[41] They offered a system of thought that unified conservative,[42] Christian, monarchical leanings with a socially progressive
agenda. They adhered to certain key liberal principles, but only within
the precepts of idealism as it was inherited from the British idealists,
who in turn borrowed from the Germans.[43] One clear voice for this
conservatism whose work played a formative role in the maturation
of Canadian politics was that of Canadian philosopher John Watson
(1847–1939), one of the many students of the British idealists to immi-
grate to Canada to teach. Watson had an enormous influence on Canada. He was instrumental in developing the principles for the United
Church, he was among the foremost teachers of moral philosophy, and
he had an indirect influence through his students who went on to become the country's elite. Unlike his idealist colleagues in the United
States, Watson and other Canadian idealists could move their ideology
into the mainstream, because the country was open to an organic collectivist conception of community that promoted human freedom with
that framework. Canadians were committed to a certain political system, but one that welcomed divergent ideological influences. Intellectual historians such as A.B. McKillop, Leslie Armour, and Doug Owram
have done extensive research in this area and revealed that idealism
gave twentieth-century Canada its uniquely communitarian ethos. So
why do Ajzenstat and Smith merely mention Watson in an endnote in
their introduction? They suggest that "Watson's ideas and influence
merit further study by Canadian political theorists."[44] Why have they
not followed their own advice? To answer this we might consider what
it was that they were trying to achieve. If their aim is indeed to promote Lockean liberalism in Canada and blur the distinctions between
Canada and the United States, then idealism is not going to suit their
purposes.

Canadian idealism is a philosophical movement that was brought to
Canada in the mid- to late nineteenth century by students of the British
idealists. It is critical of classical liberalism's conception of the self as an
atomized individual whose membership in society is only through self-
interest and contract. Idealists conceive of individual fulfilment as the
realization of rational autonomy, which necessarily involves acknowledging the self as embedded in a particular historical and cultural
moral framework and intersubjectively united with others in society

through the common ethical project and a deep need for recognition. Freedom, or autonomy, involves rationally engaging with the ethical life of one's society. Idealists oppose the empiricist approach to human nature, as with Locke's theory of natural right, and conceive of reason as combining the concept and the concrete. Idealism had a receptive audience in Canada at a time when a traditional Christian and agrarian society struggled to make sense of the world being increasingly moved by the materialist philosophies that accompanied industrialization. This idealism has a contemporary presence in the work of Charles Taylor, among others. For instance, Taylor's conception of community is an example of the traditional idealist project. His theory of deep diversity is meant to reconcile the principal conflicting modern ontologies, such as those that underlie substantive and procedural formulas for citizenship, which is a reformulation of the Hegelian project to reconcile the Romantic holistic society and the Enlightenment contractualist state. Another important aspect of this idealism is the defence of positive liberty and the criticism of atomism. These political views are anchored by an epistemology and theory of agency that acknowledges the formative role of culture (ideas) on identity. For the idealist, freedom is more than the absence of obstacles to one's pursuit of satisfying sensory appetites, but involves a commitment to a social whole that includes an ethical horizon that is integral to one's own fulfilment.

By overlooking the idealist tradition, Ajzenstat and Smith make an ironic mistake. Unaware of Taylor's debt to this tradition, they invoke his arguments to justify their interpretation and approach. They claim that Taylor promotes republicanism as a solution to the modern malaise of citizens who feel disconnected from their political community.[45] In fact, one gets the impression that Taylor's work was the impetus for their arguments and that they believed they were following his lead when they sifted through Canadian history looking for influential republicans. In "Cross Purposes: The Liberal-Communitarian Debate," Taylor portrays the Quebec crisis as a conflict between Rousseauian and Lockean political cultures. He also shows how these two views need not be mutually exclusive and that even the liberalism of the United States, with the influence of civic republicanism, entails a holistic conception of community and therefore can afford to be tolerant of a culture that has a Rousseauian sense of a general will.

Ajzenstat and Smith claim to be agreeing with Taylor that the current political malaise is aggravated by the rise of a rights-based liberalism and that this can be overcome by reviving the "communitarian-republican element in the Canadian political tradition."[46] But neither in "Cross Purposes" nor in his other writings does Taylor suggest that Canada is republican or that it could benefit from becoming republican. He clearly states that he discusses republicanism only to illustrate to those who support American procedural liberalism that a holistic conception of community and a notion of positive liberty does not threaten the integrity of the "American way." He hopes to show that republicans need not fear his communitarianism, and he also seeks to explain that the liberal-communitarian debate must be approached and settled on the level of ontology.[47] In fact, in "Cross Purposes" and elsewhere, Taylor explicitly asserts that republicanism could not work in Canada because it would conflict with the national culture of Quebec.[48] Moreover, when Taylor mentions the presence of Lockean procedural liberalism in Canada outside Quebec, he presents it as a foreign American import,[49] thus refuting the other half of Ajzenstat and Smith's depiction of Canada.

In addition to mistaking Taylor's position regarding republicanism, Ajzenstat and Smith ignore his recommendation to study these issues on an ontological level. Whereas Taylor concerns himself with questions of identity, they approach the problems of community politics by first imposing their republican-liberal thesis on the political writings of a few historical figures, such as Lord Durham, John Beverley Robinson, William Lyon Mackenzie, and John A. Macdonald. They then extrapolate, arguing that they have defined Canada as a whole. Ultimately, Ajzenstat concludes that Canada has been formed by constitutionalists and therefore fits the procedural model, whereas Smith tries to keep hold of the holistic view of community by concluding that Canada is truly republican. They eventually delve into ontology by accident. In their dialogical concluding chapter they face off, forcing one another to address the questions that their arguments beg and thus push one another into ontological waters that seem to be too deep for them. Ajzenstat criticizes Smith for attempting to cling to collectivism by asserting that Canada must be procedural because there is no distinction between Canada and the United States. Smith responds with Taylor's republican patriotism argument, arguing that citizens must identify with the common purpose of the state for society to flourish. This argument is effective, so Ajzenstat retreats into an as-yet-unmentioned defeatist Straussian conclusion about moral relativism and the decline of Western civilization. However, she wins a point by arguing that republicanism has a homogenizing effect on pluralistic societies. Then Smith too becomes despondent, craving a better form of communitarianism. He dreams of a model that can accommodate liberalism, somehow failing to appreciate the lengths to which Taylor has gone to provide exactly that in his notion of deep diversity. In the end, their deontological neo-new contextualism leads them to conclusions that cannot withstand their own honest analysis.

There are two things to keep in mind when reading the works from the Azjenstat-Smith school of Canadian political thought. First, their methodology allows them to construct a new mythology, and second, the myths that they have constructed serve to suppress Canada's distinctive intellectual history in favour of cultural and, ultimately, political continentalism. I do not suggest that their research is disingenuous, but only that their method allows them to disregard historical realities that do not fit their assumptions. So if their political views are largely informed by an American-dominated political theory discourse, it is natural that their present-centred view of the past will reflect that. In some cases, they not only begin with American assumptions, but they borrow the formulas of American historians, such Pocock and Bailyn, and impose them on Canadian history. For instance, they recast the United Empire Loyalists as displaced American liberals. In approaching history this way, they not only repeat Bailyn's mistake with respect to Hartz, but they do not meet the methodological standard set by Bailyn.

One valuable element they have disregarded is the role of idealism in Canadian history. Had they been open to seeing it, not only would they have been obliged to reconsider their interpretation of those figures they studied, but they would come out with a very different sense of Canada's political culture, one that is importantly different from that of the United States, and one that, despite its many flaws, manages to avoid the tendency towards absolutism that has continually plagued the American struggle to live up to its own liberal standards.

Conclusion

Ours is a time of increasing pressure for deep North American integration, just as the troubles that inspired Hartz forty years ago seem to have returned with a vengeance in the United States. How we conceive of human agency, freedom, and the role of government in the market determines how we arrange our society. The positive freedom of the idealists and the negative liberty of classical liberalism will bring forth radically different policies on matters including health

126   Robert Meynell

care, market regulation, and tolerance of difference. If the Hartz-
Horowitz thesis is correct, and if it is true that liberal absolutism is
once more run amok in the United States, then it is increasingly important to remember what it is that has distinguished Canada, that we
may nurture it and be prepared to answer the query, "Why is Canada
a separate country anyway?" It is important to remember that the tory
touch laid a foundation in Canada for tolerance of competing ideologies. Hartz is being restored in American political thought. Hartz-
Horowitz should be restored in Canadian political thought, and with
it should come further analysis of the road Canada has travelled since
Confederation and the importance idealism has played in its political
development.

NOTES

1 Canada's new Conservative Party has effectively silenced the toryism that
   had once influenced Canada's conservatives and adopted a neoliberal
   agenda that has traditionally been at home among the American right. The
   pull in this direction is also evident to varying degrees in provincial politics
   and the federal Liberal Party.
2 Paul Roazen, introduction to *The Necessity of Choice*, by Louis Hartz (London: Transaction Publishers, 1990), 8.
3 In this Hartz is following Tocqueville, arguing that the Enlightenment and
   the social contract were evident at the outset with the Mayflower Compact
   and Plantation Covenants of New England. Louis Hartz, *The Liberal Tradition in America: An Interpretation of American Political Thought* (New York:
   Harcourt, Brace & World, 1955), 49; Hartz, ed., *The Founding of New Societies:
   Studies in the History of the United States, Latin America, South Africa, Canada,
   and Austrialia* (New York: Harcourt, Brace & World, 1964), 73–5.
4 "Being part of a whole is psychologically tolerable, but being merely a part,
   isolated from a whole, is not.... The Puritan must convert Puritanism itself, the one thing he has, into a new nationalism which denies the humiliation of the old. He must convert it into 'Americanism,' a new national spirit
   under the sun, grander than anything the world has ever seen" (Hartz,
   Founding of New Societies, 11).
5 Ibid., 9.
6 Hartz, *Liberal Tradition in America*, 6.
7 Ibid., 56.
8 Ibid., 58–9.

9 We might add also the excesses of the Bush administration following the terrorist attacks of 11 September 2001.

10 Hartz, *Founding of New Societies*, 22.

11 He regards French Canada as predominantly feudal.

12 Hartz, *Founding of New Societies*, 34.

13 Other leading historians, political scientists, and philosophers who have described Canada's history similarly include Donald Creighton, Hugh MacLennan, S.M. Lipset, W.L. Morton, and George Grant.

14 Gad Horowitz, "Conservatism, Liberalism and Socialism: An Interpretation," in *Party Politics in Canada*, ed. Hugh G. Thorburn (Scarborough, ON: Prentice Hall Canada, 1996), 150.

15 Ibid., 149.

16 Ibid., 148.

17 Ibid., 151.

18 As one might expect from absolutists who have been shown their blemishes, the first reaction to Hartz was a defensive denial. The most widely adopted denial was that it is not contractual individualism that defines the United States but rather civic republicanism. In 1967, Bernard Bailyn composed what has become known as the republican thesis, asserting that individualism and property rights were not truly the primary concern of those formulating the U.S. Constitution. Instead of Locke, the Founding Fathers were filled with dread that, like the Roman Empire, the republican elements of the British system would descend into tyranny as the empire expanded. Bernard Bailyn, *The Ideological Origins of the American Revolution* (Cambridge, MA: Harvard University Press, 1992), 25. Bailyn's work gave rise to a deluge of revisions of early American political thought, to the point that within a generation Hartz's thesis had fallen entirely out of favour. Prominent among these was J.G.A. Pocock's historical study, which contends that a Machiavellian civic republicanism had been the principal force directing the Founding Fathers. J.G.A. Pocock, *The Machiavellian Moment: Florentine Political Thought and the Atlantic Republican Tradition* (Princeton: Princeton University Press, 1975), 509.

19 Janet Ajzenstat and Peter J. Smith, eds., *Canada's Origins: Liberal, Tory, or Republican?* (Ottawa: Carleton University Press, 1997). More recently Ajzenstat published *The Once and Future Canadian Democracy: An Essay in Political Thought* (Montreal and Kingston: McGill-Queen's University Press, 2003), in which she further argues that there is no significant distinction between Canadian and U.S. political culture, though here she replaces civic republicanism with romanticism. She attributes her earlier mistake about civic republicanism to being misguided by Smith (Ajzenstat, *Once*

and Future Canadian Democracy, 8). In this more recent book she replaces
Bailyn's template with Isaiah Berlin's liberal-romantic account of modernity. Though Berlin never wrote about Canada's political culture, pre-
sumably his assessment of modernity was sufficiently astute to act as an
interpretive template for all modern societies. Though I do not have space
to address this new tack here, I believe she is repeating her earlier mistake
with very similar political implications. She has also co-edited with Paul
Romney, Ian Gentles, and William D. Gairdner a selection of foundational
political documents, *Canada's Founding Debates* (Toronto: University of Toronto Press, 2003). In this volume substantial portions of the original texts
were excised for the sake of space, though not without affecting the authors' message.

20 Ajzenstat and Smith, *Canada's Origins*, 3, 8.

21 While Bailyn, Pocock, and their colleagues do some valuable historical dig-
ging to identify many of the particular aspects of the political discourse
of eighteenth-century America, they do not successfully refute the point
that, generally, Locke's influence was predominant. A considerable body
of literature has emerged to make this case. See Joyce Appleby, *Liberalism
and Republicanism in the Historical Imagination* (Cambridge, MA: Harvard
University Press, 1992); John Diggins, *The Lost Soul of American Politics: Virtue, Self-Interest, and the Foundations of Liberalism* (New York: Basic Books,
1984); Steven M. Dworetz, *The Unvarnished Doctrine: Locke, Liberalism and
the American Revolution* (Durham, NC: Duke University Press, 1990); Jerome
Huyler, *Locke in America: The Moral Philosophy of the Founding Era* (Lawrence, KS: University Press of Kansas, 1995); Isaac Kramnik, *Republicanism and Bourgeois Radicalism* (Ithaca, NY: Cornel University Press, 1990);
Barry Alan Shain, *The Myth of American Individualism: The Protestant Origins of American Political Thought* (Princeton: Princeton University Press,
1994), including an empirical study that has found that American Lockean absolutism and its attendant intolerance is alive and well. A study by
Jack Citrin, Beth Reingold, and Donald P. Green has found that the values
Hartz and others identify as characterizing the American nationality are
indeed firmly in place: "Democracy (republicanism, popular sovereignty),
liberty (freedom), equality (of opportunity, in manners), and individual
achievement (individualism, self-reliance)." Jack Citrin, Beth Reingold,
Donald P. Green, "American Identity and the Politics of Ethnic Change,"
Journal of Politics 52, no. 4 (1990): 1129. They contend that there is considerable empirical evidence that "Americanism" as a symbolic predisposition
continues to manifest itself in "liberal and ethno-cultural or exclusionary
elements." Joyce Appleby, a rigorous intellectual historian, was struck by

the contradiction between America's blind affirmation of liberal values and the efforts of Bailyn and others to deny it. She found that despite points of discord, the Founding Fathers did come together on the core assumption of Locke's liberalism.

22 They do mention the work of William Christian and Colin Campbell, but this is quickly dismissed with a cursory reference to Kenneth McRae and David Bell's argument that the Loyalists were "not bearers of a strain of Tory conservatism, but typical bourgeois liberals, like most citizens of the United States in the Revolutionary era." Ajzenstat and Smith, *Canada's Origins*, 4.

23 Ibid., 2.

24 For the monstrous, see the surprisingly regressive essay by Rainer Knopff, "The Triumph of Liberalism in Canada: Laurier on Representation and Party of Government," in Ajzenstat and Smith, *Canada's Origins*, 159–97. This triumph of liberalism is effectively a triumph of tyranny. He celebrates the most rudimentary and coarse form of liberalism and attributes it to Wilfrid Laurier and Canada's party system. While the other advocates of the republicanization of Canada adhered to some notion of human virtue, Knopff is less sanguine. Laurier and Canada, he says in "Triumph," are Hobbesian.

25 Hartz was aware of the republican influence, as he was aware of other ingredients, but this does not pose a problem for his thesis (Hartz, *Founding of New Societies*, 80). It was Locke's dark account of human essence and natural law that prevailed, as is evident in a constitution that relies heavily on checks and balances.

26 It is interesting to note that the artwork on the cover of *Canada's Origins* consists of brief sentences on a red background. They read, "Canada is a toothpick on the dashboard of a pickup truck. Canada is a cigarette. Canada is a table filled with beer...." The list goes on. This in itself could be a criticism of the book's approach to intellectual history. If one looks closely enough, Canada can be anything and everything to the point of being nothing in particular. The concern of Hartz and others is to identify the large overarching themes.

27 Ajzenstat and Smith, *Canada's Origins*, 6.

28 Ibid., 127.

29 Ibid., 113.

30 Ibid., 125.

31 Ibid., 270.

32 Ibid., 142.

33 Ibid., 210.

34 Ibid., 152

35 Jeremy Rayner, "The Very Idea of Canadian Political Thought: In Defence of Historicism," *Journal of Canadian Studies* 26, no. 2 (Summer 1991): 2.

36 Ibid., 13.

37 Ibid., 14.

38 Ibid., 11.

39 Ibid., 11–12.

40 See H.D. Forbes, "Hartz-Horowitz at Twenty: Nationalism, Toryism and Socialism in Canada and the United States," *Canadian Journal of Political Science* 20, no. 2 (June 1987): 287–315.

41 Though there were many prominent Hegelian idealists in the United States in the late nineteenth and early twentieth century, idealism did not achieve the same degree of mainstream success. For more on this, see Frances A. Harmon, *The Social Philosophy of the St Louis Hegelians* (New York: Columbia University Press, 1943); and William H. Goetzmann, ed., *The American Hegelians: An Intellectual Episode in the History of Western America* (New York: Alfred A. Knopf, 1973).

42 Using *conservatism* here as a term for a type of Burkean liberalism that values traditional institutions and gradual social reform.

43 It is worth noting that, beginning with Hegel and Schelling, idealism has indeed looked to the example of the civic republicanism of the classical world, but this is only another part of their system and does not nearly account for its holistic perspective.

44 Ajzenstat and Smith, *Canada's Origins*, 18.

45 Ibid., 12.

46 Ibid.

47 Charles Taylor, *Philosophical Arguments* (Cambridge, MA: Harvard University Press, 1995), 202.

48 Ibid.; see also Charles Taylor, *Reconciling the Solitudes* (Montreal and Kingston: McGill-Queen's University Press, 1993), 40, 50, 199.

49 Ibid., 25, 94–5, 127, 174.

PART THREE

Spirit and Power

8 Gad ben Rachel ve Aharon: *Parrhesiastes*

SHANNON BELL

Gad Horowitz is what Michel Foucault identifies as a *parrhesiastic* thinker, a truth-teller; that is, a thinker who speaks truth, new truths, and in speaking new truths opens horizons in knowledge terrains. "The *parrhesiastes* is someone who says everything he has in mind: he does not hide anything, but opens his heart and mind ... through his discourse."[1] Foucault refers to truth-telling, *parrhesia*, as speech activity. It is an activity that entails risk, goes against dominant thought and speech, and is often dangerous speech. *Parrhesia*, as a bringing-forth, as an opening in existing thought, as a revealing of potential in what is, is the energy that drives radical thought.

The intent of "Gad ben Rachel ve Aharon: *Parrhesiastes*" is to situate Horowitz as a truth-teller and to engage his diverse body of work concentrating on (1) four of Gad's political theoretical works – *Repression: Basic and Surplus Repression in Psychoanalytic Theory: Freud, Reich and Marcuse* (1977), "The Foucaultian Impasse: No Sex, No Self, No Revolution," *Political Theory* (1987), "Groundless Democracy," *Shadow of Spirit: Postmodernism and Religion* (1992), and "Aporiah and Messiah in Derrida and Levinas," *Difficult Justice* (2006); and (2) Horowitz's political pedagogy, as developed in his graduate/honours seminar "The Spirit of Democratic Citizenship: Sanity and Democracy" (1994–2010), in which Gad, employing a politicized interpretation of Alfred Korzybski's work in General Semantics, teaches skills for radical engaged thought. Additionally, new thought emerging from "Berlin Dharma," a five-day video-audio Berlin event-interview (14–19 February 2007), undertaken to facilitate and document thinking on location, in motion, in a new location will be threaded in. The directing assumption is that thought is materially induced, thus new locations give rise to both new thoughts and fresh extensions of previous thinking.

Two aspects of *parrhesia* come into play in Horowitz's work: radical political truth-telling and pedagogical *parrhesia*. Radical political truth-telling goes against the dominant power, whether it be governmental (institutional) or theoretical (intellectual); it sutures critical preaching, scandalous action/thoughts, and provocative dialogue. The second type of *parrhesiastic* role that Gad performs involves the duty to improve other people as well as oneself;[2] it involves individual personal relations to oneself and to others.[3] It is this pedagogical *parrhesia* that inspires and structures Horowitz's seminar "The Spirit of Democratic Citizenship: Sanity and Democracy."

Radical Political *Parrhesia*

I will begin with what I consider Gad's most seductive work, *Repression*. It certainly seduced me in 1979, to the political potential of what could be done with theory, to Freud, to bisexuality, and later to the author himself. *Repression* is a cold, precise, reclamation of the radicality of Freud, tearing him away from the Freudians, from Freudo-Marxist feminists, and even from Marcuse, who just couldn't get the inherent radicality of Freud because he couldn't get the accident in Freud's text. The accident: the female cock,[4] upon which Horowitz erects chapter 4, "The Renunciation of Bisexuality." Or so it is in my reading. And let me say, *Repression* is the text I have always wanted to fuck (with). Perhaps because it is a hard read.

Horowitz wrote *Repression* before the Federation of Feminist Women's Health Centers redefined the female clitoris as one really big outside/inside unified erect organ in *A New View of a Woman's Body* (1991),[5] before alternative-soon-to-become-a-burgeoning-sub-genre-of-porn flooded the market with female ejaculation, and before Queer Theory invented itself as a field of study and an academic discipline.

The radical distinction of basic and surplus repression, Horowitz argues and proves, was assumed, taken for granted, by Freud himself. Armed with Marcuse's proposition "that normal psychosexuality is the product of surplus repression," Gad states his project in *Repression* as "explor[ing] the Freudian texts with the hope that those texts can be illuminated by Marcuse's proposition and that Marcuse's proposition can be solidly grounded in the texts thus illuminated."[6] This was an event in both Freudian and Marcusean scholarship. Interestingly, what Gad did to initiate this event was hold a fidelity to Freud's original texts, a fidelity that was overlooked in Marcuse's philosophical hurry to construct a philosophical synthesis of Marxism and psychoanalysis.

What Horowitz, in *Repression*, displays is fidelity, as understood by Alain Badiou, to the trajectory that led to the event. "To be faithful to an event," Badiou writes, "is to move within the situation that this event has supplemented, by thinking ... the situation 'according to' the event."[7] Fidelity, for Horowitz, in *Repression* was to the presence of the unthought concepts of basic repression and surplus repression, already there in Freud's work.

Nowhere is this more obvious than in chapter 4, "The Renunciation of Bisexuality," not, perhaps, coincidentally the middle chapter, the mean of the text where Straussian scholars like to situate their most pithy truths. This is Gad's most pithy truth: the Freudian establishment could never really hold the duality of activity and passivity in all bodies. This is Freud's gift – a thought revealed and then unthought in the homogeneous heterosexual appropriations and renditions of the Oedipal complex by Freudians and in the feminist critiques of these Freudians and of Freud himself.

In a sense, Gad is doing what Gilles Deleuze does with Henri Bergson[8] and what Deleuze suggests be done with all philosophers: take them from behind to produce an offspring that is different. Deleuze discloses, "I imagined myself getting onto the back of an author, and giving him a child, which would be his and which would at the same time be a monster. It is very important that it should be his child, because the author actually had to say everything that I made him say. But it also had to be a monster because it was necessary to go through all kinds of decenterings, slips, break-ins, secret emissions."[9]

Gad takes, not Freud from behind, but Marcuse. He goes behind Marcuse to regenerate a lost part of Freud, the queer Freud. Once you have read the queer Freud through Horowitz, Freud can never be straightened again. That's the brilliance of writing your text over the original so that the original comes alive in a different way, a way that the intellectual event of deconstruction put on the scholarship map.

Gad queers prior to the Queer Theory blueprint for queering the text. Queer, in the words of David Halperin, not only "reorder(s) the relations among sexual behaviours, erotic identities, constructions of gender(s)" but also reorders "forms of knowledge, regimes of enunciation, logics of representation, modes of self-constitution and practices of community." Queer "acquires its meaning from its oppositional relation to the norm. Queer is by definition whatever is at odds with the normal, the legitimate, the dominant."[10] Queer disrupts all forms of normativity.

Gad points out that while Freud did "consider the development of exclusively heterosexual and 'supergenital' sexuality to be the 'normal' development ... he considered this to be the result of a combination of biological and cultural factors, the relative weights of which are very difficult to distinguish."[11] "It is because normal masculinity and femininity are not 'natural' but products of the repression of bisexuality, a repression which is both biological and cultural, that Freud must constantly warn against the simple equation of 'activity with maleness and passivity with femaleness.'"[12]

Reading and presenting Freud against legitimate Freudian and feminist understandings and against Marcuse's own taking of Freud, Gad reorders Freud according to the disruptions in Freud's own texts. Gad provides a clue towards the end of *Repression*: "Like every thinker who develops his ideas dialectically, Freud constantly 'contradicts' himself."[13]

Gad, in *Repression*, delivers three radical political truths: the feminist truth, the female phallic truth, and the truth of Marcuse's Freud.

Feminist Truth

Gad reveals that while the assumption of the renunciation of activity and desire for the mother by the female child, and of passivity and desire for the father by the male child are unquestionably "male chauvinist logic ... it is not Freud's logic."[14] Rather, "It is the logic he uncovered, the logic of patriarchal, surplus repressive civilization, the logic which pervades and gives form to the deepest structure of that civilization, the patriarchal family."[15]

What feminist critics of Freud take as Freud's position and "mercilessly condemn" is actually Freud's "uncovering [of] the psychological mechanism which sustains"[16] – masculinist domination as a key component of what Marcuse postulates as surplus repression.

Horowitz's most pithy of feminist truths in Freud: "The penis is superior in our civilization, not because Freud is 'phallocentric,' but because our civilization is phallocentric."[17] Gad contends that "the feminist dismissal of Freud ... deprives the women's liberation movement of the most profound insights into the nature of the oppression of woman"[18] – a nature that is embedded in the psychological structure of the biobody and subsequently was fleshed out by Jessica Benjamin in *The Bonds of Love* (1988).[19] Gad reveals the mesh of the biological underpinning of the social and the corresponding social creation and recreation of the biological foundation. In a definitive feminist *parrhesiastic* statement, Gad proclaims, "The repudiation [of super-femininity, the product of thousands of years of increasing surplus repression,] is indeed biological, for the natural tendency of libidinal energy is to be active, to flow outward toward the world and take possession of it, not to be restricted to passive aims."[20]

Female Phallic Truth

Interestingly Horowitz, Deleuze, and Félix Guattari read Freud's undertext of the active female girl renouncing activity and becoming woman. For Deleuze and Guattari, "the girl ... is defined by a relation of movement and rest, speed and slowness ... she never ceases to roam upon a body without organs. She is an abstract line, or a line of flight. Thus girls do not belong to an age group, sex, order, or kingdom: they slip in everywhere, between orders, acts, sexes."[21]

While for Deleuze and Guattari the girl is molecular movement, between the dualism of gender, refusing molar solidification into woman, for Horowitz the girl is activity. She is bisexual, refusing containment: "There are no grounds for believing that the girl is more passive than she is active, for she is not yet a woman (that is, she has not yet renounced her activity.)"[22] And then the most radical *parrhesiastic* statement: "If the little girl could be given a penis she would really become superior in our culture."[23] Horowitz did in theory what the posthumously discovered Henry Darger did in American folk art: he revealed the girl's penis. Darger's work featuring *The Story of the Vivian Girls* has become one of the most celebrated examples of outsider art. The only way the art establishment could stomach Darger was to repeatedly claim that he was an innocent, had never seen a little girl's body, and therefore drew it the same as a little boy's. Standing with Gad at the Kuntswerk Institute for Contemporary Art Exhibition *Into Me / Out of Me* (February 2007, Berlin), in front of one of Darger's prepubescent girls sadistically 'castrating' the evil forces of child slavery, one couldn't help but notice: the girl with cock castrates patriarchy. And, as Horowitz discloses from Freud, "sadism is merely an extreme of activity."[24]

Marcuse's Freud

Marcuse's Freud loses the dialectical tension between basic and surplus repression. Gad shows Marcuse's confounding of basic and surplus repression in his reading of Freud as analogous to Hegel's equation of objectification with alienation. "For Hegel (and for Marcuse's Freud) alienation is eternal because surplus repression is confounded with basic repression."[25]

Horowitz's *parrhesiastic* move is to reveal Freud's understanding of the latent concept of surplus repression as close to or neighbourly with a rendering of Hyppolite's position on alienation: "Alienation is not confounded with objectification; the discontent involved in humanization can be reduced; but humanization (objectification / basic repression) is *in itself* a painfully difficult process."[26] The two tensions of basic and surplus repression interpenetrate. "From a tory-Freudian point of view ... it is possible to criticize Marcuse's red-Freudian program for the abolition of surplus repression ... on the ground that basic, not surplus repression is the primary source of renunciation and neurosis, of the 'discontent' which pervades the human existence."[27] Gad states that the tory view would have been the view "which Freud himself would have been inclined to take."[28]

Principal Thought: Relative Weights of X and Y

Horowitz claims (and this is a *parrhesiastic* truth) that it is "impossible ... to demonstrate that either basic or surplus repression is the primary determinant of human discontent."[29] It is in this context that Gad utters his principal thought, which is rethought and redeployed in the variety of knowledge contexts that constitute his body of work. This main thought reiterated concerns the relative weights of two or more terms. In a sense Gad's foremost thought is a process of investigation: a strategy of thinking. As he said in the "Berlin Dharma" event-interview, "I am always asking something about two levels. There is a structural thing that keeps repeating itself in my work. A formal structure: the relative weights of X and Y."[30]

In *Repression* it is the relative weights of basic and surplus repression. Gad asserts, "The relative weights of biological and cultural factors are very difficult to distinguish."[31] The problem is that Marcuse over-weights the cultural, the social, the economic; what is sacrificed is the "relative weight" of basic repression. Gad explains, "Let's call basic repression X and surplus repression Y. People who don't understand relative weight say, if we take away surplus repression, X remains – you still have basic repression to deal with, and all the messianic talk about fundamental transformation is utopian. But Marcuse's suggestion is that X minus Y doesn't give you X. Rather, it gives you X prime, it gives you a fundamentally different form of X. When you remove surplus repression, then the same old basic repression does not persist, because the essential quality of the experience of basic repression depends on whether surplus repression persists or not."[32]

Relative weight, in Horowitz's recurrent way of thinking, what Martin Heidegger refers to as a "thinker's one only thought,"[33] is present in his famed Canadianist essay, "Conservatism, Liberalism, and Socialism in Canada: An Interpretation," in his later work on Marcuse and in his latest work on Derrida and Levinas. "We have the relative weight of toryism in Canada, and this is the structural aspect, then we have the relative weights of basic and surplus repression, and then in my later work the relative weights of basic and surplus repression in Levinas, Derrida, and Marcuse."[34]

Interestingly, while Gad takes Marcuse from behind in *Repression* to reveal Marcuse's omissions, Marcuse's work haunts Gad's later work on post-structuralist Continental theory, Buddhism, and Judaism. In fact, in his work on Foucault and Derrida and Levinas, it is Marcuse who facilitates Gad's *parrhesiastic* interventions. In a way, Gad deploys Marcuse to bugger Foucault and give him the monster child Foucault abandoned in his conception of self. All the while, Horowitz adheres to Deleuze's condition of "immaculate conception," which is that "it is very important that it should be the author's child." "The author," Deleuze specifies, "actually had to say everything that I made him say."[35] The monster child for Foucault turns out to be Horowitz's child generated and incubated in his previous ménage à trois with Freud and Marcuse. The monster child is the prepersonal, prediscursive, love-needy child. One could see how this would be a monster child for Foucault.

Gad makes three strategic, searing *parrhesiastic* pronouncements in "The Foucaultian Impasse: No Sex, No Self, No Revolution" (1987). Gad's *parrhesiastic* strategy is to use precisely what and who Foucault is writing against in *The History of Sexuality* (1978), repression à la Freud and Marcuse, as the antidote to what he identifies as Foucault's stalemate "that can be rectified only if it strives for an accommodation with something like the Marcusean position."[36] The clue for Horowitz is that Foucault attempts to enliven the power/counter-power or power/resistance structural oscillation in the deployment of sexuality with "bodies and pleasures."[37] Gad divulges that Foucault thinks that "he (Foucault) has discovered 'bodies and pleasures' as something *other* than Freud's sexuality," and makes precisely it "the rallying point for an attack on that sexuality."[38] Gad sardonically exclaims, "He seems not to realize that it was Freud who [had already] redefined *sexuality* as the drive to obtain *pleasure* from zones of the body."[39] This leads Gad to his *parrhesiastic* re-entry of Freud: "Beneath the actually existing sexual forms [is] the generalized prediscursive, prepersonal bodily pleasure potential of the It – and beneath that, the prepersonal, prediscursive childhood need for love."[40] It is this monstrous love-needing child, Gad contends, on which Foucault's no-self with the actualized potential of multiple foundationless identities must gestate, otherwise, shifting identities can be colonized and harnessed to the liberal democratic political project in which the postmodern identity is "an ambiguous achievement of modernity."[41] Gad offers a truth on groundless self and identity: "The self is not only constructed from moment to moment in the here and now. Adult identity is constructed out of a prepersonal, love-needy child.... If with Foucault, we throw out the child with the bathwater, we end up, with Foucault, providing grist for ... the defense of the identity now given us as 'an ambiguous achievement of modernity.'"[42]

Here it is, Freud's truth reiterated newly by Horowitz: "Even deeper than the need for love is the terror that Freud found in the infant deprived of love. It is the terror of annihilation."[43]

Gad's conclusive *parrhesiastic* utterance is a both/and statement that echoes his recurrent thought of relative weights. "Discourse theory needs radical psychoanalysis just as much as radical psychoanalysis needs discourse theory."[44] The former needs the latter "for a fuller understanding of the way in which psychoanalysis has been caught up in self-disciplinary technology."[45] And here is the unifying kicker that brings Foucault back full circle to his jumping-off point in *The History of Sexuality*. Gad proclaims, "What Foucault ... needs to learn from Freud is that identity cannot be resisted and transcended unless the child no longer craves attachment to identity in order to ward off the terror of falling apart or falling forever into the other. The abolition of surplus repression allays the terror with which we cling to identity and makes it possible for us ... to live the contradiction of simultaneously assuming and negating our identities."[46]

Thus Horowitz conjoins the hegemonic discourse that Foucault was responding to at its most intense point to discourse theory, perhaps deploying Foucault to show that hegemonic knowledge and its counter-discourse are unified.

In "Groundless Democracy" Gad pursues groundless self, identity, and agency again, but this time in the context of the groundlessness of radical democracy. Much the same as the way he took Foucault from behind armed with Freud and Marcuse, Horowitz takes radical democratic post-structuralist thinkers Ernesto Laclau and Chantal Mouffe, but not from behind, rather sideways, from the other side of Western philosophy: Buddhism. Mouffe and Laclau have got themselves and radical democracy in the dilemma of how to hold difference inside the frame of radical equality, or as Horowitz puts it, the quandary "between democracy … as a system of radical equivalence and democracy as a social formation intrinsically marked by the tension between equivalence and difference."[47] While Horowitz is not the first to identify this dilemma, he is the first to go outside Western philosophical discourse, eastwards. Horowitz declares, "In my opinion, the way out of this quandary is not clearly indicated anywhere in the philosophical tradition of the west."[48] He advises, "It is necessary to go eastwards to the Buddhist philosophical masters, Nagarjuna of India, Fa Tsang of China and Dogen of Japan."[49] Interestingly, Gad's is a neighbouring way to that traversed, albeit less explicitly, by Heidegger in his signature concept Being. It is perhaps in "Berlin Dharma," the five-day interview-event, where he most precisely sets out the Buddhist and post-structuralist discontinuous self:

When the speed of human living slows down, then it is possible to see more and possibly understand more of what is going on. When living is slow, in the sense of something that is conducive to awareness and self-awareness, then one can get some insight into the real discontinuity of the self. One can lose the idea of the substantial self as something that is continuous through time, one can lose the illusion of a self that remains somehow the same as it goes through changes, or as it passes through time. One can get more of a sense of what Dogen called being-time. Being is time. It is not that being happens in time, or passes through time, it is not that time happens to being, but being is time.

The process we label self is discontinuous. It renews itself from moment to moment. Almost non-metaphorically, you can say, and it has been said, that there is death every moment, that there is a gap or pause between this moment of life and the next, this moment of self and the next, a void or an emptiness, or a pause, or a death that intervenes between this moment of life and the next. In this moment one can appreciate the discontinuity of life and the possibility of freedom that this offers for liberating oneself from the burden of insensate habit that ordinarily obfuscates the possibilities of fundamental change from one moment to the next.

The speeder life gets, the more intense the illusion becomes of the continuity of self speeding through time. The possibilities of awareness and
liberation diminish as life gets speedier and speedier. All sorts of different
thinkers have touched on this: Martin Heidegger and Paul Virilio.

Samsara is existence-as-speed, samsara is speed. You can take the Buddhist notion of samsara and lay it over Virilio's concept and theory of
speed.[50]

The middle part of "Groundless Democracy" – "Emptiness of Emptiness" – is Horowitz at one of his most extreme *parrhesiastic* moments.
After its delivery, at the Shadow of the Spirit Conference (1990), "Emptiness of Emptiness" was immediately identified by the Buddhist monks
in the audience as a Teisho, a sermon by a Zen master. And in Horowitz's case, an unruly, eclectic Zen master free of the chains of the schools
of thought he draws upon in order to construct a political groundlessness that will hold the radical in democracy. Gad presents seven Buddhist truths:

All things are identical in that they are empty of identity.
Reality is in flux without any beginning or end.
Every event is distinguished from other events only in language and
    perception.
Emptiness is the essence of things as their absence of emptiness.
Neither "empty" nor "non-empty" should be declared, nor both, nor
    neither.
Every thing exists not as itself, but as every other thing manifested as
    the actual Suchness of this unique thing.
The particular validity of every empty phenomenon consists precisely
    in its radical interrelatedness with every other phenomenon.[51]

Whereas some tenets in post-structuralism can get to emptiness, or
at the very least, like Laclau and Mouffe, to a "groundlessness" "dissolution of certainty,"[52] unlike Buddhism, they cannot find their way
past the dissolution of certainty and emptiness into Suchness. That is,
unlike Buddhism, post-structuralism flounders and gets stuck in negativity. Gad holds that it is precisely "thinking through the principle of
emptiness,"[53] which contains Suchness, that allows for identity and difference (singularity) within the radical equivalence of all that is: "In ...
my own mind I find billions of worlds and other beings." "I contain
multitudes."[54]

The definitive thought that structures Gad's work is reiterated in "Groundless Democracy": the relative weight of two apparent opposite thought fields taken into a synthesis that is enhanced from both sides, in this case Western and Eastern thought. In a way, the speed of the synthesis is also a disclosure of a truth: it is not the amount of thought that counts; rather, it is the precision and intensity.

Horowitz's *parrhesia* in "Aporia and Messiah in Derrida and Levinas" begins by quickly disclosing the political problem inherent in deconstruction as justice premised on Levinasian ethics of responsibility to the other before self. Gad states, "The problem is that 'the notion of an impossible justice that arrives by never arriving ("openness") can be and has been very easily taken as somehow more or less subtly endorsing or underwriting the 'fundamentals' of the Western status quo and rejecting all revolutionary approaches."[55]

Partly this is due to Derrida and Levinas's distinction between good and bad regimes in the same terms as the Western liberal democratic manner: "The better regime is open to critique, the worse is closed,"[56] Gad argues, "Levinas' (Derrida's) apparent endorsement of the openness of the liberal regime threatens to overshadow their condemnation of injustice insofar as the regime is the framework within which the struggle for justice is pursued; the regime's openness is what makes the struggle possible. The framework itself is not condemned as unjust."[57]

Gad queries, "Remember Herbert Marcuse's question in *One Dimensional Man* 'Who countervails against the framework?'"[58]

What Gad argues is that in Levinas and Derrida "the (in)justice required by the third ... is conflated with the (in)justice required by the few"[59] in liberal capitalist democracy. He further contends, "Levinas and Derrida seem to assume that the extent or degree to which caring for one other must deprive other others, that is the degree of repression, would not vary in different orders of social relations. They seem to assume that poverty, inequality, exploitation, that is surplus-repression, will always inevitably recur in more or less the same way and 'on the same plane, where the ontologically necessary injustice of justice, necessary injustice of order,' that is, basic repression, must occur. The ontological necessity of order, basic repression, is conflated with the contingent historical necessity of the order of class society – surplus repression."[60]

Gad, however, makes a *parrhesiastic* utterance that takes Levinas and Derrida from the *aporia* in their thought, a political impasse, to the outside of their thought – Marcuse – and shows that this outside is an inherent inside. He deploys the signature concept of Levinas – the Other – on Levinas and Derrida's own work. Gad explains, "For Derrida and Levinas, to think is to think the Other of thought: the Other is the constitutive outside of thought, that is, it is inside."[61]

Gad declares, "What stands in the way of justice in our world system is … this system. This system, not system-per-se ('order') but this system, stands in the way."[62] He contends, "The failure to distinguish emphatically between justice for the third and justice of the few and to put this distinction close to the centre of the consideration of the relation between ethics and politics is what makes the Levinasian/Derridian much too easily recuperable by liberalism."[63]

The source of this failure to distinguish is the refusal to make "a distinction between the pre-originary 'always' and its historical mediations."[64] "'Basic repression' in the Freudian/Marcusean scheme corresponds in some sense … to the '(quasi)transcendental/(pre-)original' in the Levinasian/Derridian register."[65] There exists an aporetic relation of Necessity between the self, which is "response to the other," and the other; this is preoriginal and basic. The structural aporia in which "the self must be … separate from the other in order to respond … will never be surpassed."[66]

Horowitz documents that it is possible to find statements in both Derrida and Levinas that presuppose or even expressly point to the distinction between this quasi-transcendental aporia and its possible historical variability.[67] Then Gad proposes quite an interesting truth: "Far from contradicting the Levinasian/Derridian Contra-Diction, or Aporia, the semi-Marcusean moments in their writings are enabled by it."[68]

Gad comes full circle, or closes the circle, in his insertion of Marcuse's signature concepts of basic and surplus repression to politically rescue Derrida and Levinas's signature concepts of justice and the other (ethics) from liberal appropriation. Then comes the wild *parrhesiastic* action in Gad's text; in tandem with enabling the semi-Marcusean moments in Derrida and Levinas's writings, he proceeds to, not so much take Marcuse, Levinas and Derrida from behind, but rather to precede them by going way back to the Jewish mystical tradition, the Kabbalah. With theoretical precision, Gad connects the messianic moment in Derrida derived in part from Levinas's Other, the impossible justice to come, to Tikkun, "the mending or repair of the catastrophe that has been suffered by man and God since the world's creation."[69]

Gad discloses that Kabbalistic texts, although "redolent with images of ultimate mending … frequently indicate … sensitivity to the possibility of degrees of tikkun."[70] What are degrees of tikkun but "fundamental transformations short of perfect Tikkun – *possible* Messiahs"?[71] Here is the *parrhesiastic* utterance that brings together discourse, counter-discourse, and counter-counter-discourse; or rather, deconstruction, critical theory, Kabbalah; or perhaps Kabbalah, critical theory, deconstruction. "They [Kabbalistic texts] work with distinctions of what Marcuse would call degrees of repression."[72] Reading the *Lurianic Kabbalah* in the light of Marcuse's *Eros and Civilization*, Gad contends that in the tearing of the name of God YH/VH materially manifested as the broken world, "what happened was not only basic repression that could never be undone ... but also surplus repression – the release of extreme radical evil in the world."[73] Gad explains,

> The notion of *tikkun* as the *Lurianic Kabbalah* understands it and as I understand it refers to fundamental revolutionary transformations in the very nature of human existence. A fundamentally new experience of reality is something Marcuse talks about in *Eros and Civilization*. You do not have to wait for the impossible messiah who never comes, as a lot of readings of Derrida and Levinas would have it. That messiahism refers to a messiah that never comes, it is always to come. Perfection is always to come, the impossible messiah is always to come; we don't give up that idea. But there is the idea that when the messiah comes, although not everything is perfect, there is a substantial transformation in the intensity or degree of suffering.
>
> In "Aporia and Messiah in Derrida and Levinas," I quote my ancestor the Shelah, Rabbi Isaiah Horowitz, who was a follower of the *Lurianic Kabbalah,* who writes that after the messiah comes, many sexual restrictions will perhaps be lifted. This is an example of the easing of life, what Marcuse calls the "pacification of existence," that is possible with and subsequent to fundamental transformation. The Shelah points out that in evil times and in certain types of circumstances, which are conducive to evil, many restrictions are necessary which will not always be necessary – necessary repression versus unnecessary repression. There is not the notion that a time will ever come when no restrictions whatsoever will be necessary. Perhaps a time like that will come as the world to come, as *Olam Ha-Ba,* a next world in which everything is perfect, but that is not what happens immediately after the messiah comes.[74]

Gad links the overcoming of surplus repression in Kabbalistic terrain with what he identifies as "the astounding idea of Kabbalah": "descent for the sake of ascent."[75] Overcoming surplus repression by "descent for the sake of ascent" is what the Sabbataian movement did in the seventeenth century. Gad provides highlights of Sabbatai Zevi's use of descent to remove degrees of repression, or in fact of surplus repression. Sabbatai Zevi declared himself to be Messiah and then like a true Derridian messiah who never comes, converted to Islam.[76] Sabbatai would strike the Holy Ark in the synagogue and pronounce "the unmentionable name of God, JHVH, manifesting its messianic unification."[77] Sabbatai "flouted all norms of decency": he held a banquet at which men and women danced together, while he himself retired to another room together with a former wife; "he marries a woman, Sarah, reputed to be a prostitute, because she had a vision that she was going to marry the messiah," and on and on. Sabbatai Zevi declares religious fast days feast days, but not Yom Ha Kippurim. the Day of Atonement. Radical evil and overly strict religious conventions can be ended and/or transformed together, Gad suggests, in a Marcusean vein, when Thanatos, the drive for radical evil, converges with Eros, the life force. In the case of Sabbatai Zevi and his followers, the result was to produce a new Sabbataian reality principle that fascinated world Jewry "from London to Constantinople."[78] What is not overcome, however, is the basic repressive separation of the human from God and the self from the other.

Nowhere is the mesh of the Marcusean concepts of basic and surplus repression with Judaism more evident than in Horowitz's radical *parrhesiastic* understanding of Kol Nidre (All the Vows), the prayer/declaration that begins the Yom Kippur service in which the entire congregation confesses individually and collectively, as I and we, every possible sin. Kol Nidre, recited three times to make sure nobody misses it, "is a plea to God to cancel, render null and void all contracts, covenants, vows, oaths, and promises which will be made in the coming year."[79] *Kol Nidre operates according to a principle of surplus forgiveness*; the vows are always already cancelled; one is always already forgiven. "Kol Nidre does not cancel the sanctity of the vow." This is basic. "Kol Nidre, while canceling, intensifies. The prayer cancels all vows insofar as they are false."[80] The false vows are surplus.

Pedagogical *Parrhesia*: Gad the Teacher

Like the Stoic teachers, particularly Epictetus, Gad teaches what Foucault names "procedures and techniques": "a set of rational principles that are grounded in general statements about the world ... and ... practical rules for behavior."[81]

In fact, Gad, Epictetus, and the founder of General Semantics, Alfred Korzybski, all introduced programs for the care of the self that involve practices that "take the form of a constant putting on trial of all our representations."[82] Epictetus called for "an attitude of permanent surveillance with regard to all our representations."[83] Korzybski posited a new "negative epistemology" beyond what he referred to as "Aristotelianism" – the dominant form of human discourse, which identifies representation, or "map," with truth or territory. Horowitz develops and instructs his "Spirit of Democratic Citizenship: Sanity and Democracy" seminar[84] in how the general semantic techniques can be utilized to undermine "unsane" understandings of the world and teaches techniques to develop a saner orientation to reality.

Gad adapts the principles of General Semantics to democracy, and in so doing he radicalizes the rules of engagement, putting into question given representations of so-called reality. Gad contends that contemporary radical democracy needs the *techne* of General Semantics. In a talk delivered in 1999, Horowitz argued, "Among the differences of contemporary radical democracy from previous democratic movements is its concern with epistemological issues. We think that fundamental transformation will not happen in the world unless it is also a transformation of epistemology – of ways of knowing, sensing, and experiencing self, other, and world – beyond the hegemonic epistemology – the rationality of domination, the logic of the disciplinary society, the metaphysics of presence, carnophallogocentrism."[85]

Gad situates the techniques of General Semantics as sharing a commonality with the post-structuralist critique of representation. However, he specifies that, "unlike post-structuralism which deploys highly specialized esoteric languages – languages of destabilization of language – accessible only to a few tiny philosophical and literary elites – and without any actual intervention into sublinguistic and unconscious processes, general semantics was a mass micropolitical movement for a new epistemological sensibility involving, in Korzybski's terms, not only the cerebral cortex, but the thalamus."[86]

"Korzybski wanted general semantics to be not merely a discipline relating to semantics, the meaning of meaning, but a general discipline that is open to all disciplines, as well as appealing to all strata of the population."[87]

The radical truth underlying the teaching of General Semantics as a counter-hegemonic way of engaging the world is that self-change is fundamental to social change, that the Aristotelian self that has dominated knowledge and corresponding action since 350 BCE can be neuro-semantically restructured by non-elementalist, non-identity techniques. Korzybski states, "In general semantics we do not 'preach' 'morality' or 'ethics' as such, but we train students in consciousness of abstracting, consciousness of the multiordinal mechanisms of evaluation, relational orientations, etc., which bring about cortico-thalamic integration, and then as a result 'morality,' 'ethics,' awareness of social responsibilities, etc., follow automatically."[88]

Korzybski's assumption is that if one alters the manner in which one apprehends the world, then a non-Aristotelian morality and ethics will ensue. Korzybski does not disclose the content of this morality and ethics. Horowitz does. In a sense, it is Derrida and Levinas's concepts of justice and ethics rescued, as Gad does in "Aporia and Messiah in Derrida and Levinas," with the semi-Marcusean moments of the distinction between repression and surplus-repression embedded in Levinas and Derrida's concepts. One could argue that Korybski's repudiation of the "is" of identity, his signature concept – the structural differential, his mapping levels of abstraction in the construction of reality, and the neurolinguistic devices, the core techniques of General Semantics – singularity (index), historicity (date), non-allness (etc.), contextuality (chain index), and relationality (quotes and hyphens) – affect not only surplus repression but also in some sense basic repression in terms of altering the processing of the cortical and thalamic levels of the brain-nervous system.

"The practices of general semantics consist of working with a model or map of the mapping process known as the structural differential and with a set of linguistic devices."[89] The structural differential's central function is to convey a denial of the law of identity. The structural differential consists of three levels: the event level, the object level, and the label level. The event level indicates what is going on at this instant. It has "infinite numbers of characteristics" and "it represents a process which never stops in one form or another," "neither ... does it repeat itself."[90] We know the event only by means of sensory experience. The object, while nonverbal, unlike the event is the level of direct sensory experience. The label level is that of language: "words, words about words, and words about words about words."[91] The object is an abstraction from the event; the label is a further abstraction from the object. The further one traverses from the event, the higher the level of abstraction, the highest levels of abstraction being science, philosophy, etc. The structural differential maps the circular process by which sensory experience abstracts from "what is going on," and language, while abstracting from sensory experience, enables human understanding of "what is going on."

There are two related kinds of semantic blocks: what is happening at the level of actual lived experience is blocked from reaching the level of conceptual formulations (label level), and new formulations or theorizations at the label level are therefore prevented from entering the realm of lived experience. This duality of the semantic blocks is responsible for the simultaneity of ideological rigidity, with confusion and fragmentation in actually existing democracies.

The key linguistic devices include the index, the etc., the date, the chain-index, and quotes and hyphens. All of the devices take apart the law of identity. The index: "In our Aristotelian civilization we privilege similarity, we reconstruct it as sameness and ignore difference. But by using the Korzybski technique of habitually indexing words, for example woman1, woman2 … n, or democray1, democracy2 … n, at least in our minds, we produce indefinitely many proper names for the endless array of unique individuals and situations."[92] The index overturns all formulations relying on the is of identity. The index, states Horowitz, practically coerces the proliferation of distinctions in human evaluation. The etc. indicates that no matter how many ways an entity can be classified, there is always more beyond the end of all conceivable classifications, all classifications that it will ever have been possible to formulate – perhaps all the way to the Other as absolute alterity. Thus, the etc. opens closure without making it disappear. Etc. is the end of metaphysics.[93] Horowitz suggests that "recent post-metaphysicians, influenced by Levinas, would take the etc. as 'the ethical specificity of the other who always exceeds and questions the categories of the self.' That's what is meant when the other is named singular, absolutely unique and when it follows that it is in my responsibility to the other that I am unique, singular, irreplaceable – for if I were merely the sum of my particular instantiations of all my identities, I would be replaceable by all other members of the same set of sets of identity. Only as unique am I responsible for all others."[94]

The date "immediately abolishes the false stability that language assigns to things and events."[95] It places us in the "world of motion and change – yet the investigation of the processes can be arrested at any point for the purposes of analysis and communication."[96] Gad points out that "the date raises, among many other questions, political questions, such as the questions of retribution, punishment, reconciliation, of responsibility over time."[97]

The date is used together with context and situation as processed by the chain index. Gad states, "The chain index loves to soil the purity of the logocentric distinction between a person, thing, event, situation and its context or environment."[98] Gad quotes Adorno: "The thing itself is its context."[99] The chain index "brings the environment or context – which is of course always dated, i.e., historical – directly into the definition of the thing."[100] Gad asks, "What is the effect of the chain index on a concept such as human nature?"[101]

Quotes and hyphens, which Korzybski called safety devices, protect against elementalism. Quotes around "fascism," "democracy," "nation," "self, " etc. indicate that these phenomena do not contain their existence within themselves; in other words, they are empty of inherent existence. Hyphens bring back into relation phenomena that are conventionally ascribed independent existence: fascism-capitalism-imperial rivalry. Gad reiterates: "Korzybski wants you to have the structural differential and the devices always in mind, or readily accessible at the back of your mind."[102]

I asked Gad to demonstrate the techniques of General Semantics by applying the structural differential and some of the devices to a current political issue or situation. He chose to discuss the relevance of General Semantics terminology for "Trans Politics and Anti-Capitalism: An Interview with Dr Dan Irving" for *Upping the Anti.*

Irving speaks of the "systematic erasure of trans people."[103] Referring to the distinction between the object and label levels, Gad explains that this is a semantic block: trans people's personal troubles at the object level are not seen, heard, felt; they are not translated into public issues at the label level. Irving cites Vivian Namastes's book *Invisible Lives,* which "discusses the ways that trans people are made invisible by bureaucracy – the census, only M/F boxes on government forms – as well as by social service agencies and within public spaces."[104]

Irving states that the "ability to pass as non-trans men and women is taken to be markers of success."[105] Gad says, "Trans people must conform their lives to the two-valued M/F categorical system in order to be conceived as 'real' persons."[106] Gad situates Irving's observation that "trans is read as personal adversity"[107] in the context of the structural differential. He explains, "The facts of trans at the object level are labeled,

storied, in terms of personal adversity only, rather than a matter of political relations."[108] Gad observes that "this labeling also affects the trans
community's self-conceptions,[109] for, according to Irving, those who don't
"seek medical transition are viewed as not 'really' trans ... We can see
how these labels function as techniques of governance to regulate sex/
gender identities and expression."[110] "Why is trans often represented as a
reified and unitary identity when there are significant differences among
trans people? What happens to actual lived experiences"[111] at the object
level? "Possible knowledge about trans identities is determined in advance [i.e., blocked] by the binary system of sex/gender."[112]

The overarching truth of General Semantics is non-identity, for once
the is of identity is abandoned, then one can begin to "see that the object
is not the event but an abstraction from it, and the label is not the object
nor the event, but a still further abstraction from it."[113] Or, as Korzybski said, and it subsequently became the mantra of the neuro linguistic
programming movement, "The map is not the territory."[114] However, all
we have are maps.

Korzybski's intent on the practice of devices was that they would
tend to introduce a split second of "psycho-logical delay," a "cerebro-
thalamic pause" that would tend to derail the usually automatic habit
of identification of label with object and object with event, tending to
bring about a transformation of the process of human evaluation, not
only at the verbal theoretical label levels but also at the object level, the
sensory and neurological levels, the very-brain-nervous system, so that
one should not only theorize but experience at any moment that one's
experience at that moment is an experience of map, not territory.[115] This
is, according to Gad, a radically democratic way of experiencing experience. Horowitz's *parrhesia* is to infuse the truth of General Semantics
with radical democracy and teach the skills as a new democratic way
of engaging the world.

Foucault's lectures on *parrhesia*, collected in *Fearless Speech*, end with
three questions: "How can we recognize someone as a *parrhesiastes*?
What is the importance of having a *parrhesiastes* for the city? What is the
training of a good *parrhesiastes*?"[116] One can recognize in Gad ben Rachel
ve Aharon's work a relentless will to truth, new truth, which benefits
the theoretical and political agora through its honesty of engagement
and rigorous scrutiny of all that is. Radical General Semantics provides
training for "a good *parrhesiastes*" to put all that exists under continuous examination and to "develop counter-hegemonic thinking and
practice." Gad ben Rachel ve Aharon: *Parrhesiastes*.

NOTES

1 Michel Foucault, *Fearless Speech*, ed. Joseph Pearson (New York: Semiotext[e], 2001), 12.
2 Ibid., 19.
3 Ibid., 77.
4 For further discussion of the female cock and female ejaculation, see Shannon Bell, chapter 2, "The Female Phallus: Something to See," in *Fast Feminism: Speed Philosophy, Pornography, and Politics* (New York: Autonomedia, 2010).
5 Federation of Feminist Women's Health Centers, *A New View of a Woman's Body* (Los Angeles: Feminist Health, 1991).
6 Gad Horowitz, *Repression: Basic and Surplus Repression in Psychoanalytic Theory: Freud, Reich and Marcuse* (Toronto: University of Toronto Press, 1977), 4.
7 Alain Badiou, *Ethics: An Essay in Understanding Evil*, trans. Peter Hallward (London: Verso, 2002), 42.
8 Hugh Tomlinson and Barbara Habberiam, "Translators' Introduction" to *Bergsonism*, by Gilles Deleuze (New York: Zone Books, 1991), 8.
9 Tomlinson and Habberiam, "Translator's Introduction."
10 David Halperin, *Saint Foucault: Towards a Gay Hagiography* (New York: Oxford University Press 1995), 62.
11 Ibid., 84.
12 Horowitz, *Repression*, 94.
13 Ibid., 198.
14 Ibid., 106.
15 Ibid.
16 Ibid., 107.
17 Ibid.
18 Ibid., 108.
19 Jessica Benjamin, *The Bonds of Love: Psychoanalysis, Feminism, and the Problem of Domination* (New York: Pantheon Books, 1988).
20 Horowitz, *Repression*, 116.
21 Gilles Deleuze and Félix Guattari, *A Thousand Plateaus: Capitalism and Schizophrenia*, trans. Brian Massumi (Minneapolis: University of Minnesota Press, 1987), 276–7.
22 Horowitz, *Repression*, 90.
23 Ibid., 107.
24 Ibid., 92.
25 Ibid., 212.

26 Ibid., 213.
27 Ibid., 96.
28 Ibid., 196.
29 Ibid., 199.
30 Gad Horowitz, interview by Shannon Bell, "Berlin Dharma" interview-event, 14–19 February 2007.
31 Horowitz, *Repression*, 84.
32 Horowitz, interview.
33 Martin Heidegger, *What Is Called Thinking?*, trans. J. Glen Gray (New York: Harper and Row, Publishers, 1968), 76.
34 Heidegger, *What Is Called Thinking?*
35 Deleuze, *Bergsonism*, 8.
36 Gad Horowitz, "The Foucaultian Impasse: No Sex, No Self, No Revolution," *Political Theory* 15, no. 1 (1987): 61.
37 Ibid., 67.
38 Ibid.
39 Ibid., 67.
40 Ibid., 71.
41 Ibid.
42 Ibid.
43 Ibid.
44 Ibid., 73.
45 Ibid.
46 Ibid., 77.
47 Gad Horowitz, "Groundless Democracy," in *Shadow of Spirit: Postmodernism and Religion*, ed. Philippa Berry and Andrew Wernick (London: Routledge, 1992), 158.
48 Ibid.
49 Ibid.
50 Horowitz, interview.
51 Horowitz, "Groundless Democracy," 159–60.
52 Ibid., 156.
53 Ibid., 160.
54 As the American Whitman, poet of democracy, says, "I am large; I contain multitudes." As the ancient Tibetan Longchenpa says, "Every time I zero in on my own mind I find billions of worlds and other beings" (Horowitz, "Groundless Democracy," 163).
55 Gad Horowitz, "Aporia and Messiah in Derrida and Levinas," *Difficult Justice: Commentaries on Levinas and Politics*, ed. Gad Horowitz and Asher Horowitz (Toronto: University of Toronto Press, 2006), 310.

56 Ibid.
57 Ibid., 313.
58 Ibid.
59 Ibid.
60 Gad Horowitz, interview.
61 Horowitz, "Aporia and Messiah in Derrida and Levinas," 308.
62 Ibid., 314.
63 Ibid.
64 Ibid., 315.
65 Ibid., 320.
66 Ibid.
67 Ibid., 321.
68 Ibid., 324.
69 Ibid., 316.
70 Ibid.
71 Ibid.
72 Ibid.
73 Ibid., 317.
74 Horowitz, interview.
75 Horowitz, interview; and Horowitz, "Aporia and Messiah in Levinas and Derrida," 319.
76 Horowitz, "Aporia and Messiah in Levinas and Derrida," 314.
77 Ibid., 319.
78 Ibid., 320.
79 Gad Horowitz, "Global Pardon: Pax Romana, Pax Americana, and Kol Nidre," *Bad Subjects* 58 (December 2001), http://bad.eserver.org/issues/2001/58/horowitz.html.
80 Ibid.
81 Foucault, *Fearless Speech*, 165–6.
82 Ibid., 160.
83 Ibid.
84 Gad's twenty-two lectures on radical general semantics are available at http://radicalgeneralsemantics.net.
85 Gad Horowitz, "On Techniques of the Self – with a Look Back at the General Semantics Movement" (public lecture, Theory, Culture, Politics Program, Trent University, Peterborough, ON, 18 November 1999).
86 Ibid.
87 Ibid.
88 Alfred Korzybski, *Science and Sanity: An Introduction to Non-Aristotelian Systems and General Semantics* (Englewood, NJ: International Non-Aristotelian Library, 1948), 12.

89 Horowitz, "On Techniques of the Self."
90 Korzybski, *Science and Sanity*, 180.
91 Horowitz, "On Techniques of the Self."
92 Ibid.
93 Ibid.
94 Ibid.
95 Ibid.
96 Ibid.
97 Ibid.
98 Ibid.
99 Ibid.
100 Ibid.
101 Ibid.
102 Ibid.
103 Gary Kinsman, "Trans Politics and Anti-Capitalism: An Interview with Dan Iriving," for *Upping the Anti: A Journal of Theory and Action* 4 (May 2007): 61.
104 Ibid., 61.
105 Ibid., 63.
106 Gad Horowitz in discussion with Shannon Bell, 15 August 2008.
107 Kinsman, "Trans Politics and Anti-Capitalism," 69.
108 Horowitz in discussion.
109 Ibid.
110 Kinsman, "Trans Politics and Anti-Capitalism," 71.
111 Ibid., 72.
112 Ibid., 73.
113 Korzybski, *Science and Sanity*, 182.
114 Ibid., 12.
115 Horowitz, "On Techniques of the Self."
116 Foucault, *Fearless Speech*, 172.

9 What's Involved in Involution?
A Psycho-Poetics of Regression:
Freud–Horowitz–Celan

MICHAEL MARDER

If the encounter of psychoanalysis and poetry has a purpose, it involves neither a poetic approach to psychoanalysis nor a psychoanalytic appropriation of poetry. Rather, such an encounter seeks to reveal the common ground of the poetic and psychoanalytic *desires*, striving for the *Abgrund* of singular knowledge that "cannot be acquired (or possessed) once and for all" – the singular knowledge where "each case, each text, has its own specific, singular symbolic functioning."[1] Whenever two singularities meet in an asymmetrical Levinasian encounter, no exchange, no functional commerce, no economic activity will transpire between them, but only breath and breathlessness, breath as breathlessness, provoked by the other. It is in this attempt to breathe the secret (which, to be sure, does not pre-exist the other's provocation) in all its breathlessness that the relation to the other is forged as a teaching.

The teaching of Gad Horowitz, taken in the fullest sense of the term that remains faithfully aligned with the Hebrew etymology of Torah at the intersection of "instruction" and "showing," points aporetically towards what cannot be pinpointed, or pinned down, or identified, namely, something like singularity. More than anyone else, he knows that teaching requires taking into account both the closest proximity of the ear of the other for whom the whispered secret is intended and the farthest distance between the singularities resisting the direct transmissibility of knowledge. Between the Kabbalah and Buddhism, psychoanalysis and critical theory, along with Bataille and Levinas, Derrida and Marcuse, Horowitz reaches out "beyond thought, beyond the idea, beyond form" – towards the singular.[2]

Would it be possible, then, to follow the thread of singularity – singularity as a thread of this generous teaching – if the singular remains stubbornly discrete, regardless of all repetitions, wherein it announces and instantaneously erases itself? Of course, such an endeavour would be impossible and, therefore, undeniably worthwhile.[3] It is in the spirit of such an impossible possibility that I propose to bring together (and to draw apart) poetry and psychoanalysis, to leave just enough breathing space for what is singular in them, and to allow an ethical relation between them to unfold, touching and transforming the unique languages of both.

* * *

The importance of breath (*pneuma*) in Celan's poetry cannot be overstated. In the poet's words, "For me, especially in a poem, Jewishness is sometimes not so much a thematic as a pneumatic concern."[4] The theme is reduced, in a quasi-phenomenological fashion, to the breath that animates it in the first place and that subsequently freezes in it. This example (which is more than an example) portrays poetry as a medium in which thematization does not overshadow or subsume "pneumatic" concerns with breath as expiration, inspiration, and aspiration. Psychoanalytically, expiration and inspiration will connote the ego's projection and introjection of objects and desires. But on a different, psychogenetic level, they may be reinterpreted as psychical development (expiration) and regression (inspiration), as the *fort/da* dance of reality and phantasy, self and other, interiority and exteriority. The moment of breathless aspiration will then characterize the irreducible middle space between expiration and inspiration, between psychical excrescence and regression. Such will have been the excluded space that sets in motion the psycho-pneumatic complex, the excluded space in which the ethical encounter between poetry and psychoanalysis is experienced as a teaching.

The regressive drawing in of the psyche is the centripetal movement of the soul. But unfortunately, regression is one of the most neglected concepts in psychoanalysis, neglected, precisely, because its largely unexamined, under-analyzed strangeness is so subtle that it reverts into its opposite: an entirely obvious, self-explanatory, and almost vulgar phenomenon. Not merely uncanny, but the uncanny par excellence, the frightening familiarity and vagueness of regression come to light only in a pneumatic-poetic teaching. Read in the dim glow of the particular, emanating from Celan's poem *"Lob der Ferne"* [Praise of Distance],[5] Freud's writings on regression will gain the sort of vitality that is often bedazzled and lost in the radiant beams of universal explication.

"Lob der Ferne," a title that could have been undersigned by Levinas with his insistence on radical separation, is followed by these lines:

In the springs of your eyes
live the Madsea fishermen's nets.
In the springs of your eyes
the sea keeps its promise.

The "springs of your eyes" contain traces of much vaster bodies of water (the Madsea [*Irrsee*] and another, anonymous kind of sea [*Meer*] whose waves reproduce the impersonal rustling of the *there is, il y a*, in which the I will attempt to immerse itself throughout the poem. Hosting an ambivalent mix of capture and freedom, the nets and the promise, these traces yield the first evidence of the tremendous depths that open up before the movement of regression, inspiration, or involution. The deeper I delve into my "self," the closer I come to the other (the springs of your eyes) and the other of the other (the sea that keeps its promise), who will have already awaited or anticipated me there. Dive in, and your breathing, now more than ever dictated by alterity, will change in this aquatic medium! Take a plunge, and the spatiality of involution will be temporalized, as soon as the promise, which the sea keeps, turns this literally groundless, uncertain, turbulent space into the very possibility of a future that flourishes in the depths of the immemorial past, which, like the singularity of the singular, "is not *present*, has never been present, or … is withdrawn, leaving only a trace"![6]

For Freud, regression shifts the libidinal flows, returning them to the markers or fixations of psychical history.[7] It is driven by a desire to free the libido from the constraints placed upon sexual satisfaction in the course of psychical development and differentiation and to recuperate the time when "satisfaction was not withheld."[8] It should be noted that the regressive impulse is not nostalgic, or that it is, at best, nostalgic for that past that has never been present (the past of absolute satisfaction experienced by the ego). Regression, then, is our nostalgia for the future and for the promise that has not been fulfilled. But, here too, the promise ineluctably entwines itself with madness and capture; the desire to relive past pleasures in a way that frees the libido from developmental constraints is inseparable from the outbreak of obsessive symptoms in the place of past fixations. A failure to recover the lost pleasure one never had is spelled out a priori when the invocation of the undifferentiated and phantasy-saturated totality of originary narcissism compels the subject to turn away from reality, such that the distance between it and the other collapses. Subsequently, "narcissism and egoism ... co-incide" in a dreamy and hallucinatory satisfaction of needs,[9] while the promise is "kept" [*hält*] *back*, or halted, without a hope for its fulfilment.

In different ways, Horowitz and Celan realize that fixation is not a necessary attribute of regression. Still further away than the springs and the seas lies the "oceanic feeling," which does not imply an im-mature abandonment of the ego as such, but a new strength, a sign of convalescence, as Nietzsche will say: "The point is that the ego which is strong enough to neutralize rather than ward off libidinal and ag-gressive drives is not only anxiety-free, and 'egoless' in that sense, but strong enough, characterized by defenses which are flexible enough, to regress to the selflessness of the first oral phase."[10] One is "strong enough" to facilitate what, from the standpoint of the neurotic, anx-iety-ridden ego is the ultimate weakness – the relaxation of the ego boundaries on the model of the subject's fearless passivity that Adorno advocates in "Subject and Object." A defence that is "flexible enough" does not merely negate what it defends itself from but is equally ca-pable of turning against itself when the purpose it serves calls for such drastic measures. It is this flexibility that prevents the libidinal reflux from lapsing into the sweet illusion of narcissism.

Celan's poetic movement, too, takes precautions in order not to fall into the snares of narcissism and egoism. First, it transfers the "topogra-phy" of regression from the terra firma of fixations onto the fluidity and uncertainty of the seas and the springs. Instead of the libidinal flows that burrow psychic territory, the new topography dictates a more suit-able metaphor of currents and counter-currents, of the powerful and immanent streams of water in water (in the style of Bataille's animal-ity), returning without repetition again *and* for the first time to the sign-posts of the promise unfixed, unfixated, rendered infinite.

The other lesson of Celan is that the locus of my regression is in the eyes of the other. Instead of a defensive "flight" of the libido into the ego[11] and its subsequent re-channelling into a therapeutic relationship where the other is nothing but a screen for my self-projections, regres-sion entrusts my inner world to the other, in whose eyes alone I am able to live. If "regression can be a holiday from ego boundaries which in itself strengthens the strong ego's capacity to control the drives,"[12] then it no longer needs to lead me ever deeper into my monadic seclusion. Better yet, when it does throw me into these unfathomable depths, it, thereby, hurls me outward, into the eyes of the other. This surprising move, already intimated in the second stanza of the poem, has nothing to do with the Hegelian constitution of intersubjectivity as the source of objectivity that surfaces when, watching myself being watched by the other, I contemplate myself from the standpoint of the other and discover what has been inaccessible to my eyes alone. Rather, in this place, "here," I find myself both outside the sphere of Oedipalization, or the sway of the superego, and on the hither side of primary narcissism:

> Here, as a heart
> that abode among humans,
> I throw off my clothes and the glare of an oath.

"Here": as if one arrived at the impossible end of regression that led Freud "constantly further backwards" until it became a direction[13] devoid of the final destination akin to Levinas's metaphysical desire: "here" the distance of regression inaugurates the heart's "abode among humans." The sojourn of the heart in the middle, among humans, is what allows them to become human in the first place, to "learn" their humanity in the distance, thanks to the *spacing* (neither purely spatial, nor purely temporal) that will remain untraversable, unlike any given segment of space or stretch of time. In this ineluctably excluded middle, the heart exists in the modality of a breathless aspiration to the other, between the moments of expiration and inspiration, psychic excrescence and involution. Yet the "here," to which the being-*there* of Dasein regresses, is not a place of respite and of a final homecoming. On the contrary, it is what instantiates the uncanny, *unheimlich* unrest of *pneuma* returning time and again "to the former *Heim* [home] of all human beings, to the place where each one of us lived once upon a time and in the beginning."[14] Once upon a time and in the beginning was the Word (which became flesh or, for Freud, the womb), but before the Word (that is, before the beginning) was the act of drawing a breath to pronounce it. Radical regression aspires to, without ever reaching, what was before the beginning, before Logos, just as the heart itself craves air, requires the dynamics of inspiration and expiration, in short, is in need of what it helps set in motion.

In this "here," in this almost animal immanence, I am de-Oedipalized as soon as "I throw off my clothes and the glare of an oath." The gesture of throwing off one's clothes is symbolic of the transgressive self-exposure and the loss of shame characteristic of regression in melancholia, for instance.[15] But perhaps more importantly, I dispose of "the glare of an oath," which is not the same as the promise that the sea holds. In contrast to the latter, the oath is a swearing in, an act of initiation into the incest taboo that performatively creates the superego and, more generally, militates against the singularity of the other in the very attempt to respond to him or her: "the 'pledge,' 'oath,' or 'vow,' the 'jure' of my responsibility for the singular other, and violation ('parjure,' 'perjury') of this vow for the sake of the third, are aporetically inscribed in one another, contaminating one another."[16] To take an oath of initiation into sociality, into a decent, civil, fully clad realm of the third is to forget the exclusive promise, the thoroughly indecent proposal given to the other ("I will do everything for you and much more, though never enough").

Conspiring against the promise, the oath is still marked in its very origin by what it conspires against, for it shines with a glare (*Glanz*) of borrowed light that does not emanate from it directly. This is the predicament of the mutual contamination of the vow and its violation described by Horowitz, and this is the point Freud misses when he reduces the other to the father. If I were to put it in Freudianese, I would say that in the course of preserving both the earliest object-choices of the id and reaction formations against these choices, the superego has to resort to the "borrowed strength" it has been borrowed from the father.[17] The borrowed strength of the superego is precisely that glow of paternal authority, which reduces all promises to sworn oaths of allegiance (to the flag, the country, the Queen, etc., as instantiations of the father). There is no longer an aporetic imbalance between the reflecting and the reflected, given that the borrowed strength of the superego is a direct emanation of the father's power. It is not enough simply to regress to the earliest object-choices, leaving reaction formations against them behind, in order to break the spell of Oedipal oath. We ought to remember that the id's object-choices are, themselves, maintained on the terms dictated by our debt to what prevents their satisfaction, to what does not permit the ego to become "strong enough" to let go of itself. The act of repaying this immense loan is nothing short of a messianic return to the promise of the sea that is more ancient than any oath, thanks to a shattering of the shell (of Oedipal subjectivity) that transmits a virtual echo of its waves.

The refusal of the oath's glare does not conceal my nakedness under the cover of darkness: "Blacker in black, am I more naked." "Blacker in black" harks back to the streams of water in water, to Edmund Jabès's "oblivion in oblivion" and "sky blue in blue sky,"[18] to the seas that left their imprints "in the springs of your eyes." Such is a denuding where, refractory to all light, whether it is reflected or not, I am unable to crawl into myself, to hide in the cave or the cavity of my body but am mercilessly exposed to exteriority through my skin, whose pores – it should be noted – breathe, regardless of any conscious regulation on my part. Yet the paradox of this spatial exposure pales in contrast to the reflux of "temporal regression" into the "timeless" unconscious: not temporally ordered or altered by the passage of time or having any reference to time.[19] What Freud identifies as a "special capacity for involution"[20] – the capacity of chronological time to recoil into the atemporal constitution of the unconscious – is a psychoanalytic reduction of clock-time or world-historical time to the lowest stratum of psychic time, which conditions and erases itself from these "objective" temporalities, becomes incomprehensible and atemporal from their standpoint. I refer to regression as "a psychoanalytic reduction," because it takes us back to the founding level of experience and temporality itself, to the unconscious spacing that immemorially temporalizes everything it contains, to the innermost domain of subjectivity that turns out to be superficiality and nudity themselves, to the most jealously guarded secret that there is no secret, to the deepest breath that expires all the faster.

The regressive concern, then, is pneumatically expressed in inspiration, if to regress is to turn "blacker in black" in an attempt to breathe in without breathing out. But on the same line, Celan's expiration ("am I more naked") already suggests that regressive inspiration faces a permeable barrier – my skin – that, through its pores, derails the desire to hold my breath, even before the capacity of my lungs runs out. The more I recoil into myself and veil this recoiling with the colour that does not reflect any light, the more assuredly I expose myself to the other. Finally, the comma, separating two parts of the sentence and drawing a barely visible line of demarcation between inspiration and expiration, functions as a syntactic representative of aspiration.

Another, still more stubborn desire to keep to the path of regression is expressed in the proclamation "Apostate only am I true." Devoid of any religious connotations, apostasy is literally "standing away," a still turning away from reality to the world of phantasy, and from "word-presentations" to "thing-presentations."[21] Thanks to this turning away, melancholic regression gives its sufferer "a keener eye for the truth,"[22] which, coupled with the lack of shame more "real" than the reality principle, supplements and perhaps becomes a part of the I's nakedness. Along with the clothes and the glare of an oath, language is swept aside as a cause of complications and untruths standing in the way of originary narcissism and the subject's reunification with its objects. For a melancholic, the truth of the I is unattainable through language because "we learn to speak the language of other people,"[23] who inevitably overdetermine and distort this truth. Yet we should not rush to tabulate the presumed wholesale abandonment of language in regression, along with the other artefacts that remain of the regressive search for immanence. If regression is, indeed, a vector of psychoanalytic reduction, then it undoes what is said in the empirical systems of signification to uncover the saying that animates them in the first place. In a Levinasian deduction, Horowitz writes, "The saying, signification itself, is prior to all signs … The said belongs to Being. The saying is otherwise than the said, otherwise than being, prior to being, and its condition."[24] It is only the said, not the saying, that is shed in regression; it is "only" being, not the otherwise-than-being that one declines in melancholia. The promise [*Versprechen*] of the sea that survives or, literally, outlives itself as an aspiration in the eyes of the other and glimpses distance *as* truth, is silent, regardless of its linguistic association with speech in general and with the slips of tongue in particular. It can be kept only in something like the pregnant silence of the secret, the unutterable saying in anticipation of speech.

If the first line of the third strophe confronts the involution of inspiration with the limit it finds in expiration, and the second line attempts to hold on to involution at all costs, then the third line – "I am you, if [*wenn*] I am I" – causes a permanent revolution both in the pneumatic motions of the subject and in the philosophy of German idealism. In this climactic line, at the heart of the poem, the praise of distance is enunciated through what I earlier referred to as the internal break with narcissism and egoism taken to their logical and psychological extremes. The wish to assert that "I am I," in my nakedness and truth, is symptomatic of an attempt to hold on to self-identity and self-sameness, leading the subject to the vertiginous depths of regression. In Celan's poetics, *if* this wish is finally granted, it generates a diametrically opposed effect, insofar as the I becomes the other outside of any psychotic breakdown. In fact, this can be read as a sign of what Horowitz calls *post-personal freedom from identity* that does not naively resist that from which it will be liberated from the outside but practises self-awareness "for the nonpurpose of observing and experiencing from moment to moment the process of self-construction, and in this way transcending that process."[25] Pneumatically, the deepest inspiration finds its limit and expires in the othering of identity that cannot be sustained as such. Logically and grammatically, the customary priority of this unsustainable identity is preceded by its othering (the line under scrutiny starts with "I am you ...").

In light of these observations, Freud's depiction of regression as a "long detour"[26] gains new significance, since the "detour" is now understood as the circuitous passage through the involution of the psyche to its othering. Interestingly enough, the psychoanalytic mechanics of regression mirror Celan's ingenious formulation: the movement of involution depends on the substitution of object-choice with identification, in which "the ego assumes the characteristics of the object."[27] But this analogy calls for a theoretical detour through a rethinking of identification that internally produces cracks and fissures in the edifice of identity, of its subtle approach to and transgression of various ontological thresholds, as well as of the effects it has on the stability of the subject and object alike.

On the first threshold, "Mourning and Melancholia" is concerned with the melancholic regression from object-choice to narcissistic identification with its return to orality and a mimetic incorporation of the lost object into the ego that "can consent to its own destruction."[28] While, conventionally, identification is taken to stand for the "saming of the other" integrated as an object into the psychical apparatus of the subject, the poetic refusal to thematize pneumatic concerns construes it as the "othering of the same." Freud himself leans on the second interpretation when he contends that "the shadow of the object" that falls upon the ego[29] overpowers it, such that the economy of the same is drastically and irreparably disrupted. Despite the melancholic desire of the ego to hold onto difference within the framework of identity, this framework collapses under the weight of the object's (weightless) shadow. Instead of reassuring the subject with the utterance, "I am you (the other), *when* I am I," as the English translation of Celan suggests, the melancholic ego is forced to chose the second sense of the German word *wenn* and to admit that "I am you (the other), *if* I am I." The "open wound"[30] of melancholia shamelessly exposes what is inside to the outside world and situates involution at its inherent limit ("if"), where the I, in all its finiteness, "is" unlimited as the other, for whom it expires. This explosive undermining of identity finds regression in "a no-place beyond power, where the grown-up child plays with identity" and is on the verge of experiencing "our fundamental nonidentity, our freedom from all power and any truth whatsoever."[31]

On the second threshold that regresses from the more radical meaning of regression, "Splitting of the Ego in the Process of Defense" may
be aligned more neatly with Celan's official English translation. Here
the child turns away from reality, but *"in the same breath"* he recognizes
the danger of reality … and tries subsequently to divest himself of the
fear."[32] The regressive involution yearning for the lost pleasure acknowledges reality negatively insofar as it rejects reality's unbearable
elements in the mode of disavowal; "in the same breath," inspiration
pretends to expire without expiring. What Freud diagnoses as "a rift
in the ego which never heals but which increases as time goes on"[33]
is a by-product of the internalization of distance betraying the promise with the temporal and spatial simultaneity of difference in identity
("I am you, *when* I am I"). This appropriation and, indeed, manipula-
tion of negativity, of reality's danger recognized and sent away with the
stamp of recognition, diverges from the melancholic resignation to the
internalized lost object. The splitting of the ego in the name of defence
disavows a part of identity only to perpetuate an endless asphyxiated
involution of the I into itself, doing away with reality in order to have
it. The "rift in the ego" is not the same as the opening of the melancholic
wound; on the contrary, it is a closure preventing the subject's excrescence, a cul-de-sac of knowing that one simply doesn't want to know
what one already, in some sense, knows. Although less daring and, indeed, more conservative than the first threshold of regression, the reap-
propriation of difference on the second threshold highlights a crucial
problem that has been overlooked in the revolutionary zeal of the first,
namely, the problem of surplus repression that nullifies the self-tran-
scendence of identity and stalls us forever *on the verge* of "experiencing
our fundamental non-identity."[34]

To return to the modification of the Celan translation, I believe that
it offers a concrete example of the kind of teaching that can take place
only in the encounter of singularities, when the indeterminate and dis-
carded content (e.g., the English rendition of *wenn*, the textual "value of
no value: singularity attributed to base matter")[35] becomes decisive for
the constitution of meaning on a different scale. Nor should we forget
the injunction of poetic analysis to learn how to interpret Freud, if it is
at all possible to interpret the father of interpretation, again *and* for the
first time. The re-conceptualization of identification as the othering of
the same through Celan's "I am you, if I am I" casts the identification
of the ego in terms of its "id-entification," which is the ego's becoming

other in its return to the *arche*, the id. What I transcribe as the id-entification of the ego *with*, or *in the company of*, its objects will acquire the meaning of the ego's becoming other *with* the very objects that provoke this becoming; it will transform the ego into a complex of transcendence in immanence, whose inside ceaselessly passes into the outside. We may now add another piece to the puzzle of the psychoanalytic reduction: like Husserl's phenomenology, it wants to reactivate the irreducible "origin" (in this case, the unconscious), but such awakening ineluctably spells out the becoming-other of whatever or whoever is founded on it, if not of the origin itself.

Consider, with Freud, "a small piece of regression" in a situation, where "instead of choosing her mother as a love-object, she [the patient] identified herself with her" and "she herself *became* her mother."[36] On this "small piece," on this singular moment, turns the entire othering of the patient's ego and of the "mother-object." The becoming he carefully italicizes has nothing to do with the ego's introjection or projection of the mother, but it has everything to do with a peculiar reanimation and alteration, an altered reanimation, of the *arche* and of the earliest phantasies of the id, where the I is transformed into its own parent, or the "you" in Celan's verse, on the hither side of the autonomy/ heteronomy dualism. At the same time, the you will not assume the features of yet another I, owing to the kind of id-entification that unfetters the ego from the ontological confines of either "being" or "having" the object and that allows it to become other along with its object (mother). It is thanks to this unfettering of the ego that "regression is ... a tremendous step *forward* in the history of civilization."[37] The *fort/da* dance of regression has begun!

If "I am you, if I am I," then identification itself can appear only in the guise of becoming-other. With this, we are transported back, we regress to the heart's "abode among humans," the breathless, albeit not asphyxiated, dwelling of the I in the distance of "your eyes," such that the *unheimlich* overtones of "here" recur in the *arche*'s awakening in the course of id-entification. And, in general, from this point on, the poem undergoes a process of involution expressed in its self-citation, as if poetic time recoils into itself and the ink runs back into the poet's pen, whose point leaves nothing but a white indentation on a white sheet of paper:

In the springs of your eyes
I drift on [*treib ich*] and dream of spoils.

The repetition of the first line in the aftermath of regression driven past its multiple thresholds gives way to the transgressive drive [*treib*] and the "dream of spoils." This transgression is reminiscent of the abandonment of the oath and the overcoming of shame in favour of the sea's promise. Perhaps the only difference one can still detect in the fold, on the crease of the poem is that the "I" in these lines is not the same "I" who played with the promise and the oath, because the process of regressive identification brought the subject out of itself, made it expire in the deepest of inspirations, unsettling any semblance of its self-identity.

But this difference makes all the difference. More specifically, it uncovers yet another register of regression: the register of instinct and its defusion. Freud's alternative explanation of regression hinges upon the "detachment of erotic components" or "the defusion of instinct," which is tantamount, simultaneously, to "a harking-back to the past" and to a "shrinking-back from life."[38] The excess of interiority carefully gathered and folded back into itself, the surplus of phantasy as a substitute for "unperformed actions,"[39] the immersion in the dream and in the past as a diversion from life – all of these psychical phenomena join forces to overprotect the ego, along with its idealizations, *to* death. (Note that I am not saying, "to overprotect the ego … *from* death.") The regressive itinerary of instinct runs parallel to the subjective track outlined above; just as the involution of the I internally opens up to the other, so does the "shrinking-back" of instinct lead inspiration to its absolute expiration in death, in the most undifferentiated state lacking all tension, for, as Levinas is fond of repeating in his proto-Heideggerian mood, death and the other appeal to us from the same region of transcendence.

In addition to the drive, however, the dream of spoils conjures up the following enigmatic lines:

A net snared a net:
embracing we sever.

The first line reveals as much as it conceals to the extent that it renders the answer to the question, "*Who or what* was ensnared?" absolutely undecidable. Does "A net snared a net" throw us back to my involution in the eyes of the other, the nets of the *Irrsee*, and the fact that I now inhabit the aquatic media of alterity qua the other? Or to a materialization of my instinctual dream to catch the other as "spoils"? Do we witness the subject's regression to the protective confines of the mother's womb?[40] Or its mothering of itself as other, as in the case of

Freud's "female patient"? Moreover, this indecision signalled by the entanglement of the nets is but a prelude to the emergence of a community, passing through the open-closed gates of the colon, after which we gain the dubious right to say "we": "embracing we sever." "We" – the I in the eyes of the other, the other (perhaps in the eyes of the I), and possibly another other in the eyes of the I, or of the other – this "we" of the infinite multitude of singularities comes together in separation and separates in coming together.

Promising distance without alienation, the non-totalizable community in severance engenders the hope for an other sociality, variously enunciated by Horowitz as a Levinasian "communism" or a Marcusean new reality principle characteristic of a civilization no longer based on *surplus*-repression. In both cases, it is a matter of regressing to a more progressive social arrangement, whether it is governed by the anarchic ethics as first philosophy, which cannot be transmogrified into liberal/social democracy and to which, in the last instance, all ontology is reducible, or by a dialectical recovery of "primitive matriarchy" that overthrows the performance principle.[41] It is this backward footwork that paves a way for the forward leap towards the other and towards the infinity of other others. A disjointure in the communal embrace indicates that the subject enters the process of mourning the loss of omnipotence that has never been, of learning something like the modesty of thinking, which is not to be conflated with Oedipal shame, and of curtailing the imperialism of being. What appears to be the first act of sociality, the embrace, is unfathomable without the a priori severance or radical separation of singularities – an image that contains, in a beautifully condensed poetic form, the entire problematic of a non-relational relation, of my excrescence indebted to a psychic involution, and of a decentred navel that remains in place of a non-existent umbilical cord. "Embracing we sever."

The fragility of this last locution threatens with two extreme catastrophic effects: a suffocating totalization of the unrelenting embrace and the absolute severance that has lost touch with the embrace and has irrevocably ruptured all sociality. The latter effect seems to conclude without concluding Celan's poem:

> In the springs of your eyes
> a hanged man strangles the rope.

"In the spring of your eyes" there are no more nets and no more I's. In the now unstoppable regressive reflux of poetic time, the net is undone into a rope, while the I is transformed into "a hanged man." The un-weaving of the net into the rope it was made of (but the rope itself must be woven!), the dissolution of form into matter, is the last stronghold of regression to the state of passivity and, ultimately, death.[42] Analo-gously, the final lines of the poem unfurl and tear apart the very textile of interpretation, whose weavers and spinners are asked to account for the extraordinary activity of the hanged man who "strangles the rope" and is left breathless without suffocating. These lines, finally, urge us to reconsider the equation of breathlessness with suffocation and to place finality in a dialogue with the "altered reanimation of the *arche*."

The activity of *ein Gehenkter* (the hanged man) is, of course, the first act in the game of *fort/da*, where the distancing expressed in the going away of the deceased (*Fortgehen*) comprises a "game quasi-complete unto itself."[43] "Quasi-complete" because, on the stage of psychoanaly-sis, after the completion of the first act, the audience always expects the second. With bated breath, its members await the joyful re-apparition of what was gone, precisely because the stakes of the play get too high and the play itself too serious, work-like after the spectators have iden-tified with this absence. Regression and psychical development, invo-lution and excrescence, cannot help but constantly come back to this game of disappearance and comeback, finding both their objects and their motivations in *fort/da*. Moreover, psychoanalysis has learned to ally itself – in the guise of a curtain-puller, to be sure – with and to learn from the regressive play of the past and the present, of reality and phantasy, of the death drive and the life drive, and of the stages (more theatrical and performative than developmental) that are now *fort* and now *da*. "This regressive direction became an important characteristic of analysis. It appeared that psycho-analysis could explain nothing be-longing to the present without referring back to something past."[44]

Thus, *ein Gehenkter* is gone, the curtain is drawn, and the experience is past. And yet one can expect a comeback, first of all because the rope remains in the curtain-puller's hand, because the same string makes the spool go away and come back.[45] Still, because of its incorrigible ide-alism, psychoanalysis cannot rid itself of the compulsion to master its own objects of counter-transferential desire. In their work of mourn-ing, Sigmund and Ernst, the grandfather and the grandson, are playing the same game of a wilful annihilation and recreation of their love-objects, sending them off and making them reappear again. But the real play, one that happens wholly beyond the performance principle, be-gins only when the hanged man's breathlessness ceases to signify the finality of the last breath, that is to say, only in the internal breach of the subject's monadological closure in itself, the othering of identity, and the reanimation of the *arche* that permits me to say, "I am you, if I am I." What makes the uncanny *da* of the hanged man strangling the rope plausible is the enabling failure of involution that delivers me to my becoming-other "in your eyes." Without this delivery (if not "deliverance"), the death of the merely self-identical subject would have been the poem's tragic and trivial finale. Conversely, the very possibility of pure death is precluded if I am and am not you, if I outlive my demise as I drift on in the eyes of the other and of the other's other … disseminated in a non-totalizable community. Foregoing psychoanalytic mastery, *ein Gehenkter* returns, the curtain is raised again, and the experience is restaged in a different mode altogether, namely, in the mode of reparation.

At this point, I forewarn the reader that she should not expect the event of a glorious resurrection, nor anticipate a dramatic climax. The return of the hanged man is the kind of Derridian "messianicity without messianism" that is appropriate to the mundane irreality of regression. Attuned to what is incomparably more insignificant than the grand messianic *Tikkun* that unifies judgment and love, *Din va'Hesed*, Horowitz recognizes, in his argument against liberal appropriations of Derrida and Levinas, the singularity that often passes below the radar of a maximalist attitude coldly indifferent to the specificities of historical embeddedness: "And the Kabbalist texts … frequently indicate exquisite sensitivity to the possibilities of degrees of tikkun – of fundamental transformations short of perfect Tikkun – *possible* Messiahs."[46] The poetic reanimation of the hanged man is, therefore, a lower degree of tikkun devoid of any effect in the "real world." It is an exercise of what Benjamin famously calls "weak Messianic power," whose frailty is due to its ineffectiveness in the order of actuality (as opposed to the realm of possibility), if not due to its limited scope that hinges on a secularized redemption of the past by the current "generation."

Melanie Klein's notion of reparation, too, does not produce a change in "what has already occurred."[47] Instead of miraculously resurrecting the hanged man, it initiates a phantastic and phantasmagoric restaging of the past seen through the lens of "commemoration of that initial loss [of original difference] *as loss*."[48] In a literal and purposefully naive reading, the task of reparation, of mending, of placing a patch on the most vulnerable spot where the fabric is at its thinnest is not a part of the formal economic circuitry of value, but a singular, often gendered and classed, act of mourning the thing's past. The knitting thread – a very fine rope – facilitates this commemoration of depleted use at home, without any monetary recompense. Instead of discarding an old thing (such as a piece of clothing) nearing the end of its rope, those who sew a patch and repair it impel it into a phase of its afterlife, into an era of use beyond the confines of a properly economic life that takes into account only the calculus of value's depreciation. In the same way, breaking with the idea of dying as a depreciation of life, the *fort* of death regressively supplements the *da* of life, which is always a survival, a surplus of life above its actual "value," and a mourning of the pre-originary difference in the afterlife. In the involutions of afterlife the rope's end and the end of the rope are reached in a non-proprietary commemorative gesture, in a recommencement of the *fort/da* game that will throw, and catch, and pull, and strangle, and unfurl, and reassemble this end.

* * *

In the beginning of "On the History of the Psycho-Analytic Movement," Freud chides the analysts who wish to evade the problem of regression and unambiguously proclaims that "scientific regression is represented by the neglect of regression in analytic technique."[49] But the father of psychoanalysis himself exhibits a rather strange attitude to this psychical phenomenon. He tends to confine it to parentheses, isolates it from the rest of the text, mentions it without mentioning it, and treats it only in passing.[50] Perhaps, in these textual practices, Freud plays his favourite game of *fort/da* with the *fort/da* of regression, or perhaps, he utilizes a consistent inscriptive defence against it. If the "weak" power of a poetic reading is not capable of sorting these hypotheses out, it can (nonetheless) bring to bear the otherwise imperceptible pneumatic concerns of psychoanalysis with the regressive inspiration/involution, with the excrescence of psychical development, with the way the former passes into the latter through the relation to the other, with the rhythmic dynamism of breathing as a return, with the deepest inspiration that internally opens up to exteriority, with the transcendence of the last breath's finality, and so on. If the force of psychoanalysis as such is insufficient for the interpretation of a poem, it can (nonetheless) provide us with a unique access to a dimension of poetic sensibility, for which the difference between a promise and an oath grows into an abyss, for which the relation between the I and the you inverts the classical philosophical principles, for which beginnings and ends shed their absoluteness and finality. What, then, transpires between these singular knowledges, if not a desire to mend and to patch – without ever sealing – the untraversable distance that separates them, the desire that marks the teaching?

NOTES

1 Shoshana Felman, "Psychoanalysis and Education: Teaching Terminable and Interminable," in *Yale French Studies, The Pedagogical Imperative: Teaching as a Literary Genre* 63 (1982): 31.
2 Gad Horowitz, "Bringing Bataille to Justice," *Public* 37 (2008): 138–43.
3 I deposit a trace of my recent conversation with Gad Horowitz here.
4 Quoted in Andrew Benjamin, *Philosophy's Literature* (Manchester, UK: Clinamen, 2001), 151.
5 Paul Celan, "Praise of Distance," in *Selected Poems and Prose of Paul Celan*, ed. and trans. by J. Felstiner (New York and London: W.W. Norton, 2001), 24–5.
6 Gad Horowitz, "Aporia and Messiah in Derrida and Levinas," in *Difficult Justice*, ed. G. Horowitz and A. Horowitz (Toronto: University of Toronto Press, 2006), 308.
7 Sigmund Freud, "An Autobiographical Study," in *The Freud Reader*, ed. P. Gay (New York: W.W. Norton, 1995), 22.
8 Sigmund Freud, *Five Lectures on Psychoanalysis* (New York: W.W. Norton, 1977), 55.
9 Sigmund Freud, *On Metapsychology: The Theory of Psychoanalysis* (New York: Penguin Books, 1991), 230.
10 Gad Horowitz, *Repression: Basic and Surplus Repression in Psychoanalytic Theory; Freud, Reich and Marcuse* (Toronto: University of Toronto Press, 1977), 204.
11 Freud, *Metapsychology*, 267.
12 Horowitz, *Repression*, 208–9.
13 Sigmund Freud, "On the History of the Psycho-Analytic Movement," in *The Standard Edition of the Complete Psychological Works of Sigmund Freud* (*SE*), ed. J. Strachey (London: Hogarth, 1957), 14:10.
14 Sigmund Freud, "The 'Uncanny,'" in *The German Library: Psychological Writings and Letters*, ed. Sander Gilman (New York: Continuum, 1995), 146.
15 Freud, *Metapsychology*, 256.
16 Horowitz, "Aporia," 311.
17 Freud, *Metapsychology*, 374.
18 Edmund Jabès, *The Book of Resemblances II: Intimations; The Desert*, trans. Rosemarie Waldrop (Hanover: University Press of New England, 1991), 26.

19 Freud, *Metapsychology*, 191.
20 Freud, "Thoughts for the Times of War and Death," *SE* 14:286.
21 Freud, *Metapsychology*, 235.
22 Ibid., 255.
23 Ibid., 218.
24 Horowitz, "Bringing Bataille to Justice."
25 Gad Horowitz, "The Foucaultian Impasse: No Sex, No Self, No Revolution," *Political Theory* 15, no. 1 (February 1987): 77.
26 Freud, "On the History of the Psycho-Analytic Movement," 10.
27 Sigmund Freud, *Group Psychology and the Analysis of the Ego* (New York: W.W. Norton, 1959), 48–9.
28 Freud, *Metapsychology*, 261.
29 Ibid., 258.
30 Ibid., 262.
31 Horowitz, "Foucaultian Impasse," 78.
32 Freud, *Metapsychology*, 461–2, my emphasis.
33 Ibid., 462.
34 Horowitz, "Foucaultian Impasse," 78.
35 Horowitz, "Bringing Bataille to Justice."
36 Sigmund Freud, "A Case of Paranoia Running Counter to the Psychoanalytic Theory of the Disease," *SE* 14:269.
37 Horowitz, *Repression*, 181.
38 Sigmund Freud, "From the History of an Infantile Neurosis," *SE* 17:53.
39 Ibid.
40 Sigmund Freud, "Inhibitions, Symptoms and Anxiety," *SE* 20:127.
41 Horowitz, "Aporia," 312; Horowitz, *Repression*, 182.
42 Freud, "Inhibitions, Symptoms and Anxiety," *SE* 20:114.
43 Jacques Derrida, *The Post Card: From Socrates to Freud and Beyond*, trans. A. Bass (Chicago: University of Chicago Press, 1987), 325.
44 Freud, "On the History of the Psycho-Analytic Movement," 10.
45 Derrida, *Post Card*, 321.
46 Horowitz, "Aporia," 316.
47 Deborah Britzman, *After-Education: Anna Freud, Melanie Klein, and Psychoanalytic Histories of Learning* (New York: SUNY, 2003), 168.
48 Gayatri C. Spivak, *A Critique of Postcolonial Reason: Toward a History of the Vanishing Present* (Cambridge, MA: Harvard University Press, 1999), 198, emphasis in the original.
49 Freud, "On the History of the Psycho-Analytic Movement," 11.
50 Freud, "Autobiographical Study," 22; Freud, *Five Lecturess*, 49; and Freud, *Metapsychology*, 80. This is but a small sample of the much larger pool of Freud's unique inscription of regression.

10 The Sexed Body of the Woman-(M)Other: Irigaray and Marcuse on the Intersection of Gender and Ethical Intersubjectivity

VICTORIA TAHMASEBI

According to Luce Irigaray, in traditional Western philosophical and psychoanalytical discourses the relation between the mother and the child is an object relation. In psychoanalysis, the mother is the child's first object or partial object and never a social subject; she represents the nature side of the nature/culture dichotomy, the side that has to be sacrificed for the child's successful entry into the symbolic order. The maternal body, as the site of the natural, signifies what is sublime, all-powerful, and so is always a threat to the life of the social subject. To put it differently, the discursive association of the maternal body with the death instinct requires that to escape the abyss of death and to enter the social, the child must at the same time escape the maternal body. To overcome its threat, the child has to disavow the maternal body and form an ego through the process of separation.[1] For Irigaray, this traditional characterization of the maternal body has always made a taboo of the time spent in the mother's womb and accordingly has made no attempt to come to terms with the losses and scars involved in the separation from that original home and that primary caregiver. The abandonment of the maternal body to the pre-social has created nostalgia for that primal unity, which in turn has only caused violence to the mother. For this reason, within phallocratic discourse, the debt to the mother is expressed either by a nostalgic yearning and desire that is never fulfilled or an immediate flight to an infinite, disembodied transcendental.

In her rereading of traditional Western texts, Irigaray offers an eloquent illustration of her argument. She returns to Plato's allegory of the cave and explores the way in which subjectivity is constituted. She focuses on *antre*, the cave's inner space (corridor, neck, conduit), rather than the sun, to work through Plato's metaphor.[2] In Plato's representation of the cave, Irigaray deconstructs the age-old representation of the earth-nature-womb-mother as a disposable container that must be disavowed. Platonic representation tries to detach the subject, the man in the cave, from the earth-womb, pushing him forward towards the sun, since the cave represents only the shadow of the truth. Likewise, shadows on the wall cannot be the truth, since there is a multiplicity of shadows. Truth can only assume a singular form; it is always one, or one is always the truth. And so the subject is always unified rather than differentiated.

In Platonic imaginary, the sun is the anchor of origin, yet its own disembodiment speaks to the transcendental quality of knowledge, setting a hierarchy and a binary distinction between the intelligible world of the forms and the realm of the sensory. This dichotomy, as Irigaray argues, is a crucial dividing point between the masculine subject and the feminine object in Western discourse. This is the reason why in Platonic representation, she argues, vision and sight are privileged over all other senses. The knowledge of the eye, seeing and being seen, is synonymous with knowledge and truth. Marcuse presents a similar argument when he discusses Plato's project. Plato, according to Marcuse, breaks the alliance between Logos and Eros, resulting in the dominance of Logos. What emerges is a scientific rationality based on general laws of abstract forms. Marcuse points out that "true knowledge and reason demand domination over – if not liberation from – the senses."[3] Both Irigaray and Marcuse, then, bring into focus the disembodied nature of Western knowledge and the dichotomizing process through which the Western subjectivity is produced.

If the structure of Western discourse is one of the predominance of the visual and of solid forms with fixed boundaries, then the woman-mother is marked by indefinability from the outset. In a discourse that claims to define everything, the woman-mother lacks a proper Form. Her body represents "the repellence of matter, the horror of blood, the ambivalence of milk."[4] The woman-mother's body affirms the incompleteness of any form and hence is the limit of all representation. This body is represented and representable only as the negative, the reverse of the only visible and definable organ: the penis.[5] Similarly, her sexual organ represents the "horror of nothing to see";[6] since it is neither one nor two, it is counted as none. This organ has nothing to show of itself; it simply represents a lack or a hole – like Plato's cave – and as such has to be excluded from the scene of representation. This hole is what we have left behind us in our coming to the world; it acts as a fissure that Western discourse, ever since, has tried to close up through the phallocratic economy of solids.[7]

What Irigaray calls the phallocratic economy of solids connotes the metaphoric substitution of one solid or form for another. Unlike metonymy, which is based on contiguity, connoting fluidity, touching, and formlessness, metaphor is based on the logic of mutual exclusion; one object is always substituted for another. The maternal body is forever excluded from the symbolic social, with no access to discourse except through the phallic system of representation, which is based on solid mechanics.[8] For Irigaray, the symbolic phallus exhibits a profound tendency to privilege rational, abstract form over other senses. As a result, the subject's resignation to the law of the father is, by its definition, the triumph of the solid over the fluid, and of the principle of constancy over contiguity; it is the triumph of rationality.

Yet Irigaray does not attempt to explore why such a pre-eminence has been historically allocated to the solid. Or, beside its circulation among competing discourses, what ensures the maintenance of this economy? One viable answer lies within Marcuse's analysis of the circuit of market economy. Marcuse contends that market economy needs a closed cycle of production and reproduction of goods and services, or signs and symbols, in which reification and commodification are generated. He points out that "technological rationality reveals its political character as it becomes the great vehicle of better domination, creating a truly totalitarian universe in which society and nature, mind and body are kept in a state of permanent mobilization for the defence of this universe."[9] Therefore, Marcuse's elaboration on Marx's concepts of commodity, value, and exchange illustrates that, under capitalism, not only the economy but also social relations are governed by commodity and exchange relations.

This economy, in turn, can thrive only upon a solidified, reified psychic structure wherein human beings – sometimes as a whole entity but mostly as fragmented pieces – are transformed into things. The exchange of commodities can best operate on a system of symbolization that grants precedence to total forms; as such, it can define, control, and predict the movement and circulation of products within the cycle of production and reproduction. Effectively, not only does the coordination of the cycle become more manageable, but also the recycling and redistributing of these commodities can be best organized.

In addition, the rationale behind the cycle of perpetual production and consumption is the fact of scarcity, according to which, for human needs to be satisfied, pleasure must always be delayed, constrained, and mediated by work; the pleasure principle is therefore irreconcilable with reality and so must be repressed. Marcuse suggests that in societies geared towards domination, a specific kind of scarcity operates. This historically specific organization of scarcity is based on a hierarchical distribution of scarcity that is not in accordance with individual needs. In such a society, the kinds of goods produced do not necessarily satisfy libidinal needs; rather, the system of production, distribution, and consumption is geared towards maintaining domination, which is bound up with and guided by the interest of particular social groups. In order to sustain its privileged position and to have a lesser share of pain and greater share of gain (in economic, social, and psycho-emotional terms), this minority needs to preserve the irrational surplus scarcity, want and constraint. In other words, we are dealing with a psychosocial arrangement in which both pain and gain are unequally distributed among its members.[10]

But the question still remains. Why it is that this irrational surplus scarcity continues to hold sway upon social subjects, authenticizing itself, each and every time, as an absolute necessity. Marcuse does not adequately attend to this question, but Irigaray's intervention and her gender analysis can deepen our understanding of the survival mechanism of this cycle. Part of the answer may lie in the ways in which goods are produced partially in response to libidinal needs for the satisfaction of the pleasure-seeking drives. In other words, surplus scarcity must rely on some kind of infrastructure to legitimize its existence, and to nourish and renew its cycle. The circulation of the woman-mother, as scarce commodity, has a pivotal role in the maintenance of the cycle of production and reproduction. Although phallic existence manifests itself through culture, language, and technology, which are set up and dichotomized against nature and bodily reality, the phallic subject is still corporeal and so needs a link to nature and bodily unity. The woman-mother acts as the male's body, as an infrastructure or vital link to the pre-social. The woman-mother's body, although it remains in the periphery of the social, is essential to the life of the social insofar as it provides the infrastructure for its maintenance and continuity; it nourishes all social/psychic foundations while it is itself forcibly silenced. In this way, the woman-mother's body functions as a scarce

commodity subject to the law of exchange through which it is circulated among male subjects, both textually and materially.[11] In this context, the woman-mother in the guise of mother-wife-prostitute becomes
important in the economy of scarce commodities.[12]

For this economy of scarce commodities, Marcuse coins the term "repressive desublimation of the pleasure principle,"[13] to describe a situation wherein the release of the pleasure principle and its derivatives
still remains within, and as a result intensifies, the regime of commodity exchange. He suggests that in order to have "free sublimation," the
release of the libidinal drives must be accompanied by a transformation
of the pleasure principle from mere sexuality into re-eroticization of
the entire personality.[14] What makes Irigaray's insight relevant to Marcuse's discussion is that one of the prerequisites of realizing Marcuse's
re-eroticization is the undoing of the figure of the woman-mother as a
scarce commodity. Therefore, in pursuing this relation between Irigaray's and Marcuse's critical insights, it is possible to see the close affinity between phallic desire – as what is unfulfillable – and the psychic
structure of consumer society, which Marcuse so rigorously criticizes.
The intersection of Irigaray's feminist critique and Marcuse's criticism
of consumer society can account not only for the interplay of gender,
market economy, and subjectivity, but also, and perhaps more crucially,
for their mutual constitution.

For both Irigaray and Marcuse, the cycle of production and reproduction constantly produces its own excesses; this residue is what remains
after all attempts have been made to construct absolute transcendental form. Yet whereas for Marcuse this excess takes a non-gendered
utopian dimension,[15] for Irigaray, the excess is feminine sex. Irigaray
maintains that it is distinctively the woman-mother who embodies the
reminiscence of what is irrational. Irigaray's deconstruction of Lacanian psychoanalysis attempts to demonstrate that Lacan's lack is precisely the woman-mother body, which is always either a lack within
the social or an excess outside the social. In other words, the woman-
mother is that fluid that always remains at the periphery of the economy – as reproduction – and the discourse – as senses. So, Irigaray
claims, the woman-mother's body is that excessive signification, which
always means more than it may be taken to mean in any context. This
remainder, this fluid that resists symbolization, keeps returning in various forms to disrupt the phallic discourse with the promise of, if not liberty, at least utopian fantasies. For both Irigaray and Marcuse, this is the

return of the repressed; it manifests itself in the form of hysteria for the former and in utopian fantasies and liberatory impulses for the latter.

For Marcuse, this excess is the outcome of a clash between what claims to be inside the social and what is forcibly left outside. For him, the subject's ambivalence towards the maternal body is intrinsically interconnected with the historical modulations of pleasure and reality principles. Although repression seems to be a necessary component of human social existence, Marcuse argues that what he calls "surplus repression,"[16] or the excessive repressive methods used by civilization, is a historically specific phenomenon used by a civilization, which progresses through organized domination, so that the antagonistic conflict between the pleasure principle and the reality principle is a socio-historic conflict. Since Marcuse locates the development of these two principles in a socio-historical context, the interplay of these two forces is also subject to social conditioning, and so, open to contestation. This is the reason why Marcuse suggests that the enforced submission of the pleasure principle to the reality principle is never complete, secured, or finalized. In fact, the rule of the reality principle has to be continuously reproduced and intensified in multifaceted forms. For Marcuse, the prevailing unhappiness and misery of civilized individuals indicates that the pleasure principle is not once-and-for-all defeated and that, to some degree, it still retains its active existence. The libidinal drives that strive for gratification still express themselves in the realm of fantasy, which reproduces and recalls images of integral freedom, of yearning to break free from social constraint. The ongoing work of the reality principle to overcome and smooth over contradictions and conflict within the libidinal structure is the source of constant tension between the pleasure and the reality principles. In order to resolve this tension, the reality principle must constantly reproduce new forms and methods of domination, repression, and subjugation to maintain its control over the bodies of its subjects. The pleasure principle, although it is relegated to the pre-social and allowed to manifest itself only under the tyranny of the performance principle, constantly reproduces new forms of liberatory imagination, images of freedom, and collective and individual erotic possibilities, only to repress them all over again. Thus for Marcuse, the pleasure principle, with its derivatives, manifests itself as a regenerating process whose aim is freedom from repression; as a result, the pleasure principle, of all mental structures, is least susceptible to domination.

In contrast, for Irigaray, the liberatory impulses of the pleasure principle can be sought only within the morphology of the woman-mother's body. The woman-mother's body participates in a metonymy of pleasure, which, unlike the logic of metaphor, is not based on substitution: "the pleasure of vaginal caress does not have to be substituted for that of the clitoral caress";[17] this body is multiple, diffuse, and in continuous touch. Phallocratic discourse, which is based on a rigid rationality of foreclosed boundaries, runs against the fluid reality of women's corporeal existence. So, for Irigaray, the woman-mother's body speaks to a metonymy of fluids that do not replace each other; rather, they run into each other, caress and touch one another; this body manifests itself in "milk, luminous flow, acoustic waves, ... gasses inhaled, emitted, ... of urine, saliva, blood, even plasma."[18]

The beautiful imagery that Irigaray invokes is an attempt to imagine a different, non-phallic subject space. Irigaray depicts a woman-mother's body that is already two; unlike the phallocentric body, which must touch himself through an instrument, be it his hand, a woman's body, or a disembodied knowledge, the woman-mother and her body do not need mediation. She touches herself, for "her genitals are formed of two lips in continuous contact."[19] In other words, the woman-mother's body is pregnant, charged, and plural from within. Irigaray seeks to open a radical space that blurs the line between what gives and what takes; a subjective dimension that may undermine phallic subjectivity.

Irigaray's criticism of phallic subjectivity stops just short of articulating how this subjectivity came to be. More than this, Irigaray's model does not think through how it is that gendered subjects – males and females – establish different relations with the other; instead, she only states it as an a priori fact. In other words, Irigaray does not locate the development of the gendered subject within socio-historical processes. What this means is that insofar as the phallic subject only ever embodies the male subject, Irigaray's model is based on an essentialist foundation. Irigaray's reliance on morphological embodiment as the indicator of subjectivity deprives her model of the ability to imagine multivariant forms of engendering, or of subjectification. While this problem of essentialization (to which I will return later) runs throughout Irigaray's conceptualization, one of its implications is crucial here: within Irigaray's model, there is no process of gendering; rather, a gendered body, and its a priori sexual specificity, exists even before the subject unfolds within its specific historical, social, psychological terrain. As a result, the subject emerges, not as an open-ended process, but rather as a finished product, either male or female. Therefore, ultimately, Irigaray's model, I argue, is the other side of theories that insist on the autonomous essence of the subject. Without a socio-historical account of subjectification, Irigaray's model is unable to overcome its essentialist foundation.

Like Irigaray, Marcuse is interested in the figure of the mother both in terms of decentring the patriarchal reality principle and, or as a result, undoing the logic of the subjectivity that reduces the other to the same. However, in his approach, any return to the maternal body that aims to challenge phallic subjectivity must address two problems. Broadly speaking, first it must give an account of why the memory of infantile gratification, which is rooted in intimate relation to the maternal body, encounters such a hostile and excessive defence mechanism. Second, it must account for the socio-historical dynamics that make subjectivity tend towards reducing the other to the same. As such, it is not the morphology of the maternal body, per se, that provides a rapture within the patriarchal reality principle. Rather, it is the relationship that the subject conceives between itself and that pre-Oedipal, pre-genital memory of being one with the maternal body. It is only through reconceptualizing this relation that a space can be opened for the constitution of a non-instrumental, non-antagonistic subjectivity.

One implication of Marcuse's model for Irigaray's is that since Marcuse's subject is grounded within the social and not within its own morphology, remembering the maternal body becomes a social practice rather than a metaphysical reality; in other words, how and who remembers is more pressing than what there is to remember. Although for Marcuse, like Irigaray, the liberatory vision is grounded in remembering the maternal body, remembering, as a social and interpretive act, is not a transparent activity; in Marcuse's model, therefore, remembering is always mediated by the social and so is problematized.

It is important to note that Marcuse's critique of Western subject formation rests on a concept he coins as "repressive sublimation." Sublimation, according to Marcuse, has not only psychic but also social content, so that sublimation under domination is towards intensified domination and not towards free gratification of libidinal needs. Insofar as sublimated activities are at the service of domination and alienated labour, they constrain pleasure and enforce superfluous abstinence; in other words, they involve surplus rather than basic repression.

Gad Horowitz, in his book entitled *Repression*,[20] gives a definitive formulation to these two forms of repression. For if basic repression, restraining and constraining the libido, is necessary for human growth, surplus repression, on the other hand, is unnecessary and the by-product of domination and exploitation. Horowitz's argument demonstrates that sublimation under the condition of surplus repression leads to an illusion of freedom while the chains are still everywhere. A subjectivity that unfolds in and through surplus repression can only remember what Irigaray calls "the phallic mother" – the maternal body as an omnipotent container. Consequently, repressive sublimation is always effected through the renunciation and the condemnation of the pleasure principle so that guilt functions to enforce modifications.[21] Under the reality principle, the above processes make sublimation a tool of oppression rather than an internal mechanism through which libidinal drives extend themselves to the outer world.

For that reason, Marcuse regards the incapability of the subject to imagine or remember the maternal body in any other way as closely tied to the socio-historical processes of repression and domination. For Irigaray, this incapability does not seem to beg a socio-historical explanation, since it is rooted within the morphology of the male body. So, insofar as the practice of remembering unfolds within a subjectivity that itself operates within social and historical parameters, it needs to be examined rather than taken as an immediate, transparent act.

Irigaray's conviction that there is an inherent non-reciprocity between the maternal body and the male subject stems from her essentialist approach to the libidinal drives. According to Irigaray, the underlying pre-Oedipal edifice of culture accounts for the different self-positioning of men and women. For both Freud and Lacan, she argues, libido is always masculine,[22] and "I" usually refers to masculine identity. On a deeper level, the structure of phallocratic discourse is organized to allow for the imaginary only as it pertains to the symbolic father-phallus. For Irigaray, in contrast, there is not one but two separate libidinal economies even before the Oedipal situation. So the gendered subject, Irigaray maintains, exists before any symbolic distinction between feminine and masculine; in other words, there is a fundamental asymmetry of the two sexes based on their morphology.

The implication of this theoretical framework is Irigaray's own suggestion that there are two absolutely irreducible sexual universals, each with its own authentic difference, separate origin, and morphological specificity. Irigaray argues that "the natural is at least two: male and female.... In order to go beyond – assuming this is necessary – we should make reality the point of departure: it is two."[23] Therefore, within the

Irigaray's pre-Oedipal gendered economy, sexual difference is independent of its constitutive relationship to the other. So, unlike Marcuse's
conception of Eros as sexually undifferentiated, in Irigaray's articulation, Eros manifests itself in human embodiment and so is always preceded by a sexual differentiation that hinges upon the morphology of
the body; this autonomous sexual essence, these two separate natures,
are the foundation of Irigaray's theory of gender.

Irigaray's origin, I argue, is an inverted form of a heterosexual model,
since it is based on opposition and on an assumption that women's,
or men's, relationships with their bodies/sexes are immediate and
transparent. Irigaray may be able to tell us how and why women are
oppressed, but her model cannot adequately respond to the problem
that many women are oppressed by having to be a "woman." If what
we start with is already a female and a male, then we are not setting
up difference but rather dichotomy, since it is only through the sexual
specificity of the one that we can outline the specificity of the other.
Ultimately, Irigaray's insistence on irreducible gender difference forecloses the possibility of imagining gender in any other way and, as a
result, reaffirms the present-day status of heterosexuality.

Contrary to Irigaray, for Marcuse, if sexual drives have an origin,
it is a polymorphous, undifferentiated, pre-genital sexuality. Following Freud, Marcuse argues that sexuality from the beginning is "poly-
morphous-perverse":[24] the body in its entirety is the object of cathexis.
In other words, pleasure can be derived from a variety of erotogenic
zones. Further, sexuality, in both its object choice and aim, is diffuse
and open to multiple configurations. It is only after the reality principle
takes hold that gendered libidinal economies, and their separation into
two separate universes, appear. And it is precisely the polymorphous
structure of sexuality that is not tolerated by the project of domination;
however, as socialized bodies become ghettoized and contained within
two separate economies, the organization of libidinal energy is increasingly manageable. This process is simultaneously accompanied by a
de-sexualization of the body, so that partial sex instincts and pre-genital
sexual drives are transformed into the primacy of genital sexuality. In
turn, the social body is required to renounce a range of polymorphous
pleasures in order to participate in a social life based on genital supremacy and reproductive sexuality. Consequently, this organization of
adult sexuality in the service of reproduction frees the rest of the body
to be utilized in the realm of necessity, under the logic of instrumental
rationality.

The primacy of genital intercourse excludes the rest of the body from the flow of libidinal instincts and so forcibly compartmentalizes the human body for other uses – mainly for alienated labour. As Gad Horowitz succinctly puts it, "'normal' psychosexuality is the product of surplus repression";[25] it conditions hetero-normative gender boundaries. Horowitz's formulation allows us to immediately decipher the ways in which the process of non-gratifying, alienated labour (read "surplus repression") requires that the human body be perpetually desexualized, yet not de-gendered. In other words, for individuals to be instruments of labour and to be productive, most of their sexual energy has to be repressively sublimated.[26] The result of subjugating polymorphous sexual instincts to the function of procreation is the almost complete transformation of sexuality from an autonomous principle into a means to an end, a technical skill, a specialized tool for a specific goal. According to Marcuse, this condition is critical for the performance principle to congeal, since the restriction and confinement of libidinal relations make the human organism the subject-object of socially useful performances and roles. The human body, becoming the subject of sets of instrumental performances, contributes to the perpetuation of domination.

Consequently, under the rule of two distinct libidinal economies geared towards genital supremacy, sex and social utility become one and the same, and the critical distance between erotic reality and the social given is eliminated. In other words, the fundamental antagonism between sex and domination is blurred so that even liberated sexuality itself coincides with profitable conformity. As Marcuse puts it, "In their erotic relations, they keep their appointments with charm, with romance, with their favourite commercials."[27]

The de-sexualization of the body and the negation of the original desire for the maternal body are therefore central to the project of domination and alienated labour. If humans are to be subjected to the project of mastery over nature and other humans, and of transforming their bodies into instruments of labour, then the desire for separation must be the ontological core of subjectification. The result is that the maternal body and the "perverted," pre-genital sexuality, insofar as they halt civilization's progress and growing productivity, symbolize the ultimate identity of life and death instincts or the submission of life to death.[28] For this reason, Marcuse, unlike Irigaray, maps the development of libidinal economies within socio-historical contexts, grounding the male subject's desire to disavow the maternal body not in his morphological specificity, but rather in the requirements of patriarchal, instrumental, social order. It is within this context that Marcuse's formulation of sexually undifferentiated libido far surpasses Irigaray's model of two separate and innate libidinal economies, since Marcuse's theory not only allows for a multiplicity of gender formation but also carries within itself the possibility of imagining another ontological relation to reality.

Therefore, Marcuse states, in order to reinstate the critical distance, and the tension, between the actual and the possible erotic future, in order to imagine a new reality principle, and finally, in order for sex instincts to be able to generate lasting erotic relations, all erotogenic zones must be reactivated, and pre-genital polymorphous sexuality must re-emerge. This is not possible unless the channelling of sexuality into monogamous reproduction, the primacy of genital sexuality, and the taboo on sexual "perversions" can be undone. If, for Irigaray, re-eroticization means a symbolic return to the specificity of sexual bodies, for Marcuse it entails a non-repressive regression and a dialectical return to undifferentiated, diffused, and polymorphous Eros. Such an Eros would require a regressive leap in human civilization, a dialectical regression that would revive yet transcend early stages of libidinal sexuality, by returning to a point before the mystifying forms of the given.

Marcuse agues that, although under a non-repressive social arrangement, re-sexualization of the body can ultimately grow to re-eroticize all of human existence, Eros signifies not only a quantitative but also a qualitative enlargement of sexuality. According to Marcuse, Eros enlarges the sexual instincts so that the objective of the instincts becomes neither just one specific other, nor exclusively the desire for bodily gratification, but rather the establishment of a non-antagonistic, receptive relationship with living organisms in their entirety. In this sense, Eros, unlike sexuality, need neither inhibit its aim nor change its direction; as Marcuse puts it, "The modifications of sexuality are not the same as the modifications of Eros."[29] Marcuse's argument seems to indicate that, in fact, the whole point of the re-eroticization is to remove the repressive measures that stop the flow of erotic feelings from expanding into the organism's whole life. Unlike Eros, sexual energies in many instances are still aim-inhibited and so their sublimation requires repressive measure, but again, these restraints originate in the order of gratification and so they constitute basic rather than surplus repression; in other words, this process is non-repressive sublimation.[30]

Marcuse makes two major points concerning non-repressive sublimation: first, non-repressive sublimation does not intend to do away with basic repression; rather, it intends to make a distinction between repression under the logic of domination and repression guided by internal necessity. In repressive sublimation, Eros itself goes through repressive changes, but in non-repressive sublimation, constraints are initiated by the order of gratification and so do not require the repressive modification of Eros. In other words, non-repressive sublimation emphasizes the ascendancy of Eros and does not proceed against the instincts but functions as their affirmation; it is an extension and expression of libido, a release of inherent libidinal forces rather than a constraining deflection.[31] Second, and a more important point, is that non-repressive sublimation always contains some degree of de-sexualization; that is, it is a departure from sexual gratification organized around genital sexuality; it can, however, dispense with de-eroticization. In Marcuse's image of Orphic play, although playing a harp is a de-sexualized activity and, as such, needs some degree of basic repression of sexuality, it springs from the erotic relationship of Orpheus with his world. Not only does the harp-playing Orpheus not need to deflect his erotic aim, but the fact that his Eros is not deflected allows his language to be song and his work to be play.[32]

Now, Irigaray has argued on this point, that while it might be possible to sublimate partial drives, "nothing could enable us to sublimate genital drives, those corresponding to sexual difference *per se.*"[33] Marcuse's Eros, read against Irigaray's model, is a chaos that phallocratic discourse labels as life drives. It is chaos since it is a male or a neutral attraction based on a non-individuated subjectivity whose only aim is violent penetration of the maternal body and destruction of its cohesion. In Irigaray's formulation, this is a phallocratic Eros, which is always driven by a desire to return to the maternal body in order to enjoy exclusive possession of her fertility. Eros, in its sexually undifferentiated form, is just the loss of the woman-mother's identity through fusion and so is a return "to the level of tension that is always identical."[34] The only way in which Eros can represent a life-generating process, a respect for the other, and a non-phallic intersubjectivity, is for it to be grounded in the morphology of the woman-mother's body.

For Irigaray, the woman-mother's body is itself the originator of intersubjective recognition. Irigaray starts with the assertion that the maternal body already includes social relations; she refutes the notion that a third party – the father or the phallus – is necessary in order to make the mother-child dyad social. Instead, she explores the social within the maternal body itself. Irigaray finds it ironic that the maternal body – the original provider for the infant's need – must suddenly and violently be left behind, excluded from the economy of desire and speech. She argues that the traditional psychoanalytic construction of the mother as an all-powerful container, able to meet the infant's every need, but without access to desire, is an image of the phallic mother that does not correspond to the corporeality of the woman-mother's body.[35]

For her, the woman-mother is already a desiring body, always in-relationship, and so is always social. Therefore, Irigaray argues, we do not need to violently abject the maternal body in order to become social.

Irigaray claims that if language could speak the woman-mother's corporeality and subscribe to its contours (instead of to the phallocratic economy of solid and the visual), then it would be able to allow for alterity. For Irigaray, the woman-mother's body is already impregnated with alterity, leaving her indefinitely other in herself and so always in dialogue with herself. The woman-mother is never simply one but always remains several. Woman's sexuality is plural; she has sex organs spread through her entire body; "fondling the breasts, touching the vulva, spreading the lips, stroking the posterior wall of the vagina, brushing against the mouth of the uterus,"[36] among other caresses, contribute, irreplaceably, to woman's pleasure. So the woman-mother already has the other within her, which is both at one with and different from her at the same time.

Contrary to the metaphor of the phallus as the sun, the symbolic that is solidly self-sufficient, self-referential, and disembodied, Irigaray claims that her own image calls for an interlocution within the woman-mother's body, acknowledging the corporeal existence of the other. Within this scene of representation, Irigaray believes, desire is no longer Lacan's lack based on the logic of metaphoric substitution; rather, it is the "wonder-full" excess between the self and the other, an exchange or an interval between two that cannot be reduced to one. The relationship between the mother and the other within her is marked neither by property nor by appropriation, but by nearness. As such, the mother-child dyad represents both nature and culture, need and desire, and so acts as an alternative model for a new kind of intersubjectivity based on the ethics of proximity in place of the phallocratic law of the father.[37]

Certainly there is much to be learned from Irigaray's attempt to bring the woman-mother's body into the symbolic. For Irigaray, this means that language does not privilege sight, and representation is not in clear-cut forms. Rather, the corporeality of language, instead of inhibiting the bodily encounter, speaks corporeally and takes each sign back to its source in the tactile and the tangible, the body. Irigaray convincingly demonstrates that the woman-mother cannot emerge in phallocratic discourse, since her absence as a desiring subject is the logical requirement of a social order whose transcendence refuses the body; within this discourse, the woman-mother is the "prediscursive reality" that threatens to disrupt the transcendental.[38] I agree with the position Irigaray takes against the enforced disembodiment that produces a subject who sees an increase in abstractions as his only route to redemption. As Irigaray says, "Qualities of love are not inconsistent with the carnal act; on the contrary, they give it its human dimension."[39]

Nevertheless, I disagree with Irigaray's positioning of carnality as the origin of subjectivity, and worst of all, as its only possible origin. Ironically, Irigaray's model is itself caught within the Western progressive and developmental model of subjectivity; in applying a hierarchy to human erotic development, Irigaray herself appeals to this model wherever she sees fit. For example, in arguing against Freud's pre-Oedipal/undifferentiated Eros, Irigaray describes it as "primitive desire that preceded any human incarnation,"[40] an "undifferentiated elemental state,"[41] and "always the lowest, with neither development nor growth."[42]

Since Irigaray reads gender difference not as a social construct but as nature itself, her theory leaves these separate libidinal economies necessarily immune to critical inquiry and to social practices; this prevents a radical critique of heterosexuality and forecloses the possibility of other gender positions. As it stands, Irigaray's model cannot account for social subjects who assume gender positions outside the heterosexual definition of male and female. Freud's theory has forever destabilized the unproblematic transparency of the relationship between sex and gender. Irigaray's notion of two separate libidinal economies presents the problematic relationship between sex and gender, once again, as a natural given. As a result, what we are left with is a repressive regression (to use Marcuse's terminology) to what is clearly a pre-Freudian moment. For example, when Irigaray claims that the "unisex male order" manifests itself in the libidinal economy of drives without genitality,[43] to what can she be referring but the heterosexual equation of male and female with their genitals? Moreover, even if Irigaray's notion of the placental economy can work as a suggestive image, she still has to account for her universal claim regarding an innate and specifically female desire – or male desire for that matter.

Finally, a question still remains to be answered: what happens to the boy, the adult male subject, and other gender positions? Irigaray's model only allows for, and assumes, a non-antagonistic intersubjectivity between the mother and her daughter. It is only the daughter who is capable of establishing a non-subsumptive relationship with the mother, since she is herself "potentially a mother."[44] For Irigaray, there are two universes, male and female, and only the latter is capable of representing the most highly evolved social and ethical possibility, with the former caught within his primitive incestuous and violent desire for the mother. Irigaray's formulation implies a necessary, if unwanted, conclusion: this time, it is the maternal body, and not the phallus, that signifies the social; it is the maternal body's relation with its own alterity – with the daughter – that signifies intersubjective relation.

Irigaray's model falls short of Marcuse's in its formulation of the libidinal drives. Irigaray does not perceive the historical character of the instincts as separate from their nature. For Marcuse, however, the nature of the drives is historically acquired. Irigaray's identification of the historical and natural characteristics of the instincts prevents a conceptualization of the reality principle as contingent and open to change. As a result, Irigaray's essentializing approach has the inadvertent effect of dismissing the possibility of alternative development of the instinctual drives.

Marcuse's insistence on locating these principles within their specific histories opens up the possibility of imagining a new reality bound up not with the father but with the reality first experienced in the child's libidinal relation to the mother, one in which the child's experience of the world and the Other is far from hostile. For Marcuse, this new reality encompasses not only the separation of self and other, humanity and nature, but also their unity. Yet unlike Irigaray, Marcuse does not ground this new reality in an autonomous essence, nor in a pre-Oedipal gendered subject; rather, his theory rests on the non-gendered status of a pre-Oedipal desire, which is open to various possible signifying positions. Moreover, through the reformulation of this long-abandoned, but not forgotten, primordial desire, Marcuse undoes the historical and representational bond between the mother and nirvana. The mother no longer represents the threat of humanity's annihilation by the "overpowering womb,"[45] but rather the state of primordial unity without pain or want, the unconditionality of being. And when suffering and want recede, nirvana is no longer destructive in its manifestations, while death becomes a biological fact, not an existential angst.

In Marcuse's conception of a mature civilization, primary narcissism towards the maternal body represents a completely novel kind of relation between self and other. Marcuse is convinced that Freud's notion of sexually undifferentiated libido carries within itself the possibilities of imagining this kind of intersubjectivity. According to Marcuse, beyond all immature autoeroticism, primary narcissism contains the germ of an alternate reality principle: remember, Narcissus does not love only himself, in fact he does not know that the image he admires is his own. If Freud is right in asserting that all sublimation takes place through the initiatives of the ego, which changes sexual object/libido into narcissistic libido and then gives it another aim, then all sublimation originates in the reactivation of narcissistic libido, and its subsequent extension to objects. This, for Marcuse, indicates the possibility of a non-repressive mode of sublimation. Marcuse's conceptualization makes the harmonious integration of the narcissistic ego with the objective world a possibility rather than a mere fantasy.

So Marcuse envisions an ethics that is based on a dialectical regression to the pre-Oedipal, pre-genital memories of the child's identification with the mother, which operate within the "superid," which contains within itself the instinctual barriers to immediate gratification.[46] Unlike the morality of the superego, which grows out of the child's acceptance of the law of the father and the fear of castration, the libidinal morality of the superid is based on the wish for castration and the remembrance of unity with the maternal body. This libidinal morality recalls the integral identification of the human race with nature and with an original unity with the mother.

Yet there is a significant absence in Marcuse's theory: Marcuse does not see woman as an active historical agent so he offers no analysis of female desire, either within the Oedipal situation or within the theory of primal horde. Nor does Marcuse's theory attempt to account for woman's self-experience of desire within the dynamics of ego development. In Marcuse's theory, the maternal body provides only a utopian vision for the son; in other words, it treats the maternal body as a mere object rather than a desiring subject. Moreover, as long as Marcuse's theory does not take into account the agency of the mother-woman, his own recollection of the figure of the mother is tied up in the narcissistic masculine desire for the same, which constructs not the woman-mother but the phallic mother and longs for her omnipotence. It is understandable that Marcuse does not want to associate the maternal body with the woman, since there is always a danger of reducing his discourse to ontology. Still any discussion of the maternal body has to take into account the social oppression of the female subject, and its production as woman, under phallocratic conditions.

In contrast, Irigaray's notion of two autonomous, separate universals bypasses the question of tension between the self and its alterity by subsuming intersubjectivity under the woman-mother's morphology. Marcuse, on the other hand, introduces tension between Eros and Death, between the realms of necessity and freedom, between the self and the other, as the foundation of the social. This tension can either solidify domination or offer liberatory potential and the possibility of freedom; it indicates the mutual constitution of the self and its alterity, one always requiring the recognition of the other in order to signify its own meaning. This necessity of mutual recognition opens the intersubjective relation to the possibility of domination and subordination.

What emerges from Irigaray's and Marcuse's criticisms of phallocratic subjectivity is that we need non-phallic metaphors in order to be able to imagine intersubjective recognition. Both writers use the maternal body as a utopian moment to allow the possibility of an intersubjective recognition. Yet, as my own critique illustrates, there is a crucial polarity between the work of Marcuse and the work of Irigaray, a polarity between an account of dynamics of oppression and a discourse of the oppressed. While Marcuse's work secures an immanent critique of civilization and the production of its subject, it is unable to describe women's oppression or to locate women as historical actors. And while Irigaray's own model secures the voice of the woman-mother, it lacks an account of the social construction of this voice. Instead, Irigaray returns the woman-mother to the essentialized realm of pre-Oedipal female desire. Through a synthesis of Marcuse's polymorphous state of Eros with Irigaray's metaphor of the woman-mother's body we can, I believe, overcome the lacuna in each of their theories. On one hand, without Irigaray's account of the maternal body as a desiring subject, Marcuse's Eros is only the son's desire for the memory of an objectified maternal body. On the other hand, Irigaray's return to the morphology of the women-mother's body cannot succeed as a disruptive force without Marcuse's re-eroticization; what is crucial in the economy of the woman-mother's body, what makes possible a recognition and support between intimates, is not the sexual specificity of the maternal body but Eros itself. It is erotic love for existence in its undifferentiated – but not chaotic – form, blind to sexual or other polarity, that makes this moment of intersubjectivity possible.

NOTES

1 Luce Irigaray, *The Irigaray Reader*, ed. Margaret Whitford (Oxford: Blackwell, 1995), 50–1.
2 Luce Irigaray, *Speculum of the Other Woman*, trans. Gillian C. Gill (Ithaca, NY: Cornell University Press, 1985), 243, 246, 280.
3 Herbert Marcuse, *One-Dimensional Man* (Boston: Beacon, 1964), 147.
4 Irigaray, *Irigaray Reader*, 54.
5 Luce Irigaray, *This Sex Which Is Not One*, trans. Catherine Porter (Ithaca, NY: Cornell University Press, 1985), 26–7.
6 Ibid., 25–6.
7 Irigaray, "Volume without Contours," in *Irigaray Reader*, 54–5.
8 Irigaray, *This Sex Which Is Not One*, 84–5.
9 Marcuse, *One-Dimensional Man*, 18.
10 Herbert Marcuse, *Eros and Civilization* (Boston: Beacon, 1955), 35–6.
11 Irigaray, *This Sex Which Is Not One*, 170–1.
12 Irigaray, "Women-Mothers: The Silent Substratum of the Social Order," in *Irigaray Reader*, 48–9.
13 Marcuse, *One-Dimensional Man*, 72.
14 Marcuse, *Eros and Civilization*, 201–3.
15 Ibid., chap. 9.
16 Ibid., 36–46, 206–7.
17 Irigaray, *This Sex Which Is Not One*, 28.
18 Ibid., 113.
19 Ibid., 24.
20 Gad Horowitz, *Repression: Basic and Surplus Repression in Psychoanalytic Theory: Freud, Reich and Marcuse* (Toronto: University of Toronto Press, 1977).
21 Marcuse, *Eros and Civilization*, 17–18.
22 Irigaray, *This Sex Which Is Not One*, 35.
23 Luce Irigaray, *I Love to You: Sketch of a Possible Felicity in History*, trans. Alison Martin (New York: Routledge, 1996), 35.
24 Marcuse, *Eros and Civilization*, 49.
25 Horowitz, *Repression*, 4.
26 Marcuse, *Eros and Civilization*, 80–2.
27 Ibid., 95.

28 Ibid., 49, 51.
29 Ibid., 206.
30 Ibid., 206–7. Marcuse's distinction between re-eroticization and re-sexual-
    ization become confusing, since in some chapters in *Eros and Civilization* he
    uses them interchangeably. However this, I argue, is due to the develop-
    ment of his discussion that occurs at several levels of abstraction simulta-
    neously. Therefore, sometimes (for example, on page 208), he talks about
    sublimation without de-sexualization, which might be interpreted as Mar-
    cuse denying the basic repressive sublimation of sexual energies. But the
    sexuality he refers to, and de-sexualization that he objects to, at this spe-
    cific point, is one that is "not sexual in the sense of organized genital sexu-
    ality" (208) and as such is Eros itself.
31 Ibid., 202–9.
32 Ibid., 169–71.
33 Luce Irigaray, *Thinking the Difference for a Peaceful Revolution*, trans. Karin
    Montin (New York: Routledge, 2001), 96.
34 Ibid., 99.
35 Irigaray, *This Sex Which Is Not One*, 30–3, 102.
36 Ibid., 28.
37 Ibid., 31.
38 Ibid., 79–89.
39 Irigaray, *Thinking the Difference*, 94.
40 Ibid., 97.
41 Ibid., 95.
42 Ibid., 99.
43 Ibid., 109.
44 Ibid., 110.
45 Marcuse, *Eros and Civilization*, 230.
46 Ibid., 228.

11   The Spark of Philosophy: Hartz-Horowitz and Theories of Religion

COLIN J. CAMPBELL

I

It may be a telling irony that the theory of political culture developed by Louis Hartz specifically for his American audience in the 1950s seems to have had its most lasting impact in Canada. Ironies of fate aside, we can say at least that Hartz presented a uniquely coherent and elegant analysis of the global spectrum of modern political ideologies: from the tory, defined by traditionalism, a vision of society as collective and the individual as subordinate or even insignificant; to the liberal, defined by his rationalism and egalitarianism, and his view of society as being an association of pre-existing and freely contracting individuals; to the socialist, defined by some alchemical combination of the tory's sense of collectivity and community and the liberal's rationality and opposition to inequality. These three positions, with various shadings and in various combinations, were used by Hartz and his students to illuminate a wide array of actual political positions, and to explain some of the unexpected allegiances and oppositions that have developed in political history.

In the 1960s the young Gad Horowitz, a student of Louis Hartz, argued that in the Canadian context it is precisely the persistence of an explicitly traditional, organic-hierarchical "Tory touch" in an otherwise liberal Canadian polity that explains the relative-historical – and he hoped, future – success of the socialist movement in Canada. According to what has become rather widely known in Canadian political science as the "Hartz-Horowitz" theory, in the largely liberal North American environment, old scions of the British-Canadian aristocracy in Canada might be found contributing to change in a socialist or egalitarian direction. Horowitz offered as evidence the contribution of an otherwise staunch Canadian tory, George Grant, to the founding NDP document, *A Social Purpose for Canada*.

This is not at all to say that Hartzian theory has been *unanimously* accepted in Canada. As Donald Forbes notes,[1] Hartzian-Horowitzian theory has left many questions unanswered, not least the one of how or even whether one can make an accurate political analysis that does not reflect inherent biases in one's own political views. Horowitz, although he may have been open and generous in his descriptions of the motivations of Canadian liberals and tories, was neither a liberal nor a tory – he is an avowed socialist. Hartz himself seemed committed to a liberalism of some as-yet-unknown form, one that would be substantially cured of the ailments he saw to be plaguing its American variants. Forbes and other sceptics therefore ask whether it is not possible that such sympathies with socialism or liberalism may impinge on the accuracy of theoretical appraisal.

Hartz's answer to this kind of question was that his theory was speculative, intended to illuminate the political realities, not categorize them in an absolute sense. His allegiance to liberalism, furthermore, was not by any means unconditional. He was indeed concerned in his day with the way that in his time the absolute commitment of liberalism to the freedom of the lone individual, in the absence of balancing elements from other ideologies, had apparently flipped over into its dialectical opposite – the paranoia of McCarthyism.[2] But the "fuzziness" of Hartz's dialectical liberal logic has remained unconvincing to many analysts, or only convinced them more of a Hartzian "bias." Today, although the Hartzian theory still appears to generate interest in political and social science in Canada, it seems at the very least that the theory has come to a kind of impasse, if not yet a fateful silence. As with so many academic pursuits in our time, it often seems that those who come to agree with the theory would have agreed with it from the very beginning, while those who oppose it could never be convinced by any "merely academic" argument. More and more we discover that we are preaching to the converted, while those with views fundamentally unlike our own appear to be constitutionally unable even to begin to understand what we mean.

I suggest that we can describe this situation in another way: more than methodological problems, it is the importance and persistence in public life of religion and religious ways of thinking that appears to vitiate the conclusions Hartz developed in his classic texts, *The Liberal*

Tradition in America and *The Founding of New Societies*. Hartz believed or hoped that the opening of the "fragment cultures," the New World European colonies – especially the "monolithically liberal" United States – to the Old World of the European past would reignite "a spark of philosophy" that the strains of the voyage to the New World had smothered.[3] The "spark of philosophy" cannot happen without sensitivity to the full range of ideological positions, including the toryism that has been excluded from American liberalism. Philosophy, Hartz suggests, can help us come to terms with what narrow liberalisms forget: that as individuals we are only parts of a larger whole. Philosophy, born out of a sensitivity to ideological diversity, is an expression of collective memory: "In other words, we are fated to 'remember' what an earlier generation 'forgot.' And yet what is involved here, of course, is not a return to the original colonial situation. One of the buried sources of fear in the face of a modification of the fragment nationalisms is undoubtedly the sense of that past situation, the intolerable ambiguity of being a part of whole and isolated from it. But not only is it in the nature of the current situation for isolation to end, but also the 'whole' that is returning is wider than the old European nation."[4]

Hartzian theory, understood as part of a larger movement of collective remembering, is explicitly philosophical. The practice of philosophy, however, appears to be inherently connected with the work of reason. It therefore must be distinguished from the experience and meaning of faith, even if we can use philosophical arguments to reconcile philosophy with faith after the fact. Indeed, in its origins in archaic Greece, philosophy emerged precisely as a questioning and criticism of traditional religion by isolated individuals. Whatever the explicit conclusions of a given philosophical enterprise, it is clear that from the outset it presumes a degree of free individual speculation that does not easily enter into the crucibles of faith. Philosophy asks difficult and even dangerous questions about the ties (explicit in the original Latin sense of the word, *re-ligio*) that bind us. If Hartz opted for the "spark of philosophy" against the religious experience, it might well be argued, he placed himself on one side of an impassable chasm.

The question of the relation between rational theories and traditions of faith is important for Hartz, but it resonates beyond him as well, raising the question of the relevance of philosophy in general in (post) modern pluralist social orders. If philosophy, the love of wisdom, cannot speak in principle to anyone and everyone, if it knows furthermore from the beginning that a whole category of educated and articulate people would never be willing or able to hear what it says, the question of its relevance must surely arise. Even if the truth it finds is dialectical (e.g., that there is no one truth), the practice of philosophy is grounded in the possibility of a truth beyond itself. At the very least, people doing philosophy must be open at the outset to the possibility that they will find common ground through discussion and dialogue. The negotiation of a mere truce in which we merely tolerate the other's beliefs (which we nevertheless find "erroneous," "immoral," etc.) does not satisfy the aim of philosophy, though it may well make philosophy seem superfluous. Philosophy aims for a shared truth, what J.J. Rousseau called a "general will." If a philosophy cannot aspire to any truth that transcends the particular individuals who happen to advocate it at any given moment, it might well be asked what makes it different from a kind of role-playing game, aimed at confusing the impressionable, or to put it more colloquially, "messing with people's heads."

If anything could make Hartzian philosophy still broadly relevant in our plural world, could give it a claim to a larger truth, it would be that something deeper and wider than philosophy itself motivated the Hartzian interest in philosophy. Hartz's commitment to the values of egalitarian *community*, to human progress not only beyond the dogmatic, hierarchical authoritarianism of traditional societies but also beyond the dogmatic, atomistic, competitive, and self-destructive rationality of modern liberal-capitalist ones like the United States, drove him to call the prevailing order of things into philosophical question. Undoubtedly, as the sceptics will remind us, this philosophical and political "bias" colours the entirety of the Hartzian theory. It allowed Hartz to relativize or downplay certain problems that remain absolute from the liberal point of view, such as distinguishing between fair and oppressive impositions on individual liberties by collective interests. It also allowed Hartz (and Horowitz) to reconcile apparently irreconcilable positions and individuals – the socialist and the pre-liberal tory, for example – who themselves might likely as not resist and repudiate this reconciliation.

Forbes points out that one of the distinguishing weaknesses of Hartzian theory (besides its speculative nature) is its neglect of religion.[5] I argue in this essay that this criticism is both founded and unfounded. It is founded in the sense that in his classic texts Hartz never explicitly discusses religion at any length except in terms of its social and political effects – for example, the role of established churches in feudal society and in the feudal fragment cultures of Quebec and Latin America.

But it is unfounded in the sense that the Hartzian social and political theory *as a whole* implies a deep appreciation of the history and living reality and power of religion and how it limits and enables political action. That Hartz's last, most ambitious, and never-published theoretical work, entitled "A Synthesis of World History," took up the problem of human culture in its fullest religious dimensions indicates that Hartz was in no way unappreciative of the religious dimensions of his political theory. It suggests that its truth at a more general level could be construed as a religious truth.

Because this work was never published, our view of Hartz as explicitly a theorist of religion must necessarily remain fragmentary and ambiguous. Nevertheless, I argue that a religious perspective is already inherent in his published "secular" social theory of political ideology. Whether or not Hartz ultimately believed that change had to come in a more liberal direction, he always insisted that liberalism is in need of a full and uncompromised memory of the feudal order, of the preliberal society that was the host for the "contagion" that produced liberalism, along with the various other reformist and revolutionary political movements.[6] A full and uncompromised memory of feudalism, to be true to its object of study, would necessarily give a central place to religion, which was clearly a fundamental element of life in feudal societies.

It is with a view to illuminating as sharply as possible the implicit religious dimensions of Hartz's theory of the pre-liberal past that I turn to the theories of René Girard and Georges Bataille, two thinkers who are explicitly theorists of religion. Admittedly, Girard and Bataille are much further from the mainstream of contemporary Canadian political science than Hartz-Horowitz. However, though they have been relegated academically to a different department – largely literature and literary theory – they function very well indeed as "unexpected allies" of the Hartz-Horowitz approach. In Bataille and Girard we find formulated in explicitly religious terms insights that are strikingly similar to Hartzian theory. As such, they can help us give voice to the implicit theory of religion in Hartz. The religious underpinnings of the distinction Hartz drew between liberalism and toryism need to be illuminated, and it is precisely these differences that obsess both Bataille and Girard.

II

René Girard's first major publication, *Deceit, Desire, and the Novel*, might appear to be an unlikely beginning for a scholarly career in the theory of religion, let alone a resource for the study of politics. It is an examination of the development of the European novel from Cervantes to Dostoyevsky and Proust. However, Girard's greater theoretical design is evident from the beginning. Girard insists that literary criticism, against both postmodernism and premodern obscurity, must be systematic, and furthermore that it will be systematizing an insight, already present in literature itself, on par with or exceeding the insights of mainstream philosophy and science. He argues, "To maintain that criticism will never be systematic is to maintain that it will never be real knowledge."[7] Girard's literary theory is as logically argued and as systematic as any scientific theory. But the output of what seems to be an elegantly simple logical structure will not be formulaic or a mere empirical datum. Girard announces that his goal in this text is to embrace, comprehend, and make communicable the substantial truth of literature: "triangular desire."

When Girard talks about "triangular desire," he is not only specifying a fictional psychological structure aimed at producing drama and tension in storytelling (though it is this as well). He refers to a deeper truth: that, to a degree not characteristic of other animals, human beings' motivations and actions are defined and engendered by imitation. What I truly want, the desires that most define my striving and work in life, my very sense of self, is in fact not the original, self-originating phenomenon it often seems to me to be. It is in essence a copy, something learned. My desire, any "biological" human desire, no matter what parts of it could be deemed as "purely physiological," is *human* to the extent that it has been framed and shaped by following an example from someone else, whom Girard refers to as the "model" or "mediator." For Girard, a great novel is great to the extent that it teaches this truth about human desire in the form of a story.

For Girard, the line between the human sense of self and the object of that self's desire is seen mistakenly by social or psychological science as directly analogous to animal instinct: a vector directly connecting the self with the object. Far more powerful and determinate for human beings than any immediate "instinct," says Girard, is the line that connects me with a model whom I imitate. At the very basis of the personality, in earliest childhood, the "me," like all forms of verbal language, exists only because "I" begin (if "I" is not an autistic statement) at some time in my infancy to imitate that way another person says "me." Our desires, like our cultural habits and everything else that makes us different from other animals, are learned from others, not produced autistically. What we could call "pure instinct" is from the beginning layered over with language, with the necessity of communicating about "what we feel," and the inevitability of the fact that what we feel is *changed* by the act of communicating about it. This, says Girard, means that even our "purest wishes" are inspired and shaped by imitation.

For Girard, insight into the "triangular" nature of desire is the substantial and even scientific truth of the European novel. The irony and humour of *Don Quixote* truly lies not in the prodigious originality of the protagonist's desires, but in the fact that he is absurdly and anachronistically imitating the desires of a much earlier hero, Amadis de Gaul, a twelfth-century chivalric knight. Quixote's imitative desire, furthermore, is itself humorously imitated by his companion-follower, Sancho Panza. But even if we grant that this theory of desire might raise important psychological questions, what do they have to do with the Hartz-Horowitz theory?

It turns out that the specific ways in which imitative desire is structured go beyond the level of personal dramas, fictional or real. They speak to the whole configuration of a society and a way of life. Girard finds it notable that Quixote is separated from his model Amadis de Gaul by a great historical distance, and Quixote's own imitator, Sancho Panza, is separated from Quixote himself by a force at least as strong: class difference. Panza would never feel as if he were an individual equal to Quixote and thus actually deserving of the same things, though he might imitate his desires more generally. He relates to Quixote as Quixote in turn relates to Amadis de Gaul: as a kind of total externality, a person, but one from whom he is qualitatively separated by birth. Admiration for the model is thus never tinged by jealousy, which would be the immediate desire to actually possess what a present rival possesses. This is why the imitation in *Don Quixote* is a kind of whimsical dream, an essentially happy desire, an ideal safely stowed within the imagination, or relegated to an unknown future. Girard calls this essentially non-conflictual form of triangular desire "external mediation."

It is in the idea of "external mediation" as a historical phenomenon that we see the first key element in Girard of a theory of what Hartz and Horowitz call "toryism." A "tory" or feudal society, for Girard, is one characterized by the active presence of viable non-conflictual external models, whose desires we can freely imitate without fear of rivalry over the object of desire. Girard emphasizes how such external models make possible a real kind of freedom: freedom from jealous conflict and guilt, both personal and political.

Girard emphasizes again and again in *Deceit, Desire, and the Novel* that the defining social, political, and religious characteristic of a modernizing, democratizing, and secularizing Europe is the rise and spread of *internal* mediation. This changing socio-political context is reflected clearly in the novel as art form after the time of Cervantes. The individual in a liberalizing universe has less and less recourse to ideal figures who remain separated from him by lines of birth, tradition, or sacred law. The old idols fall as the process of enlightenment wears away the intricate networks of traditional authority, patriarchal domination, and servitude. All that eventually remains in the enlightened liberal imagination is a rational, abstract ideal: the equality of all individuals. Early liberal philosophers suggested radically that nature, rather than tradition, could be a guide for action for enlightened action. But Girard argues trenchantly that this is actually no solution, because *our nature as human is to imitate*. According to Girard, the imitative nature of desire explains how the rise of modern, bourgeois individualism coincides with internal mediation in the proliferation of a deeply conformist anxiety:

> The impulse toward the object is ultimately an impulse toward the mediator; in internal mediation this impulse is checked by the mediator himself since he desires, or perhaps possesses, the object. Fascinated by his model, the disciple inevitably sees, in the mechanical obstacle which he puts in his way, proof of the ill will borne him. Far from declaring himself a faithful vassal, he thinks only of repudiating the bonds of mediation. But these bonds are stronger than ever, for the mediator's apparent hostility does not diminish his prestige but instead augments it. The subject is convinced that the model considers himself too superior to accept him as a disciple. The subject is torn between two opposite feelings toward his model – the most submissive reverence and the most intense malice. This is the passion we call hatred.[8]

Freed from the bonds of feudal class-privilege, too enlightened to be caught "imitating their betters," modern bourgeois individuals, says Girard, only rush into a new and far more insidious trap: jealous imitation of their neighbours. Desiring above all to be "above the crowd," to be original, each individual is simply becoming more and more like his or her neighbour, who is both a model for and obstacle to the satisfaction of his or her desires. Girard says that the end-state of the individualizing process at the social level is reversion back to the collective, but one shorn of external models, rooted directly in the jealousy and rivalry of internal mediation. This is the modern totalitarian universe reflected in the work of Franz Kafka, in which the keeper of the door of the law (who could be interpreted in Girardian terms as the mediator of triangular desire) proclaims sadistically, "This door was meant for you and for no one else, and now I am closing it!"

Girard's theories of feudalism, liberalism, and totalitarianism, though they are literary in the origins, resonate strikingly with many of the concerns Hartz voiced about the "pure" liberal democratic fragment cultures like the United States. If we are sensitive to the imitative nature of human desire, if we do not hide behind masks of invincible self-reliance, we can suddenly perceive how the ideal of individual self-reliance easily flips over into its opposite – exclusive, jealous, and even paranoid conformity. We can see how the emergence of an unquestionably "objective" and "unbiased" concept of "human nature" in the new human sciences, for example in the nineteenth-century liberal-individualistic fragment cultures of the United States and South Africa, served at the same time to legitimate new forms of slavery, more exclusive and brutal than the old feudal hierarchy, based on the new definition of certain races as "subhuman": "In a bourgeois community where the Negro is either an item of property or an equal human being, a free Negro under conditions of slavery is an enormous paradox. How can an object of property be 'free'? Or if it can be free, it must be human and hence all Negroes must be free. But in a feudal context, where the slave is accepted as human and given a status, this paradox does not exist. Manumission is merely a rise in status. It does not threaten the rationale of slavery itself, and it does not threaten the fragment ethic as a whole since that ethic is grounded in social differentiation."[9]

What Hartz describes as an ethic grounded in social differentiation could be described in Girardian terms as an ethic where my own sense of well-being does not depend on my neighbours being the same as me. Girard and Hartz would agree that racism is not an inherent "instinct." It is rather the reaction of highly "rational" individuals who are desperately trying to convince themselves that their co-racialists have that superior essence, worthy of imitation, that their sense of sameness with each other implicitly denies. Underlying the prejudice of racial difference is not hatred of difference per se but an intolerable sense of *sameness* that can be accepted only by way of a mythic projection of that intolerable feeling onto scapegoats, such as the victims of the lynch mobs. What Hartz calls an "ethic grounded in social differentiation" could be described as a bulwark against the jealous and allergic sense of sameness Girard calls "internal mediation." The Girardian theory makes clear the value of social differentiation in religious terms: it permits me to imitate my models without confronting them in rivalry.

Of course, in European history, the ethic of social differentiation is also an ethic of *patriarchal* and *hierarchical* differentiation. So far, it might be easy to conclude that Girard, most unlike Hartz, is a "pure tory" much like his forbearer Joseph de Maistre, for whom it is self-evident that the loss of the divine influence of a universal Catholic Church can only mean the apocalypse. And indeed, Girard appears at times in *Deceit, Desire, and the Novel* to be not just a literary but a religious and political tory, calling for the re-establishment of a hierarchical traditional social order. Girard might appear, that is, to be giving an absolute value to pre-liberal societies, where for Hartz the value is relative, being the lesser of two evils, or perhaps only a different kind of evil.

But in the end it is not the actual political trappings of feudalism, but the *general possibility of external mediation* that Girard is concerned with. The positive or absolute value Girard may seem to ascribe to toryism turns out to be as relative as Hartz's, though in a different sense: a literary one. Girard is interested in the religious and literary depiction of external mediation, not tory ideology. Girard finds in the novelists he loves a deep sense of what has been lost in the transition to the modern capitalist world, a loss so painful that the necessity of some kind of radical change appears as an implicit cry or command. The isolated, atomic individual of the liberal social contract is for Girard a deeply mutilated human being. But it is clear that the old feudal order cannot be restored.

And if feudalism cannot be restored, all of Girard's work after *Deceit, Desire, and the Novel* makes abundantly clear that it is not desirable to restore it anyway. His explorations of anthropology, psychology, and the classics all point for him towards what we will summarize here as the "scapegoat theory." Aristocracy, monarchy, and other tory societies of external mediation were never really the idyllic models of social life they sometimes appear to be in romantic or novelistic retrospect. It turns out, Girard finds, that the problem of internal mediation – essentially, jealous rivalry over objects of desire – is not unique to modern liberalizing societies. External mediation was, it fact, *only ever produced at the apex of an out-of-control cycle of internal mediation.*[10] This apex is what Girard calls "sacrifice." A community made up of jealous rivals lacking external mediation, all imitating and hating each other, might suddenly "decide" (likely without being aware of doing it) there is one person to blame for *all* of their troubles. Because they are imitating each other so fiercely, it is easy for their desires to converge in such a way. Because they live a world structured by myth, it is not hard for them to make a range of accusations ("evil eye," "demon-possessed," "witch," etc.) that seem utterly fantastical to our rational minds. The community as a whole might converge and murder their scapegoat, and in a symbolic act of retribution (symbolic, because the scapegoat cannot really be said to have been the cause of their troubles) they conduct an act of *sacrifice* that returns the community to a "peace that passeth all understanding." The scapegoat may now be feared and even revered for the great power he had to harm, and in death, to heal. Because he is no longer present, he can now be the central figure for external mediation. Girard insists in all of his works after *Deceit, Desire, and the Novel* that the jealous murder of a scapegoat lies at the roots of external mediation. The scapegoat, the "stone that was cast away," is the cornerstone of all pre-liberal social orders, in Europe and elsewhere. Internal mediation, for all its problems, is also a sign that the brutal "contagion" generative of external mediation has been contained.

But if he is not a Maistrian tory, nor a secularist liberal, Girard is not by any means an advocate of socialism either. In fact, where Girard discusses socialism or communism, they are more or less equated with the other forms of internally mediated desire that generally characterize modern ideologies. Secularist liberalism and socialism, for Girard, are going down the same river in different boats – a river of destructive, jealous imitative desire. As moderns we are "deprived" by Christian illumination, of the possibility of finding a satisfactory scapegoat, and so we are unable to attain the "peace that passeth understanding," the mythical peace of external mediation. At our best we maintain a uniquely sensitive concern for the victims of collective violence. At our worst, in horrors like the Holocaust, we extend the sacrificial process ad infinitum, on an industrial scale, in the futile hope of restoring a mythic sense of social cohesion that Christianity has made impossible.

Girard's discussion of political themes ends in a kind of religiously enthusiastic but politically ambiguous liberalism. He might best be summarized politically as being much closer to Burke than Maistre: he is a situational conservative. As much as he reviles the world as it is, the world as it is still reverberating from the Christian revolution, and this is what he wants more of: "Our society is the most preoccupied with victims of any that ever was. Even if it is insincere, a big show, the phenomenon has no precedent. No historical period, no society we know, has ever spoken of victims as we do. We can detect in the recent past the beginnings of the contemporary attitude, but every day new records are broken. We are all actors as well as witnesses in a great anthropological first."[11]

Christian enthusiasm in politics, for Girard, does not mean fundamentalist fervour, it means a deep-seated commitment to maintaining the status quo and to mitigating those aspects of the status quo that seem most likely to destroy it. The Christian religion (and literature that leads us to the Christian situation) is the only way Girard has found to prevent this destruction. Like Hartz, Girard is even-handed in his treatment of the limitations of available ideological alternatives. Unlike Hartz, he has no hope for a new ideological configuration that might address these limitations.

III

Georges Bataille seems at first to be completely incompatible with Girard: Bataille perversely embraces the most extreme ideological positions. At times he appears to be a Stalinist, at others to harbour fascist sympathies. And yet deep lines of connection can be drawn between Bataille and Girard if we think in terms of the Hartzian idea of toryism. In a kind of mystical sense, Bataille glorifies "all human activities – sciences, arts and technology – insofar as they have a communifying value, in the active sense of the word, that is to say, insofar as they are the *creators* of unity."[12] One of Bataille's central presuppositions is that society as a whole is a "being": "In addition to the individuals who make up society, there exists an overall movement which transforms their nature."[13] What Girard calls imitative desire, the electrified, ecstatic Bataille glorifies as the obscure but powerful movement of "communification" – that is, the sacred violence that gives birth to community by way of sacrifice.

What Girard calls "external mediation," Bataille calls "sovereignty." What Bataille means by "sovereignty" or by "sovereign desire" is not at all what we generally mean in modern political theory by sovereignty – the monopoly of violence exercised by the government of a territorially limited nation state. By "sovereignty," Bataille means instead something that lies, unbeknownst to us, at the foundation of every community. As for Girard, for Bataille this foundation consists in sacrificial violence. The difference between Bataille and Girard is that Bataille does not share Girard's "modern concern for victims," and he never uses the term "scapegoat." He instead *celebrates* the general capacity of sacrificial ritual for *destroying or giving without expectation of return*. The violence done to a particular scapegoat is not Bataille's central concern. The life of the sacred for Bataille is at its roots a life of useless destruction *in general*, a life antithetical to the everyday world of work and self-preservation. Participating in sacrifice brings us collectively into a world without clear delimitations between means and ends, between me and you, between individual and collective. This is the world of the orgy, the riot, or the sacrificial festival: it is a violent as well as sacred experience.

According to Bataille, what we call political sovereignty was in its origins a religious institution, nothing but an expression of this "wild" sacred experience. The ultimate or "purest" form of sovereignty in Bataille's sense is therefore not what embodies the largest territorial sweep, which exercises the most unquestioned degree of power and control. Power is rooted in the ability to marshal and preserve the order of everyday work activity – what non-Western religions often refer to as the world of the "profane." Sacred violence represents a danger to the productive order that power creates, and it is prior to and beyond political orders. It is the very power of death, and power is not sovereign in Bataille's sense if it does not risk its own death too: "Life devoting itself to death is the passion of one lover for another; in it angry jealousy is a factor at work, but never 'authority.'"[14] In Hartzian terms, Bataille would say that power in a tory society differs from power in modern societies to the extent that it emerges out of sovereignty, on the capacity to consign resources (including human resources) to a glorious destruction.

Girard and Bataille are similar in that they draw attention to how such a desire to destroy is an indelible aspect of the human experience. But Bataille is most unlike Girard in that he actively *desires* such destruction, a desire that must surely seem ludicrous from the perspective of political theory. However, in his madness for sovereign violence, Bataille also opens a theoretical door to a redefinition of sovereignty that speaks to crucial and often misunderstood aspects of the Hartzian theory and political theory more generally.

For Bataille, feudal sovereignty is antithetical to contractual or voluntary bonds of association, not because it aims at accumulating *power*, but because of its capacity or propensity to *destroy without calculated return*. The more that feudal authorities aimed at accumulating power, says Bataille, the more they were undermining their power as a class. Only the image of a sovereign sacrificing useful wealth could induce his subjects to imitate him and sacrifice themselves to him. This is the very meaning and mystique of nobility, and the explanation for the demise of feudal institutions. The ancient Roman formula, *do ut des*, "I give that you may give," was already a contractual reduction of what sacrificial sovereignty involves. Sovereignty in its "pure" state would be nothing but "I give." Bataille's sovereignty means that I am *nothing* in relation to the whole of which I am part; I am bound to my sovereign because he embodies that whole that includes me and facilitates the sacrifice of useful goods to its ends.

Sovereignty, Bataille says enthusiastically, is the impulse to give no matter what, to give violently and to give violence. Sovereign giving is not a transfer of a recognized value, which would imply the obligation of return. It is not a rational agreement. The gift of a sovereign is first and foremost violence – if I am sovereign, my violence is a gift to you, even if that means killing you. No sovereign would ever have been *chosen* by a group of freely associating people in the state of nature. Hobbesian theory in fact quietly implies that it is precisely the sovereign's "natural" violence that enjoins and maintains the transition out of the state of nature, and that his institutional power merely commemorates a more elemental, and indeed antisocial, sovereign role. Bataille makes vividly clear Hartz's insight about Lockean liberalism: that it never really solved the problem of Hobbes's *Leviathan*, it merely repressed it and the memory of what sovereignty really means.

Among other things, Bataille's redefinition of sovereignty allows us to further expand and explicate the Hartzian theory of toryism. "Toryism" need not be hierarchical. The pre-liberal world goes back even before the age of the divine right of kings; it goes back to the time of the *sacrifice of the king*, and beyond that, to the relative egalitarianism of the earliest human cultures. Here, as Gad and Asher Horowitz suggest in their text *Everywhere They Are in Chains*, it is possible to see more clearly how collectivism connects toryism, or at least aspects of the feudal experience, with socialism.

However, because Bataille's prime mover is not equality, but sovereignty, it would seem impossible to develop a "realistic" Bataillian political theory. In fact, like Girard, when Bataille actually considers solutions to political and social problems in the modern world, he usually appears surprisingly moderate, or else confused. As an example of giving without expectation of return, for example, Bataille suggests the

Marshall Plan. Of course, rumours do circulate about Bataille's involvement in the 1930s in Paris in surreal cults of human sacrifice. But what
Bataille's wartime writings communicate, more than anything else,
is his feeling of failure and finitude, of how small his "sovereignty"
seemed in the face of the infinitely more powerful engines of annihilation represented in modern industry and total industrial war. The
modern world is one deprived of the outlets represented in premodern sovereignty and is totally devoted to the accumulation of productive wealth. But for Bataille, though we may have deprived ourselves
of official outlets, the unofficial one we call war has officially stepped
up to accept all the sacrificial victims Christianity claims to have saved,
and more. We are now prepared to make a sacrifice on a scale unimag-
ined by the most brutal Aztec warrior: the annihilation of the earth as
a whole.

   Faced with the world-annihilating machinery of post-industrial ro-
botic warfare, what Bataille calls sovereignty, in the end, is as a practical
matter essentially historical and literary, and any Bataillian "political
theory" pleads for the indulgence of its readership: a desperate, lost,
and isolated intelligentsia. Like Hartz and Girard, Bataille is even-
handed in his treatment of the limitations of available ideological alternatives. Unlike Hartz and more like Girard, he has no hope for a new
ideological configuration that might address these limitations. Girard
and Bataille are in equal measures repelled and attracted by the world
as it already is.

IV

Whatever the hopes it raised, the grounds for scepticism about Hartzian theory should by now appear in a clearer light, and perhaps seem
all the more justified. The tory world that Hartz seems to treat with
equanimity, sometimes even contrasting it favourably with the liberal
one, was one characterized by the ludicrous, pointlessly destructive sacred violence Bataille inexplicably loves. In Girard's terms, it is one that
makes scapegoats. Bataille and Girard, precisely in their deep literary
appreciation for illiberal social orders, only reveal all the more starkly
why liberals oppose them.

   Bataille and Girard partake in rich and colourful images of the history of ideologies, ones that I have argued here also implicitly inform
Hartzian political theory. But in the pragmatic world of political science, many readers of Hartz must surely feel that he is playing with fire.

He seems at times to minimize the moral demand that gives rise to and is represented by liberal ideals of individual rights and freedoms, the ideal of a conscious and voluntary definition of social norms. When he describes "feudal collectivism," we feel he is describing too neutrally a world of mythic fear and uncontrolled violence. When Hartz says there "is a process of contagion at work in Europe, enormously subtle and ramifying, in which ideologies give birth to one another over time,"[15] we could say he is also describing a kind of religious contagion, in precisely Girard's sense of the mimetic desire in scapegoating. The revolutionary socialist doctrines of Europe share with toryism the character of uncontrolled violence that the Hobbesian monopoly of violence and liberal social contract theory aim to prevent.

But it seems incredible that Hartz was ignorant of these problems. We could go further: perhaps his vision of the tory world was just as clear as those of Bataille and Girard, with the crucial difference that it was not as marked by the kind of ambivalent desire that both Bataille and Girard show. Hartz offered, we might say, a more dialectical perspective. Hartz remained politically committed to the value of a rational conception of the community, the ideals of liberal community and philosophy against blind faith in tradition. But for all this he was not satisfied with the liberal status quo. Above all else, he suspected it of failing to meet its own standards, or, dialectically speaking, of *being too successful by its own standards.*

To use Gad and Asher Horowitz's metaphor in *Everywhere They Are in Chains*, we might say the liberal society "negatively hallucinates" its tory baggage. Bataille and Girard have the virtue at least of openly declaring this baggage. From the land of literature, they give voice, even to the border guards of political science, to the sense that liberal orthodoxies and social contracts have not fully enough justified their own existence. What liberalism forgets are religious truths: that we are moved at root by currents of imitative desire, that we exhibit deeply irrational forms of collective behaviour, none more irrational and wasteful than war. We believe we live in a liberal "market" and have transcended the tory "hive," but in reality the hive lives on, stronger than ever. Our hatred of anything illiberal, of all forms of "extremism" or "terrorism," even our dogmatic assertion of our private economic rights expresses the sacrificial ambiguity of secularism. What can never be fully perceived in the public discourse of monolithically liberal societies, what Bataille, Girard, and Hartz are as one in drawing attention to, is the intimate connection between liberal individualism and totalitarianism.

But Bataille and Girard, for all their intellectual brilliance and religious truths, cannot conceive of any reconciliation of individual and collective in a world beyond the market-hive. All they can do is express the wildly contradictory inner life of the individual under liberal capitalism as it currently exists. They oscillate involuntarily, or voluntarily oscillate, between the values of market and hive. Neither Girard nor Bataille quite as clearly as Hartz perceives or expresses the interconnectedness of hive and market *at every moment*; in this they are qualitatively different from and, from a socialist perspective, "behind" Hartzian theory.

Gad Horowitz employed Hartzian theory to argue that we Canadians have, in our "tory touch," a small fragment of a real (i.e., more than literary) experience of pre-liberal politics, one that is not accessible to the American "new world order" of monolithic liberalism. As a result, we have, or at least once had, a spark of collective memory that was more quickly smothered in the American market-society. It is the extent, we could imagine Hartz or Horowitz saying, to which we collectively and institutionally conserve this memory, and not some mythically Canadian sense of the value of the toleration of differences, that makes us more sensitive to how the iconoclastic values of modern individualism can easily become their own paranoid mythology. The absolute belief in the freedom of the individual slips without a pause into a collectively reinforced, ontological inability to conceive of the individual as anything but entirely separate, voluntary, self-creating.

Liberal individuals might give a community their allegiance, or they might explode against it in literary iconoclasm. What is forgotten either way in monolithically liberal fragment culture is that, for better or for worse, the community is dialectically speaking the *essence* of the individual. The Hartz-Horowitz thesis says nothing more to begin with than that to actually realize the laudable moral and religious concerns expressed by documents like the Declaration of Independence – concern for individual free creativity, concern for the minimization of arbitrary collective violence – we need first of all to come to terms with what this liberal society has actually always been.

NOTES

1 Donald Forbes, "Hartz-Horowitz at Twenty: Nationalism, Toryism and Socialism in Canada and the United States," *Canadian Journal of Political Science* 20, no. 2 (June 1987): 287–315.

2 There is surely no more striking or resonant echo of McCarthyite paranoia in our time than the hysterical accusations that have accompanied President Obama's attempts to reform health-care provision in the United States. The common thread underlying these accusations is that a public-funding option abandons the principle of the freedom and responsibility of the individual and is therefore socialist, fascist, racist, totalitarian, etc.

3 Louis Hartz, ed., *The Founding of New Societies: Studies in the History of the United States, Latin America, South Africa, Canada, and Australia* (New York: Harcourt, Brace and World, 1964), 65.

4 Ibid., 64.

5 Forbes, "Hartz-Horowitz at Twenty," 315.

6 Hartz, *Founding of New Societies*, 6–7.

7 René Girard, *Deceit, Desire, and the Novel: Self and Other in Literary Structure*, trans. Yvonne Freccero (Baltimore: Johns Hopkins University Press, 1965), 3.

8 Ibid., 10–11.

9 Hartz, *Founding of New Societies*, 55.

10 In the interest of brevity I am not able to reproduce the fuller contours of Girard's incredible revelations here; my report must remain schematic. For further reference, the reader is directed to Girard's texts *Violence and the Sacred, The Scapegoat,* or his more recent and accessible *I See Satan Fall like Lightning*.

11 René Girard, *I See Satan Fall like Lightning*, trans. James G. Williams (New York: Orbis Books, 2001), 161.

12 Georges Bataille and Roger Caillois, "Sacred Sociology and the Relationships between 'Society,' 'Organism' and 'Being,'" in *The College of Sociology*, ed. Denis Hollier (Minneapolis: University of Minnesota Press, 1988), 74.

13 Ibid.

14 Georges Bataille, *Inner Experience*, trans. Leslie Boldt (Albany, NY: SUNY, 1988), 72.

15 Hartz, *Founding of New Societies*, 6–7.

PART FOUR

Political Philosophy

12 Transcendental Liberalism and the Politics of Representation: Possessive Individualism Revisited

SEAN SARAKA

The two overarching themes of Horowitz and Horowitz's *"Everywhere They Are in Chains"* are the relationship of the individual to the totality, and the subterranean connection between conservatism and radicalism.[1] Each of these themes can be seen to have a more and a less proximate source of inspiration. The nature of the individual and her relationship to the totality is the great theme of Western Marxism, both in its classic formulation in the work of Georg Lukács, and also in the work of the Frankfurt school. More immediate to the concerns of political theory is the work of C.B. Macpherson, whose *Political Theory of Possessive Individualism* identifies a conception of individual self-ownership as the defining element of modern political thought.[2] The theme of the relationship between conservatism and socialism is an implicit theme in the work of Rousseau, and the explicit thesis of "Conservatism, Liberalism, and Socialism in Canada: An Interpretation," Gad Horowitz's most famous work, and a revision of and response to Louis Hartz's fragment theory of political culture.[3] At the risk of complicating the symmetry of this scheme, we may note that Rousseau too takes subjectivation as his theme in the second *Discourse*, the *Social Contract, Emile*, and elsewhere.[4]

The claim that the individual stands at the centre of modern political theory is hardly novel, but this centrality has nevertheless posed a long series of problems for political theory and philosophy. This is perhaps best illustrated by Macpherson's study, which, despite the self-evidence of its central claims, has been perennially embroiled in controversy.[5] In *"Everywhere They Are in Chains,"* Horowitz and Horowitz superimpose a series of overlapping discourses of politics and subjectivity, including Macpherson's, in a double attempt to negotiate the complexities of modern individualism. This double strategy can be tentatively characterized as dialectical; it is defined by two antithetical tendencies: on the one hand, an analysis of images of political organization and of the institution of the social in early modern political thought, for which purpose the authors introduce the categories of "market" and "hive," as well as the notion of a historico-anthropological progression from "early" to "high" classless society. On the other hand and at the same time, Horowitz and Horowitz describe a libidinal politics of the modern subject, which establishes a countervailing tendency to any claims of historical progress, and which they identify with the thought of Rousseau, Hegel, and Marx.

This attempt by Horowitz and Horowitz to execute a dialectical reading of modern political thought manifests a number of remarkable features, not least of which are the authors' reticence regarding the impetus and aims of their project, and the many theoretical complications that arise from their reading, especially the disordering of history that occurs in the space between their developmental anthropology and their psychology of the modern subject. In what follows, I will relate these silences and reversals to the contemporary literature of subjectivity and subjectivation. With reference to the work of Slavoj Žižek and Étienne Balibar, among others, I will show that the apparent idiosyncrasies of "Everywhere They Are in Chains" are hardly capricious, but are rather rigorously determined by a nexus of relationships between subjectivation, history, and representation.

I

Horowitz and Horowitz state their intentions at the outset of "Everywhere They Are in Chains," in a preface that consists of one short and one long paragraph. They write, "Our purpose in this book is to explore its unifying theme: the critique of the 'market-hive.' Where standard treatments of political theory play the market off against the hive, we attempt a new interpretation by moving beyond what seems to us a false dichotomy" (ix). In a peremptory statement, the authors acknowledge that "Everywhere They Are in Chains" is not quite a book (ix). It is neither comprehensive in the manner of a textbook, nor exhaustive in the manner of a scholarly monograph. It traces a progression only from Rousseau to Marx. It announces no explicit methodology and does not make its logic of organization quite clear. If, on the one hand, the impetus for the book is explicitly stated, on the other hand this statement rests on idiosyncratic concepts, which are only cursorily explained.

The irritation that such evasions might produce is sharply felt by Florian Bail, an early reviewer who finds that *"Everywhere They Are in Chains"* is "sociological" and "politically uninformative."[6] "Underscored by a romantic perspective of history," he complains, the book "offers the sentimental view of a politics still mediated through a parochially socialized self and locates political thinking on an unhappy continuum between anamnesis of a naïve past and intuition of an emerging pacific realm." It is noxious to political theory itself: "Precisely because the authors chose to comment on the seemingly sociological links between Rousseau, de Bonald, de Maistre, Burke, Bentham, James Mill, John Stuart Mill, Hegel and Marx and the 'market-hive' reality of modern society, they fail to appreciate the political merits of theoretical attempts to render political rule simultaneously just, effective and beneficial."

Bail's particular objections aside, *"Everywhere They Are in Chains"* is a strange book, all the more so because it is not what Bail says it is. Horowitz and Horowitz's concern for the relationship between the individual and whole is emblematic of Western Marxism, but despite initial appearances, market and hive are not quite social forms in a Lukácsian sense. They are less binding agents of the social whole or points of condensation for social contradictions than ideological images of the social totality. As such, Horowitz and Horowitz supplement a Lukácsian analysis rooted in the theory of fetishism, with an ideological analysis of liberalism and conservatism that both cleaves closer to the conventional concerns of political science and suggests significant revisions to a Western Marxist approach. The methodological revisions that Horowitz and Horowitz enact are informed by a Rousseauian, anthropological concern for the nature of the social bond, a sociology of knowledge inspired by the Frankfurt school, and a critique of reason common to both. It is this constellation of theoretical imperatives that lead Horowitz and Horowitz to shift in their introductory chapter from market and hive as images of totality, to an anthropological history of forms of human community, to the Enlightenment idea of reason and its critique. They write, "Reason is the solvent of community, the solvent of the hive. What is left after it has done its work of separation and purification is the free, rational individual."[7]

If Bail implies that the book obeys a kind of Hegelian-Marxist historical logic that secures its "intuition of an emerging pacific realm," this teleology is perhaps less certain than he suggests. In fact, a kind of historical stasis hangs over *"Everywhere They Are in Chains,"* and it is this very lack of historical movement that leaves its authors' intimations of the future as little more than intuitions. The book traces only a brief interval in the development of modern political thought, one that can be said to culminate with Marx, but also one over which decisive historical change cannot be said to have occurred. This apparent stasis marks what is in effect a movement of retrogression: not only do Horowitz and Horowitz draw many of their examples from the anthropology of tribal cultures, but this reversal structures the very interval in discourse they have undertaken to study. In *"Everywhere They Are in Chains,"* retrogression is an index of theoretical progress: the reader learns that "Rousseau is the founder of post-liberal thought precisely because he looked *forward* to the restoration of primitive anarchy, social individuality, spontaneity, and priority of the community."[8] Marx's superiority over Hegel is established by his *"retreat ... to the materialist rationalism of the Enlightenment."* Rousseau, because he "diagnosed human reason itself as an expression and facilitation of an aggressive, dominating attitude toward external and internal nature," is "in a sense" superior to Marx.[9] The epoch of modern thought runs, as in the title of the book's final section, "From Marx to Rousseau."

Adopting a quasi-sociological approach and presenting a historical narrative that is purposively disordered by its authors' reading of the canon, *"Everywhere They Are in Chains"* is a study of political theory in search of new concepts. It is possible to read this curiously acephalic quality as a formal analogue to the representational limits asserted by thinkers such as Adorno, or even as a thematic repetition of Rousseau himself, whose central governing concepts, as Horowitz and Horowitz amply note, concern individual psychology and the relationship of the individual to the social whole. What distinguishes *"Everywhere They Are in Chains"* from other works of Western Marxism in this respect is its refusal to place emphasis on the indeterminate orientation of the subject to the totality, or the attendant problems of perception and figuration, but rather on the constitution of the subject itself. This attention to subjectivation remains at a level below the statement in *"Everywhere They Are in Chains,"* even as it saturates the book. What is Naikan therapy if not a practice of subjectivation, and what else could Rousseau be said to reveal, if not the existence of processes of subjectivation and their necessary role in the formation of the political community? It also determines Gad Horowitz's contemporaneous encounter with Foucault, and his study of Marcuse.[10]

Horowitz and Horowitz do comment on the importance of subjectivity in passing in the beginning of a chapter on John Stuart Mill: "The priority of the individual is not the idea that the human being is an inherently worthy entity who ought to be positively affected by the social order. There is no one who does not believe that.... You can play the game of 'law and order' from within any point of view. You can shower the individual with love or discipline him strongly from a socialist or tory or liberal point of view.... It is not a debate between 'order' and 'freedom.' It is not a question of how much 'worth' to give the individual and how much to reserve for society, but rather a debate about what the individual *is*."[11]

In this context, Rousseau is the thinker who maps the subject's relationship to both nature and society and who takes the ontological formation of the subject as the central problem of politics. If Rousseau can serve as the thinker who initiates the series examined in *"Everywhere They Are in Chains,"* it is because he is critically aware of the sublimated violence that politics entails. In "The Foucauldian Impasse" Horowitz objects to Foucault's failure to distinguish as Marcuse does between primary and surplus repression. It is clear that what Foucault and Rousseau do share with Marcuse is a recognition of the implicit violence contained in subjectivation.[12] Foucault's critique of Hobbes in the lectures that comprise *Society Must Be Defended* might be read to suggest Rousseau's superiority over the latter as a theorist of modern politics: "Rather than asking ourselves what the sovereign looks like from on high, we should be trying to discover how multiple bodies, forces, energies, matters, desires, thoughts, and so on are gradually, progressively, actually and materially constituted as subjects, or as the subject.... [R]ather than raising the problem of the central soul, I think we should be trying ... to study the multiple peripheral bodies, the bodies that are constituted as subjects by power-effects."[13]

Foucault's description of the dilemma of modern subjectivity in the late programmatic essay "What Is Enlightenment?" notably parallels the tension between the development of social institutions and the preservation of individual liberty which emerges in *On the Social Contract*. For Foucault, the stakes of the problem of Enlightenment "are indicated by what might be called 'the paradox of the relations of capacity and power.'"[14] If Rousseau's attempted resolution to this paradox differs markedly from Foucault's, Foucault's formulation of the problem is nevertheless one that he might share: "How can the growth of capabilities be disconnected from the intensification of power relations?"

This interest in the formation of subjectivity determines the sociologism of *"Everywhere They Are in Chains."* The analysis of modern political forms might therefore be thought to devolve to the examination of processes of subjectivation: the conditioning of the subject is one lesson that Marx is known explicitly to have taken over from Rousseau, in "On the Jewish Question."[15] C.B. Macpherson, for his part, argues in the *Theory of Possessive Individualism* and elsewhere that the constitution of subjects as individuals is not simply one axiom among others in modern Western ideology, but constitutes the ground of "a western democratic ontology."[16] In the work of the Frankfurt school, as in the work of Rousseau, the consolidation of modern individualism coincides with alienation, domination, and atavistic regression. For Foucault, the question of political obligation is supplanted by an investigation of the institutional discourses that form the subject. Market and hive as images of the social totality thus correlate with processes of subjectivation and images of political power.

II

The movement of retrogression – from Marx to Rousseau – traced by *"Everywhere They Are in Chains"* is neither nostalgic nor retrograde. It does not manifest a blind spot so much as trace a rigorously determined hiatus around the problem of the subject. In Marxian terms, this is the problem of ideology, according to which the formation of the subject implies the suspension of history. This is the point of Althusser's claim that ideology (which, for Althusser, is always the ideology of the subject) has no history.[17] History manifests as something outside of the subject, whose sense of historicity is the effect of a synchronic symbolic construction. For the later Marx, the counterpart of this congealed sense of historicity is the "scandal" of the dialectical method, which exposes "every historically developed form as being in a fluid state" and in so doing traces the process of abstraction itself.[18]

The ideological exchange between history and the subject has the same formal structure as Marx's conception of commodity fetishism in the first chapter of *Capital*, which similarly manifests a congealment of social processes. The collateral effect of a process of exchange that "goes on behind the backs of producers," fetishism sees an exchange of the characteristics of labour between labour and its products.[19] Yet value itself also emerges from this scene, if not exactly as an ex post facto symbolic construction, then as a "concrete abstraction," the very extraneous standard according to which production is organized. It is value, perhaps, more than any other concept that is the "sum of many determinations": it is not the product of a mental process of reflection, but rather is the practical result of producers' actions themselves.[20]

According to Marx, then, the concept of value that arises in exchange has two principal characteristics. In the first place, it is the product of a material process, although Marx complicates its material status by distinguishing use-from exchange-value and price as symbolic forms of appearance.[21] At the same time, the realization of value is the moment of an exchange of ideologemes, according to which that which is dynamic and productive exchanges qualities with that which is passive and inert. This exchange of qualities is accompanied by a thoroughgoing de-historicization, through which exchange-value comes to appear as a naturalized measure of worth.

The temporal structure of fetishism elaborated by Marx and Althusser dictates that all histories are an a posteriori symbolic construction, and further that these constructions constitute a necessary support of subjectivity. The subject "always-already" exists precisely because its formation inaugurates the experience of history itself. This can be taken to account for the temporal vacillations of *"Everywhere They Are in Chains,"* wherein Horowitz and Horowitz discover a historical void as they attempt to disentangle the modern political subject from the various ideologies in which it is enfolded, even as they advance critical reflections that are themselves decorated with pendants of an idiosyncratic historicity. Rousseau is here again the prime exemplar, with his attempt to void the state of nature of the detritus of society and his coeval acknowledgment the necessity of symbolism in the *Social Contract*'s many reversions, both tacit and explicit, to the fiction of the lawgiver, civil religion, classical republicanism, Sparta and Plato.[22] At the level of practical politics, this cements a relationship between socialism and conservatism: both ideologies define a certain relationship to history that may exert a libidinal pull as nostalgia. Here the fundamental empirical insight of "Conservatism, Liberalism, and Socialism in Canada" shades into the theoretical analysis of *"Everywhere They Are in Chains,"* in which the analytical force and rhetorical appeal of both Rousseau and Marx is understood precisely in terms of their admixture of conservatism and radicalism.[23]

Is it possible categorically to disavow such nostalgia? Rousseau, for his part, doggedly exposes the violence of political power in the second *Discourse*, only to wish in the *Social Contract* for a power that "can compel without violence and persuade without convincing."[24] Reading Rousseau in light of "Conservatism, Liberalism, and Socialism in

Canada" and *"Everywhere They Are in Chains,"* one might take his reversions as an implicit or explicit acknowledgment of the symbolic foundations of authority, or even as a practical strategy of political persuasion
and mobilization, but this is precisely Marx's concern in the *Eighteenth
Brumaire*, where he laments that previous revolutions have remained
fatefully circumscribed by the historical symbols through which they
have found expression.[25]

On what conditions can political power be made visible, and can this
visibility be sustained? For Marx, fetishism dictates that the manifest
symbolization of exchange coexists with value, a concrete abstraction
that is not explicitly conceptualized. Reading Marx, Slavoj Žižek argues
that not only is the unconscious element in fetishism properly ineradi-
cable, but that Marx has in fact discovered the form of the human unconscious in general.[26] Žižek argues that fetishism is the counterpart of the
Lacanian conception of fantasy, which, far from masking reality, serves
as "a support for our 'reality' itself": "'Reality' is a fantasy-construction
which enables us to mask the Real of our desire."[27] Ideology serves not to
distort reality but to structure it; the basis of subjectivity therefore cannot
simply be brought to knowledge, but rather the appearance of knowledge acts as a support that prolongs the fetishistic illusion.

The difference in Žižek's scheme is apparent in his treatment of the
fetish-object. In commodity fetishism, as in fetishism in general, it is not
simply that an illusory exchange of qualities has taken place. Rather,
the structure of fetishism is such that the ideological fantasy is not an
object of conscious belief but is sustained by the subject's actions. Individuals may very well be aware that commodity fetishism obscures
the nature of value, or may adopt a cynical attitude towards capitalist
ideology, yet their participation in the system of commodity exchange
nevertheless serves concretely to reproduce capitalist ideology. The fetish-object, far from retaining an illusory power, represents for the subject an indigestible kernel of the Real. In this way, the fetish is more real
than "reality" itself, and any attempt to dispel the illusion ultimately
constitutes a form of neurotic avoidance.

Žižek consequently criticizes Althusser both for the implication
that abstraction occurs primarily in thought, and for his failure to account in the theory of interpellation for the kind of circularity dictated
by the Lacanian theory of fantasy.[28] Yet Žižek's criticisms also indicate
a deeper disagreement with Althusser regarding the relationship between representation and ontology. While both theories emphasize the
role of the symbolic in the formation of subjectivity, Althusser's theory

of interpellation grants a specific role to the exercise of political power, whereas Žižek's Lacanian framework ostensibly posits subjective lack as a primary phenomenon, prior to any determinate exercise of power or coercion. In the following sections, I will explore the implications of this dilemma for practices of theoretical representation, through an examination of C.B. Macpherson's theory of possessive individualism, in particular as it is treated by Étienne Balibar in a series of essays on the nature and origins of the modern Western subject.

III

The controversies surrounding *The Political Theory of Possessive Individualism* have revolved around C.B. Macpherson's framing of possessive individualism as a unitary phenomenon characterized by a high degree of internal consistency and a history of interrupted development.[29] While commentators such as Ashcraft have objected strongly to Macpherson's portrayal of Locke as an apologist for capitalism,[30] perhaps the boldest and most problematic of Macpherson's gestures is the attribution of common conceptions of property and individualism to Hobbes and Locke alike. Such claims are of a piece with Macpherson's overarching thesis, namely that, contrary to appearances, the formulations of all of the principal figures in early modern political thought hold in common a latent conception of subjectivity as self-ownership. Macpherson's aetiology of possessive individualism thus serves his larger project of disentangling democracy from capitalism by demonstrating that there is no pre-existing original of democratic theory innocent of capitalist individualism to which contemporary theorists may appeal, and therefore that a new properly egalitarian account of political obligation is necessary.[31]

But if Macpherson's theory of possessive individualism turns on a typically Marxist critique of private property and has excited the predictable ideological denials, complaints against his work stem equally from the conceptual difficulties that attend any attempt to theorize the relationships between subjectivity, property, and power in the modern period. In "'Possessive Individualism' Reversed: From Locke to Derrida," Étienne Balibar returns to Macpherson's study to perform a series of historical corrections and conceptual emendations, three of which are of particular note here.[32]

Firstly, Balibar remarks that Macpherson's desire to present possessive individualism as a unitary phenomenon produces a reading of early modern political thought that is "rather forced."[33] Whereas Macpherson claims that the seven tenets that he ascribes to possessive individualism "are clearest and fullest in Hobbes," Balibar notes that "there are essential reasons why Hobbes would *absolutely refuse* the notion of 'self-ownership' as a *political* notion – since it would establish competing authorities and obligations."[34] Yet the issue is not simply that Macpherson has misread Hobbes; rather, Balibar's reading suggests that Macpherson's "privileging [of] unity over diversity, subjecting the 'points of heresy' to the establishment of a general *doxa*" leads him into a different kind of misapprehension.[35] Clarity is precisely the attraction of Hobbes's text vis-à-vis Locke's, whose formulations can seem only muddy by comparison. Macpherson, in his desire to formulate possessive individualism as a parsimonious system, and encouraged by the notional atomism of both Hobbes's and Locke's formulations, is led to posit a strong identification between the two that privileges the former over the latter.

Conversely, Balibar suggests that it is precisely Locke's lack of clarity that is his greatest advantage. Whereas Macpherson frames a single conception of possessive individualism, Balibar posits "at least two": "I prefer to consider that possessive individualism never existed if not in the form of a conflict, with an initial division at its core."[36] Within this multiplicity, termed by Balibar "a proper *dialectics of possessive individualism*,"[37] the difference and advantage of Locke's formulations inheres precisely in his conception of self-ownership, which both efficiently describes the property relation at the core of capitalist subjectivity and establishes a regime of representation sufficiently ambivalent to engender a long series of theoretical and ideological disseminations.

Secondly, then, like Horowitz and Horowitz, Balibar emphasizes the significance of images of the subject in modern political thought. Yet whereas the former perform a critical operation similar to Macpherson's, arguing that behind market and hive subsists an indifferent conception of the rational subject that unites, as Balibar writes of Macpherson, "the most opposite projects,"[38] Balibar examines the implications of the notion of self-ownership itself, which he traces through a series of transformations in the work of Rousseau, Marx, and Derrida. Unlike Macpherson, who reads Locke through the lens of a Marxian conception of the alienation of labour-power and the exclusion of the working class from political participation,[39] Balibar seeks to interrogate the complications internal to the Lockean subject. On this count, Balibar seeks not only to correct Macpherson's unitary conception of possessive individualism, but to show that modern political subjectivity is itself essentially divided.

Balibar's reading of Macpherson comes at the end of a long series of essays in which he overturns a number of historical and philosophical commonplaces regarding the formation of the modern subject.[40] The overarching thesis that connects these individual studies is that modern subjectivity is divided and contradictory at its core. In terms of the history of philosophy, Balibar argues that, contrary to the claims of master thinkers such as Heidegger, it is with Kant and not Descartes that the subject as a category of modern thought is consolidated. This claim is the product of a close reading of the key texts of modern philosophy and political theory, which allows Balibar to point out that substance is the more important category for Descartes, and that it is in the context of the holistic philosophies of Spinoza and Leibniz, rather than the putative individualisms of Descartes, Locke, and Hobbes, that a modern concept of individuality is developed.[41] Yet Balibar finds that this concept of the individual is not equivalent to the modern conception of the subject, the complications of which are signalled by its ambiguous relationship to the Roman legal categories of *subjectum* and *subjectus*, neither of which is plainly equivalent to the modern conception of a free and equal individual.[42]

A principal impetus of Balibar's research is to demonstrate that the modern subject is not in fact free. If Kant can be taken to complete the concept of modern subjectivity, it is because he explicitly presents the modern individual as the subject of the law. "The puzzling nature of what is called 'modernity,'" Balibar writes, is that "the individual can be a citizen effectively only if he or she *becomes a subject again.*"[43] The modern individual is characterized by this double constitution, on the one hand as a free citizen, and on the other as the subject of multiple internal and external discourses that secure its subordination. Citizens, as the subjects of liberal discourses of governance, are in principle neither singular individuals nor free political agents, but are rather identical forms organized in series and subordinated to the whole through a constellation of disparate internal and external discourses.[44]

This image of the modern individual belies Macpherson's conception of possessive individualism as a triumphalist, self-regarding doctrine. In both sociological and philosophical terms, Balibar shows that the apparatus of contemporary individualism is not compact and self-sufficient, but distributed across a constellation of sites and terms that serve to supplement each other, and which manifest the interpenetration of mutually distinct imperatives and objectives. Accordingly, Balibar frames a concept of multiple *"modes of subjection* ... [that] combine relations of power, an economy of language, and imagination of the body and soul."[45] Given the importance of the symbolic in this formation, Balibar argues that *"on the issues of the subject* ... only *philosophical* work can be critical work," as it is uniquely capable of tracing the substitutions and displacements that occur in the transcendental dimension of modern subjectivity.[46]

By the same token, this project of "philosophical anthropology" is foundational for philosophy itself, as it "has no metatheoretical position or external vantage point in relation to the signifying composites that constitute it."[47] Unlike Macpherson, who apprehends possessive individualism largely as an accessory to the early modern development of capitalism, Balibar argues that the symbolic component of possessive individualism has an ontological function with respect to modern subjectivity, which warrants examination in its own right.

IV

Privileging "points of heresy" over any notional unity, Balibar discerns two forms of possessive individualism, associated with Hobbes and Locke respectively. The first turns on a conception of economic competition "as war waged 'by other means'"; the second, "as reciprocity and exchange culminating in the legal dispute, whose 'natural' scene is not the battlefield but the tribunal."[48] These are, Balibar writes, "two different ways of introducing the play of metaphor into the representation of the market."[49] Negatively, this takes the form of an attempt to ascertain the limits or boundaries of the field of the political. Presupposing the ineradicability of violence, Hobbes places himself in the tradition of conservative thinkers such as de Bonald and de Maistre, for whom the political order supplies the only guarantee against human barbarism.[50] At the same time, this threat of violence underlies representation itself, which Hobbes makes clear cannot alone hold disorder at bay.[51] Hobbes therefore proposes to contain the negativity underlying representation by buttressing signification with political authority and the threat of sovereign violence. In this way, the exclusion of violence constitutes not only a precondition for the establishment of an orderly commonwealth, but of representation itself.[52]

Whereas for Hobbes individuals can be represented only by other individuals in a relationship of direct authorization, for Locke the belonging of individuals to the political community is mediated via their property, or things, which are secured through the activity of labour. Hobbes is concerned to limit individuals' public expression of their internal states, but Locke's formulation explicitly relies on parallel conceptions of labour and self-consciousness as capacities immanent and internal to the individual, the public expression of which is the condition of belonging itself. Accordingly, Locke's conception of individual self-ownership simultaneously positions the subject as a participant in the commercial market and the subject of law, and it is for this reason that Balibar identifies Locke as the first modern thinker of the subject and a precursor to Kant.[53] Yet the representational scheme described in Locke's work is no more able to recognize political violence than Hobbes's. If Hobbes's atomism bore the implication that individual bodies could always be recombined or decomposed, and therefore were always implicitly susceptible to violence, Locke's framing of the subject as transcendental and indestructible both establishes the overwhelming political and philosophical primacy of the proprietary individual and simultaneously disavows any recognition of formative or systematic violence. Locke's conception of personal identity reduces all history to the scope of the individual consciousness, transcendental in its unity and immanent in temporality.[54]

According to Balibar, then, representation is crucial to Locke's conception of subjectivity, because the coherence of the subject rests on the ability of the individual to identify with the actions and things by which she is represented to the community. For Balibar, this proprietary form of identification is part of a broader and more parsimonious trope of "appropriation" that both comprehends and exceeds Macpherson's conception of possessive individualism.[55] Perhaps most significantly, it calls into question the adequacy of Macpherson's own attempts to provide an alternative to liberal democracy, insofar as he addresses the economic and institutional, but not the metaphysical, dimensions of self-ownership. Alternatively, the critique of reason offered in *"Everywhere They Are in Chains"* more closely identifies modern subjectivity with its transcendental predicates, yet Horowitz and Horowitz ultimately accede to a Marxian vision according to which the latent persistence of the "hive" offers the possibility of a full recuperation of reason via a dialectical reversal won by the forces of production.[56]

If Balibar is correct that only philosophical work on subjectivity can be critical work, how is it possible to undo the constitutive relationship between representation and subjectivity that lies at the core of modern being? What new form of representation is possible that might displace modern subjectivity and provide the basis for an alternative account of political right? In "'Possessive Individualism' Reversed," Balibar considers three such attempts to move beyond the Lockean-Kantian doctrine of representation as mediation in the work of Rousseau, Marx, and Derrida.

Whereas the Lockean conception of self-ownership dictates that individuals constitute the community via the action of appropriation, Rousseau reverses this schema so that it is the community that legitimates the property of the individual. According to Balibar, this "establish[es] dispossession at the very heart of property, in an irreversible manner," insofar as the precondition of the legitimation of property by the state is a "total alienation" of all property and propriety on behalf of individuals.[57] To wit, this also constitutes an admission of violence into political representation, which not only establishes the very need to legitimate property for Rousseau but also informs some of his most provocatively anti-liberal assertions regarding the relationship of the state to the individual.[58]

For Balibar, Rousseau's ambivalence regarding the priority of the individual versus the community holds the implication that individualism is always an institutional fiction, but Rousseau's "total dispossession" also has the collateral effect of subordinating the individual to the law.[59] The constitution of the individual comes at the price of subjecting the enjoyment of property to the law of the community, in recognition of the fundamental violence that property entails. Yet this subordination also contains an implicit recognition that belonging to the community entails the suppression of the non-identity between the individual and the whole, an abiding alienation at the core of subjectivity that cannot be overcome. Consequently, self-ownership is displaced "in the direction of an impossible unity with oneself," which Rousseau projects into a past prior to the constitution of property and subjectivity as such.[60] This is to say, as well, that Rousseau's presentation of the law is itself no less ambivalent. Insofar as law serves as a mechanism of moral legitimation, its own violent excesses are displaced, as in Locke, onto the act of consent.

If Rousseau effects a reversal of priority between the community and the individual, Marx seeks to undo possessive individualism via a dialectical negation of the negation according to which private property is sublated through an act of collective expropriation. Balibar reads this strategy as a radical revision of the formulations of both Locke and Rousseau. With respect to the former, Marx asserts the divisibility of labour, precisely what Locke posits as indivisible.[61] For Marx, labour cannot serve to establish private property because it is in reality not an individual, but rather a collective, capacity. Like Rousseau, Marx thus recognizes a formative violence and alienation in the constitution of individual private property; but whereas Rousseau reassigns the mediating function of property to the community, Marx posits the collectivity as the proper subject of self-ownership. Marx deconstructs the concept of individual self-ownership only to reaffirm the Lockean notion that the subject is formed in an act of legitimate appropriation, which, in equally Lockean fashion, "seems to conceal a secret aporia that concerns the capacity of individuals to identify *subjectively* with the teleology of socialized labour."[62]

Marx in effect undertakes to separate individuality from subjectivity and to mediate the relationship between the two via the operation of the dialectic, but Balibar argues that this only serves to pose the relationship between the collectivity and the individual as an "an impossible choice."[63] As with Rousseau, this choice ultimately rests on the possibility of enjoyment, which in Marx's work takes the form of the question of the possibility of leisure versus the necessity of labour.[64] In representational terms, this introduces a certain form of reversibility into Marx's formulations. The ambiguous relationship between the individual and the collectivity gives rise to a dilemma regarding the status of the act of collective appropriation itself. For Marx, Balibar writes, "in a contradictory manner, collective appropriation *is and is not representable* as a 'process of subjectivation' or subjective individualization."[65]

Derrida's relationship to possessive individualism is ostensibly more oblique, but Balibar argues persuasively that the persistent themes of capital, the gift, the proper, and ex-appropriation in Derrida's work constitute "[a] new strategy of reversal" that "reveals better than any other the eschatological element that was latent in the classical discourse of 'possessive individualism,' and uses this revelation to question the implications and functions of eschatology. [It also] succeeds in discovering within the concept of the 'subject' associated with a constitutive concept of 'property,' the 'own,' and the 'proper,' or with possessive individuality, the same antinomic (hence violent) elements that are also constitutive of the concept of sovereignty."[66]

Derrida's deconstruction of figures of propriety consists of a double strategy that, on the one hand, posits a general movement of

"propriation" prior to any properly appropriative origin. This constitutes a repetition of the gesture through which Locke grounded the
notion of individual self-ownership in the *arche*-ownership of each individual by God. On the other hand, then, Derrida calls attention to
the curious atemporality of the origin of property and to the implicit
teleology according to which the non-identity of the subject is deferred.

This temporal deconstruction of the proper dictates that, unlike
Rousseau or Marx, Derrida's reversal of possessive individualism cannot rely on the implicit or explicit projection of a notional unity into
the future or past. As such, Derrida presents time as what, contrary
to the movement of appropriation, constitutes the absolutely inap-
propriable, and thus marks an abiding negativity at the very heart of
representation.[67]

In recognition of this negative, Derrida frames the concept-metaphor
of "ex-appropriation" to designate an impossible "property without
property," a transcendental gesture "where[by] the 'proper' becomes
reversed into a 'universal' that *belongs to nobody*."[68] Balibar speculates
that this impossible reversal might turn on "the idea of a community
that has no 'property' in itself, and therefore no 'common good' (or
commonwealth) to protect, appropriate, and identify with, but can be approached only in terms of its ever to-come requisite of justice, openness
to the other – a reciprocity beyond reciprocity founded on the loss of
property that is the core of the subject's resistance to identification."[69]

But even here, Balibar argues, "a certain 'form' has been preserved."
For Locke, "it is ... *identity* and the *identical* that becomes preserved as the
inalienable self ... [w]hereas in Derrida it is rather deconstruction as such
that constitutes the undeconstructible.... So in a sense it is 'alienation' radicalized ... that has become inalienable."[70] Derrida's solution can consequently be understood as a redoubling of Rousseau's, in that it radicalizes
the alienation that is necessarily effaced in the constitution of subjectivity.
But what persists from Locke to Derrida, and which Rousseau and Marx
similarly fail to evade, is the preservation of "a certain ... antinomic form
that has to do with the alternative of gain and loss, and which ... would
inscribe our ethical discourse in the eschatological horizon of justice."[71]

V

In place of a conclusion that might recommend a decision between
these different attempts to constitute and reverse possessive individualism, Balibar has described a certain form of reversibility within
which all such attempts are located. His interest in doing so is not to

present possessive individualism as an absolute limit to all efforts to arrive at a new politics, but rather to demonstrate the durability, if not the necessity, of Locke's formulations. This durability is a function of Locke's parallel efforts to describe the relationship between the individual and the community, and between the mind and nature, with recourse to mediating representations. In this particular respect, Locke's formulations prove remarkably supple in comparison with those of Hobbes, Rousseau, Marx, or Derrida, insofar as his conception of mediation proves remarkably capable of accommodating ambiguities and excesses of meaning. His conception of subjectivity as a set of potentials immanent to the individual body both posits existence of the subject as a function of external actions, and secures it coherence through self-identification.

The counterpart of this internalized self-consciousness is a conception of law immanent to the individual, given final form by Kant. Natural law subjects the Lockean individual to norms of behaviour that are similarly explained in terms of property (in this case, the ownership of all individuals by God), and subjects her actions to the norms of reason. This indefeasible link between the liberty of the individual and her subjection not only establishes a set of regulatory norms that govern behaviour, but also pre-empts any consideration of the nature and origin of the law itself. Law, like the unitary subject, is transcendental and therefore does not admit of the kind of inquiry into origins that might raise questions regarding the role of violence in politics.

In Locke's labouring world, the key elements of politics and community emerge, like Marx's value, behind the backs of individual actors, as the unconscious product of their collective actions. It is precisely for this reason that those thinkers who would seek to reverse possessive individualism, Marx among them, have sought to foreground the role of the symbolic in the construction of subjectivity. For Rousseau, this project takes the form of a conscious founding of the law in full awareness of its violence. For Marx, this entails both a critique of modern individualism and a corresponding attempt to develop a concept of "transindividuality,"[72] which might effect a dialectical mediation between the individual and the whole. If Balibar demonstrates that these attempts ultimately founder on their inability to move beyond a conception of the unitary subject, we may also recognize a certain commonality between conservatism and socialism here, in that both seek to supplant transcendental liberalism by reinserting the subject into a rich history of development, and by advancing a politics that appeals to the promises of subjective fulfilment implied therein.

232   Sean Saraka

NOTES

1 Asher Horowitz and Gad Horowitz, *"Everywhere They Are in Chains"*: Political Theory from Rousseau to Marx (Toronto: Nelson Canada, 1988).
2 C.B. Macpherson, *The Political Theory of Possessive Individualism* (London: Oxford University Press, 1962).
3 Gad Horowitz, "Conservatism, Liberalism, and Socialism in Canada: An Interpretation," *Canadian Journal of Economics and Political Science* 32, no. 2 (May 1966): 144–71; Louis Hartz, *The Liberal Tradition in America: An Interpretation of American Political Thought since the Revolution* (New York: Harcourt Brace, 1955). For a recent discussion of the Hartz-Horowitz debate, see Katherine Fierlbeck, *Political Thought in Canada: An Intellectual History* (Peterborough, ON: Broadview, 2006), 87–92.
4 See Asher Horowitz, *Rousseau: Nature and History* (Toronto: University of Toronto Press, 1987).
5 For a critical discussion of the historical and theoretical controversies surrounding Macpherson's thesis, see James Tully, "The Possessive Individualism Thesis: A Reconsideration in Light of Recent Scholarship," in *Democracy and Possessive Individualism: The Intellectual Legacy of C.B. Macpherson*, ed. Joseph Carens, 19–44 (Albany, NY: SUNY, 1993).
6 Florian Bail, review of *"Everywhere They Are in Chains"* by Asher Horowitz and Gad Horowitz, *Canadian Journal of Political Science* 21, no. 4 (December 1988): 865–6. All quotations are taken from these two pages.
7 Horowitz and Horowitz, *"Everywhere They Are in Chains,"* 7.
8 Ibid., 13, emphasis in original.
9 Ibid., 285, emphasis added.
10 Gad Horowitz, "The Foucaultian Impasse: No Sex, No Self, No Revolution," *Political Theory* 15, no. 1 (February 1987): 61–80; Horowitz, *Repression: Basic and Surplus Repression in Psychoanalytic Theory; Freud, Reich, and Marcuse* (Toronto: University of Toronto Press, 1977).
11 Horowitz and Horowitz, *"Everywhere They Are in Chains,"* 168, emphasis in original.
12 In *"Everywhere They Are in Chains"* the distinction between primary and surplus repression is rehearsed in relationship between Marx and Hegel. Whereas Hegel apprehends all objectification as alienation, Marx holds out the prospect of a non-alienated use of reason, of objectification without alienation (284–5).
13 Michel Foucault, *"Society Must Be Defended": Lectures at the Collège de France 1975–1976*, trans. David Macey, ed. Arnold I. Davidson, Mauro Bertani, and Allesandro Fontana (New York: Picador, 2003), 28–9.

14 Michel Foucault, "What Is Enlightenment?," trans. Catherine Porter, in *The Foucault Reader*, ed. Paul Rabinow (New York: Pantheon, 1994), 47–8.
15 See Karl Marx, "On the Jewish Question," trans. David McLellan, in *Selected Writings*, 2nd ed., ed. David McLellan (Oxford: Oxford University Press, 2000), 64.
16 C.B. Macpherson, *Democratic Theory: Essays in Retrieval* (Oxford: Clarendon, 1973).
17 Louis Althusser, "Ideology and Ideological State Apparatuses (Notes towards an Investigation)," in *Lenin and Philosophy and Other Essays*, trans. Ben Brewster (New York: Monthly Review, 1971), 160.
18 Karl Marx, *Capital*, trans. Ben Fowkes (London: Penguin, 1976), 1:103.
19 Ibid., 1:135.
20 Karl Marx, "Introduction to the *Grundrisse*," in *Karl Marx: Texts on Method*, ed. and trans. Terrell Carver (Oxford: Blackwell), 72. On the a posteriori nature of abstraction, see "Introduction," 78. The unconscious character of concrete abstraction is discussed at length by Alfred Sohn-Rethel in *Intellectual and Manual Labour: A Critique of Epistemology*, trans. Martin Sohn-Rethel (Atlantic Highlands, NJ: Humanities, 1978); and by Slavoj Žižek, in *The Sublime Object of Ideology* (London: Verso, 1989).
21 See Gayatri Spivak, "Scattered Speculations on the Question of Value," in *The Spivak Reader*, ed. Danna Landry and Gerald Maclean (New York: Routledge: 1996), 114.
22 For Horowitz and Horowitz's commentary on Rousseau's reversions, see *"Everywhere They Are in Chains,"* 48–9. Bonnie Honig's *Democracy and the Foreigner* (Princeton: Princeton University Press, 2001) contains a more recent and direct examination of Rousseau's lawgiver and the symbolic construction of history. On another point, Althusser is particularly attentive to the tension established in Rousseau's work as a result of his desire to create a void – see Louis Althusser, "The Underground Current of the Materialism of the Encounter," in *Philosophy of the Encounter: Later Writings, 1978–1987*, ed. François Matheron and Oliver Corpet, trans. G.M. Goshgarian (London: Verso, 2006), 191, 195. I owe this last point to Warren Montag and his essay "The Late Althusser: Materialism of the Encounter or Philosophy of the Void?," paper presention, Rileggere Il Capitale: La Lezione di Louis Althusser, Venice, Italy, 10 November 2006.
23 E.g., Horowitz and Horowitz, *"Everywhere They Are in Chains,"* 238. An equally striking example of their tacit appraisal of conservatism is Horowitz and Horowitz's characterization of Hegel's philosophy as "a rationalization of Burke's" (231).

24 Jean-Jacques Rousseau, "On the Social Contract," in *Jean-Jacques Rouseau: Basic Political Writings*, trans. Donald A. Cress (Indianapolis, IN: Hackett, 1987), 163.
25 Karl Marx, *The Eighteenth Brumaire of Louis Bonaparte*, trans. C.P. Dutt (New York: International, 1963), 15–18.
26 Žižek, *Sublime Object of Ideology*, 11–53.
27 Ibid., 45.
28 Ibid., 19 and 44.
29 See note 5.
30 Richard Ashcraft, *Revolutionary Politics and Locke's Two Treatises of Government* (Princeton: Princeton University Press, 1986); and Ashcraft, *Locke's Two Treatises of Government* (London: Unwin Hyman, 1987).
31 James Tully, "The Possessive Individualism Thesis: A Reconsideration in Light of Recent Scholarship," in *Democracy and Possessive Individualism: The Intellectual Legacy of C.B. Macpherson*, ed. Joseph Carens (Albany, NY: SUNY, 1993), 20–3.
32 Étienne Balibar, "'Possessive Individualism' Reversed: From Locke to Derrida," *Constellations* 9, no. 3 (September 2002): 299–317.
33 Ibid., 300.
34 Macpherson, *The Political Theory of Possessive Individualism*, 264; Balibar, "'Possessive Individualism,'" 301, emphasis in original.
35 Balibar, "'Possessive Individualism,'" 300.
36 Ibid., 301.
37 Ibid., emphasis in original.
38 Ibid., 300.
39 See Tully, "Possessive Individualism Thesis," 30–1. Macpherson's introduction to Locke's *Second Treatise of Government* (Indianapolis: Hackett, 1980) is also instructive in this respect. In his introduction, Macpherson comments on both the exclusions of political representation (xix) and the ambiguities of Locke's conceptions of human nature and the state of nature (see especially xiv).
40 See Étienne Balibar, "Citizen Subject," trans. James B. Swenson Jr, in *Who Comes after the Subject?*, ed. Eduardo Cadava, 33–57 (New York: Routledge, 1991); Balibar, "Subjection and Subjectivation," in *Supposing the Subject*, ed. Joan Copjec, 1–15 (London: Verso, 1994); Balibar, "The Infinite Contradiction," trans. Jean-Marc Poisson and Jacques Lezra, *Yale French Studies* 88 (1995): 142–64; Balibar, "What Is 'Man' in Seventeenth-Century Philosophy? Subject, Individual, Citizen," in *The Individual in Political Theory and Practice*, ed. Janet Coleman, 215–41 (Oxford: Clarendon, 1996); Balibar, "What Makes a People a People? Rousseau and Kant," in *Masses, Classes*

and the Public Sphere, ed. Mike Hill and Warren Montag, trans. Erin Post, 105–31 (London: Verso, 2000).

41 Balibar, "What Is 'Man,'" 217–18, 226–9; Balibar, "Citizen Subject," 33–6.

42 Balibar, "Citizen Subject," 40–4; "Subjection and Subjectivation," 8–10.

43 Balibar "Infinite Contradiction," 153, emphasis in original.

44 See Tully, "Possessive Individualism Thesis," 32–3, 38.

45 Balibar, "Infinite Contradiction," 156, emphasis in original.

46 Ibid., 154. Balibar continues, "It is ... quite illusory to rely on disciplines other than philosophy in order to display the margin of freedom or capacity of variation that these problematic notions [i.e., of subjectivity] conceal ... unless, under the name of this or that discipline, what is really taking place is philosophical work – as is the case, to offer some examples, in Max Weber, Kelsen, Mauss, Freud, Benveniste, and Lacan."

47 Ibid.

48 Balibar, "'Possessive Individualism,'" 301.

49 Ibid.

50 See Horowitz, *Repression*, 214.

51 Thomas Hobbes, *Leviathan*, ed. Edwin Curley (Indianapolis: Hackett, 1994), 39: "The secret thoughts of a man run over all things, holy, profane, clean, obscene, grave, and light, without shame or blame; which verbal discourse cannot do farther than the judgment shall approve of the time, place, and persons."

52 See Foucault, *"Society Must Be Defended,"* 96–9.

53 Balibar, "What Is 'Man,'" 236.

54 Ibid.

55 Balibar, "'Possessive Individualism,'" 302–3; "What Is 'Man,'" 234–5.

56 Horowitz and Horowitz, *"Everywhere They Are in Chains,"* 284.

57 Balibar, "'Possessive Individualism,'" 305–6.

58 Among these assertions, I have in mind the most celebrated: that citizens who do not obey the general will, will be "forced to be free." See Rousseau, "On the Social Contract," 150.

59 Balibar, "'Possessive Individualism,'" 306–7.

60 Ibid., 307.

61 Ibid., 308.

62 Ibid., 310.

63 Ibid.

64 Ibid.

65 Ibid., 311.

66 Ibid.

67 Ibid., 312–13.

68 Ibid., 311, emphasis in original.
69 Ibid., 315, emphasis in original.
70 Ibid., emphasis in original.
71 Ibid.
72 Ibid., 308. See also Balibar, "What Is 'Man,'" 228–30; and Étienne Balibar, "Spinoza: From Individuality to Transindividuality," *Mededelingen vanwege het Spinozahuis* 71 (1997): 3–36.

13 From the Narcissism of Small Differences to the Vertigo of Endless Possibilities: Horowitz among the Levinasians[1]

OONA EISENSTADT

Scholars who seek a political philosophy in Levinas tend, whatever their political stripes, to agree on a single delimiting axiom: Levinas holds that all regimes, states, institutions, communities, ethnic groups, clubs – all political structures whatever, whether egalitarian or hierarchical; liberal, socialist, or totalitarian; voluntary, circumstantial, or biological – necessarily overlook the uniqueness of the singular human being and thus do violence; they therefore must be subjected to continual critique. Beginning with this axiom we find our thoughts severely circumscribed. A few scholars refuse to go any further, arguing that Levinas gives us no criteria for a ranking of regimes. Most, however, draw a minimal criterion from the axiom itself, arguing that regimes that welcome critique must be better than regimes that prohibit it, and though this amounts to little more than asserting that liberalism is better than totalitarianism, it might be said that a small victory is won when we find ourselves able to draw a standard out of an anti-foundationalist philosophy. In any case, this is the commonest position: Levinas supports an open regime, but he cannot tell us what that means, since to pin down details would preclude the critique that defines the regime's virtue.

It is agreed, then, that a Levinasian political philosophy requires an extra-Levinasian theoretical layer, and subsequent arguments over his politics treat the question of which layer is most appropriate – this being a matter of bringing to the table whatever political allegiance one happens to cherish. On one end of the spectrum we have Enrique Dussel, the Latin American liberation theologian, frustrated at the fact that the minimal position cannot help us envision a post-revolutionary regime, and supplementing Levinas with Marx. On the other end we have Alain

Finkielkraut, the French public intellectual, delighted with the minimal position, since it allows him to read Levinas as supporting the freedom of the individual under a classical liberal assimilationist (French) state; though he is less likely to admit that Levinas requires supplementation, his Levinas is, in fact, generously spiced with Enlightenment thought. In the middle we have the majority of Levinas scholars, thoughtful left-wingers who see in Levinas a way to defend democracy supplemented with such things as a stronger welfare state, a more hospitable foreign policy, and perhaps a heightened communitarian ethos.

Does Levinas really say so little that all these interpretations are legitimate? No one has done more than Gad Horowitz to bring this question into focus. Though Horowitz does suggest thinkers and positions that might supplement Levinas politically, he does so only after a close reading of the passages in which Levinas points towards a politics, or declines to point towards a politics. His argument in a nutshell is that while Levinas does indeed at times support the minimal position, such support is at odds with other, perhaps more trenchant aspects of his thought. Thus while scholars are justified in drawing from Levinas a check on their affiliations, a curb on their enthusiasms, to argue that this is *all* we can learn from Levinas about politics requires a series of philosophical slippages facilitated by selective reading and motivated by political inertia, for there do exist indications in the corpus of a positive politics.

The first slippage to which Levinas scholars are prone – and I include myself in the list of those who have leaned too far in this direction – follows from what might be called Levinas's realism, his understanding that ethics, even at its best, is insufficient to the suffering of other human beings, and that politics curtails the possibility to alleviate suffering even where it reaches out to try. In the rare passage in which Levinas praises revolution, attesting that we ought to "revolt for a society that is other," he adds the dampening qualification that it must be "a revolt that recommences as soon as the other society is established": always a new revolt "against the injustice that is founded as soon as an order is founded."[2] The slippage is the path from this realism to political apathy; many of us are inclined to call an indefinite halt to our moral and political aspirations in the face of the striking insight that failure is inevitable. What Horowitz points out appears obvious only after it is grasped, namely, that one need not slip from the realization that justice is always injustice into inactivity, or, in his more critically clarified terms, that the fact that basic repression is inevitable does not lead logically to the notion that any transformative or emancipatory politics is a fool's errand. So much, then, for the tendency towards lethargy. More interesting is the question of how scholars slip from unaffiliated indifference to a support for the liberal status quo.

We can begin with a question: who (or what) is the Levinasian other? A simple question, one might think, but in fact it is fraught for Levinasians, who argue ceaselessly over whether alterity is something I meet in the everyday world as well as a diachrony existing in the mode of a gap between the present and a pre-original past or an extra-temporal future, whether it is experienced in the conscious gaze as well as in secondary reflection, and whether "the face" can be the face of another human being as well as the non-phenomenal structure of alterity itself. What interests us, however, is the way scholars sometimes draw from these complexities two relatively uncomplex and erroneous understandings. The first conflates the Levinasian other with the other of sociology or postcolonial thought where the term refers to a marginalized group of people who have been marked by a dominant and oppressive group and who deserve redress that can be grounded either in inclusion or identity politics. A number of studies of Levinas, particularly those produced in the 1990s, have taken this interpretation and on its basis postulated conceptions of a Levinasian politics, most of which are forms of multiculturalism. Certainly such arguments are worthwhile. But none of them has anything to do with Levinas, whose other cannot be a collectivity. This is well understood now, with the interesting result that many are adopting a second mistaken understanding of the other, in which the term is taken out of its relational role and made to refer simply to the human individual.

The shift begins in the difficulties I sketched above about the nature of the other, and particularly in the recognition that Levinas sometimes speaks as if his whole thought is intelligible without any concrete other at all – as if the other could be replaced by an abstract structure of alterity, or an alienation interior to human beings and institutions. For instance, Levinas allows for the idea that one might attack a hegemonic institution – like language – in the name of an other who suffers under its homogenizing force; from here it is only a short step to attacking institutions on principle without any reference to an actual other. For a second instance, Levinas suggests that institutions are born in the brokenness that emerges from the ethical encounter and that they somehow carry that brokenness within them. This opens the door for a reader to think that totalities break themselves, and to rephrase Levinas in a neutral way, again omitting any mention of another human being. Third, part of the conundrum of alterity is the question of whether what I respond to in each concrete other isn't always the same thing – difference, alterity, not-me-ness, infinity – and whether this doesn't introduce a note of anonymity where there should only be particularity; once again, people exterior to the subject do not figure here except as abstractions. Fourth, and finally, following this thought, there is the question of reflection: if I think of the shock of alterity as something that has its full impact after the fact in my consciousness rather than coming to me from an actual face, then alterity is a movement of thought I perform alone, even a quasi-Cartesian movement.

It is, I think, Derrida who offers the "otherless" reading of Levinas in its best form. He shows a consistent tendency in his own thought to borrow ideas from Levinas and to rephrase them such that alterity's role is downplayed. Beginning with a translation of the Levinasian idea that *the other ruptures my totalities* to the more complex Derridean idea that *the other in me ruptures totalities* – a translation that carries great weight as an interpretation of Levinas – Derrida goes on to argue that text deconstructs itself, peace ruptures itself, and law embodies an aporia by which it calls itself into question. The *différance* inherent in the French passive/reflexive form aids the slippage but does not create it. On the contrary, it is created consciously and for a particular purpose, namely, in order that Derrida can, without abandoning a Levinasian framework, make policy statements. Why Derrida wishes to make policy statements is an open question. It might have to do with the scandals of 1987, the year in which Paul de Man's anti-Semitic writings were published and the question of his (and also Heidegger's) Nazism was forcefully raised in the French consciousness – 1987 being around the time Derrida's books began to be less literary and more political. Or it might simply be that Derrida, like many Levinasians, is frustrated by the fact that Levinas speaks so little about political realities. What is certain is that an otherless reading of Levinas makes for an easier entry into political debate, for, with the idea of the face of the other, Levinas calls into question the distinction on which much political philosophy is based, the distinction between the one and the many, the individual and the society. According to Levinas, responsibility can originate in neither of these spheres; on the contrary, it is introduced only when the subject is faced with the single other human being and arises from nothing more or less than the fact that any given other individual must have experienced things the subject has not. In other words, for Levinas, one alone cannot learn or give; three or more do not learn or give; only in the relation between two is learning and giving possible. Derrida knows this: he points out in his 1967 essay "Violence and Metaphysics" that *the face* is Levinas's profoundest contribution to philosophy, and perhaps his sole original thought. But the face, understood this way, does not play well in public debate, which continues to focus on the difference between the one and the many.

To work Levinas around until his philosophy is applicable is a task begun by Derrida (whose interpretations remain, however, interesting and loyal to their source) and continued by many other scholars (whose interpretations are often neither interesting nor loyal). The limit case is Alain Finkielkraut, who believes that Levinas's "other" is "a discrete individual" whom Levinas "describes and analyses ... in the true Enlightenment tradition."[3] But it is not only right-wing thinkers who translate the other into the individual: many left-leaning Levinasians have also ceased speaking of an "ethics of alterity" to speak instead of an "ethics of singularity." In general they are using the terminology for one or another sophisticated phenomenological purpose. But the language does its own damage. As singularity, the face is wholly reconciled to the discourse of standard liberal political theory, in which the individual must be protected from social forces and its good weighed against the common good; denuded of its relational force, the face now plays a merely rhetorical function, since, to speak crudely, it sounds more noble to criticize prevailing institutions on behalf of the "other" than on behalf of the "individual" who could be myself. It is *like* Levinas, but it is not Levinas.

The other main slippage that allows us to read Levinas as a liberal begins in the question of the relation of ethics to politics. As Levinas uses the terms, politics cannot be ethical and should not try: it *cannot* be ethical because its job is to totalize, to distribute fairly, rather than to infinitize, or to take on endless obligation to the single other; it *should not try* because to found a regime on ethics is to build dystopia. How then does ethics enter the political sphere? A very common answer is that, after its original formative entry in which the ethical for-the-other is extended into the political for-the-others, ethics enters the realm of politics only in the form of critique. As an answer, this has the great virtue of guarding against unsalutary utopian aspirations. More significantly, it appears to be the only answer that is adequate to the paradoxical nature of politics: that politics is, as Annabel Herzog puts it, "both the origin and the cure of hunger."[4] If politics begins as an attempt to alleviate suffering, then, when it fails, what it needs is evidently to be reminded of what lies at its core, to be pinched into consciousness of its origins. Thus it is often said that the only prescriptive teaching Levinas offers in an overwhelmingly descriptive body of thought is, "remember the description": remember the ethical demand at the root of your daily actions and political constructions. Ethics appears in the political realm as a call for a kind of phenomenological reduction, one that is performed as criticism of the prevailing structures in the name of those who suffer under them.

Levinas has an account of how it works, offered obliquely in a description of Talmudic method. The rabbis of the classical era knew that "general and generous principles can be inverted in their application. Every generous thought is threatened by its Stalinism. The great strength of the Talmud's casuistry is to be the special discipline which seeks in the particular the precise moment at which the general principle runs the danger of becoming its own contrary, and watches over the general in light of the particular."[5] The thought is familiar; it is everywhere in the Talmudic readings, in such forms as his praise of the tent of meeting, the place in which the biblical laws were modified or overturned on a case-by-case basis, and more generally in the way he refuses to harmonize rabbinic opinion, arguing that deeper meanings can be drawn from conversations than from conclusions; the thought is also a way of describing the difference between Hebrew and Greek. When Levinasians say that ethics enters politics in the form of critique, they are using the word *critique* broadly, to represent all the qualities associated with the Hebrew mode: listening, dialogue, hesitancy in judgment, and specifically the overturning of the general in light of the particular.

The slippage arises when we note how well all these qualities are enshrined in our contemporary political institutions. Our leaders debate; our press is free; and our legal system is based in a distinction between legislature and judiciary that allows general rules to be modified or overturned on the basis of the particular circumstances of individuals who are encountered by judges on a face-to-face basis. Perhaps the bridge between Talmudic political debate and liberal political debate owes something to the Spinozistic idea that our modern democratic principles embody the best of the ancient Jewish political insights. But there is more in operation here than an extension of the *conatus* into the checks and balances of the social contract. Levinasians who wish to apply his thought seek the moments in our political discourse where we acknowledge obligations to one another more fundamental than our freedoms. Scott Davidson, for instance, finds such a moment in article 29 of the Universal Human Rights Declaration, which, he argues, reorients the document in a Levinasian direction by speaking not of our rights but of our duties.[6] In his work, as in that of many others, there is an assumption that our regime embodies Levinasian principles, looking after singularities both by underwriting the individual's freedom and by acknowledging an obligation to unfortunates. No doubt the regime needs to be criticized. But even the work of a scholar as acute as Davidson assumes that such critique is possible and indeed is taking place. Our tradition of debate, the story goes, exists so that we can bring the violences of our institutions to mind; with only a small stretch we can say that it encourages us to become aware, as we meet other people, of the ways they are not encompassed by our wider social understandings or served by our political structures.

Of course there is truth in this progression of thought. But at least two things have been left unstated. First, the idea that ethics enters politics only in the form of a critical call to remember a founding desire for justice rests on the notion that politics does indeed originate in such a desire. While this may be true for Levinas in a very basic sense, it cannot be true that any given regime has all of its roots in a for-the-others, for regimes have many roots and there are many kinds of injustice. It is all very well to say that every generous and general thought is threatened by its Stalinism and must be reminded of its generous origins. But to have stood before Stalin crying *Zachor! Remember!* would not have done much good – and it is possible that acts like this do little or no good in a liberal regime either. In fact, Levinas is well aware of this. He knows that critique is not enough. The idea that his prescriptive teaching is limited to a re-rupturing re-membering, attractive as it might be to the logic of his argument, is far from being the whole picture; in actuality his thought is riddled with prescriptive teachings. "The Torah demands, in opposition to the natural perseverance of being in his or her own being (a fundamental ontological law), care for the stranger, the widow and the orphan, a preoccupation with the other person. A reversal of the order of things!"[7] The commands to listen and to give do not constitute merely a description of pre-original responsibility, always already there and emerging in a scruple or a blush as we go about our dirty business in the realm of sociality.[8] They are a hortative call on every level and in every sphere.

Second, and more importantly, the idea that liberal debate enshrines a Hebraic concern for the particular other rests on the interpretation of alterity as singularity. If, as I have argued, Levinas is less concerned about what collectivities do to individuals and more concerned about what collectivities do to relationships, then the problem cannot be addressed by any discussion of human freedom or human rights, even one that acknowledges abstract duties. What politics betrays, for Levinas, is not the singularity. It betrays ethics, that is, the command to approach the other with full hands and an open ear. It is *this* betrayal that cannot be eliminated but can perhaps be reduced. The question is thus whether our society, which goes a long way to protecting singularity, also provides resources for the protection of alterity. Does it offer us the opportunity to feel obligation and to respond to it? Horowitz argues that the present social structure denies us this opportunity: it blinds us to the existence of the underclasses, relegating poverty and violence to its margins while at the same time institutionalizing them; it encourages us in limited ways to reach out to the poor to improve their relative situation, and thus precisely relies on the continued existence of the poor qua poor. He offers an incomplete list of the conditions of our society that both enshrine oppression and prevent our noticing it: "extreme socio-economic inequality, spiritual constriction, economic exploitation, joyless servile jobs (or 'redundancy')."[9] To reduce the betrayal, to allow us to turn to one another with full hands, would these conditions not have to be eliminated?

Levinas would no doubt be wary of this leap into radical politics. But how wary would he be? Why not use Horowitz's framework to rethink Levinas? Or, at any rate, why not think about why we don't? Pierre Bourdieu describes the academy as home to a "secret resistance to innovation and intellectual creativity, [an] aversion to ideas and to a free and critical spirit," relating this to "the effect of the recognition granted to an institutionalized thought only on those who implicitly accept the limits assigned by the institution."[10] Surely Levinasians are at the very least obliged to ask themselves to what extent they are suffering under such limits.

The question of whether our society serves or denies the face is perhaps most forcefully raised in Levinas's 1934 essay, "Reflections on the Philosophy of Hitlerism." Here he traces the degeneration of the ideal of freedom from Judaism's conception of repentance and pardon as breaking the stranglehold of history, through Christianity's pseudo-philosophical liberation of the soul from the prison of the body, to liberalism's notion of an autonomous and mastering reason. Under the liberal regime, Levinas tells us, the ideal can degenerate further: while the soul that has risen above its limits chases the illusion of an assimilative harmony of minds, freedom becomes a goal in itself, thought becomes a game, and authenticity gives way to fashion. His argument culminates in the claim that this was the condition that dominated in Germany in the 1920s and facilitated the Nazi rise to power. Hitler offered Germans the authenticity they lacked: without giving up the idea that the superior soul was absolutely free – or bound only by the duty to spread that freedom across the globe – Hitler's followers could overcome the paranoia of absolute freedom by immersing themselves in a greater whole. The essay closes with a description of a coercive fascist expansionism, fuelled by the universal potential of the disembodied spirit, and a non-coercive liberal expansionism, fuelled from the same source.

In the course of the article, Levinas offers two alternatives. One is Marxism, for in championing the idea that human beings are bound by historical forces it stands as a critique of the Christian conception of miracle-working freedom. Marxism, however, appears to be insufficient for Levinas both because it is lacking the ancient Jewish insight that the stranglehold of history can be broken, and because when it does move in the direction of a freedom from history it does so through the instrument of consciousness, that is, through a form of mastering reason. Levinas then offers a second alternative, one that he calls "more radical." It is embodiment: the understanding that human beings are matter before they are mind, that the body is not a contingent thing to be tolerated but the defining human characteristic, and that "the whole of the spirit's essence lies in the fact that it is chained to the body."[11]

There is nothing in the piece that suggests that Levinas does not see liberalism, in the vein of the critics of modernity, as the best of the bad. Nevertheless, the critique of liberalism is very strong. This we see when Levinas argues that human beings are not fulfilled in liberalism's defining quality, freedom, but in "a certain bondage," when he compares liberal expansionism to fascist expansionism, and when he declares, in the preface he wrote for the piece in 1990, that his intention was to raise the question of whether liberalism is "all we need." One can speculate that his critique would be even stronger were it not held in check by a consciousness of his personal debt to the liberal West. But more important to us is that here – already in 1934 – he makes an attempt to define the freedom and scepticism of liberal thought as something different from the freedom and scepticism of Jewish thought, for though throughout his corpus he champions the free-wheeling, disputational liberty of rabbinic argumentation, he would never say that it bore the risk of becoming a game. What appears to hold it back from such degeneration is its allegiance to corporeality, for although he does not call embodiment a Jewish idea, it is critical to note that it is only with the second movement in his morphology of freedom, the Christian movement, that the body is downgraded or associated with sin.

Since the Hitlerism essay contains Levinas's strongest critique of liberalism, we might think to look there for hints of an alternative. Insofar as a positive political ethos emerges in the piece, it begins with the Jewish breaking of history with repentance and pardon. But it is well to recognize that repentance and pardon can be made to play cunning tricks, tricks that are explored in depth in two recent essays: Horowitz's "Global Pardon" and Jacques Derrida's piece on *The Merchant of Venice*.[12] One thing we learn from the from the latter is that the act of repentance can solidify social oppression: this can be seen both in Shylock, forced to his knees to beg for his life, and also in the charming story Derrida tells us of John Paul II, the pope of apology, stepping off an airplane on his way to ask, yet again, forgiveness for the sins of the historical church, sighing, and saying to an aide, "I notice that it is always *we* who are asking forgiveness" – in the sigh we see how it rankles him to beg for mercy, but also how the very act that confirms Shylock's inferiority here confirms the pope's superiority. Another thing we learn from Derrida's essay is that pardon or mercy is an assimilative force, the key move in Portia's murderous legal case as well as the critical *Aufhebung* in Hegel's dialectic. It is perhaps because Levinas is aware that repentance and pardon are often tools of the oppressors that, in the Hitlerism essay, he supplements his description of Judaism as freed from history by these things with the idea of a bondage to the body. The political picture that emerges from the essay remains very thin, but it is possible to say that insofar as Levinas follows the critique of liberalism to offer a different political form, that form involves repentance and pardon, as well, more importantly, a focus on the body. For Horowitz, this utopia of the body would be a matter of the elimination of surplus repression and the awakening of a new psychoanalytic-political mode, an erotic reality principle, a Marcusean "maternal, libidinal morality."[13]

If we are to stretch Levinas in the direction of an erotic reality principle, we are going to have to pull very hard. The relationship between two people is at the heart of his thought, and perhaps for this very reason he takes pains everywhere to distinguish it from a sexual one. It is the main burden of section 4 of *Totality and Infinity* to place eros beneath ethics in the Levinasian pantheon. And the same point can be drawn more quickly from his Talmudic reading "And God Created Woman," where he argues that the story of Eve's creation from Adam's rib, rather than putting women in their place, is putting eros in its place: "It is not woman who is secondary ... it is the relationship with the woman that is secondary."[14] What is more, Levinas speaks here directly and scornfully of the association between eros and revolution. "What is challenged [in the biblical story] is the revolution that thinks it has achieved the ultimate by destroying the family so as to liberate imprisoned sexuality. What is challenged is the claim of accomplishing on the sexual plane the real liberation of man."[15] At only one point in the reading is there a hint of an opening towards erotic liberation, when he writes that "sexual liberation, by itself, would not be a revolution adequate to the human species." Here he suggests that sexual liberation could be a part of such a revolution; perhaps he raises the possibility of a sexual liberation for-the-other, of an erotic embodied proximity that could form the ground of a new totality; and certainly he seems to assume that revolution – albeit a more adequate revolution – is a desideratum. We may recall at this point that Levinas was appalled by the riots of 1968 and wrote some of his harshest material on libidinal politics in response to what he saw as its juvenile excesses. "When youth is in rapture and when there is optimism on the boulevards, that does not at all prove the coming of the Messiah. Let us not confuse eroticism and messianism ... For youth, animated by pure vital impulse, which is not always the equivalent of a pure impulse, messianic times are always near."[16] This critique, like the one in "And God Created Woman," seems to indicate a disappointment with the shallowness of Parisian revolutionary politics. Levinas despises a politics that does not think, a radical politics that attacks even the customs and mores that protect the proletariat. To the advocates of this politics, he says, "How can you act politically while ignorant of the nature of evil, while ignorant of its metaphysical and spiritual reason?"[17] But perhaps this is a question that permits of answer.[18]

What, in light of Levinas's qualified dismissal of sexual liberation, are we to make of the idea of a politics of the repentant body? Annabel Herzog makes an argument that treads the same ground as Horowitz while avoiding the orthodox Levinasian counterclaims. She begins her piece with a careful examination of the aporetic nature of Levinas's politics, opening with a discussion of his "yes" and "no" to politics itself, and moving to a discussion of his "yes" and "no" to liberalism. There are moments, she points out, where he seems to endorse, at least to some extent, the train of thought I questioned earlier, moments where he suggests that ethics enters politics primarily as critique and that such critique is the foundation of the modern liberal democracy. Thus she cites him describing "the liberal state" as "a permanent revisiting of the right itself, a critical reflection on political rights, which are only de facto laws."[19] I have already argued that this idea, while strong, stands in opposition to other thrusts in the corpus, thrusts suggesting that liberal critique is not entirely adequate to Levinasian critique, or, more precisely, not entirely adequate to the model of rabbinic critique that Levinas proffers. Herzog does not make this argument, but neither can she stop with Levinas's endorsement of liberalism; she is fully aware that he seeks to move beyond it towards something else. "The entire life of a nation," she cites him saying, "carries within itself ... men who, before all loans have debts, owe their fellowman, are responsible – chosen and unique – and in this responsibility want peace, justice, reason. Utopia!"[20] *In* their responsibility they *want* utopia: in other words, while the pre-original state of responsibility is a given, it is not the sole expression of political morality but pushes beyond itself towards concrete political forms.[21] Above all, Herzog draws our attention to the points at which Levinas calls for a political surplus: a "surplus of sociality and love."[22]

For Herzog this call for surplus cannot be answered with attempts to represent under-represented minorities. People who are not part of the political process cannot be dragged into it: to force such people to represent themselves is both impossible and rude, and to represent them in their absence is merely to make them play roles in a politics that has nothing to do with them. There are people in every regime who are radically absent from the political world; our response to them has to be "something beyond, something infinite." Grasping for a trope with which she can describe this something, Herzog turns to some under-quoted lines from Levinas's Talmudic reading "Judaism and Revolution": "To a certain degree, when feeding another, it is necessary to humour his fancy ... Sleep and food. Sublime materialism!... Sublime materialism concerned with dessert."[23] Her article culminates in a distinction between regular politics, which must provide food, and utopian politics, which must provide puddings. "Liberalism," she writes, "is not all we need to achieve an authentic dignity for the human subject because this dignity needs dessert."[24]

The argument is perhaps not as absurd as it might appear. I have often noticed that beggars do better when they ply their trade near Levinas conferences. A group of Levinasians approached by an other on their way to dinner will shower her with coins, each perhaps afraid of appearing inadequately Levinasian before the others. But Herzog's argument reminds me of a dilemma I faced one day in San Francisco, when I happened to be on my way to dinner alone. A homeless man asked for a dollar to buy some wine and, as I was taking out my wallet, another man rushed up and instructed me not to give my dollar to the first fellow, who would only waste it on alcohol, but instead to give it to him for his homeless shelter where he provided such men beds and nourishing dinners. There I was, caught between the other and the third. What was I to do? Classes of undergraduates to whom I've put the question can't see the dilemma at all. I once had a class of a hundred outraged at the fact that I didn't immediately give everything I could spare to the representative of distributive justice. But, as Herzog points out, we have both political and utopian duties. Wine is my dessert, and I gave to them both. To be sure, I was not at that moment enacting an ethical politics. I was enacting the distinction between ethics and politics. But that is because San Francisco exists in a liberal state: a state that tries its best to put dinners before us and in doing so blinds us to the duties of dessert. Is it not possible to imagine with Herzog – and with Horowitz – a politics that holds luxury as essential as necessity, that ranks desire as need's equal?

Herzog notes that it is representation that is the problem with politics: politics must re-present or totalize the other. In Horowitz's interpretation of Levinas, representation is the problem with social existence as such. For the Levinasian, aporia is really the simple truth that we cannot reach a relational good that is pure. There is no pure hospitality, for "please enter my house" cannot be said without an underlying, "the house is mine, not yours." There is no pure gift, for I always get something from giving, be it only self-esteem. There is no pure ethics, for not only can I not give everything to the other (I do not have it; the more I give the less I have to give; eventually I will die) but the impulse is immediately attenuated by my awareness of the needs of the other others. And, finally, there is no way I can know you. Another way of saying all this is to say that original aporia is the aporia of the original: I can never touch the original but only seek it through its replicas; it is only present insofar as it is represented: the singularity withdraws and "all sins, events, phenomena partake of the nature of the trace of withdrawn singularity."[25]

The face evokes in us desire to know, to answer the call, to get through to the original. It is this that stands as the origin of language and thought, and this that emerges as goodness, a goodness that, however, is dependant on our failure to grasp the evasive singularity, a goodness that exists as a going towards, an obsession with what is not given, a sickness called forth by the absence of what is sought. Faced with a unique other who stands before me, I am faced with the presence of absence; this is desire; it is eros. In my quest for the singularity, I do not ignore the representations; I do not call them false. Rather I enter into them, cherishing them, studying them. "To see the invisibility of the other doesn't mean I ignore or overlook his particular features; on the contrary my desire, my obligation, is to attend, to enter into them, into the details of the details, endlessly."[26] Where Herzog's utopian gesture is to feed the other cake, Horowitz's is to elevate the senses of touch, smell, and taste to the level of the sense of hearing, to the level of conversation. Both gestures acknowledge the insoluble problem of representation, both lament it in a gesture akin to repentance, both pardon the absence of the object of desire, both involve a surplus materiality, both are erotic.

Levinas's sobering, if qualified, dismissals of eros are drawn from his Talmudic readings, from his Jewish works. But there are less sober strands in Judaism. There is, for instance, Isaac Luria, whose famous cosmology, as Horowitz points out, maps perfectly onto Marcuse's account of basic and surplus repression. Luria's fundamental concern, Horowitz reminds us, is with the divine attribute of *din*, or judgment. He recognizes that the power of judgment is also the power of the limit: without judgment everything is part of the undifferentiated whole. But the tight knot at the core of his cosmology, over which Kabbalists continue to ponder, is that the power of the limit holds too much sway: there are too many boundaries, judgment is too harsh. In short, the power responsible for existence of the material world is also responsible for everything wrong in that world, and that power is limitation – or repression. Luria's is not a gnostic cosmology; he does not see the power of *din* as demiurgic, and he does not wish to eradicate it and reenter a state of cosmic oneness. He sees the material world, basic limitation or basic repression, as not merely necessary but good. The error can be corrected; the world can be rid of the excessive power of the limit, rid of surplus repression. On a cosmological level, this correction is effected as the reuniting of the two halves of God's name: the YH of judgment persists, but it is bound to the VH of love, such that "material and spiritual suffering will not be abolished but radically ... diminished."[27] So too with Marcuse, and thus Luria and Marcuse come together structurally – but not only Luria and Marcuse, Levinas as well, for Marcuse's basic repression, which is Luria's *din* in conjunction with *hesed*, is surely also Levinas's "yes" to political order. And Marcuse's surplus repression, which is Luria's *din* unchecked, is Levinas's "no" to political oppression.

The transformation is not brought down from on high but is effected by human beings: on this point almost all the Kabbalists are in agreement. For most Lurianists (and almost all believing Jews are in one way or another Lurianists) the way to go about it is through prayer and good deeds. Each good deed, each *halachic* act, releases a spark from the "other side," which rises to the supernal realm and enables the entities there to couple. But there is a strand of Kabbalah for which the *halachic* laws themselves are in part a product of surplus repression. Horowitz points to two examples: the Shelah, who argues that sexual prohibitions will be loosened in the days of the messiah, and Sabbatai Zevi, whose principle of "redemption through sin" appears to have included such things as calling women to the Torah, open use of the divine name, and sexual licence – a list that may read, in our time, as a series of relatively mild attacks on surplus repression.

According to Horowitz, Levinas disassociates himself from these excesses not only because he is uneasy with libidinal politics but because he is uneasy with radical politics per se. His Kabbalist of choice is Rabbi Hayim of Volozhin, from whom he "has adopted a much muted version of Lurianic theology that stops short of envisioning any future radical Tikkun of God-and-world," focusing instead on obedience to the divine will.[28] This is true, to be sure, but it cannot be the whole story, for the man of *halachic* obedience is also a Kabbalist, a philosopher. The distinction between the Hasidim (like, say, Horowitz) and the Mitnagdim (like Hayim and Levinas) is not that the former envision a radical future and the latter do not, it is that the former believe in the open promulgation of such visions while the latter believe that to promulgate them is to cheapen them. In Horowitz's language this is to say that to advocate openly for the elimination of surplus repression is to invite into your bed those who would try to rid us of basic repression: those whose libidinal politics would overlook, as Levinas might put it, what I owe to the other, or as Hayim might put it, that when I atone, God atones with me. We are not permitted to forget that the embodied, Jewish politics of which Levinas spoke in the Hitlerism essay, while it may liberate the senses of touch, smell, and taste, must at the same time retain remorse and repentance. These things are not fun, but they are what break the stranglehold of historical forces, returning to us the past.

The Kabbalist Gikatilla also speaks of endless details.[29] Gikatilla's details are the "cognomens," or names of God: these names are the structuring principles of the world through which we glimpse God's purposes and can therefore be described metaphorically as God's clothing, revealing the outlines of the divine body they conceal. God is thus present to us insofar as he is represented – by robes, natural laws, names – and each representation is cherished and studied – details of details, endlessly – for this is the way we know God. The exercise is not fruitless; it gives us knowledge of the world and makes us care for it. Moreover, an ascent is implied, the culmination of which is to speak, in awareness, the great name, YHVH, in saying which "you carry all the Sacred Names, and it is as if you bear on your lips and on your tongue the Holy Name and all the Holy Names, it is as if your lips bear the responsibility of the world and all that it contains."[30] To be aware of absence, to study the representations, and to speak the word that draws all together bearing all responsibility would seem to be enough.

But this is not all Gikatilla has to say. And it is not hard to see that there is something wanting in this continual study. Those who are pleased with the sobriety of the realization that God's clothes are all we can see become lost in the details of the armour, or ornamentation. But others may go further. Gikatilla tells us that there are three levels of intimacy. Before his ministers and servants, the king appears fully clothed. At home, before his household, he removes some of his clothes. And "at times the king desires privacy, and no one is present except his queen. Then the king is not inhibited from undressing."[31] When "God unites with the righteous and the pious, the fathers of the world and the mighty ones, then he removes all his cognomens, and God is exalted alone."[32]

Gikatilla's phrase "at times" suggests that uniting with the naked God in his bedchamber is something the pious can do at any point in history. But the main thrust of his chapter on the cognomens gives a strong sense that the union is a unique historical moment, for the prevalence of the cognomens is connected to the exile, and, he tells us, when the *shechinah* returns to her proper place, Israel en masse will be gathered into the bedchamber.[33] On a third reading, it has already happened. *I removed my cloak, how will I put it back on? I have washed my legs, how could I soil them?*[34] For Gikatilla these lines mean that those who dwell on the cognomens are dwelling in sin. Exile appears here as a metaphor for blindness to reality. God has stripped and bathed, and it is the confused among us who are covering him with dirt, dirt we heap on him in lieu of the clothes we have spent our lives studying, dirt that shelters us from the truth and allows us to continue gazing at an outline. The third reading reconciles the first two: the potential is here, the God is stripped, now the world must stop dragging him through the mud. When this happens, Gikatilla says, the "erasable" names will be erased. Only the "inerasable" names will remain, to give structure to the world.

When Gikatilla switches from the terminology of clothes to the terminology of erasable and inerasable names, he suggests that we cannot remove the last of the cognomens. But it remains the case that the desire evoked by cognomens is the desire to strip them off. It may be that we cannot have what we desire. But is it necessary over and above this limitation to do violence to our desires? A limited transformation is perhaps possible. And who knows where it would end? We can certainly imagine a politics that took upon itself the provision of dessert. Perhaps we can also imagine that, under such a politics, the meaning of the sentence that expresses the eternal verity of inequity – my house, not yours – might change. In a politics that freed us through repentance and bound us through the body, the meaning of the terms *house, my, yours* might be given a new sense.

NOTES

1 A shorter account of some of these ideas appeared in my article "Anti-Uto-pianism Revisited" for a special edition of the journal *Shofar: An Interdisciplinary Journal of Jewish Studies* 26, no. 4 (Summer 2008): 120–38. I would like to thank Dara Hill and Rebecca Nicholson-Weir, the editors of that issue, for allowing me to present this revised and extended version, as well as the North American Levinas Society, where, in spring 2007, I delivered a first sketch of these thoughts. In addition I should thank Robert Gibbs, Diane Perpich, and Scott C. Davidson, each of whom said things, at the 2007 meeting of the Levinas Research Seminar, that were invaluable to my analysis in section 4.

2 Emmanuel Levinas, *Of God Who Comes to Mind*, trans. Bettina Bergo (Stanford: Stanford University Press, 1998), 9; cited in Gad Horowitz, "Aporia

and Messiah in Derrida and Levinas," in *Difficult Justice: Commentaries on Levinas and Politics*, ed. Asher Horowitz and Gad Horowitz (Toronto: University of Toronto Press, 2006), 327n10.

3 Judith Friedlander, "Translator's Introduction," in *The Defeat of The Mind* by Alain Finkielkraut (New York: Columbia University Press, 1995), xiii.
4 Annabel Herzog, "Is Liberalism 'All We Need'? Levinas's Politics of Surplus," *Political Theory* 30, no. 2 (April 2002): 211.
5 Emmanuel Levinas, *Beyond the Verse*, trans. Gary D. Mole (Bloomington: Indiana University Press, 1994), 79.
6 Scott C. Davidson, "Taking Responsibilities Seriously: Levinas and Human Rights," paper delivered at the annual meeting of the Levinas Research Seminar, Hamilton, ON, spring 2007.
7 Emmanuel Levinas, *In the Time of Nations*, trans. Michael Smith (Bloomington: Indiana University Press, 1994), 61.
8 See Emmanuel Levinas, *Otherwise Than Being or Beyond Essence*, trans. A. Lingis (Dordrecht: Klewer Academic Publishers, 1991), 6.
9 Horowitz, "Aporia and Messiah," 313.
10 Pierre Bourdieu, *Homo Academicus*, trans. Peter Collier (Stanford: Stanford University Press, 1988), 95.
11 Emmanuel Levinas, "Reflections on the Philosophy of Hitlerism," trans. Sean Hand, in *Difficult Justice*, 9.
12 Gad Horowitz, "Global Pardon: Pax Romana, Pax Americana, and Kol Nidre," *Bad Subjects* 58 (December 2001), http://bad.eserver.org/issues/2001/58/horowitz.html; and Jacques Derrida, "What Is a 'Relevant' Translation?," *Critical Inquiry* 27, no. 2 (Winter 2001): 174–200.
13 Horowitz, "Aporia and Messiah," 318.
14 Emmanuel Levinas, *Nine Talmudic Readings*, trans. Annette Aronowicz (Bloomington: Indiana University Press, 1994), 169.
15 Ibid., 170.
16 Ibid., 194.
17 Ibid., 110.
18 This paragraph draws heavily on Matthew Guy, "'Not to Build the World Is to Destroy It': Levinas on Holy History and Messianic Politics" (paper presentation, Inaugural Meeting of the North American Levinas Society, Purdue University, May 2006). For a more politically positive reading of these essays, see Mitchell Verter, "Levinas: For the Kids!" (paper presentation, Second Annual Meeting of the North American Levinas Society, Purdue University, June 2007). Verter offers a compelling comparison between Levinas's position on the Paris riots and that of Raoul Vaneigem's contemporary manifesto, *The Revolution of Everyday Life*, 2nd ed., trans. Donald Nicholson Smith (London: Rebel, 1994).

19 Emmanuel Levinas, *Entre Nous: Thinking-of-the-Other*, trans. Michael Smith and Barbara Harshav (New York: Columbia University Press, 1998), 205. To this we can add that at another moment Levinas makes a similar argument that appears to give full justification to Scott Davidson, writing that "the defense of human rights corresponds to a vocation outside the state, disposing, in a political society of a kind of extraterritoriality.… The capacity to guarantee that extraterritoriality and that independence defines the liberal state and describes the modality according to which the conjunction of politics and ethics is intrinsically possible," *Outside the Subject*, trans. Michael Smith (Stanford: Stanford University Press, 1997), 123.

20 Ibid., 231.

21 The strongest passage expressing this idea is cited by Gad Horowitz and Asher Horowitz in their piece on the Hitlerism essay. It is *Otherwise Than Being*, 177, wherein Levinas challenges "us Westerners" to find "another kinship," one that will not see the other as a product of the forces of being or history but will make room for encounters, one that "will perhaps enable us to conceive of this difference between me and the other, this inequality in a sense absolutely opposed to oppression." I would point out that an inequity opposed to oppression takes us back to the ideas of "Messianic Texts." Horowitz and Horowitz stress, even more importantly, that Levinas speaks here of something new rather than the re-emergence or recollection of a primordial kinship. See Asher Horowitz and Gad Horowitz, "Is Liberalism All We Need? Prelude Via Fascism," in *Difficult Justice*, 20.

22 Emmanuel Levinas, "Peace and Proximity," in *Emmanuel Levinas: Basic Philosophical Writings*, ed. Adriaan Theodor Peperzak, Simon Critchley, and Robert Bernasconi, trans. Peter Atterton and Simon Critchley (Bloomington: Indiana University Press, 1996), 165.

23 Levinas, *Nine Talmudic Readings*, 97.

24 Herzog, "Is Liberalism All We Need?," 222.

25 Horowitz, "Aporia and Messiah," 308.

26 Ibid., 309.

27 Ibid., 317.

28 Ibid., 321.

29 R. Joseph Gikatilla, *Gates of Light: Sha'are Orah*, trans. Avi Weinstein (Walnut Creek, CA: AltaMira, 1998).

30 Ibid., 165.

31 Ibid., 166.

32 Ibid., 177.

33 Ibid., 186.

34 Song of Songs, 5:3; Gikatilla, *Gates*, 178.

14   Adorno and Emptiness

ASHER HOROWITZ

I

It is not uncommon to hear from different directions that Adorno's *Negative Dialectics* fails as either philosophy or as theory that can find a unity with practice. There are many reasons for Adorno's gradual slide into neglect and indifference. Yet it is likely that *Negative Dialectics* is ignored or dismissed because its *aims* cannot be assimilated to either the main thrust of the Western philosophical tradition or to the vast majority of attempts to offer alternatives. Adorno could be far enough ahead or outside of the curve in the West that the aims of *Negative Dialectics* are not sufficiently grasped, and the work as a whole remains open to misplaced judgments. It might, then, be useful to look outside the West for movements that share at least similar aims and procedures in order to better position to understand that work. This is admittedly an unfamiliar procedure: to look outside one's own culture, in this case to the Madhyamika philosophy that initiates and underpins much if not all of Mahayana Buddhism, for something like an analogue that will aid in grasping something that appears to be inside it. But if this "inside" work is in fact a radical challenge to the very culture in which it appears, to look to the outside may help in its appreciation. This encounter would not remain a one-way street. Adorno also offers something to Buddhism that it has not been able to develop (much) on its own: a relation to the "project" of liberation as historical and social.

Madhyamika philosophy and its founder and chief proponent Nagarjuna (first to second century CE) are frequently compared to and aligned with the sceptical tradition in the West, Wittgenstein's attack on essentialism,[1] the process philosophy of A.N. Whitehead,[2] and more recently Derridean deconstruction.[3] More interesting is the frequent and correct characterization of Nagarjuna's thought as a "negative dialectic."[4] Long before the appearance of a thoroughly negative dialectics in the West, albeit in radically different circumstances and with different means, there arises a thoroughgoing and comprehensive attack on what Adorno will later term "identity thinking," one that will be refined over many centuries, reanimate a world "religion," and result in a profusion of myriad schools and practices of enlightenment. Nagarjuna owes the impetus for his new direction in Buddhist philosophy to Buddha's famous silence on metaphysical questions, to the clash of opposing metaphysical positions in Indian philosophy, and to what he perceived as the tendency in earlier Buddhist thought (the Abbidharma schools) to hypostatize the analysands of self, things, and experience (the five aggregates) and their relations (the twelve links of dependent origination) to the point where metaphysical claims about a fundamental and unchanging reality were tacitly re-emerging.

For Nagarjuna and his Buddha, the stubborn persistence of such "views" (*drsti*) was not a matter to be met with anodyne indifference. It would be vital to the practice of liberation from the suffering of cyclic existence to repeat the Buddha's silence much more loudly. That silence was not simply impatience with matters diverting attention and energy from more important pursuits. Silence on such matters was for Madhyamika philosophy the enunciation of a *critical* perspective,[5] which took "views" to be more than symptomatic, to be the actual performance of the "root delusion" perpetuating the repetition of grasping and attachment at the heart of *dukkha* (the suffering and discontent referred to in the first noble truth). The constant flow and fluctuation of desire and aversion, including the desire for the continuation of desire and the desperate fear of its annihilation, are paralleled in the drive to find and believe in, to hold and possess permanence, independence, timelessness, and indestructibility. On the plane of conceptually mediated experience there is inherently generated a hypostatization and reification of entities. Abstractions become more real than the flux of experiential conditions from which they were abstracted. They are, as idealism discovers, the most transcendent and indestructible things, and not separate from the "I" that conceives them. The race is on to posit somewhere the inherent existence of a Reality that transcends or subtends the flow in experience, whose apparently fixed and independent elements are themselves in a state of transience and relation. Such positing, whether explicit or implicit, whether by metaphysicians or in commonsensical belief, is the generation of *drsti*. For Nagarjuna, the proper Buddhist perspective becomes radically critical and takes the analysis of the root delusion down to the very level of the conceptual as such, in that the concept carries with it the appearance of permanence, invariance, and the power of indestructibility; also the promise of being able to explain and account for what appears (at least to the conceptualizing agency) to be the non-conceptual, to generate the other out of itself.

For Nagarjuna, the problem of hypostatization went well beyond the older concern in Buddhism to avoid the notions of a permanent self or the complete non-existence of self, "eternalist" or "annihilation-ist" extreme views. Instead, he "understood the basic message of Buddha to be the elimination of all hypostatic theorizations."[6] All of the fundamental categories of metaphysics could be demonstrated to be ultimately unreal, though conventionally useful. Attainment of the ultimate perspective, in which liberation takes place in the silence of mental fabrication, is itself dependent, however, on categories, thoughts, and language that do not escape convention, even though they are to be left behind. Thus Nagarjuna extends his destructive analysis to include concepts of time, motion, cause, agency, elements, becoming, actions, wholes, process, and even relations. This list is not exhaustive. Nagarjuna's method is anything but piecemeal, and its scope is universal. It does not aim at the refinement of the conceptual schematizations of experience but at their thoroughgoing destruction, when conceived of as composed of essences, of permanent, self-identical entities in relation with one another, when, in other words, concepts or the phenomena to which they refer are taken to have "inherent existence" (*svabhava*). However, when concepts are thoroughly known to be subject to dependent origination (to the causal-relational processes to which all things are subject), when this knowledge includes even the concept of dependent origination and phenomena are not reducible to one ultimate reality, the phenomenal world is recovered as or in its suchness. And the conventional understandings of phenomena will allow and even, for some of Nagarjuna's progeny, require empirical judgments of relative truth and falsehood.[7]

Nagarjuna's famous tetralemmas, his negations of all possible forms of assertion (S is P; S is not-P; S is both P and not-P; S is neither P nor not-P) convict various "views," and views as such, of incoherence. They do this negatively, primarily by reductio ad absurdum, by driving all *drsti* towards awareness of their own inherent incoherence (which might appear in the forms of tautology, mutually exclusive contradiction, or infinite regress); and they do this through exploiting the dependence of views on (1) the apparently real, i.e., apparently inherently existent but actually reified entities that are the bases of assertions, and (2) a basic and inescapable dilemma of identity and difference in the reification of the entities that become the bases or referents of assertions, "the dilemma of their identity or difference":[8] entities, that is, essences with permanent and invariant identities, cannot be what they are, cannot possess identity, without negating, without *not* being other entities; entities as such, as instances of identity, presuppose differences from other entities. But difference, in its turn, also presupposes the very identity it must negate to be different. With one stroke, but a stroke repeated in many different contexts, both the extreme views, those of eternalism and nihilism, along with all their implications, are convicted of incoherence because each presupposes and negates the other. They are incoherent because, when driven to their logical conclusion, they cannot account for the experience of which they are the abstraction. The real is neither a single, self-identical, unchanging, unified entity or system; nor is the real what difference without identity would necessitate, that is, "such radical discontinuity, disjunction and lack of intelligibility that even the most mundane things would become incoherent and inexplicable."[9] Garfield's authoritative commentary refers to this basic dilemma of identity as following from the requirements of inherent existence:

> If an entity is inherently existent [is an essence or is self-identical], it must be independently established as an entity with its own nature. So no entity could be established as inherently existent through dependence on any other entity [i.e., through difference]. Only inherently existent entities could be independent. To establish something as inherently existing through its dependence on something else is incoherent. So since entities can be established neither through independence [which would be tautological], nor through dependence [which follows from difference], there is no way to establish anything as an entity in its own right.[10]

But if there are no entities in their own right, no self-identical essences within or at the bottom of the phenomenal, it might seem that there is nothing, that nothing has being. What Nagarjuna is doing, however, is leading his reificationist interlocutors away from the assumption, given by formal logic and promoted by language in its necessary employment of substantives, that to exist is to exist inherently. If to exist means to exist inherently, to be independent, eternal, invariant, to possess a self-nature, then there are only two alternatives: either there is a being or beings (or the Being of beings) or there is nothing.

Nagarjuna's dialectic is sufficient to destroy the first alternative, but it would be a gross error to suppose that this necessarily implies the second alternative, nihilism, because opposition of the two alternatives is itself a function of the logic of identity and difference. Existence is not a negative function of nothingness. The only thing that is a negative function of nothingness is *inherent* existence, own-being. The point is to get outside this logic, and this does not yield nothing; instead it yields sunyata or emptiness, and ultimately, liberation from the suffering perpetuated in the repetition of samsara.

Emptiness is the central non-negative category of the Madhyamika systems and remains central in succeeding Mahayana movements. Literally, *sunya* means "void" (and sunyata = voidness). This has allowed the attribute of nihilism to be attached repeatedly to Madhyamika philosophy. But it cannot be judged nihilistic because sunyata is not used as a predicate of the Real. Nagarjuna himself points out that "'Empty' should not be asserted. / 'Nonempty' should not be asserted. / Neither both nor neither should be asserted. / They are only used nominally."[11] Madhyamika, despite the accusation that the rejection of metaphysical views necessarily implies the acceptance of an alternative metaphysics, takes no position on the ultimately real and holds no *drsti*. Its language does not assert, but "ostends."[12] To hold no view of ultimate reality means that one should also consider "emptiness" to be empty. But this does not amount to a view, since sunyata does not refer to an essential void beyond illusory appearances. Sunyata is not a substance independent of its attributes but points instead to the essencelessness and lack of identity of the categories constituting both conventional and metaphysical views of reality.[13] Nagarjuna is able to deflect the charge of nihilism because, having extricated himself negatively from the consequences of the dialectic of identity and difference, he does not and need not share the assumption of his reificationist opponents that "existence and emptiness are opposites."[14] To demand essence or inherent existence of reality is, for Nagarjuna, actually to subscribe to an untenable theory of the real, which, if true, would make it impossible for things to exist. The equation of existence with inherent existence results in the paradoxes, contradictions, and absurdities of his opponents' views. As the upshot, his negative dialectics of the realization of sunyata means undoing the "force of the delusion of reification,"[15] which becomes in metaphysics a redoubling of the world into the apparent and the real. But sunyata is not a reality hidden from appearance; to know it means to recognize the very conventionality of the real-as-reified.

It frequently becomes tempting to forget that the *madhayamika*, the middle path, does not mean the assertion of an Absolute, whether that absolute is conceived to be accessible or, like the Kantian noumenal, not accessible to mind. Thus, even though Nagarjuna's is a critical philosophy with significant parallels to Kant, the similarities can be overdrawn. Like Kant, Nagarjuna conceives of the categories as generated a priori and not by association.[16] But sunyata does not refer to a noumenal reality, taken as an absolute, which the categories of the understanding cannot reach and whose extension into the non-empirical embroils reason in paralogisms and contradictions. Nagarjuna has no necessary but unknowable ground for the empirical world.[17] Yet there is clearly something like absoluteness in the suchness that is not a notion, in the freedom from conceptual construction. C.G. Nayak puts this nicely: "It is not that the Reality of an altogether different order hidden behind the appearance is grasped in wisdom, but it is like something getting revealed in our understanding which was all the while there unnoticed in front of us."[18] It is not possible anymore, on this basis, to make a truly strict distinction between the apparent and the real, or between *explanans* and *explanandum*, and all dualisms are necessarily brought radically into question, without the reassertion of any monism. Nagarjuna does not merely reject all positive thought constructions *about* a reality that transcends phenomena, he rejects all assumptions that a transcendental reality *exists*.[19]

It thus turns out that the removal of essentialist thought-constructions, the dis-identification of things and the de-reification of concepts results not in something or in nothing or both (Hegelian "becoming"?), or neither. But how can the real as suchness (itself a non-concept), as *sunya*, be *not neither* something nor nothing? To put the question in this form (to ask even negatively about identity) is already to distort Nagarjuna's meaning. He is here rearticulating but also refining and radicalizing the most central doctrine of the Buddha, the dependent origination (*pratityasamutpada*) of all things. He announces this in the dedicatory verse: "I prostrate to the perfect Buddha / ... who taught that / Whatever is dependently arisen is / ... without identity, / And free from conceptual construction." Against earlier Abbidharma schools, which took dependent origination to imply causal laws according to which evanescent momentary things appear, Nagarjuna takes *pratityasamutpada* to refer to the interrelation of experiences and their concepts as always mediated by the dilemmas of identity and difference. Neither something nor nothing should be asserted if both something and nothing, and therefore neither something nor nothing, are dependently arisen, that is, internally related through both identity and difference, neither of them having a fixed essence of their own, not able to establish their own identity (or pure difference) outside of all relation.[20] Sunyata is not something mysterious inhering in the phenomenal but simply the dependently arisen phenomenal world in its lack of essence(s). Emptiness and the dependently arisen phenomenal world are not two distinct things, but alternative characterizations of the same thing.[21] The first is (only) *apparently* negative to the point of being nihilistic; the second (only) *apparently* positive to the point of being metaphysical. In reality there is neither nihilism nor metaphysics, but the middle path. This is not to say that the lack of mystery means the absence of wonder.

To say that sunyata and *paratityasamutpada* are obverse and reverse also means it remains possible to make true and false statements, but only in conventional terms. Concepts are rejected only from the ultimate standpoint, and Nagarjuna makes a crucial distinction between the conventional and ultimate truth. The ultimate truth cannot even be reached except through the terms of the conventional. Conventional terms, along with the frameworks of identity and difference they carry along with them, are not arbitrary. But they are partial, interested, and themselves determined. *Given* the conventions that prescribe identity to concepts, empirically true or false statements can be made.[22] The problem is that the dilemma of identity and difference makes it impossible for those conventions of identification to establish criteria that distinguish things absolutely from their conditions. From their own side, things remain free "in essence" from the identities and differences conceptually imputed to them, which establish essence.[23] That is, they do not inherently exist, they are empty, they are dependently arisen. The point is to be able to use such conventional terms and truths up to a point, the point at which the necessarily reified terms are taken to be the real. For Nagarjuna, therefore, a central distinction is the distinction between causes and conditions. A cause would be an event or state that, as part of its essence or nature, has the power to bring about an effect. Conditions are similarly events, states, or processes that can be used to explain other events, states, or processes but without any commitment to hidden or purely logical connections between *explanandum* and *explanans*. The connection of conditions to effects is therefore neither through absolute difference nor absolute identity.[24] Dependent origination thus means the lack of inherent existence in phenomena, their emptiness.

The distinction between conventional and ultimate truth is not the distinction between illusion and a transcendent reality. The relation of the ultimate truth to the conventional or the ultimate truth about the conventional is that the conventional is simply conventional; the identities it plays with are functions of the play of identity and difference that inhere in our grasping. Its terms and relations are empty of inherent existence. The dialectic is put in play to get us to see we are enmeshed in such a predicament, "trapped in conventional reality through the force of the delusion of reification"[25] *and* that we can emerge from it. "The ultimate truth is that every concept is *sunya* in the sense of being essenceless, and when one is firmly entrenched in this truth he is said to have realized the highest truth … as distinguished from the conventional truth … and that is all. That is why it is said to be *tathata*, that is thusness or suchness."[26] Or as Garfield puts it, "When all error is abandoned and we see the world aright, we are no longer ignorant of the true nature of things. But this is not because we then apprehend things and their true nature. Rather we apprehend that there are no things, per se, and that those posited from our side have no nature to understand."[27]

One of the most surprising and productive consequences of emptiness as the middle path was the breakdown in the strict distinction between samsara and nirvana (or liberation), without which the rise to such prominence in the Mahayana of the bodhisattva ideal with its limitless compassionate action on behalf of all sentient beings, would be difficult to imagine. The notion that "*samsara is nirvana*" is often incorrectly attributed to Nagarjuna, for whom such a judgment of the ultimate identity of opposites would be nonsensical. The negation of an absolute difference does not imply the necessity of an identity.[28] Nirvana, although it cannot be positively described, is not something nonexistent. It is the release from the identification through which samsara is reproduced as the belief in and grasping after inherently existent entities.[29] Nirvana or liberation is not a different place or a future time, but another way of being here and now; not escape from the world, but awakened and enlightened engagement with it.[30] "*Nirvana* is thus nondifferent from critical insight par excellence which is free from all essentialist picture thinking."[31] Such insight cannot be conveyed by way of representations. Instead it finds its expression not in positive theorizations and in remaking the world, but in silence, "the highest end for a philosophically enlightened person."[32] For Nagarjuna, referring to action in the sense of grasping, of trying to make something one's own, or capable of being one's own, "The root of cyclic existence is action. / Therefore the wise one does not act. / Therefore the unwise is the agent. / The wise one is not because of his insight."[33]

Although critical-destructive, the soteriological purpose is central. It is certainly not an end in itself but is meant as a vehicle of deliverance. Nagarjuna makes use of the stock Buddhist metaphor of the raft that can and should be left behind, once the far shore is reached. Negative dialectics is meant to disappear and negate itself once its aims are achieved. In exploding essentialist thought-constructions through the exposition of their fundamental incoherence, it is aimed at the root conditions of endless misery: "Action and misery come from conceptual thought. / This comes from mental fabrication. / Fabrication ceases through emptiness."[34] Deliverance from reifying thought is deliverance from the egoism in which one grasps after material things, achievements to call one's own, and especially one's own identity. To realize the emptiness of these things is to accept that they neither exist absolutely nor fail to exist. They are insubstantial, transient, and unworthy of the furious and inevitably frustrated passion directed to them. "There is little scope for indulging in a rigidly self-centered existence arising out of a desperate clinging to immutable essences on the part of one, be it an individual or a nation as a whole, who simply takes *sunyata* seriously, not to speak of one who has realized the truth of *sunyata* in *nirvana*."[35]

In the history of Mahayana Buddhism, taking sunyata seriously led to the replacement of the *arhat* ideal with that of the bodhisattva. The *arhat* eliminates in himself or herself all passions and suffering, while the bodhisattva, through the realization of the emptiness of the distinction between samsaric existence and nirvana, becomes engaged in/ by the vow to strive for the salvation of all sentient beings. As Gad Horowitz points out in response to Robert Magliola's Buddhist deconstruction,[36] Buddhism seems to lack an account of the *ethically obligatory* quality of such a vow. He suggests that the insight into emptiness is, at bottom, the ethical discovery of the for-the-other of the human self, as understood in the work of Emmanuel Levinas: "The obligation, in the darkness of the Other … is the no-space in which the light of insight-compassion can appear."[37] Thus Buddhism could benefit from a "Western" insight into its own condition of possibility. Sakyamuni's enlightenment was itself due to the ethically obligatory bodhisattva vow experienced prior to his historical moment of enlightenment, after which he was faced with the decision of whether to teach or not. I will suggest in sections II and III below that Buddhism might also be able to benefit from Adorno's transposition of negative dialectics into the realm of the natural-historical, the socio-individual reproduction of samsaric suffering.

II

Adorno and Nagarjuna are separated by enormous cultural and historical differences. But their soteriologies are astoundingly similar in aim and, up to a point, in method. Adorno, unlike Nagarjuna, is operating in a philosophical context in which metaphysics is all but universally agreed to be moribund. Hegelian metaphysics is exhausted. Various positivist and pragmatic approaches have taken its place to underwrite the activities of a society progressively losing the ability to distinguish between instrumental action oriented by self-preservation and power, and liberated experience. Such a culture expresses a thoroughly perverse unity of samsara and nirvana, or in Adorno's terms, of myth and enlightenment. The dominant, and in Adorno's eyes, utterly reactionary response to the rise of scientific philosophy is Heidegger's fundamental ontology, in which sentient beings are reduced to the role of facilitators of the anonymous and veiled utterances of unfeeling Being. In this context, unlike Nagarjuna, Adorno will not aim simply to undercut metaphysics, but to draw from it a hope that can be further secularized. His sympathy for and solidarity with metaphysics "at the time of its fall" also includes the acknowledgment that the uncompromising drive to identity in idealist metaphysics carried with it the sense of contradiction between the actual and the real lost in positivism. Thus, in *Negative Dialectics*, his principal interlocutors are Kant and Hegel. Nagarjuna was facing many viable metaphysical positions. In the administered society, where "satisfactions" and the needs that sustain them are induced and doled out to promote and intensify activities whose overriding purpose is a quiescent and willing contribution to the endless expansion of the reproduction of capital, to samsara in extremis, it is at least very difficult to take to heart the Buddha's first and second noble truths, that life is *dukkha* and that its cause is the craving that gives rise to renewed existence (*samsara*). Nagarjuna's audience probably did not need much urging on this point. He could concentrate on the third and fourth truths. Negative dialectics,[38] however, must aim first at bringing its audience back to an unhappy consciousness, to an experience of "reduced experience."

Adorno's *Negative Dialectics*, much like Nagarjuna, begins by rejecting the notion that dialectics implies a view. "It does not begin by taking a standpoint."[39] It is not the march of Reason through history, realizing the ultimate identity of identity with non-identity, unifying all partial views in the Absolute, in Reason. "The crux is what happens in it, not a thesis or a position."[40] It is, in this sense, thoroughly anti-metaphysical, not aiming to name the real, even negatively, a *via negativa* but not a negative theology. Instead, it is unending critique to the *n*th degree, a "meta-critical turn against *prima philosophia*,"[41] meta-critical because, unlike Kant, it does not ground any ultimate categories transcendentally.

Negative dialectics, Adorno announces, "is not a program of knowledge"[42] but a protest against the mechanism of thought's conceptuality.[43] He recognizes and even intends that it will offend – and it certainly does offend the pretensions of thought to finality and unity, certainty and primacy. It will be experienced as vertigo and denounced as bottomless and even nihilist by the bureaucratic mentality, which is the inheritor of dogmatic metaphysics.[44] But it is not nihilist, at least inasmuch as it aims beyond and "eschews" relativism[45] and renders "binding statements without a system,"[46] truths that are "suspended and frail" because of their "temporal substance." To say that the *substance* of truth is frail and temporal is to imply, as Nagarjuna implies, that neither identity nor difference qualifies the real, and also that there is a distinction to be made between the conventional and the ultimate truth. The latter distinction appears not only in the use of the concepts of the philosophical tradition, but in Adorno's constant recursion to the limited and temporal truth-value of the positions subjected to dialectical scrutiny, to what Critical Theory calls determinate negation.[47] *Negative Dialectics* begins to assume the lineaments of the middle path, neither nihilist nor eternalist. Such adherence is also visible in its relation to systematic thought, especially idealist systematics. Although negative dialectics identifies the system, the aim to reduce all possible experience to the smallest number of universal and necessary propositions, as "belly turned mind," as a "paranoid zeal to tolerate nothing else" and detects that "rage is the mark of each and every idealism,"[48] he insists that negative dialectics is not the flight into the opposite of systems, since it aims to perceive the individual moment in its immanent connection with others.[49] This is its inheritance from systematic metaphysics, in parallel, as we shall see, with Nagarjuna's adherence to conditions rather than causes.

Thus a "possible definition" of negative dialectics, which Nagarjuna might have appreciated, is "a thinking against thought."[50] This is not a blanket rejection, neither complete silence nor meaningless babble; it recognizes the need to use the conventional truths and concepts as vehicles to transcend the delusions that the concept brings with it. But it still traffics in the currency of thought and does not lead to its "vanishing."[51] Yet it aims to "transcend the natural context and its delusion without imposing its rule on this context." And because of this it is like a raft. It will pass like the antagonistic society of which it is the frail and temporal truth.[52] It must even turn against itself, "in the very negation of the negation that will not become a positing"; its "form of hope" is that "it will not come to rest in itself as though it were total."[53]

It is *against thought* – not simply these or those thoughts, or against ideologies, although this is crucial, but against the delusions that follow from the traps set by the concept, by identity thinking, even though "one cannot think without identifying."[54] "To think is to identify," while dialectics is "the consistent sense of non-identity."[55] Negative dialectics is thus not a new form or system of positive thought, although it contains moments of critical positivity. The primary delusion in identity is that it "depreciates a thing to a sample of its species."[56] Identity grasps after what transcends conditioned existence, proclaims itself and to an extent whatever falls under it, to have inherent existence, thus maintaining the delusive duality of subject and object,[57] which in its turn orchestrates the possibilities of a purely instrumental action underlying the development of social domination. And domination ends up in the endless social-systemic repetition of a self-enforced self-preservation that can persist only by denying the difference that defines it, the domination of so-called nature. In the administered society, domination becomes the samsara it always was, and vice versa. As Nagarjuna put it, "Action and misery come from conceptual thought. / This comes from mental fabrication."[58] Unfortunately for Adorno, and for the rest of us, he was able to witness the reductio ad absurdum of identity or inherent existence beyond anything Nagarjuna could have imagined. This reductio was made visible at Auschwitz, where it was "no longer the individual who died, but a specimen."[59] "Genocide is the absolute integration ... Auschwitz confirmed the philosopheme of pure identity as death."[60]

The identity required by thought is anything but innocent or neutral. But where Nagarjuna conquers identity with it own weapons, by way of the dilemma of identity and difference, Adorno approaches what he terms "the disenchantment of the concept"[61] by a different yet compatible route. From Adorno's perspective, what Nagarjuna is doing makes eminently good sense, because contradiction indicates the un-truth of identity, "the fact that the concept does not exhaust the thing conceived." In dialectics, contradiction is necessary because "the appearance of identity is inherent in thought itself, in its pure form." But since the total identity towards which thought strives "is structured to accord with logic ... whose core is the principle of the excluded middle, whatever differs in quality comes to be designated as contradiction. *Contradiction is non-identity under the aspect of identity*."[62] And it is true that Nagarjuna cannot achieve the thoroughgoing destruction of identity (including the identity of nihility) without a sometimes tacit appeal to aspects or qualities of experience that do not fit with inherent exis-tence, but do fit with emptiness. The emptiness of inherent existence, the non-identity screened by identity, is not found a priori, without ex-perience.[63] For Adorno, to say that "objects do not go into their con-cept without leaving a remainder"[64] is tacitly to assert the emptiness, in Nagarjuna's sense, of the concept. Thus both no longer exclude the middle between identity and difference.

But Adorno divagates by appealing directly to the experience that escapes the concept. In part this is because metaphysics already has in the modern West many critics and quite a bad name, but also because he is concerned with powerful political and philosophical ideologies, including orthodox Marxisms, that propagate and/or are limited by identity-thinking. Ideology is not defined by its content but by the sub-sumption of something primary, something independent and substan-tial, permanent and inherently existent.[65] But for Adorno, the concept also tacitly reaches beyond its own identifying function. It is not only identification, for it presupposes contact with realities that call for their formulation. To be able to be rid of "conceptual fetishism"[66] is to pos-tulate an already existent "capacity to experience the object,"[67] which shows up in sensibility as the ability to discriminate.[68] In the construc-tion of identities, the discrimination of qualities that takes place at the perceptual level is transformed into the negative difference, the logic of mutual exclusion, through which the delusion of unity and perma-nence, or inherent existence, can be established.

This thinking against thought, which recognizes both the dependence of thought on sensibility and thought's own recoil against the passiv-ity of sensibility into the purity and independence of essence, does not,

like the tradition, aim at unity.[69] To aim at unity already presupposes
a duality to be united, while pursuing identity is exactly the production of that reduced experience, which production is for *Negative Dialectics*, as it is for Nagarjuna, the root delusion. Negative dialectics instead
has as its goal not to take identity for the goal,[70] to cancel the aim of
capturing the infinite in the finite.[71] This end requires the thoroughgoing disenchantment of the concept. Rather than offer direct analyses of
the incoherence of assumptions of inherent existence, which Nagarjuna
develops, however, Adorno thinks that the central shift required is a
second Copernican turn beyond the Kantian. This would mean the initiation of a subject-object dialectic[72] but one unlike the Hegelian, which
left the subject's primacy over the object unchallenged.[73] Primacy for
the object does not mean granting inherent existence to either subject
or object, or both.[74] But it does entail recourse to what Adorno calls the
object's "preponderance." The concept opens itself dialectically to this
reversal and this preponderance out of the very striving for identity inherent in it: what Adorno appropriates from Hegel's dialectic is not the
goal of identity, or the demonstration of its attainment, or the logic of
categorial contradiction and synthesis, but the supposition and procedure from the *Phenomenology* (primarily from its preface) that "because
the subject does not make the object, it can really only 'look on,' and
the cognitive maxim is to assist in that process."[75] For Adorno, a "cognition that is to bear fruit" would mean the subject, in relinquishing its
goals of identity and identification, "will throw itself to the objects *a
fond perdu.*"[76] It means that "if the thought really yielded to the object, if
its attention were on the object, not its category, the very objects would
start talking under the lingering eye."[77] Not that their ultimate identification would be made. The importance of aesthetics to Adorno lies
primarily in art's all-but-self-conscious practice of failing at identification while looking on and speaking for things, often enough for their
agony. Adorno's analysis often ironically mimics the Hegelian dialectic,
but only up to a point, the point at which the object, such as "enlightenment," turns into its "opposite," "myth," which turns out to have already been what it seemed to negate: already "enlightenment." It is the
consistent practice of identification that thus ends up working against
itself, producing its own apparent difference. The tactic of negative dialectic is to reflect on and reflect the self-positing and eventual self-
destruction of identification, and this tactic follows from the consistent
practice of "only looking on," from the consistent sense of non-identity.
The result is not any form of positive knowledge of the object, but the

bare "emptiness" (not non-existence) of the concepts and phenomena it subjects to scrutiny.

The experience of non-adequation in the concept, and thus the failure of reconcilement, is the motor of its potential disenchantment.[78] Such disenchantment *may* open the concept and the knower to the radical insufficiency of identity – to its own emptiness, to its non-difference from difference. The object's preponderance does *not* mean the positing of a transcendent Reality making possible our experience, like the Kantian noumenon; nor does it mean access to an immediate experience of objectivity.[79] A minimum of the thing outside the subject's categories is sufficient to spoil identity as a whole, and this minimum is not beyond, but already in the realm of *possible* experience.[80] Disenchantment requires no unknowable but necessary ground for the empirical world. It does imply, however, the relinquishment by the subject of its claim to constitute the world. The categorial schemata through which a de facto constitution takes place are themselves relative and determined, themselves conventional, *historical* phenomena with a *relative* truth-value to be ascertained in reflection. As with Nagarjuna, the ultimate truth is not a truth about a transcendent reality beyond the realm of illusion, but a truth about the emptiness of conventional categories. Thus Adorno notes that Kant's categories of subjective experience are not cognitive ultimates, but that with progressive experience cognition can break through them.[81] The aim of thinking against thought is a "knowledge of the absolute which is not an absolute knowledge."[82] This would mean that in the insight into the emptiness of the categories, what is recovered is suchness. The recovery of such suchness is also a function of the aesthetic recourse to "semblance," which Adorno strictly differentiates from illusion.[83] The preponderance of the object follows from the meta-critical turn Adorno gives to Kant's Copernican revolution, and vice versa. Adorno relativizes and makes conventional both the Kantian categories of possible experience and the transcendental subject correlative with those categories. As with Hegel, the subject and the categories of subjectivity have a history. Unlike Hegel, that history is the non-teleological, material, and pragmatic "natural-history" of "a society unaware of itself,"[84] one that is "samsarically" imprisoned in its own survival mechanism[85] and repeats in ever more technically sophisticated but destructive forms the paroxysm of identification, which is its primordial form of attachment to its world.[86] The transcendental subject so closely linked to bourgeois society as its apparently substantial source is empty because it is a function of this history. The supposedly spontaneous and constitutive I turns out to be more of a thing than its own psychological content, which, from the Kantian perspective, is seen as naturalistic and reified.[87] Metaphysical freedom turns out to be a function of its constitution with and by a society driven by identity taking the form of the rule of equivalence required and propagated by the capitalist mode of production. It is not true that the object is a subject, but it is true that the subject is an object;[88] that is, true that the subject has no inherently existent essence, that it is empty. It is an object in the sense that it is its otherness.[89]

As with Nagarjuna's, Adorno's thinking against thought remains a thinking. For the former, the destruction of inherent existence not only leaves open the realm of conventional truths but affirms the dependent origination of all things. The distinction between causes and conditions that follows allows for the explanatory, aetiological, and soteriological employment of the twelve links of dependent origination.[90] Yet none of these links can be taken any longer as inherently existent, as ultimate or prior. The suffering subject cannot be finally reduced to any one or even a set of them. Adorno's echo is in the notion of thinking in constellations, which, following from the preponderance of the object is, among other things, meant to replace the metaphysical bent of the many forms of Marxian reductionism. Thinking in constellations involves the retention of concepts, but concepts used as if without identity in themselves and referring themselves to the non-identical. The *explanandum* of the constellation, as with Nagarjuna's "conditions," cannot even be easily separated from the *explanans*; both are moments of a process that cannot be reified in a logic. "Cognition of the object in its constellation is cognition of the process stored in the object. As a constellation, theoretical thought circles the object it would like to unseal, hoping that it may fly open like the lock of a well-guarded safe-deposit box: in response not to a single key or a single number, but to a combination of numbers."[91] The box, it must be understood, is ultimately "empty." As a product of natural-historic activity it originates dependent upon the very forces of identification now aimed at unsealing it. None of the categories of negative dialectics are ultimate, prior, or final.

III

As with Nagarjuna, the root delusion of identification is for Adorno a function of the grasping that is a part of embodied, samsaric existence. Nagarjuna: "Conditioned by feeling is craving. / Craving arises because of feeling. / When it appears there is grasping."[92] For Adorno there are no facts of consciousness not mixed with pain and pleasure, desire and aversion – feeling and craving. All mental things are modifications of physical impulse, and both body and mind are abstractions of their experience.[93] The root delusion of identity in the concept is, for him, a function of the *mimetic* impulse, similar to what Nagarjuna calls, in very traditional Buddhist terms, "grasping." However, with the concept of mimesis, Adorno begins not so much to part company with Nagarjuna, but perhaps to supplement him in a way that could indicate to Mahayanists a possible extension of their soteriology into history.

Mimesis is misunderstood as being simply the urge to imitate, copy, represent, or take on the characteristics of something other on the part of a self or subject. It is, "primordially" one might say, the desire to be what there is contact with before there is a self to make contact. But even this formulation too much separates subject and object, for in the mimetic relation the desire of being is granted once and for all. "One" is "the object." And that is all there is. There could be nothing more powerful, more seemingly permanent, more seemingly inherently existent. In negative dialectics, it is the mimetic impulse that stands behind and inside all historically differentiated and developed forms of identification, be they cognitive, psychological, or practical. And mimesis is understood not simply as a condition of individual existence, but as internally mediated by the social forms that mediate the mimetizing individuals who embody and, in perception, cognition, and action, reproduce those forms along with all of their tensions and contradictions. According to Nagarjuna, and fundamental to all of Buddhism, is the notion that the tendency to reify is innate and is one of the root delusions, a "primal ignorance" that is separate from mere social convention[94] and underpins the fundamental "defilements" of greed, hatred, and confusion. The insight into emptiness, in eliminating the fabrication of essence, undoes this delusion and liberates the enlightened being from compulsive reification. To reify, to think that things either exist inherently or fail to exist, will be to overvalue oneself, one's possessions, achievements, performances.[95] Adorno's "mimesis" is also arguably innate. But it is, as dependently originating and empty, more than that as well, and he would find the Madhyamika treatment of it to be one-sided. The social institutions of domination require, in passing historical forms, the very subjects of the root delusion, who in turn adapt to, adopt and repeat those institutions as "natural," as inherently existent. Mimesis may be innate but it is never pure. Can Nagarjuna accept this? Yes, because reification itself would have to be seen as empty of inherent existence, otherwise full liberation would be impossible. To borrow from Marcuse, Adorno's colleague in negative dialectics, there is the need to differentiate, albeit conventionally, between a basic and a surplus mimesis. For Adorno, the mimetic is even essential to undoing the identification of which it is the root. Both poison and (at least part of the) cure. This is because the concept must refer back to the contact and perceptual discrimination of infinite qualitative differences of which it is the abstraction. Thus even, perhaps especially, the most identifying of theories already carries with it the guilty knowledge that as it identifies it fails in identification.

For Buddhism it is possible for some, perhaps a relatively very few, to cut through the surplus and the basic delusion and, with the aid of a teacher, "on their own." But the root delusion is both constituted and modulated in a social reproduction that takes place earlier than and over the heads even of bodhisattvas. Nagarjuna's distinction between the conventional and the ultimate truth would be both accepted by Adorno and found wanting. The ultimate truth needs to be put to use not only to enlighten individuals, whole nations of individuals one at a time, but to destroy the ideologies that sustain the institutions of domination that produce the individuals who cannot but reify – and thereby those institutions themselves. There are much, much better and much, much worse conventions and conventional truths. Not all conventional truths are merely conventional truths. Some conventional truths are moments of ideologies of domination. Negative dialectics in general needs to move beyond the categories and assumptions of metaphysics into the critique of the ideologies of domination, and in such a way as to preserve the emptiness of the truths with which the ideological is perceived *as* ideological. This is what Adorno does.

Buddhism has developed myriad forms of teaching, of community and of social engagement. But it does not seem to have addressed the socio-historical sources (and a source is not a cause in Nagarjuna's sense) of the root delusion. Nothing should stop it from doing so, from becoming historico-soteriological. In doing so it would find Adorno and Critical Theory a valuable ally. There are small signs that as part of the process of the absorption of Buddhism in the West the notion of a Marxian-Buddhist alignment is possible. One recent exhortation to effect such an alignment argues that Buddhism and Marx are compatible and that the former addresses the sources of internal suffering, while the latter addresses the sources of external suffering.[96] This way of approaching the issue tends to reify "internal" and "external." But Adorno's negative dialectics goes a step beyond in addressing the internal sources of external suffering and the external sources of internal suffering without reifying either. If either positive knowledge or instrumental action is the criterion of success, then Adorno will have failed. But if emptiness and liberation from identity-thinking are to be the criteria, then it is only through the conventions of a hyper-samsaric existence that Adorno's glass is seen as failed, as empty.

NOTES

1 Jay L. Garfield, "Epoche and Sunyata: Skepticism East and West," *Philosophy East and West* 40, no. 3 (July 1990): 285–307; Garfield, *The Fundamental Wisdom of the Middle Way: Nagarjuna's Mulamadhyamakakarika* (Oxford: Oxford University Press, 1995); G.C. Nayak, "The Madhyamika Attack on Essentialism: A Critical Appraisal," *Philosophy East and West* 29, no. 4 (October 1979): 477–90.
2 Jay McDaniel, "Mahayana Enlightenment in Process Perspective," in *Buddhism and American Thinkers*, ed. Kenneth K. Inada and Nolan P. Jacobsen, 50–60 (Albany, NY: SUNY, 1984); Robert C. Neville, "Buddhism and Process Philosophy," in Inada and Jacobsen, *Buddhism and American Thinkers*, 120–42.
3 Robert Magliola, *Derrida on the Mend* (West Lafayette, IN: Purdue University Press, 1984); Magliola, "In No Wise Is Healing Holistic: A Deconstructive Alternative to Masao Abe's 'Kenotic God and Dynamic Sunyata,'" in *Healing Deconstruction: Postmodern Thought in Buddhism and Deconstruction*, ed. David Loy, 99–117 (Atlanta: Scholar's, 1996); David Loy, *Nonduality: A Study in Comparative Philosophy* (Amherst, NY: Humanity Books, 1988); Loy, "Dead Words, Living Words and Healing Words: The Disseminations of Dogen and Eckhart," in Loy, *Healing Deconstruction*, 33–51.
4 Garfield, *Fundamental Wisdom*, 94–5; T.R.V. Murti, *The Central Philosophy of Buddhism: A Study of Madhyamika System* (New Delhi: Munshiram Manoharlal, 2006), 40, 49, 75, 121–2, 124, 140.
5 Murti, *Central Philosophy of Buddhism*, 40.
6 Dan Lusthaus, "Nagarjuna," Yogacara Buddhism Research Association, http://www.acmuller.net/yogacara/thinkers/nagarjuna-bio.html.
7 Garfield, *Fundamental Wisdom*, 275.
8 Ibid., 132.

9 Lusthaus, "Nagarjuna."
10 Garfield, *Fundamental Wisdom*, 194; see also 111–12, 118, 179, 218. Garfield sums it up succinctly: "The only way that difference or the identity of a different thing as different could be shown to exist inherently would be for that difference to be present independently of the existence of another different thing. But that is not so. The only alternative would be to argue that difference is present independently in single things. But this ignores the relational character of difference" (218).
11 Nagarjuna, *Mulamadhyamikakarikas*, 22.11.
12 Garfield, *Fundamental Wisdom*, 213, 280.
13 See ibid., 91–2.
14 Ibid., 308.
15 Ibid., 282.
16 Murti, *Central Philosophy of Buddhism*, 73.
17 Garfield, *Fundamental Wisdom*, 198n.
18 Nayak, "Madhyamika Attack on Essentialism," 485.
19 Ibid., 479.
20 In this regard it should be noted that Nagarjuna is also not reducing things to their relations, as though the relations were as inherently existent underlying the things they constituted. See Nagarjuna, *Mulamadhyamikakarikas*, chaps. 14, 20, and 21.
21 Garfield, *Fundamental Wisdom*, 305.
22 Ibid., 200n.
23 Ibid., 101–2.
24 Ibid., 103–5.
25 Ibid., 282.
26 Nayak, "Madhyamika Attack on Essentialism," 486.
27 Garfield, *Fundamental Wisdom*, 291.
28 Lusthaus, "Nagarjuna."
29 Garfield, *Fundamental Wisdom*, 322–8.
30 Ibid., 341. In this connection, see in particular Hershock, who gives a very novel view of the dramatic quality of sentient impermanence beyond "the processive nature of things." Peter D. Hershock, *Liberating Intimacy: Enlightenment and Social Virtuosity in Ch'an Buddhism* (Albany, NY: SUNY, 1996), 46. In this interpretation of Ch'an Buddhism, what is key is the realization of emptiness in "ready responsiveness" within the world.
31 Nayak, "Madhyamika Attack on Essentialism," 489.
32 Ibid., 487.
33 Nagarjuna, *Mulamadhyamikakarikas*, 26.10.

34 Ibid., 18.5.
35 Nayak, "Madhyamika Attack on Essentialism," 489.
36 Gad Horowitz, "emmanuel, Robert," *Journal of Contemporary Thought* 14 (Winter 2001): 83–91.
37 Ibid., 87.
38 Adorno's *Negative Dialectics* is far from the only instance of his negative dialectics. The work, which was published near the end of his life, can be seen as, among other things, a retrospective meta-theoretical exploration of the methods, epistemological postulates, and some of the consequences of the negatively dialectical works of his earlier career, primarily with respect to his co-authorship with Horkheimer of *Dialectic of Enlightenment*, and to *Minima Moralia* as well.
39 Theodore W. Adorno, *Negative Dialectics*, trans. E.B. Ashton (New York: Seabury, 1979), 5.
40 Ibid., 33.
41 Ibid., 13.
42 Ibid., 160.
43 Ibid., 153.
44 Ibid., 31.
45 Ibid., 34.
46 Ibid., 29.
47 Ibid:, 34.
48 Ibid., 22–3.
49 Ibid., 25–6.
50 Ibid., 140.
51 Ibid., 149.
52 Ibid., 141.
53 Ibid., 406.
54 Ibid., 149.
55 Ibid., 5.
56 Ibid., 145.
57 Ibid., 174–5.
58 Nagarjuna, *Mulamadhyamikakarikas*, 18.5.
59 Ibid., 362.
60 Ibid.
61 Ibid., 13.
62 Ibid., 5; emphasis added.
63 This dependence on object-experience is something that Yogacara Buddhism and the Buddha-nature theory that follows from it seem to have incorporated into their critiques and/or critical extensions of Madhyamika

philosophy. See Sallie B. King, *Buddha Nature* (Albany, NY: SUNY, 1991), 9; and Lusthaus, "Nagarjuna."

64 Adorno, *Negative Dialectics*, 5.
65 Ibid., 40.
66 Ibid., 12.
67 Ibid., 45.
68 Ibid., 43.
69 Ibid., 20.
70 Ibid., 149.
71 Ibid., 13.
72 Ibid., 174.
73 Ibid., 38.
74 Ibid., 174–5.
75 Ibid., 188.
76 Ibid., 33.
77 Ibid., 28.
78 Ibid., 186.
79 Ibid., 184.
80 Ibid., 183.
81 Ibid., 187.
82 Ibid., 405.
83 See ibid., 373, 393, 404.
84 Ibid., 177.
85 Ibid., 180.
86 Keiji Nishitani, one of the most prominent of the Kyoto school's Zen philosophers, in considering the question of whether Buddhism is ahistorical, has produced a trenchant critique of the self-centredness at the heart of the Judaeo-Christian West's philosophies of history. In these religio-philosophical histories, meaning for the unique events of a rectilinear history is inevitably tied up with the preservation of self-centredness, a self-centredness from which escape is not possible by means of self-denial. From the viewpoint of *sunyata*, the self tied up in a rectilinear *project* (whether God's or humankind's or, as with Hegel's, "both") of historical conciliation of self and other would be still wrapped up in and reproduce karmic unfreedom and *avidya*. Nishitani maintains that the Buddhist conception of time is, however, both rectilinear *and* circular and that the standpoint of *sunyata* internally related to such a conception would be the logical and radical conclusion of historical self-consciousness. Such an enlightenment would correspond to the emergence of a realm of play and ethical compassion beyond "autotelic" self-sufficiency. See Keiji Nishitani, *Religion and*

Nothingness, trans. Jan Van Bragt (Berkeley: University of California Press, 1982), chaps. 5, 6. It would unfortunately go far beyond the framework and confines of this chapter to pursue the parallels and possible interplay between Nishitani's Mahayanist notion of historicity, with its great debt to Nagarjuna, and Adorno's understanding and critique of "natural-history."

87 Adorno, *Negative Dialectics*, 177. This theme is pursued in somewhat greater detail in Adorno's "On Subject and Object," in *Critical Models*, trans. Henry W. Pickford, 245–58 (New York: Columbia University Press, 1998).

88 Adorno, *Negative Dialectics*, 179.

89 Ibid., 161.

90 See Nagarjuna, *Mulamadhyamikakarikas*, chap. 26.

91 Adorno, *Negative Dialectics*, 163.

92 Nagarjuna, *Mulamadhyamikakarikas*, 26.6.

93 Adorno, *Negative Dialectics*, 202.

94 Garfield, *Fundamental Wisdom*, 299n, 314n.

95 Ibid., 152.

96 See Kevin M. Brien, *Marx, Reason and the Art of Freedom*. 2nd ed. (Amherst, NY: Humanity Books, 2006), appendix.

15 horowitz dances with wolves: inquiries pursuant to the thought of gad horowitz

peter kulchyski

to gad

this address is directed, however much it may miss its mark, towards gad. i speak not for him, as one who attempts to bear his "legacy" of critical thought in canada, but to him whose thinking in this moment/conjunction is more urgent for us than ever. i hope to influence his work at this stage rather than celebrate or entomb it: to you i have things to say, in the hope we will see more from you.

i welcome the rest of you, our third, to "listen in" or read along for whatever value you might find in these admittedly informal words.

gad, i am going to confine my remarks here to several passages and thoughts provoked by your famous early work on *canadian labour in politics*, and by your perhaps less known but even more urgent later work, especially your essay in *difficult justice*. in the shadow of these reflections i hope to show the manner in which your conceptual work both limits and opens insights into the particularities of indigenous resistance in canada, a subject far from your own terrain in some respects, and surprisingly close in others, as will become apparent.

one last preface: *dances with wolves* is the very well known kevin costner, academy award–winning film about an american soldier who joins the lakota sioux. the film has both its critical-utopian moments while being deeply saturated in ideology. the central character is named by lakota "dances with wolves," when they see him, rather than trying to destroy the wolf pack that lives near his home, embrace and dance with them, a foreshadowing of the way he ultimately joins lakota. while his finding a "white woman" as romantic interest and the treatment of lakota enemies in the film as "savage savages" are both among its problematic or ideological elements, one of the most critical filmic moments occurs when he is captured by the american cavalry. the particular look of disgust his captors give him as they throw him in a makeshift brig represents a mechanism of dominant cultures as they cast out those within who have "crossed to the other side." gad long ago left the pieties and strictures of north american society and culture, dancing with the wolves in his life and thought.

oh canada (my confession)

canadian labour in politics is embedded in the moment in which a leftist movement attempts to seize the national project as its own. this is a left i identify with: i too have made canada the site of my reflective practice. but, yet, however, in the movement of my own thought, concerned as it is with indigenous resistances, i have come to see "canada" as the most powerful ideological device of the settler colony: the first and primary violence of the letter that in its being denies the being of nitassinan, innu atsche, denendeh, nunavut, manitou-baa, n'dakai menan, haida gwai, and so on.

it is not from a socialist internationalism that i pursue this insight (though I also do not reject out of hand that line of thought), but paradoxically from the grounded struggles of the communities i work with. it is my view now that these structures of identification, let's say nitassinan, should not be identified as nations, even first nations, though they do constitute peoples and territories.

there is an internationalism that closely relates to my project, an emergent indigenous internationalism only now finding its own distinct voice. i am inspired now by the hemispheric struggles of indigenous peoples from chiapas to bolivia, and the promise that bleeds from those struggles that challenges the structure of the nation as it has been designed to serve capitalism: by erecting barriers to human movement, maintaining cultural divisions between peoples, and controlling the movement of labour.

in view of the mindless, knee-jerk nationalism that surrounds us, i think at this conjunction it demands a repudiation. hence, at a respectable conference in fall 2011, full of critical-thinking, left, national types, decent, thoughtful scholars and writers, my desire to scandalize could hardly find an outlet, though i finally felt satisfied in enunciating the three words not to be spoken in our time and place: "i hate canada." you can see how far i've travelled from *canadian labour and politics*.

the then and the now

here are two quotations from your work that struck me and that moved me as i reread them for this work. the first is from 1968: "the prevalence of doctrinaire Marxism helps to explain the sectarianism of the American socialist party. The distinctive quality of a sect is its 'otherworldliness.' It rejects the existing scheme of things entirely; its energies are directed not to devising stratagems with which to lure the electorate, but to elaborating its utopian theory."[1]

the second quote is from 2006: "one could deploy the aporia in a revolutionary direction in some such manner as this: On the one hand, 'the promise can't fail to break its promise, and this comes of the structure of the promise.' On the other hand (which is, on the other hand, the very same hand), this structure of the promise – messianicity, as oriented to the absolute unpredictability, uncontrollability of the future, the Other – must involve a promise of Messiah not only as infinitely deferred, non-arriving, impossible, but also and by the same token, as the possibility of the actual arrival in history of a 'new meaning of life,' 'new relations with others,' and so on – the possible Messiah."[2]

you know of course that this second statement is part of what you characterize as an "unsatisfactory" approach, yet you also know this essay on the messiah is in fact a discussion of the utopian in a manner that far exceeds what the american marxists were theoretically fighting about.

i am tempted to say that you were so much older then, you're younger than that now, and leave it at that.

i cannot, because this very issue is in my marrow at this stage of my life, as i grapple with the question of whether i should pursue a course of elaborating a theoretical position or engaging in real world politics. but then, your reflection on the utopian (our secular messiah), or more precisely your criticism of levinas and derrida, is precisely directed towards their ahistoricism. perhaps 1968 and 2006 are not so far apart, as a surface reading would indicate. it might even reflect a structure where the other hand, on the other hand, can be the very same hand, in which case i would have to hand it to you.

some other stories of red tories

your early work is known and respected in part for its identification of what is called the "red tory," a political species that developed and had an influence in canadian politics. you see it as a product of the specific "left-right" dynamic that emerges in canada as a result of the comparative strength of the labour movement in this context, if i may drastically simplify. reading this essay today, we would criticize it unrelentingly for its lack of an analysis of the place of women in the construction of the national political identity (has this been done?), and pursuing that thought in a more sympathetic vein we might ask some questions about the longer term impact of the women's movement, whether it had distinctive features from the u.s. movement as a result of labour's strength, and so on. i point this out to illustrate that more work could follow, supplements as it were, and certainly this would be a central line of questioning. my own supplement is to add an indigenous rights spin to your story.

as tony hall (who identifies as a "red, red tory") and I are at pains to point out,[3] central to the american revolution was a decision to abrogate aboriginal rights, to tear up the royal proclamation of 1763: a racist imperial project was at the centre of the united states project, ultimately a major reason why its utopian value was vitiated. the loyalists who influenced canada's political development were forced to adopt the crown's policy of "protection" of indigenous land rights. hence indigenous issues were at the heart of the founding of canada and the united states as distinct entities.

one stream of conservative thought and practice in canada played a role in defending at least the idea of aboriginal rights and elements of its practical implementation. i give you justice jack sissons, jurist of the north, inventor of the circuit court in the late fifties and early sixties, as quoted in the book i've co-written with my friend frank tester, in his decision r. v kogoglalik, 20 April 1959:

> I think the Royal Proclamation of 1763 is still in full force and effect as to the lands of the Eskimos. The Queen has sovereignty and the Queen's writ runs in these Arctic 'lands and territories.' This is the Queen's court and it needs must be observant of the 'Royal will and pleasure' expressed two hundred years ago and of the rights Royally proclaimed. The Queen's Justice is a 'loving subject' and would not wish to incur the 'pain of the Queen's displeasure.' The lands of the Eskimos are reserved to them as their hunting grounds. It is the Royal will that the Eskimos 'should not be molested or disturbed in the possession of these lands.' Others should tread softly, for this is dedicated ground.[4]

the opponent of sissons was none other than gordon robertson, perhaps the leading liberal mandarin of the following decade. although sissons was himself very likely a liberal for much of his life, i think his attitude clearly expressed a tory loyalty to the crown and concern for inuit and dene communities. his struggle is repeated today, when we have a supreme court that firmly insists on respect for aboriginal rights and a federal government that, quite simply, confines the decisions to their singular sites and refuses to apply them in any way. i would then go so far as to say that the species, red tory, in its constitution was inflected with a certain kind of respect for aboriginal rights, perhaps even respect for the value of community, and that the issue would deserve some further thought. red tories and aboriginal peoples – at least, those who self-designate as treaty nations – may be the only distinct groups of people in canada for whom respect for the crown is a vital issue. this is not just a curiosity or accidental conjunction but a key factor in canada's continuing constitutional development.

the dance of anthropology and philosophy

it is my view that european philosophy has been engaged in a dance with anthropology since the shock of the new world contributed towards challenging the universal absolutism of western philosophy. the dance, a marathon, continues, though the dancers cling to each other for support. your own concern with comparative ethnographic study is emblematic of this, but i think much in philosophy involves a slow-burning response to that fact that in other cultural contexts what our philosophy takes as definitive of the human condition is not relevant, or not relevant in the same way, or takes on an unrecognizable form. and in your essay on derrida and levinas it erupts here and there, in the passage where you note that "derrida admires mandela's admiration of early African society,"[5] but most especially in the criticisms of the "eurocentrism" in levinas and derrida as a result of their refusal to historicize the miseries of the other.

and, i must say, i am one who reads in derrida his strongest insights coming from an anthropological space of critique of eurocentrism: as in the passages in *of grammatology*, where he argues against the notion that "primitive peoples" do not possess writing; his essay on the gift, half of which is a close reading of marcel mauss's work, and i could go on. in fact, i agree with your critique. it inclines me to the perspective that undoing eurocentrism is a project of each generation, and that perhaps in rousseau we find the beginnings of that lengthy process (or, perhaps, in las casas, if not herodotus). but for me, derrida is the sign of a critique of the metaphysics of presence more than of an aporetic structure of thought.

your anthropology is, of course, what you take from your extensive reading. and you have an anthropology (twentieth-century critical thought can be divided down a line that marks those who have an anthropology and those who do not). mine owes to that, but also as you know involves being at the dance, hearing the story, walking into the homes. an anthropology in canada is not innocent: it is deeply implicated in the politics of dispossession. your insights into this terrain are multiple and fold over each other in a few ways i want to elaborate below.

political culture

one thing that retrospectively strikes me about your 1968 essay is the stress you place on cultural politics. your discussion is of "English-Canadian political culture"[6] but you do not use the term in an unreflective manner. you write, "Institutional analysis can show why permanent, significant third parties arise, but it cannot explain why one of those parties should be socialist. The cultural analysis is necessary to explain the relative strength of a socialist ideology in Canada; the institutional analysis is necessary to explain why this ideology can easily find expression in a permanent separate party."[7]

i would say your essay inaugurates and opens the space for an understanding of the importance of culture to politics. it is my view that strong currents in marxism, which allocate culture to the realm of "mere" superstructure, miss an opportunity to offer insight at the level on which people live and breathe, the level at which meaning is created. today, critical thought must have both institutional analysis, which i would call political economy, and cultural studies; together these inform a materialist cultural politics. a cultural studies divorced from political economy becomes apolitical and endlessly self-reflective. a political economy divorced from cultural studies is left with the task of shouting the same slogans at higher decibels. your 1968 study is materialist, in my view, because it is genealogical, substantive (you even use data!), comparative, and class based. i want to emphasize the last point, because in both 2006, which ends with a reminder of the importance of thinking the economic if we are to think the ethical, and in 1968, with its attentiveness to social class, you demonstrate or enact a reminder of the importance of thinking class issues at all levels of inquiry, from thinking of utopic social forms to thinking of the place of organized labour in politics. perhaps class analysis must be "wizened, and kept out of sight" (to borrow benjamin's phrase), but it remains insistent in your work. yours is also a study in cultural politics, and aboriginal politics are, as i've suggested in the subtitle of one of my own books, first and foremost cultural politics. i might even go so far as to suggest that the theme of surplus repression so central to your thought may be seen as the critical question to ask of any particular culture and of cultural politics in general.

post-structural liberalism: towards a new didacticism

i think your most trenchant critique of derrida and levinas has to do with how their work is co-optable by liberalism, and i note that liberalism is the strategic enemy in both 1968 and 2006. in 2006 you write: "Levinas and Derrida and most of their followers seem to distinguish better from worse regimes in the time honoured western liberal democratic manner: the better regime is open to critique, the worst is 'closed,' 'totalitarian.' The problem with this is that the notion of an impossible justice that arrives by never arriving ('openness') can be and has been very easily taken as somehow more or less subtly endorsing or underwriting the 'fundamentals' of the western status quo and rejecting all revolutionary approaches as 'apocalyptic,' 'totalitarian,' 'utopian,' 'nostalgic,' and so on and on."[8]

i myself have noted how a certain strain of thought in homi bhabha, and even in michel foucault, lends itself to co-option by liberal discourse to the extreme detriment of indigenous calls for social justice. though bhabha and foucault cannot be held entirely responsible for the misreadings and appropriations of their nuanced and challenging work, it is nevertheless worrying that, for example, alan cairns's or sherril grace's endorsement of hybridity theory[9] allows them to say "anything goes" in contemporary aboriginal identities. as i say elsewhere, the aboriginal corporate executive who plans more capital-intensive resource-extraction projects is for cairns and grace as aboriginal as the trapper being dispossessed. being an old-fashioned postmodernist and somewhat substantivist when it comes to culture, i beg to differ: on *and* on!

our mutual criticisms lead me to believe that "theory," much as i love it, and post-structural theory may at points be too clever by half: some degree of orientation to historical agents in struggle is demanded, and in this i feel i join your criticisms of the problem of ahistoricism in levinas and derrida. to some extent (though i've already railed at the problem of shouting the same slogans at higher decibels), i think a new didacticism in art and criticism may be necessary (perhaps benjamin's project?). in this world in this time we must name the bastards and we must fight them. i find the courage to do this increasingly rare, and the best minds cannot be allowed to hide their politics behind obscure formulas.

a critique of judgment: historicizing utopia

now that i'm almost finished i can safely come to my main point. in 2006 you illustrate how the problem with not distinguishing between surplus and basic repression is closely related to the problem of ahistoricism in derrida and levinas. this points me to the question of thinking about grounded utopic social forms: utopia as historical, somewhat in the manner of your discussion of sabbatai zevi. so, for example, imagine if you will an america of peoples with no need for centralized state direction, practising ecologically sustainable land use, affluent in a form of wealth that can be called "time," egalitarian both in gender and in other social terms, sharing land with as much generosity as today we share air, and engaging in a marked respect for individual personal autonomy. these might be intergenerational productive communities of artists and storytellers and the daring and the humble. in fact, this anti-lockean america does not need to be imagined but rather remembered; ethically these communities must be remembered if a project of social justice is to have any substance. although benjamin wrote that the thought of enslaved ancestors was more powerful a spur to revolutionary sentiment than the thought of liberated successors – appropriate enough to his european context – in this world it is precisely the memory of liberated ancestors, of the nature of the liberation they invented and continually reconstructed for themselves, that is a critical key in unlocking the door to fundamental social change.

the distinctiveness of the hunting cultures in the northern part of what would become america, of course, relates in a strong way to your reading of rousseau, especially. you and i play rousseau off against the official lockean culture that has assumed dominance. deploying your terms, i can also characterize at least the hunting cultures as absent the dominant, alienating forms of surplus repression prevalent in the contemporary socially constructed world, but not absent basic repression (which would be impossible, in any event). society and community function rather well, without individuals being held in check by an alien power structure. do you remember the conversation we once had about clastres and *society against the state*?[10] at the time you said the structure of his argument assumed a state form that has to be held in abeyance and thereby presumes a human nature that tends towards dominance. in this spirit i come to wonder about the use of the term *repression* as a way of characterizing at least the "basic" moment or element of the structure you posit. is what is basic the "repression" of pre-given antisocial tendencies, or is it better to think of this moment as something that is not repressed but rather nurtured: that is, not a repression or halting of individual tendencies to set no ethical limit on the self, but a positive nurturance of already and necessarily presupposed social tendencies. so perhaps among contemporary hunters the issue is not one of a different structure of repression but of a different structure of predispositions being nurtured: how we might elaborate this position is demonstrated in part by my discussion of the meeting in colville lake discussed below.

the concern is something more than an "academic" vetting of terms, ultimately perhaps reflecting on one of your more provocative but powerful and interesting reflections: must we pass through debasement, and could such a formula act as justification for the worst revolutionary excesses, the cleansing violence that does not cleanse? genet yes, mugabe no?

the current struggles of indigenous peoples in canada are in this context not insignificant: not so much the struggles of elites for a greater share of capital wealth, or of the victims of residential schools for redress, though these in their different ways compel our attention as well, but of land-based communities of production against the further degradation of the territories they need as a material basis for meaningful and intergenerational social bonds. today, on the day i am speaking these words, a day long passed for those of you who read them, the innu of quebec who have cabins in nitassinan/labrador are being told their cabins will be torn down, and are promising to burn all the cabins in nitassinan/labrador if that happens. today there is some new moment in this extraordinary historical event called "the conquest" called "the resistance."

compare these social forms with that of the modern: modern "man" is a social being slowly being stripped of her ability to discern, to decide, to make judgments; every aspect of bureaucratic life reduces our ability to respond to the concrete, the embodied. in fact bureaucracy is precisely this, a structure that holds thought itself in abeyance. contra habermas, who believes in communicative advances, i think we are slowly becoming stunted in our communicative ethics: this is one of the lessons i take from my work in fort good hope and colville lake.

one time, gad, i was the only *mola* in a meeting of dene leaders from the denendeh communities of fort good hope and colville lake. the meeting involved about thirty people and lasted about eight hours. there were very compelling and divisive issues on the table, potentially involving tens of millions of dollars – or more – in capital terms, and good relations between two close-knit communities in human terms. it began with the host chief welcoming us and the visiting chief expressing a sense of what the meeting was about. then, through the day, almost everyone in attendance spoke (except for the note-taking *mola*). some spoke for five minutes, some for twenty. about a quarter of those in attendance were female, and they spoke as freely as the men, with one of them giving perhaps the most powerful speech of the day. the only time one person interrupted another, one of the women in the room gently intervened to say "this is not our way." the interruptions ceased. there was no direct repudiation of any statement, though one speaker might address what an earlier speaker had said, and in this elliptical way sharp disagreements were aired. what struck me at the end of all this was that a full room of the most highly trained professionals in "advanced" western culture, university professors for example, could never have held such a meeting. a chair would be needed, preferably following "robert's rules," in order to maintain order. allow me to call the talk "basic repression" or in my own lexicon "social nurturance" and the chair with his rules "surplus repression." in the absence of the latter, each and every socially produced individual must learn the complex rules and ethics of speech. and, among dene, they still do learn them. "we," with our forms of writing, our laws, our policies, our rules, do not. "we" may be more effective at managing large groups of people. but all of us as singular beings are losing our ability to "read the room," to practise situational ethics, to have the very ability to make (never mind the courage to stand behind) judgments.

"one-dimensional man" appears the telos of capitalist human development. does society really "advance" to the extent that each of its members becomes a thoughtless drone? it is to your great credit that you refuse to flinch from being "judgmental," because without judgment there is no discernment and no politics.

the surprise that names the instance: two gifts

this world, "sick and hungry and tired and torn / it looks like its dying when it's hardly been born," needs you more than ever gad horowitz. never let that restless critical disposition retire! how can it, when there are more moments on the itinerary to be traversed and renewed complacencies to be subverted? it is in addressing you that i find a place not encumbered by academic grammatological structures, a voice (surely in part my own?) that refuses the same institutionalization that threatens to haunt you.

knowing as we do the aporetic structure of the gift, i would like to offer you here and now two. first, as is appropriate between scholars, my little book.[11] beyond all of this, to mark a bond more than friendship and more than mentor, a kinship of taste, of thought, of ethics, and crucially inappropriate in an academic discussion (though hardly inappropriate to the drunken revelry that marked the earliest symposia) i would at least with these written words convey to you what i could not in the moment, from my mouth to yours not the speech or words that offer deliberate and calculated meaning but the kiss that explodes it.

NOTES

1 Gad Horowitz, *Canadian Labour in Politics* (Toronto: University of Toronto Press, 1968), 26.
2 Gad Horowitz, "Aporia and Messiah in Derrida and Levinas," in *Difficult Justice: Commentaries on Levinas and Politics*, ed. Asher Horowitz and Gad Horowitz (Toronto: University of Toronto Press, 2006), 324–5.
3 See Anthony Hall, *The American Empire and the Fourth World* (Montreal and Kingston: McGill-Queen's University Press, 2005).
4 peter kulchyski and Frank J. Tester, *Kiumajut (Talking Back): Game Management and Inuit Rights 1900–70* (Vancouver: University of British Columbia Press, 2007), 181. See also Jack Sissons, *Judge of the Far North: The Memoirs of Jack Sissons* (Toronto: McClelland and Stewart, 1968).
5 Horowitz, "Aporiah and Messiah," 322.
6 Horowitz, *Canadian Labour*, 29.

7 Ibid., 49.
8 Horowitz, "Aporiah and Messiah," 310.
9 See Alan Cairns, *Citizen's Plus: Aboriginal Peoples and the Canadian State* (Vancouver: University of British Columbia Press, 2000); and Sherill Grace, *Canada and the Idea of North* (Vancouver: University of British Columbia Press, 2003); as well as my criticism of Cairns in my *Like the Sound of a Drum: Aboriginal Cultural Politics in Denendeh and Nunavut* (Winnipeg: University of Manitoba Press, 2005), 243–50, and of Grace in a review of her book published in *Études Inuit Studies* 28, no. 1 (Spring 2004): 197–201.
10 See Pierre Clastres, *Society against the State* (New York: Zone Books, 1983).
11 After delivering an earlier version of this paper, titled "From Political Cultures to Cultural Politics: Indigenous Horowitz; Horowitz Dances with Wolves!" at the panel "Contemporary Critical Theory in Canada: Essays in Honour of Gad Horowitz," Canadian Political Science Association, Congress of Humanities and Social Sciences, Vancouver, June 2008, I presented Gad with a copy of my book *The Red Indians* (Winnipeg: Arbeiter Ring, 2008).

PART FIVE

Horowitz in His Own Words

emmanuel, Robert[1]

GAD HOROWITZ

Robert Magliola's *On Deconstructing Life Worlds*[2] is motivated by the bodhisattvic desire to help others cope with evil and suffering through Buddhist/deconstructive meditative frequenting of the double binding happenings of human existence – essentially a teaching of profound *acceptance* of all goings on. However, this work is punctuated by periodic assertions of an absolute obligation binding all human beings to work for a better world and justice. Magliola's Buddhism – like Buddhism in general – does not seek to account for the *ethically obligatory* quality of the bodhisattva vow. I suggest that ethical obligation is the "prior" "condition" even of Sakyamuni's experience of enlightenment and his decision to share it with humanity. The Bodhi tree would also be Jacob's ladder.

1

Robert Magliola has been one of the foremost mediators of Buddhism and Derridean deconstruction, especially in his major work *Derrida on the Mend* (1984).[3] In his more recent work, *On Deconstructing Life Worlds* (1997) Magliola lets us know: "the main reason for this book: if you sense your life is a bind/double bind I will give you a way to cope."[4] The desire in this book is the bodhisattvic desire: to give. In this book Robert describes and gives ways of healing that he found through much travail at the (non)intersections of Buddhism, deconstruction, and Christianity. Through Derridean and Nargarjunist analytic deconstruction, and especially through deep meditation on the devoidness of all happenings, one can learn how to cope with evil and suffering, "letting the spectacle of the world go on without me (i.e., without ME) letting go, letting be," observing and affirming "the rising and cessation of all 'things.'"[5] This is a practice of *frequenting* the binds/double binds, which describe how the devoid happenings of the world devolve. "As in Derrida, the world of 'cause and effect' proceeds: it is not destroyed but deconstructed, not evaded but obviated."[6] Robert indicates that such healing follows or goes along with surrender of the "Awake-Dream of an omnipotent Creator whom we can expect to provide 'justice' and 'fairness' within our life experience,"[7] even though he makes happen or allows the happening of not only good but also evil, the triumphs of the wicked and the tortures of the innocent. Many of us will have found it necessary, like Robert, to pray to God to deliver us from belief in that God.[8] The God of healing, like the worlding of the world of "cause and effect," "seems to work as a Bind."[9] "God is a Bind/Double Bind," like Derrida's *différence originaire*.[10] Derrida "strongly compares difference originaire (the 'prior' difference enabling no and not – no talk in language) and 'God' as pure difference (the 'prior' difference making possible the 'naming' of beings and their negations).["11] "Irreducible binds/double binds ... are clues, somehow, to the very constitution of God."[12] "God is the name of this bottomless collapse of language."[13] Bind and double bind after bind and double bind, infinite retreat of binds/double binds. Only such a view of God could "make sense for me," says Robert, "out of the unspeakable injustices of human history." Surrender the expectation of justice, practise the meditative frequenting of the double binds of your existence, and "eventually the double binds become salubrious."[14] "Christ's wounds – our wounds – are turned all glorious."[15] "The enlightened person is detached from every circumstance and thus can celebrate every circumstance ... in a 'playful Samadhi' ... one can even enjoy hell."[16]

But wait, Robert cautions: "There attaches, however, a certain moral apostil: because the deconstructionist is teaching ... everyone is obliged to kindness."[17] Caveat meditator. And the question arises: *why* is the deconstructionist teaching? Why and whence this *obligation* to kindness? A search of *On Deconstructing Life Worlds* reveals numerous similar caveats: Robert rejects, at least for himself, the "kind of Buddhism which would simply affirm good and evil in the world as the inevitable play of Samsara."[18] His religious practice is not "escapism" because he believes in "direct action," even "leftist," "socialist" action to "make the world better," to "stop aggression/oppression."[19] Marx's prescription of communism – "from each according to her/his ability, to each according to her/his needs" – is for Robert a "holy maxim."[20] But why is it holy? He declares his commitment "to ethics, and to working out the project of goodness-at-all-costs."[21] Why at all costs? Like a good deconstructionist, Buddhist Robert refuses to "lay claims to absolute or universalized truth";[22] however, in a footnote, this refusal is interrupted: "Except for one conviction, which I insist is binding on all: the obligation to loving-kindness."[23] And he writes of his decision to "try [his] utmost to do good, and *for the rest* affirm (and observe) the rising and cessation of all 'things.'"[24] How does it happen that there is this exception, this absolute truth, this obligation binding on all human beings, which takes precedence over the practice of meditative frequenting of the binds and double binds of the devoid happenings of God and the world? What is the secret of the happening of this divine exception, and what kind of devoidness is its devoidness? Whence the peremptory, compulsive, compelling passion in Robert's work for doing good and for justice, which somehow assumes a kind of priority – behind his back – in relation to the teaching of analytic Derridean and Nargarjunist deconstruction and of non-clinging meditative practice? Is this passion a response to the commandment of God – not the omnipotent One from who Robert prayed to be delivered – but God the name of the Other who interrupts cause-and-effect, being-and-non-being, invoking and evoking the self as infinite obligation to the other person?

One will have recognized in these words the teaching of Emmanuel Levinas. Though Robert Magliola disavows any calling to contribute to the "theoretics of justice and expectation," referring his readers instead to "Deleuze, Guattari, Baudrillard, and so on,"[25] is it not the case that his confessions of commitment and obligation indicate, implicate, resonate not those pagans but the Jew?

Magliola's text, very much like the Mahayana Buddhist tradition to/ of which it is a contribution, does not go behind the bodhisattva's vow, the promise, to account for the *vow* – nature of the vow, that is, to explain the obligatory quality, the *must*-ness of the "I must 'do good.'" The bodhisattva vow gives no account of itself other than the familiar formulations of compassion as the manifestation, in the world of cause and effect, of insight into emptiness. But ... the question: "why the must? Why the *vow*?"

2

Emmanuel Levinas's phenomenological or post-phenomenological research indicates that this "must" precedes the ego "I," occupies, preoccupies, animates, breathes the "I" as its inescapable orientation to the other, who is not an alter ego, i.e., not "another Same" and not the other *of* the same, but the inaccessible, inconceivable, non-phenomenal, always already past and always to come, utterly powerless, vulnerable yet Authoritative Other, who shines in the faces of all actually existing others as the Face.

The vow is not freely assumed by a pre-existing "I." There is no pre-existing I. The *I* is the vow. The erring sinful creature (and God knows there is no creature, not even the most righteous tzaddik, who is free of sin/error) disavows the vow to greater or lesser extents without affecting its primordial inescapability. The bodhisattva, the bodhisattva in Robert or Whoever, Someone / No One, "Personne," is the human fully living the ethical responsibility, or more precisely the struggle with ethical responsibility, Israel, which characterizes, defines, the human.

Buddhist insight into devoidness/emptiness, whether we think of it as prior to or co-arising with compassion, is at bottom discovery of the *pour-l'autre* of the human self – its (non)essential dispossession or home-leaving. It's not a matter of I taking refuge / leaving home. Rather, leaving home *is* the I correctly understood. In Levinas's words, "Its very closing" or selfhood "is a turning inside-out ... an inside-out without an inside."[26]

The bodhisattvic self – our true nature, or Buddha nature, if it is all right to say so – shows itself in this perspective as a "putting into question of the self," which poses "itself directly as deposed, as for the other.... The departure from oneself" can only be "the approach of the neighbor."[27] That is why the bodhisattva *must* help not only by teaching the devoidness of self and of things and of all happenings but by helping in every way, by insisting on justice in this world. God just is this powerless yet obsessively authoritative insistence on justice, or as Levinas put it, "God" is the "signification" that comes to mind when the *conatus essendi* or right to life is shaken by the question: do I deserve to live? "If I am for myself, what am I?" asks bodhisattva Rabbi Hillel.

The world of cause and effect *can* be deconstructed, obviated, phenomenologically speaking, and it *must* be deconstructed, obviated, ethically speaking, because the call of the Other, the approach of the Other who has always already escaped my comprehension, has created me as desire, as response to and for the Other. What is beyond the ego, says Levinas, is its very own constitutive "non-indifference" to the Other, its "disinterestedness ... as the just judgment, and not a nothingness," i.e., not a simple spacious devoidness of ego.[28] Not simply its devoidness/

suchness then, but this devoidness/suchness *as* the incumbent pre-occupying proximity of the other, dis-possession by the other, infinite obligation to the other, impossible to discharge, finish, or fulfil. The teaching and the experience of non-importance, of devoidness, which may indeed if we are fortunate dis/empower us to be insightful/bliss-ful/compassionate even in hell, gains its significance and importance from the commandment: be ye just. So the self is bodhisattva, Buddha, Christ, saint, messiah, and tzaddik: "At the very bottom of my 'posi-tion' within myself [there is] my substitution for the Other."[29] But all of the above are not God. "God" is the signification of human signification that "cuts across all phenomenality." Cuts across, cross-hatches (the translator elaborates: "trancher: contrasts with it, interrupts it, put it to an end temporarily at least." One might add, from inside/outside)[30] ... the signification that "comes to mind" when I hear the call. Another Levinasian term that belongs here is "illeity": impersonal intersubjec-tivity, indicating not an I–Thou dialogue relation but an asymmetrical relation, between I and a commanding utterly vulnerable He – the *alter-ity* of the other person.

Immediately following Sakyamuni's experience of enlightenment under the Bodhi tree, the Buddhist legend tells us, he *has to decide* whether or not he will share, give, teach, in spite of the likelihood that others will be unreceptive or uncomprehending. According to legend he was persuaded by the god (God?) Indra. Would Levinas say that this story should be turned inside out? The struggle with obligation/decision would come first, though not in any chronological synchronic sense. The Bodhi tree would also be Jacob's ladder. The inescapable call of the Other would be the "prior" "condition" of the search for enlight-enment, and of the experience of enlightenment, the decision to teach and the teaching. As in the case of the Israelites whose response (not without struggle) to the giving of the Torah was *"Naáseh Vénishma –* we will do it and (then) we shall hear the word," it would be the elec-tion by God, even before there is any apparently or conventionally au-tonomous ego to respond to it, which would precede, condition, and evoke the ego and its insights and sharings and refusals and refusals/inabilities to share. The obligation, in the darkness of the Other (Moses sees only God's back) is the no-space in which the light of insight-compassion can appear. The ethical question faced by Sakyamuni "after" his enlightenment is "before" his enlightenment, the *first* ques-tion, the question posed to the first human born to Adam and Eve: Am I my bother's guardian? All religion, according to Levinas, answers, "Yes,

yes, that is what I am. I alone am my sister's guardian" (*shomer* – watch-person, guardian, preserver). The tree is the tree of the "knowledge" that we must first choose between good and evil. Eve is God's angel: first eat the apple, then we'll talk. The orthodox Lubavitch writer Zalman Posner puts it this way: "Yes, yes. He is omni-this and omni-that, but what do we need him for? For defining good and evil."[31] Just obey the commandments, do God's will, do good, *then* we can talk about talking about language and the "bottomless collapse of language." For Posner this is "thinking Jewish." He's not far from Levinas and, strange as it may seem, not far from the Bodhi tree.

According to the legend, the Buddha proclaims, immediately following his liberation, "I alone am the World-Honoured One." Levinas would make it more clear than has ever been done how far this is from any boastful or even not boastful assumption of Superiority or Power, worldly, churchly, or "spiritual." My obligation places upon me the burden of the entire suffering creation, weighs on me as the very *meaning* of me, on myself alone (on every myself but not as deduction from any general rule of reason, thus never on *"you"*); and this, Levinas tells us, is the "infinition of the infinite," or "the glory," "the glory of God."

Again, this is not the God from whom Robert prayed to be relieved, but the God who is nothing other than the approach of the Other: "It is as if the face of the other man, who from the first 'asks for me' and orders me were the crux of ... the surpassing by God of the idea of God and of every idea in which he would still be intended, visible, and known, and in which the idea of the infinite were denied by thematization or in presence or representation."[32] In *Fragments of Redemption*, Susan Hendelman cites Isaiah 43:10: "You are my witness, says the Lord" – and the appended Midrash: "If you are my witnesses, I am God, but if not, not."[33] Or as Moshe Idel puts it, transmitting a Kabbalistic tradition, the Torah "looks not so much for salvation by the intervention of God as for God's redemption by human intervention."[34]

In Flannery O'Conner's story "A Temple of the Holy Ghost" recounted by Robert in *On Deconstructing Life Worlds*,[35] when the hermaphrodite "freak" on display in the country sideshows admonishes his audience, "God made me this way ... if you laugh he may strike you the same way," it is the Face of the Other that speaks, commanding, imploring, don't kill me, don't make me a "freak." Robert is close to this when he suggests that this figure "is the very emblem of God's Divine out-and-indwelling." But he is far from this, I think, when he says, "How can a good God 'will' such a birth-in-the-world? O'Connor's hermaphrodite affirms and does not dispute."[36] I don't think Levinas could abide any idea of a *God* who "makes" "freaks" any more than a God who could "will" the devoid happening of Auschwitz, or, for that matter, the bombings of Dresden and Baghdad.

Is there some trepidation in relation to my language of priority, ultimacy, firstness? I think that Levinas knows as well as Magliola and Derrida that *différance originaire* or "God" or "any 'ultimate' would be asymmetrically but doubly bound into its 'traces' in the 'other-than-ultimate'"[37] "Always entrammeled, entangled (1) in ad hoc situational difference, whichever one happens to be happening at the time, and even (2) in the empty traces which 'it' (there is no self-identical 'it,' of course) is singularly 'then and there' constituting."[38] There is no logocentric "prior." Levinas says, "Even if it cuts across all phenomenality," the signification "God" always signifies in a "phenomenological concreteness."[39]

But he shows us as well that the ultimate is nevertheless in a certain most significant sense, ultimate – a kind of cross-hatching, much like Magliola's discourse of bind and double bind, but with a systematic, explicit, Judaic, ethical difference, which Robert needs if he is to account for his "musts." The priority of the ethical is not logocentric and not theocentric, has always already come "before" any "first." If we go for help in relation to this issue to Levinas's crucial distinction between the ethical call, the Saying and the commonsensical, philosophical, phenomenological, theological, or gnoselogical Said, all saids betray traces of a Saying and are uttered by a Saying that nevertheless "does not enter as a contextual or intertextual element [i.e., 'presence'] into any said." That Saying "in its contentless and nondiscursive repetition ... is always new" and has always passed when its message is heard.[40] Thus it is always coming from an "immemorial" past that has never been present, a pre-original past, from a future that will never arrive, and therefore cannot be thought of as an origin, ground, *arche*. The "primordial" ethical saying is an-archic, inaudible in itself, cutting across the devoid saids of what Robert calls "the ever erratic going on."[41]

3

"Logocentric," says Robert, is "any concept or even 'experience' taken as 'closed' so that its parts adequate ... to it and/or to each other ... (thus, even 'no frame' is a frame)." But "what really happens is measured ... by what/how much is *missed*.... In the 'less' or 'more' which is *left out* happenings really go on" [emphasis in the original]. It is "this lack" that "generates what 'goes on.'"[42]

What is let out:, alterity, for Levinas is "ultimately," in terms of human significance, the alterity of the other person, the Other; the approach, appeal, incumbency of this ever-escaping Other generates the selfing that goes on. A Buddhist might say, "What cuts across *samvrti-satya* (conventional logocentric truth) is *paramartha-satya* (absolute truth of devoidness)," but for Levinas the imperative of gratuitous love, the ethical Saying, cuts across truth, all truths of happenings-and-their-devoidness. The saying of the saids "is" what "cuts across" them. There is much cross-hatching going on, but for Levinas the arms of the cross, though equal in some sense, are ultimately not equal. And it may be that Derrida would agree, for it is not at all difficult to find a similar sense of the priority of the ethical in some of his more recent writings.

For example, in an interview with Derrida, the question is posed, "Is there a logic of ethical testimony at work in deconstruction?" Derrida answers, "Yes, it is absolutely central to it. Testimony, which implies faith or promise, governs the entire social space. I would say that theoretical knowledge [truths of happenings and their devoidness] is circumscribed within this testimonial space [the space of the ethical Saying]. It is only by reference to the possibility of testimony that deconstruction can begin to ask questions about knowledge and meaning." And referring directly to Levinas's teaching, Derrida says, "It is because" ... of "the infinity of the other ... the infinite alterity of the other" ... "that I must describe my relation to him/her ethically and not in a purely phenomenological fashion.... In order to describe things in themselves ... in order to be a phenomenologist to the end, I have to interrupt phenomenology. That is what is meant by self-interruption, which is another name for *différence*."[43] The ethical saying that cuts across, cross-hatches, interrupts all truths, all saids, all happenings, is self-interruption, *différence originaire*, the bottomless collapse of language, all of which, as we have already heard, are among the names of God.

NOTES

1 "emmanuel, Robert" was originally published as chapter 10 in *Buddhisms and Deconstructions*, ed. Jin Y. Park, 181–90 (Lanham, MD: Rowman & Littlefield, 2006).

2 Robert Magliola, *On Deconstructing Life Worlds: Buddhism, Christianity, Culture* (Atlanta: Scholars, 1997).
3 Robert Magliola, *Derrida on the Mend* (West Lafayette, IN: Purdue University Press, 1984).
4 Magliola, *Deconstructing Life Worlds*, 109.
5 Ibid., 78.
6 Robert Magliola, "French Deconstruction with a (Buddhist) Difference: More Cases from the *Gateless Gate [Wu-men-kuan] and Blue Cliff Record [Pi-yen-lu]*," *Studies in Language and Literature* 3, no. 1 (1988): 20.
7 Magliola, *Deconstructing Life Worlds*, 99.
8 Ibid., 79.
9 Ibid., 104.
10 Ibid., 158–9, 163.
11 Ibid., 159.
12 Ibid., 127.
13 Jacques Derrida, *On the Name*, ed. Thomas Dutoit (Stanford: Stanford University Press, 1995), 51.
14 Magliola, *Deconstructing Life Worlds*, 117.
15 Magliola, "French Deconstruction," 127.
16 Ibid., 19.
17 Ibid.
18 Magliola, *Deconstructing Life Worlds*, 69n32.
19 Ibid., 70.
20 Ibid., 70n34.
21 Ibid., 75.
22 Ibid., 79–80.
23 Ibid., 80n60.
24 Ibid., 78.
25 Ibid., 99n94.
26 Joseph Libertson, *Proximity* (The Hague: Martinus Nijhoff, 1982), 225.
27 Emmanuel Levinas, *Of God Who Comes to Mind*, trans. Bettina Bergo (Stanford, CA: Stanford University Press, 1998), 13.
28 Ibid., 11.
29 Ibid., 10.
30 Ibid., xi.
31 Zalman Posner, *Think Jewish: A Contemporary View of Judaism; A Jewish View of Today's World* (Boston: Spring, 1997), 22.
32 Levinas, *God Who Comes to Mind*, xiv.
33 Susan Handelman, *Fragments of Redemption* (Bloomington: Indiana University Press, 1991), 286.

34 Moshe Idel, *Kabbalah: New Perspectives* (New Haven, CT: Yale University Press, 1988), 179.
35 Magliola, *Deconstructing Life Worlds*, 127–30.
36 Ibid., 130.
37 Ibid., 168.
38 Ibid., 169.
39 Levinas, *God Who Comes to Mind*, xi.
40 Adrian Peperzak, "From Intentionality to Responsibility," in *The Question of the Other: Essays in Contemporary Continental Philosophy*, ed. Arleen B. Dallery and Charles Scott (Albany, NY: SUNY, 1989), 16–17.
41 Magliola, *Deconstructing Life Worlds*, 169.
42 Ibid., 172.
43 "Hospitality, Justice and Responsibility: Dialogue with Jacques Derrida," in *Questioning Ethics: Contemporary Debates in Philosophy*, ed. Richard Kerney and Mark Dooley (New York: Routledge, 1999), 81–2.

Bringing Bataille to Justice[1]

GAD HOROWITZ

"Intelligence ... as sensitive to pain as aching teeth"[2] is at work in both
Bataille and Levinas. Bataille is a hell-dweller and Levinas visits him
there. They confer there, through gritted teeth, discoursing on the experience of evil. They agree that evil is, in Levinas's words, "an excess, a
break with the normal and normative, with order, with synthesis, with
the world." It is "the nonsynthesizable."[3] Like death or as death, it is
wholly other. Evil is trauma, overwhelming energy, energy that over-
whelms the being, shattering its boundaries, making it impossible to
experience it in the sense of assembling it as an event in historical time,
within the mineness of the narrative of my life. Therefore, Bataille and
Levinas would agree, evil can be a salutary shock, an awakening from
the pleasant slumber of self-certitude; "without evil, human existence
would turn on itself, would be enclosed as a zone of independence, and
[this] would certainly be the greater evil."[4]

But Levinas would not agree with Bataille that the experience of
trauma *is* the experience of divinity. For Bataille, but not for Levinas,
trauma *is* God. Bataille is transfixed in trauma, dying to repeat the transubstantiation of anguish into the joy of self-loss. He prostrates himself
before this divinity, propitiating the trauma, devoting himself to the
object of his terror: "To face the impossible – exorbitant – when nothing is possible any longer," he says, "is ... to have an experience of the
divine."[5]

For Levinas, to find the God of Abraham *in* Energy, Intensity, or
Trauma, one must somehow have loosened herself from the grip of
what Levinas would call the primitive religion of taking Trauma *as* God.
Bataille writes, "Horror won't stop making me sick but it is my wish to
love this weight unreservedly."[6] This weight is for Levinas the whole

"weight of the world"[7] to which the subject, which is at bottom "sensibility," "vulnerability," "exposure to wounding," to "outrage," is subjected.[8] "The self is a subjectum; it is under the weight of the universe responsible for everything."[9] In the suffering of this evil, the human being is called to "pass from the outrage undergone" and from an ensnarement in trauma to responsibility for the other man, for the persecuted and for the persecutor; to hear this call is to hear the name of God.

Bataille had pictured the Unknowable – the otherwise than being – as "a hard alien fingertip pressing into the small of the back."[10] Like many Bataillean expressions, Levinas could have used this. Perhaps he did, for he describes the subject as "a pure sensible point,"[11] a "point of pain."[12] "All the suffering and cruelty of essence weighs on a point that supports and expiates for it…. In expiation, on a point of the essence there weighs the rest of essence, to the point of expelling it"[13] – not as in Bataille, expelled as a "pure inner fall into a void"[14] – but expelled into itself: "a subject is immolated without fleeing itself, without entering into ecstasy … it is pursued into itself, to the hither side of rest in itself, of its coincidence with itself,"[15] into itself, its self *as* "substitution" for the other.

For Bataille, "sovereignty" or "glory" is the "moral summit," "a radiant shining through," in which the "isolated being denies itself as isolated being."[16] It is the moment in which I "ruin in myself that which is opposed to ruin."[17] Glory is to "drown joyously, sinking, and laughing at one's own tragic demise":[18] "One who loses his life is a saint – it matters little to what end."[19] For Levinas, it matters more than anything. For Bataille, "sovereign," glorious, is "what you and I are, on one condition, that we forget, forget *everything*."[20] But for Levinas, to forget *justice* is to fall short of the moral summit, to fall far short of glory. In the sovereign moment of glory, Abraham *drops* the knife at the summit of Mount Moriah. For Bataille, "the sovereign is he who is as if death were not."[21] For Levinas, the self substituted for the other is he who is as if his *own* death were not: glorious is to prefer to die rather than let the other die. And we shall see that Bataille can't really forget justice: when the primitive gods sleep, he flirts with justice. Even Nick Land, the most intense Bataillean, flirts with justice when he writes, "All energy must be spent … the only questions being where and when and in whose name this useless discharge will occur."[22] "Useless" to the ego, Bataille and Levinas agree. But Levinas wants to focus on the question: in whose name?

The beyond being for both Bataille and Levinas is the beyond thought, beyond the idea, beyond form: it is the *singular*, what Bataille calls *l'informe*, the formless. "Bataille's writing," says Dennis Hollier, "is only an effort to ... [get] lower and lower," to that base matter "too low ... to be submitted to the common measure of the idea." Bataille's desire is "to *fall*"[23] to the otherwise than being – taking Socrates's hint in the *Parmenides* about the excessive distance from the Forms of such useless things as hair, mud, dirt. Bataille goes lower: spiders, spit, the big toe, cadaver, tears and laughter, shit, rot, mutilation and waste, madness, obscenity, the severed foot. The low, the formless is "outside genus," "unexplainable discrepancies."[24] "Base matter," says Bataille, is what "exists outside of my self and the idea."[25] His desire is to fall into the realm of chance, going below any will to power into the will to chance, the will to laughter: "It is alea, how the dice *fall*."[26] "Here," says Hollier, "man finds himself in Hell ... the realm of the pagan gods. The *inferni*, the places below, are divine."[27] But Levinas distinguishes two very different meanings of formless: first, the "absurdity" of what, falling outside of form, is still relevant to form: "Its uselessness appears only relative to the form against which it contrasts itself of which it is deficient." Second, the "signification of the (human) face breaking through all form."[28]

Here we only touch what in Levinas's work is most difficult and most distinctive in contrast with Bataille and all other pagan and Christian and of course post-Christian thinkers – for Bataille, though he was introduced to philosophy by the Russian Jew Lev Shestov, author of *Athens and Jerusalem*,[29] could never shed his foreskin. He could shred it but he could never shed it. Levinas distinguishes sharply the "Saying" from the content or words communicated, the sign, the "said." The Saying, signification itself, is prior to all signs. (There is no saying *outside* the said: the saying is "betrayed" in the said, leaves a "trace" in the said, but we can't pursue this matter here.) The said belongs to Being. The saying is otherwise than the said, otherwise than being, prior to being, and its condition. Peperzak says it well: "The question of being – the question of 'what is?' has forgotten that this question is asked of someone. It is a call for help. *Demande* and *prière*."[30] Questioning is what evokes, calls forth, or interpellates the "someone." Levinas writes: the theme, the said, "seems to contain the other. But already it is said *to* the other."[31] Signification, Saying, happens when the human being, always already vulnerable, exposed to wounding, already responsible in the sense of compelled to respond to the weight of being, encounters the Face of the other human being as absolutely Other, unavailable to my material or intellectual grasp, essentially beyond essence, unpredictable, incalculable, inconceivable: the other not as alter ego, another me, another version or instance of "self"; the other, signifying nothing but itself, signification itself, signification of signification. "The signifier, he who gives a sign, is not signified."[32] The face of the other, precisely because it is in its primordial materiality beyond any possibility of being grasped, arouses in me an unquenchable temptation to murder her, in every sense of the word murder, including possession, comprehension, incorporation, assimilation, reduction to the same, recognition of the other as alter ego, another "me."

At that very instant of temptation, the other becomes the Questioner, the Interlocutor who questions being, essence, *my* drive to be for myself. It is the question of justice. How can I *justify* my existence? The existential possibility of murder – of myself as lord and master, exploiter, torturer, and executioner, of which Bataille was so excruciatingly aware – poses its ethical impossibility. It is the question of the first human being born of woman, our father Cain, the first murderer: "Am I my brother's keeper?" With this question he enacted his inescapable responsibility, his response to the Face of the other, his response to the question of the other: "Will you murder me? How can you murder me?"

The question is at once the only commandment: thou shalt not murder. Cain's response was to murder and to turn away – but not to escape – from his inescapable responsibility; and Levinas's comment is, "Only beings capable of war can rise to peace."[33]

There is a similar moment in Bataille: "Philosophy," he writes, "is never supplication," but "without supplication, there is no conceivable reply: no answer ever preceded the question; and what does the question without anguish, without torment mean?"[34] For Bataille the anguish is essentially interpersonally shared by alter egos who are *with* me down here in hell. But for Levinas, what approaches is the alterity of the other, not from hell, not in hell, but from above, in another dimension, the ethical dimension of "height." This ethical relation is asymmetrical, or non-relational, in the sense that it is always the I who is obligated, always I who am obligated. It is I as being, as the same, that is put in question by the other, beyond being. The other is not simply *refractory* to representation like traumatic happenings per se: he is, has always been prior to representation, she has never *been*. The other, and my (non)relation with the other is in principle absolutely invisible from any perspective; not visible to an observer, to a third, whether myself as third (thus myself as conscious subject) or some other ego or conscious subject as third. At this level there is no possibility of reciprocity in which *each* would be other to the other, for this would require a third position from which this reciprocity could be seen. I and the other are not on the same plane, for if we were she would not be the other but "a peculiar point of my realm … [If the other were] included within a network of relations visible to a third party," the individuals would appear from the outset "as [mere] participants in the totality" – submitted to the common measure of the idea – particular instantiations of a genus – no longer singular. "The other would amount to a second copy of the same, both included in the same concept."[35] "The absolutely other is the Other. He and I do not form a number."[36] It is my non-reciprocal, asymmetrical obligation that individuates me. Thus for Levinas, I am sovereign only in the sense that no one else can be responsible in my place as "hostage" for the Other, for all the others. What the other can do for me, says Levinas, is "*his* affair. If it were my affair, then the substitution would be only a moment of exchange and would lose its gratuity…. The other may substitute himself for whomever, except for me."[37] This is asymmetry, non-reciprocity, ingratitude, or the "curvature of intersubjective space."[38]

Bataille's lowering gave us an alterity that is still caught up with being. Ethical height, for Levinas, does involve a kind of lowering in the sense that the Face of the other obliges me without having any power over me: "I call face that which … in another concerns … me – reminding me from behind [his] countenance of his abandonment, his defenselessness, and his mortality."[39] Bataille's "communication" as the *sharing* of anguish, the loss of self of all of us on the same plane, our dying together, misses the irreplaceable singularity of the subject. It does not go below, that is above, the community of those who have nothing in common to the null place where I alone, the hard alien fingertip pressing into my back, bear the burden of all the others. The Bataillean space is not curved. That's why Bataille can only beat his head against the walls of this double dilemma: first he explains, "That which I desired to be for others" (he doesn't often formulate his desire in this Levinasian way) "was excluded" by my "being for me…. Therefore the use to which I wanted to be put by others required that I cease to be … that I die…. [Thus] I was condemned to live as an unreality, as a fetus tainted at birth." And second, "I see the good of another as a kind of decoy, for if I wish the good of another it is in order to find my own." Therefore I'm left with only an "empty yearning, the unhappy desire to be consumed for no reason other than desire itself – to burn."[40] With both "therefores" Bataille turns himself around inside of a kind of symmetrically twisted-on-itself Möbius space. But Levinas would hear Bataille's helpless speech betraying its source in his election from on high, which has already produced him as inescapably himself, as self-for-the-other, prior to all possibilities on the plane of being of wishing the good of another in order to find his own. According to Levinas, "Without Saying, passivity would" doubtless "be crawling with secrets designs."[41] However, the Saying, the pure direction to the other, which is itself the condition for all possibilities of refusing or embracing this direction, ensures that what I do for the other could never be *merely* or *essentially* a modality of the for-self. And Levinas as well as Bataille uses the images of dying and burning: the Self "is a burning for the other, consuming the basis of any position for myself. He dies continuously,"[42] not, thank God, for no reason other than to burn, but for the sake of the other. Levinas would say that Bataille is mistaken about his desire, "desire itself": desire itself (as opposed to ego's need) is desire for the other. Bataille's saying, betrayed in his said, is: hineni, here *I* am, not condemned to live as an unreality but as "myself, at the service of men ... without having anything to identity with but ... [this] saying itself."[43]

The subject being just a point of pain "does not identify itself, does not appear to knowing."[44] The subject is the singular being, just "moi, c'est moi ... and nothing else to which one might be tempted to assimilate me."[45] Signification is "expression"[46] – just pure expression of self, as self, to you for you, prior to any expressed. Bataille approaches this when he writes of Manet, "No painter more heavily invested the subject not with meaning but with that which goes beyond and is more significant than meaning."[47] Levinas would ask: signifying signification? Asymmetry again: asymmetry forbids taking human beings initially from any *perspective,* theological, sociological, biological, or cosmological, and deriving somehow an ethical orientation *from* such a perspective, deriving ethics from truths of being. "Like a shunt," says Levinas, "every social relation leads back to the presentation of the Other to the same without any image or sign, solely by the expression of the Face."[48] "When taken to be like the genus that unites like individuals, the essence of society is lost sight of."[49] It is Bataille's cosmological ("general economical") perspective above all that holds him to the Möbius plane of heterogeneity-homogeneity.

For Levinas, only the subject is formless, beyond being. An arrow shot at Hegel here will also hit Bataille: Levinas notes that for Hegel, unique or singular beings are mere "bits of dust" or "drops of sweat" collected by the movement of "universal self-consciousness" – "forget-table moments" of what counts, which is "only their identities due to their positions in the system."[50] Since that's what they are for Hegel, that's what they are for Bataille: dust, sweat, spit, with their value reversed or inverted scatologically as the value of no value: singularity attributed to base matter. We come back to Levinas's distinction between the nudity of the useless, which falls outside of form *relative* to form, and that of the Face breaking through all form at every moment. Nothing falls as low as it can go, impossibly low, lower than lower than low, except the other on high. "Nothing is unique," says Levinas, "that is, refractory to concepts, except the I involved in responsibility,"[51] because the alterity of the Face is "not only a resistance to generalization, which is on the same plane…. Here the refusal of the concept is not only one aspect of its being but is its whole concept."[52] Bataille's tears, laughter, the absurd: for Levinas they are on the brink at which Bataille feels himself stymied: the human subject, says Levinas, is "called on the brink of tears and laughter to responsibility"[53] for all the others. Here Bataille has already been brought to justice.

What Levinas calls the face, Bataille can only call defacement. Bataille defines "painting as the defacement of human figure, the defacement … in which he constitutes himself as a man. In contrast to architecture, painting does not ask man to recognize himself in the mirror trap…. [P]ainting confronts him with an image in which he cannot find himself. Man produces himself refusing his image, in refusing to be reproduced."[54] Levinas's intuition of asymmetry allows him to present defacement, which is in the mode of lowering, precisely as the Face, in the mode of an ethical height, which is neither the high nor the low of being. It's no longer a question of self-defacement as self-mutilation like Bataille's beloved Van Gogh cutting off of his ear, self-mutilation as refusal, even as refusal of the choice between submitting and refusing (of the kind Bataille attributes to Baudelaire),[55] for I am *already* constituted as human, already "fallen *upward*"[56] into the human, subjected by the Saying of the other, already a pure sensible point of responsibility. It's not the ear that has to go but the foreskin. Thou shalt not make unto thyself any other cuts. For Levinas, self-mutilation and suicide are evasions of responsibility, though only "the being capable of suicide is capable of sacrifice"[57] for the other.

For Levinas, spit, sweat, cadaver, rot, waste, etc. are not yet otherwise than being but products of the fragmentation of being. "However incomparable the fragments of being" excluded, excreted by the

Idea from knowledge, usefulness, and beauty, "being weaves among incomparables a common fate ... despite their diversity.... [They] do not escape order."[58] "Disorder is but another order."[59] "Every attempt to disjoin the conjunction would be only the clashing of the chains."[60] In the *Story of the Eye* Bataille enacts among other execrable marvels the transubstantiation in the mode of lowering of the body of Christ (the scene is a Roman Catholic Church) into the sperm of Christ "in the form of small white biscuits" and the wine, His blood, into his urine. Is this the first piss Christ?

"The ecclesiastics," writes Bataille, "at the bottom of their hearts ... are quite aware that this is urine," otherwise they would have used red rather than white wine. And the hosts "obviously smell like come."[61] And obviously – would Bataille deny this? – this lowering of God (elsewhere Bataille makes Him loathe Himself and recognize Himself as pig and whore) not only lowers the God of Being but *repeats* him at a lower level, no matter how much lower still symmetrical, without breaking the Möbius circle of higher being and lower or fragmented being. Bataille writes, "Life is a product of putrefaction, and it depends on both death and the dung heap.... Death is that putrefaction, that stench ... which is at once the source and the repulsive condition of *life*."[62] Here is the circle of life and death, saving and expenditure, the symmetry of life as detour to death, presented in the tractate *Avot*, in Levinas's favourite text, the Talmud, in these words: "Where do you come from? From a putrid, stinking drop. And where are you going? To a place of maggots and worms." But the Talmud poses a third couplet: "And before Whom will you justify yourself? Before the King of Kings, the Holy One, Blessed be He." In Levinas's radical restatement of the Jewish tradition, this would be: before the Other, the Unknowable Interlocutor who questions me. Only the asymmetry, the curvature of intersubjective space, the Before Whom, breaks through the circle of being, of life and death, has always already broken through as the condition of all human experience. Life, says Bataille, moves "unceasingly from the known to the unknown." There's no escape, he says, from "this circular agitation which does not exhaust itself in ecstasy but begins again from it."[63] Recurrent impossible tension: the thirst for annihilation of the being that wishes at all costs not to disappear. From cemetery to church, from urine to wine and back, chalice ... from acéphale to the Marshall Plan[64] and back, attraction/repulsion, prohibition/transgression, territorialization/deterritorialization, eros/thanatos, self-assertion/self-dismemberment. Nietzsche, says Bataille, "thrashed about in all directions, seeking a way out."[65] Thrashing about in the Möbius of the same, no otherwise than being for Bataille other than clear awareness of this thrashing about. Well, there is the moment of supreme victory/ defeat, glory, sovereignty forgetting everything, past and future, living as burning as dying as living in the so-called moment – but this ecstasy, insists Levinas, is "but the outside of oneself of an entity always closed up at home with itself."[66] The ecstatic moment of lowering only preserves "the structure of self-knowledge ... of a quest for self, though it be led astray on obstructed labyrinthine pathways."[67] "Every opposition to life takes refuge in life and refers to its values."[68]

Sometimes we can catch Bataille on the brink of circumcision, leaving behind the pagan gods. (Hold that man down and cut off his foreskin! But don't spare the anaesthetic, we wouldn't want him to enjoy it too much.)[69] For example, when he says, "Unknowing does not eliminate sympathy,"[70] is he not on the brink of hearing why or how it is that unknowing does *not* "forget everything," that it eliminates everything but "sympathy"? When he writes, "It is insofar as an individual is not a thing that he can be loved ... the loved one cannot be perceived unless projected into death,"[71] is he not on the brink of Saying with Levinas that "fear and responsibility for the death of the other person ... is ... the secret of love ... without concupiscence"?[72] Most famously, Bataille's "I find in myself nothing" immediately moves on to "at the disposal of my fellow beings ... everything in me gives itself to others."[73]

The great rabbi of Prague, the Maharal (who, according to legend, created and destroyed the Golem), when asked to contribute to the interminable discussion about why circumcision happens on the eighth day of life, speculated that it is like the musical scale. It begins with "do." Let's call it the indifference to essence, the "expenditure" that is Bataille's "glory," and it ends with "do," the same note but at a *higher level* – let's say it's the indifference that has passed over into what Levinas calls "indifference to essence as non-indifference to another,"[74] which Levinas calls glory. This Passover is the reason that absolute unknowing does not eliminate sympathy.

Now look: what have I done? Have I come from piety to piety to a pious conclusion? Here I am on the spot Jacques Derrida pointed out in *On the Name*: now that deconstruction has taken on a certain Levinasian tone, Derrida admits that, though this is on the one hand pleasing, on the other, the left hand, he is repelled by the prospect of a "community of complacent deconstructionists." Now that we postmoderns may officially explicitly concern ourselves with ethics, obligation, and responsibility, we may fall into "a new dogmatic slumber ... Reassured and reconciled with the world in ethical certainty and good conscience ... The consciousness of duty accomplished, or more heroically still, yet to be accomplished."[75] Levinas himself often warned of the temptation of good conscience, insisting on bad conscience going from bad to worse, responsibility painfully increasing the more it is actually shouldered. But that can sound pious too. Perhaps nothing can ensure Levinas's teaching against piety and the pious Jewish and Christian clerics and the pious liberals and social democrats like the editors of *Philosophy Today*, introducing their special issue on Levinas, who line him up with Vaclav Havel and Jan Sokol, giving him partial credit for the "fact" that "human rights, fifty years after they were enshrined in the U.N. Charter, have finally become a primary obligation. At least they are in principle an obligation for world citizens."[76]

So I have come to an alternate conclusion that you were perhaps not expecting. Whenever I hear the word *Levinas*, I reach for my Bataille. Yes, I want Bataille held down and circumcised, brought to justice, but I also want Levinas lowered. He *says* the "psyche" is "psychosis," possession by the other, but he never freaks out. I want him lowered down here, bug-eyed, red-faced, raving with me and Bataille and Nick Land and all the rest of us fools, raging against the world as it is, against our damaged lives, *with* us and the murderous kids of Columbine. I want to hear that clashing of the chains, at least a little bit. Even if it is almost immediately commodified.

NOTES

1 "Bringing Bataille to Justice" was originally published in *Public* 37 (2008): 138–43.

2 Georges Bataille, *Guilty*, trans. Stuart Kendall (Venice, CA: Lapis, 1988), 66.

3 Emmanuel Levinas, "Transcendence and Evil," in *Collected Philosophical Papers*, trans. Alphonso Lingis (Dordrecht: Martinus Nijhoff, 1987), 180.

4 Georges Bataille, *Inner Experience*, trans. Leslie Boldt (Albany, NY: SUNY, 1988), 93.

5 Ibid., 23.

6 Bataille, *Guilty*, 12.

7 Emmanuel Levinas, *Otherwise than Being*, trans. Alphonso Lingis (Pittsburgh: Duquesne University Press, 1998), 128.

8 Ibid, 15.

9 Ibid., 116.
10 Bataille, *Guilty*, 12.
11 Levinas, *Otherwise than Being*, 164.
12 Ibid., 56.
13 Ibid., 125.
14 Bataille, *Inner Experience*, 121.
15 Levinas, *Otherwise than Being*, 108.
16 Bataille, *Guilty*, 104.
17 Bataille, *Inner Experience*, 120.
18 Ibid., 36.
19 Ibid., 197.
20 Georges Bataille, "Sovereignty," in *The Bataille Reader*, ed. Fred Botting and Scott Wilson (Oxford: Blackwell, 1997), 312.
21 Ibid., 319.
22 Nick Land, *The Thirst for Annihilation* (London: Routledge, 1992), 56.
23 Dennis Hollier, *Against Architecture: The Writings of George Bataille*, trans. Betsy Wing (Cambridge, MA: MIT, 1989), 102, my emphasis.
24 Ibid.
25 Bataille, *Inner Experience*, 36.
26 Quoted in Hollier, *Against Architecture*, 103, Bataille's emphasis.
27 Hollier, *Against Architecture*, 103.
28 Emmanuel Levinas, *Totality and Infinity*, trans. Alphonso Lingis (Pittsburgh: Duquesne University Press, 1969), 74–5.
29 Lev Shestov, *Athens and Jerusalem* (Athens: Ohio University Press, 1966).
30 Adrian Peperzak, review of *Beyond Being*, *Research in Phenomenology* 8 (1976): 247–8n21.
31 Levinas, *Totality and Infinity*, 195, my emphasis.
32 Ibid., 182.
33 Ibid., 222.
34 Bataille, *Inner Experience*, 36.
35 Levinas, *Totality and Infinity*, 16.
36 Ibid., 39.
37 Emmanuel Levinas, *Of God Who Comes to Mind*, trans. Bettina Bergo (Stanford: Stanford University Press, 1998), 91.
38 Levinas, *Totality and Infinity*, 291.
39 Ibid., 227.
40 Georges Bataille, "On Nietzsche: The Will to Chance," in *The Bataille Reader*, 337–8.
41 Levinas, *Otherwise than Being*, 19.
42 Ibid., 50.

43 Ibid., 149.
44 Ibid., 56.
45 Levinas, *Totality and Infinity*, 296.
46 Ibid., 297.
47 Quoted in Yves Alain Bois, *Formless: A User's Guide* (New York: Zone Books, 1997), 21.
48 Levinas, *Totality and Infinity*, 213.
49 The reciprocity of responsibility: the necessity of rationality, law, and taking care for oneself, comparison of incomparables, emerges as a secondary phenomenon – it "comes to be superimposed on the pure altruism ... of the I *qua* I." Emmanuel Levinas, *Entre Nous: Essays on Thinking-of-the-Other*, trans. Barbara Harshav and Michael B. Smith (New York: Columbia University Press, 1998), 100. This is another important and difficult matter we cannot pursue here.
50 Levinas, *Otherwise than Being*, 104.
51 Ibid., 139.
52 Levinas, *Totality and Infinity*, 118.
53 Levinas, *Otherwise than Being*, 18.
54 Hollier, *Against Architecture*, 55.
55 Georges Bataille, *Literature and Evil*, trans. Alastair Hamilton (London: Marion Byers, 1997), 57.
56 Levinas, *Otherwise than Being*, 184.
57 Levinas, *Totality and Infinity*, 149.
58 Levinas, *Otherwise than Being*, 8.
59 Ibid., 101.
60 Ibid., 182.
61 Georges Bataille, *The Story of the Eye*, trans. Dovid Bergelson (San Francisco: City Lights Books, 1987), 76.
62 Bataille, "Sovereignty," 242–3.
63 Bataille, *Inner Experience*, 111.
64 According to Peter Tracy Connor, *Georges Bataille and the Mysticism of Sin* (Baltimore: Johns Hopkins University Press, 2000), 182n34, it was said that Bataille mused for a while that he might win the Nobel Peace Prize for his general-economic advocacy of the Marshall Plan.
65 Bataille, "On Nietzsche," 340–1.
66 Levinas, *Otherwise than Being*, 178.
67 Ibid., 194n6.
68 Levinas, *Totality and Infinity*, 145.
69 I am grateful to Robert Gibbs for the anaesthetic suggestion.

70 Georges Bataille, "Unknowing and Its Consequences," in *The Bataille Reader*, 324.
71 Ibid., 325.
72 Levinas, *Entre Nous*, 130–1.
73 Bataille, *Inner Experience*, 128–9.
74 Levinas, *Otherwise than Being*, 146.
75 Jacques Derrida, *On the Name*, ed. Thomas Dutoit, trans. David Wood, John P. Leavey Jr, and Ian McLeod (Stanford: Stanford University Press, 1995), 15.
76 Caroline Bayard and Joyce Bellows, "Editors' Introduction," *Philosophy Today* 43, no. 2 (1999): 115.

An Essay on the Altruism of Nature

GAD HOROWITZ

Introduction

What can we learn ... what can we Levinasians learn from George Price? George Price was a scientist who made important contributions to neo-Darwinian theory, especially to its understanding of how processes of natural selection could have given rise to altruistic behaviour in living beings, including humans. And he was for eighteen months an incandescent practitioner of self-sacrificial altruism in the slums of London – a veritable saint of the impossible. At the end of that period he committed suicide. His funeral was attended by five of the homeless men he had assisted and two of the world's best-known evolutionary theorists. What can we learn from George Price? And what, if anything, could he have learned from us?

Kin Altruism

What Levinas, following Spinoza, calls *conatus essendi*, the driving force of being, has been identified by Darwinian science as natural selection. It is the way of being – survival of the fittest over time, more precisely, elimination of the unfit, those who are relatively unable to perpetuate their genes. For decades evolutionary science was puzzled by the phenomenon of altruistic behaviour among animals. Given the constraints of natural selection, how was it possible that for countless centuries, ground squirrels, for example, could continue to utter warning cries to warn their fellows of the approach of a predator, thus themselves becoming prey? Over time the genes underlying such altruistic behaviour should be selected out, leaving only exclusively self-serving squirrels.[1] The literature contains many examples of such behaviour in many species, from the most primitive to the most highly evolved.

In 1963 the biologist William Hamilton solved the puzzle.[2] The solution involved the clarification or revision of the meaning of the "fitness" of an individual organism to include the fitness of kin, carriers of the same gene; thus, "inclusive fitness." The squirrel who sounded the warning might perish, but many of her nearby kin would be saved. The altruistic gene would therefore actually be favoured for survival in the evolutionary process. The term *kin altruism* was soon coined by a contemporary of Hamilton to point to the kind of altruism inherent in being. Hamilton's discovery enlightens the entire realm of living being: even "amoebas can recognize and aid kin" in preference to non-kin. And human "step children are much more likely to be abused" than biological children.[3]

Reciprocal Altruism

Hamilton's contribution paved the way for the formulation of a theory of *reciprocal* altruism. The genetic substrate here would be one that gives rise to behaviours that help *unrelated* others, so long as there is expectation, conscious or unconscious, of reciprocation of some kind, either directly from the beneficiaries or indirectly from others in the course of time. In George Williams's words, "An individual who maximizes his friendships and minimizes his antagonisms will have an evolutionary advantage, and selection should favour those characters that promote the optimization of personal relationships,"[4] That's why "we will do almost anything for 'reputation' and 'respect.'"[5] Furthermore, over time, reciprocal altruism "fosters a sense of group obligation," a more diffuse targeting of indirect reciprocity, so that individuals make sacrifices for the good of the group as a whole, with the expectation of reciprocation no longer for myself directly but for the group. I expect you to sacrifice for the group as I did, and the other "members expect this too," and offenders are punished, at least via shaming, isolation, loss of reputation and of self-esteem. Perhaps, Robert Wright speculates, a genetic infrastructure might evolve in favour of larger and larger groups (and I would suggest, perhaps even the very largest group, humanity as a whole), but this could *never* involve sacrifice without regard for "ultimate" reciprocation.[6] As we shall see shortly, according to both Darwinians and Levinas, only psychosis can go there.

Deception

The theorists of reciprocal altruism move easily from the thought that giving is the best path to receiving, to the realization that the specific purpose, so to speak, of the reciprocal altruism gene is to give to the other the *impression* that I am beneficent. Perhaps the primary evolutionary function of the self "is to be the organ of impression management."[7] Thus, though deceptive manoeuvring is not uncommon in the animal kingdom[8] (e.g., some birds make false alarm calls to frighten the other bird away from her food), the evolution of Homo sapiens proceeds *pari passu* with the perfection of the capacities to deceive both the other and the self.

According to Richard Alexander, natural selection has favoured the development of more and more effective abilities to "make one's self seem more beneficent than is the case" and to "influence others to be beneficent" in a manner "deleterious to themselves,"[9] while repressing such generosity in oneself. Natural selection has also therefore driven the development of the ability to *detect* deliberate deception on the scene of reciprocity, as so, in a kind of evolutionary arms race, the ability to deceive in a way that avoids detection, i.e., to deceive oneself, so that one can deceive others without betraying the least sign of any intention to deceive. For what could serve to avoid detection more effectively than the power to appear even to oneself as more beneficent than one actually is? The whole game sinks to the level of the unconscious. Indeed, for many evolutionary theorists, these are the roots of the Freudian unconscious. On the scene of reciprocal altruism, Alexander argues, we see the elaboration of hyper-idealistic moralities that are deployed unconsciously in the service of the self. He might have quoted Ambrose Bierce: "Remember the Sabbath day to make thy neighbour keep it wholly." And, of course, we Levinasians are very much aware that it is easy "to be seduced into believing" that if I propound Truth, Goodness, etc., this can in no way be framed as "another (however subtle) power play, another means of expanding my influence and expanding my powers, in short, a matter of self-interest."[10] Jacques Derrida knows: "I perjure like I breathe."[11]

Enter George Price: Group Selection

This American scientist came to London in November 1967 to work with Hamilton on the evolution of altruism. Price was disturbed by the reduction of morality in Hamilton's work to a kind of nepotistic drive, appalled at the thought that "pure unadulterated goodness was a fiction."[12] His main technical contribution to the field was an equation (the Price Equation) that showed the exact circumstances under which natural selection could operate on genes, not only at the level of the individual but at the level of the group to favour evolution of traits that would be good not for the individual but for the group.[13] This is the idea of group selection, up until then almost universally discredited. Price showed that under certain circumstances of extreme competition between groups, self-sacrificial traits of individuals within a group might evolve in a way that empowers the group to extinguish its rival. The victorious group and its genes would thereby flourish. Hamilton revised his original theorization to take the Price Equation into account, declaring that this "effectively disposes of the problem dating back to Darwin of whether the individual or the group should be considered the unit of natural selection."[14]

Some evolutionary thinkers, following Kropotkin, had wanted to invoke group selection, involving sharing, cooperation, and even self-sacrifice for the sake of others, as testimony to a "romantic universal niceness,"[15] but it was immediately apparent to Price and almost all workers in this area that "arguing the moral superiority of group selection over individual selection is like arguing the superiority of genocide over random murder."[16] It now seemed clear that in order for real self-sacrifice to evolve, "a ruthless rival to the group was mandatory"[17] "It was a terrible irony": "goodness could be bought only at the price of cruelty."[18]

In 1968 Price was asked by his friend the political scientist Al Somit to give a paper at the International Political Science Association session on biology and politics. Price agreed to speak about "morality being nothing but a 'masquerade.'"[19] The paper was never given. Price was about to find God.

A Saint of the Impossible

Suddenly, the mathematical genius George Price finds himself in a state of mind in which he is astonished by a series of coincidences that strike him as so extremely improbable that he becomes convinced of the existence of God and the truth of the Gospels. More than likely, under the stress of certain personal misfortunes and illness, together with the failure of his scientific search for true goodness, he had unconsciously begun to search for God, and that forced him to notice the coincidences.

Price decides to become "in everything a slave to the Lord ... not like the usual 'evangelical' Christian who prays for 'guidance' and then makes his own decisions. I do not ask for 'guidance.' I ask for *commands*.[20] And then I obey them." He signs at least one letter "sincerely His."[21] His biographer writes, "As George grew crazier and crazier to the world, his scientific insight only sharpened,"[22] and he produces a number of innovative scientific papers. In September 1970 he writes to Billy Graham urging him to use his influence over President Nixon to end the war in Vietnam.[23]

In October 1972 Price decides to obey literally Jesus's admonition to "take no thought for your own life ... nor yet for your body" and to have faith that the Lord would provide for his basic needs. He eats very little, at one point surviving on a pint of milk a day.[24] He adopts the practice of periodically stopping his thyroid medication as a way of opening a space for divine commands. After collapsing from malnutrition, he decides, upon leaving the hospital, "pale and thin, his figure nails brittle and blackening,"[25] that to be a true Christian he must devote his life to serving others. His biographer suggests that this was perhaps a different kind of scientific experiment: "If George's own mathematics described a world where selflessness was always selfish, perhaps in his own actions he could prove that in humans this wasn't necessarily so.... Perhaps man could do better. Perhaps *George* could do better."[26]

Occasional visions and whispers from Jesus instruct and encourage him. Eighteen months of sainthood begin in March 1973, "around the beer-and-piss reeking, rat infested corners of Euston Station and Soho Square." He seeks out "London's homeless and helpless dregs," alcoholics, street fighters, ex-cons, thieves. "'My name is George,' he'd introduce himself. 'Is there some way I can help you?' ... Soon he learned that there were many ways he could help them. A quid here, a sandwich there, a cup of hot cider, a word to a policeman. Most of all though he could offer room and board, and beginning in April they were flocking to his home." He forms ongoing friendships with a number of them. "To all who stayed longer than overnight George provided keys." He gives out money freely, keeping only a pittance for his own minimal needs.[27]

John Llewelyn's words in *Appositions of Jacques Derrida and Emmanuel Levinas* could easily, and more truly, have been written by George Price: "I am in exile in my own home, hospitable to the point at which possessions make sense only in being given gratuitously to the ungrateful."[28]

In June he decides that he must become homeless himself, refrains from renewing the lease on his apartment, and continues his mission; he spends his nights at his office, at friends' places, at a homeless shelter where "some nights a violent drunk would fight him over his cubicle and always he would yield with a smile."[29] Is this not "extreme passivity of exposure to another"?[30] His brother, other relatives, and colleagues in evolutionary biology try and fail to convince him that his mission is irrational and unfair to himself. His friend Al Somit comes to visit, offers to give him twenty pounds to replace his ragged shoes if he would promise not to give the money away. George will not promise. Somit gives him no money and returns to the United States.[31]

Now fifty years old, "as sinewy and gaunt as an old man ... grungy and oily and shabbily dressed, his teeth were beginning to rot ... hair ... as brittle as hay, his fingers yellow from smoking," looking ill and starving, emaciated,[32] is this not "all the gravity of the body, extirpated from its *conatus essendi* in the possibility of giving"?[33]

On Christmas eve 1973 George spends the night in an old folks home. The staff sleep in on Christmas morning and wake to find that George has dressed and fed all twenty-one residents. He says good-bye and disappears into the morning.[34]

Doubt

As the eighteenth month draws to a close, George begins to suffer from doubt. Perhaps after all one cannot give a gift. He is realizing in his bones the impossibility of the gift, but this doesn't make him a more subtle philosopher. It exacerbates his misery. But he does decide that Jesus wants him to take better care of himself; he trims his beard and stops giving away almost all his possessions. As his mission continues into July 1974, he meets a twenty-five-year-old American artist named Sylvia and falls in love. As if he didn't have enough trouble.

The doubts intensify. "No matter how much he wanted to forget himself, in the end he couldn't. How could he discern if his selflessness was not just a masquerade, the self fooling the self only to please the self and nothing more? How could he know ... whether his goodness, *human goodness*, was really genuine and pure?"[35]

Levinas would say that it could not be just a masquerade to please the self, because *before* the self there is the pure altruism, beyond all calculation, of the "I qua I," and every bit of all normal human goodness is at least in some part, some sense, a manifestation of this otherwise than being. Therefore we are burdened and blessed with the knowledge that, as John Caputo suggests, we can't give a gift, and that it is only when we really know this that we can give a gift. "It is only a gift ... when you fully experience the tension, torque, or torsion ... when I know I can't give a gift, only then can I give a gift."[36] But George, having access only to his science and to his Christianity, was not blessed with this knowledge.

In October 1974 he writes, "'I have indeed been serving the Devil.' Trying to help all the homeless and old people had not been led by true love and had only done them harm ... He had just created false hope ... now is the time to confess to himself the 'deepest selfish desires'"[37] that underlie his mission. And now Jesus wants him to learn "'real love, giving love, Jesus style love,'" and in order to do that "he would have to start again with just one person."[38] That would be Sylvia. Sylvia likes and admires him but turns down several proposals of marriage.

Even after taking better care of himself for a while, George is still "skin and bones,"[39] "weak and disheveled"[40] and depressed. He confers with a psychiatrist, but a few days later, on 5 or January 1975, he severs his carotid artery with a sharp instrument and dies. At the coroner's inquest the psychiatrist discloses that George had again stopped taking his thyroid medication, that he was suffering from depression and perhaps "from the symptoms of schizophrenia."[41] His funeral was attended by five ragged homeless men and by two prominent evolutionary biologists, William Hamilton and John Maynard Smith. George Price is buried in an unmarked grave in London.

Jesus or someone has whispered to me to share George's story with the Levinasians.

Convergences

One might have thought that the neo-Darwinian and Levinasian discourses were either mutually exclusive or incommensurable. But I think they converge in a few important and interesting places. First, pure unconditional altruism is an aberration. In Levinas's words, "It is a seed of folly, already a psychosis,"[42] "pure non-sense invading and threatening signification," a "folly at the confines of reason."[43] One of the founding fathers of sociobiology, Robin Fox, put it this way: humans are capable of "excesses" of both destructiveness and altruism, which are "aberrant" from "the scientific point of view."[44] For the biologists, the life scientists, and for many other thinkers of Being, the aberration is within being, on the margins of the human. For Levinas, however, the aberration is otherwise than Being, an aberration that is presupposed by human personhood. It is not simply a marginal quirk or glitch in the machinery of natural selection, but the limit of the human that defines the human as such; it is the opening of the human otherwise than biology. (Actually one scientist, George Williams, is perhaps somehow aware of this when he writes, "Thoroughly unselfish and genuinely altruistic" acts, which we do sometimes find in humans, "cannot have been directly favored by natural selection. They must have been produced indirectly by some sort of accident.... It is on this abnormality that human ethics depends.")[45] For Levinas and Derrida the altruism of the I is the *supplement*: the marginalized term is itself central. The human person is psychotic at the core.

e'ven ma'asu ha'bonim
hayta le'rosh pina
me'et hashem hayta zot
hi niflat be'eyneynu

(from Psalm 118, in the ancient Hallel prayer)

The stone   (of non-sense, of the impossible)
rejected   (put aside, minimized, marginalized)
by the builders (the cogitators of the *conatus essendi*) and (the design *factors*
of natural selection)
will have become the cornerstone (the supplement)

This is the work of God
It is miraculous in our eyes.

The crazy altruism that George Price got from taking Jesus at his literal word for eighteen months manifests what Levinas calls the asymmetrical (non)relation with the other, the altruism of the I, I who encounter the other as Other, the I separated from all egoic relations with others (and presupposed by those egoic relations). The neo-Darwinians have no way to approach this craziness other than as an accident on the scene of reproduction and reciprocity.

During George Price's eighteen months he made no demands on anyone, politely refuted all attempts to dissuade him from his path, issued no denunciations, displayed no moral indignation, never raised his fist to the heavens to shout hey ho hey ho, someone or other has got to go. Levinas and the Darwinians would agree: this is way beyond the symmetrical, the reciprocal; this is the asymmetrical, where "one forgets reciprocity, as in a love that does not expect to be shared."[46] It is the asymmetrical, where one expects nothing of the other, where one refrains from making demands of the other: "to say that the other has to sacrifice himself to the others would be to preach human sacrifice!"[47]

And this has brought us to a second convergence: on self-righteousness, which is a species of deception-and-self-deception. The perfection of deception flowers in the uniquely human attribute of moralism, or self-righteousness. The most sincere (self-)righteousness is a stratagem of being on the scene of reciprocity, where a sense of egoic obligation arises out of the mutual dependence of egos, up to that of all the egos, as against the impossible altruism of the I, obligation without why or because. Hyper-moralistic rhetorics go very well with kin and reciprocal altruism, but they are altogether incompatible with the crazy asymmetrical orientation to the other, which paradoxically, or aporetically, they must presuppose.

A number of neo-Darwinian theorists, especially Robert Trivers and Richard Alexander, have emphasized that human self-righteousness has been a major factor in the causation and rationalization of "devastating wars" and other "pathological conditions,"[48] and they hope that natural-scientific evolutionary thinking can contribute to "a deeper self-understanding,"[49] bringing into our conscious awareness the ways we are primed to use the feelings of righteousness, righteous anger, righteous indignation, etc. to drive our self-serving behaviour, especially in international relations.[50] We are in danger, says Alexander, "of being rendered extinct by our morality."[51] We must come to understand that "morality was generated, maintained, and elaborated because of its self serving aspects."[52] "All ... moral posturing," says Robert Wright, should be subjected "to skeptical scrutiny ... [since] the feeling of moral 'rightness' is something natural selection created so that people would employ it selfishly."[53]

Pharmakon

Of Levinas's teaching we can say: *Pharmakon*. It can be poison rather than elixir, in three different but not unrelated ways. First, whenever we allow it to be misinterpreted as a hyper-idealistic moral ideology, either by its critics or by its professors. Second, when it is turned against Levinas himself. We might ask ourselves how it happens that one significant tendency in Levinas studies is the quest for flaws in his morality, from the points of view of the highly valued ego-syntonic "progressive" causes of these times: formal universalism: is Levinas too "Eurocentric"? Is he too Jewish? antiracism, anti-colonialism, feminism, animal liberation, ecology, Sabra and Shatila … Economic and social inequality haven't received all that much attention, despite my own efforts in this sense,[54] and neither have gay marriage, reproductive rights, prison abolition, legalization of drugs, Aboriginal rights. And any minute now we'll get it from the "conservative" point of view: Does the preborn child not "have a face"? Does the victim of crime not "have a face"? Do the "1 per cent" not "have a face"? Third, when it is "applied" over-enthusiastically. Perhaps it is time to temper the enthusiasm with which we endeavour to "develop" and to find more and more "applications" for Levinas's teaching, as though it were a general theory of some kind. Although it is certainly valuable to consider many possibilities of development and application, it is in my opinion important to remember to devote at least equal attention to the study, the contemplation of his teaching, as though it were a prayer which can affect our *feeling* of what it is to be a human person, that is, to be on the cusp, as it were, of the otherwise than being. Perhaps with such an attitude we could have helped George Price if we had been with him on the day before his suicide. (Or perhaps not).

NOTES

1 Robert Wright, *The Moral Animal: Evolutionary Psychology and Everyday Life* (New York: Pantheon, 1994), 157.
2 William Hamilton, "The Evolution of Altruistic Behavior," *American Naturalist* 97, no. 896 (Sept.–Oct. 1963): 354–6.
3 Wright, *Moral Animal*, 103.
4 Ibid., 190.
5 Ibid., 262.
6 Ibid., 207.
7 Ibid., 275.
8 Ibid.
9 Richard D. Alexander, *The Biology of Moral Systems* (Hawthorne, NY: Aldine Transaction, 1987), 103.

10 Jeffrey Dudiak, *The Intrigue of Ethics* (New York: Fordham University Press, 2001), 408.
11 Jacques Derrida, "Circumfession," in *Geoffrey Bennington and Jacques Derrida*, trans. Geoffrey Bennington (Chicago: University of Chicago Press, 1993), 101.
12 Oren Harman, *The Price of Altruism* (New York: W.W. Norton, 2010), 209.
13 Ibid., 221.
14 Quoted in ibid., 346.
15 Elliot Sober, "Evolutionary Altruism, Psychological Egoism, and Morality: Disentangling the Phenotypes," in Matthew H. Nitecki and Doris V. Nitecki, *Evolutionary Ethics* (Albany, NY: SUNY Press, 1993), 130.
16 George Williams, "Mother Nature Is an Evil Old Witch," in Nitecki and Nitecki, *Evolutionary Ethics*, 228.
17 Harman, *Price of Altruism*, 328.
18 Ibid., 222.
19 Ibid., 225.
20 Price's emphasis.
21 Ibid., 248–9.
22 Ibid., 249.
23 Ibid., 257.
24 Ibid., 270.
25 Ibid., 271.
26 Ibid., 363. Harman's emphasis.
27 Ibid., 278–80.
28 John Llewelyn, *Appositions of Jacques Derrida and Emmanuel Levinas* (Indianapolis: University of Indiana Press, 2002), 207.
29 Harman, *Price of Altruism*, 287.
30 Emmanuel Levinas, *Otherwise Than Being*, trans. Alphonso Lingis (Pittsburgh: Duquesne University Press, 1998), 82.
31 Harman, *Price of Altruism*, 294–5.
32 Ibid., 294.
33 Levinas, *Otherwise than Being*, 142.
34 Harman, *Price of Altruism*, 304.
35 Ibid., 364. Harman's emphasis.
36 John Caputo, at the Institute for Christian Studies Seminar, Toronto, April 1998.
37 Harman, *Price of Altruism*, 340–1.
38 Ibid., 340.
39 Ibid., 343.
40 Ibid., 345.

41 Ibid., 350.
42 Levinas, *Otherwise than Being*, 113.
43 Ibid., 50.
44 Quoted in Sober, "Evolutionary Altruism," 134.
45 Williams, "Mother Nature Is an Evil Old Witch," 229.
46 Levinas, *Otherwise than Being*, 82.
47 Ibid., 126.
48 Alexander, *Biology of Moral Systems*, 9.
49 Ibid., xviii.
50 Ibid., 248–9.
51 Ibid., 256.
52 Ibid., 249.
53 Wright, *Moral Animal*, 344.
54 See Gad Horowitz, "Aporia and Messiah in Derrida and Levinas," in *Difficult Justice: Commentaries on Levinas and Politics*, ed. Asher Horowitz and Gad Horowitz, 307–28 (Toronto: University of Toronto Press, 2006); and Asher Horowitz and Gad Horowitz, "An Ethical Orientation for Marxism: Geras and Levinas," *Rethinking Marxism* 15, no. 2 (2003): 181–95.

Bibliography

Adorno, Theodore W. *Critical Models*, translated by Henry W. Pickford. New York: Columbia University Press, 1998.
– *Negative Dialectics*, translated by E.B. Ashton. New York: Seabury, 1979.
Ajzenstat, Janet. *The Once and Future Canadian Democracy: An Essay in Political Thought*. Montreal and Kingston: McGill-Queen's University Press, 2003.
Ajzenstat, Janet, Paul Romney, Ian Gentles, and William D. Gairdner. *Canada's Founding Debates*. Toronto: University of Toronto Press, 2003.
Ajzenstat, Janet, and Peter J. Smith, eds. *Canada's Origins: Liberal, Tory, or Republican?* Ottawa: Carleton University Press, 1995.
– eds. *Canada's Origins: Liberal, Tory, or Republican*. Ottawa: Carleton University Press, 1997.
– "The 'Tory Touch' Thesis: Bad History, Poor Political Science." In *Crosscurrents: Contemporary Political Issues*, 4th ed., edited by Mark Charlton and Paul Barker, 68–77. Toronto: Thomson Nelson, 2002.
Alexander, Richard D. *The Biology of Moral Systems*. Hawthorne, NY: Aldine Transaction, 1987.
Althusser, Louis. "Ideology and Ideological State Apparatuses (Notes towards an Investigation)." In *Lenin and Philosophy and Other Essays*, translated by Ben Brewster, 127–86. New York: Monthly Review, 1971.
– "The Underground Current of the Materialism of the Encounter." In *Philosophy of the Encounter: Later Writings, 1978–1987*, edited by François Matheron and Oliver Corpet, translated by G.M. Goshgarian, 163–207. London: Verso, 2006.
Angus, Ian. *A Border Within: National Identity, Cultural Plurality and Wilderness*. Montreal and Kingston: McGill-Queen's University Press, 1997.
– "For a Canadian Philosophy: George Grant." *Canadian Journal of Political and Social Theory* 13, nos. 1–2 (1989): 140–3.

– "The Paradox of Cultural Identity in English Canada." In "Sociology in Anglophone Canada," special issue of *Les Cahiers de recherche sociologique* 39 (2003). http://www.ianangus.ca/paradox.htm.

Antonides, Harry. Review. *Guide* 18, no. 2 (February 1970): 18–19.

Appleby, Joyce. *Liberalism and Republicanism in the Historical Imagination.* Cambridge, MA: Harvard University Press, 1992.

– "Republicanism and Ideology." *American Quarterly* 37, no. 4 (Autumn 1985): 461–73.

Armour, Leslie. *The Idea of Canada and the Crisis of Community.* Ottawa: Steel Rail, 1981.

Armour, Leslie, and Elizabeth Trott. *The Faces of Reason: An Essay on Philosophy and Culture in English Canada, 1850–1950.* Waterloo, ON: Wilfrid Laurier University Press, 1981.

Armstrong, Frederick H. *Handbook of Upper Canadian Chronology.* Toronto: Dundurn, 1985.

Ashcraft, Richard. *Locke's Two Treatises of Government.* London: Unwin Hyman, 1987.

– *Revolutionary Politics and Locke's Two Treatises of Government.* Princeton: Princeton University Press, 1986.

Bachelard, Gaston. *The Formation of the Scientific Mind.* Manchester, UK: Clinamen, 2002.

Badiou, Alain. *Ethics: An Essay in Understanding Evil,* translated by Peter Hallward. London: Verso, 2002.

Bail, Florian. Review of *"Everywhere They Are in Chains,"* by Asher Horowitz and Gad Horowitz. *Canadian Journal of Political Science* 21, no. 4 (December 1988): 865–6.

Bailyn, Bernard. *The Ideological Origins of the American Revolution.* Cambridge, MA: Harvard University Press, 1967.

– *The Ideological Origins of the American Revolution.* Cambridge, MA: Harvard University Press, 1992.

Balibar, Etienne. "Citizen Subject." In *Who Comes after the Subject?*, edited by Eduardo Cadava, Peter Connor, and Jean-Luc Nancy, translated by James B. Swenson Jr, 33–57. New York: Routledge, 1991.

– "The Infinite Contradiction," translated by Jean-Marc Poisson and Jacques Lezra. *Yale French Studies* 88 (1995): 142–64.

– "'Possessive Individualism' Reversed: From Locke to Derrida." *Constellations* 9, no. 3 (September 2002): 299–317.

– "Spinoza: From Individuality to Transindividuality." *Mededelingen vanwege het Spinozahuis* 71 (1997): 3–36.

- "Subjection and Subjectivation." In *Supposing the Subject*, edited by Joan Copjec, 1–15. London: Verso, 1994.
- "What Is 'Man' in Seventeenth-Century Philosophy? Subject, Individual, Citizen." In *The Individual in Political Theory and Practice*, edited by Janet Coleman, 215–41. Oxford: Clarendon, 1996.
- "What Makes a People a People? Rousseau and Kant." In *Masses, Classes and the Public Sphere*, edited by Mike Hill and Warren Montag, translated by Erin Post, 105–31. London: Verso, 2000.
Bataille, Georges. *Guilty*, translated by Stuart Kendall. Venice: Lapis, 1988.
- *Inner Experience*, translated by Leslie Boldt. Albany: SUNY, 1988.
- *Literature and Evil*, translated by Alastair Hamilton. London: Marion Byers, 1997.
- "On Nietzsche: The Will to Chance." In *The Bataille Reader*, edited by Fred Botting and Scott Wilson, 330–42. Oxford: Blackwell, 1997.
- "Sovereignty." In *The Bataille Reader*, edited by Fred Botting and Scott Wilson, 275–342. Oxford: Blackwell, 1997.
- *The Story of the Eye*, translated by Dovid Bergelson. San Francisco: City Lights Books, 1987.
- "Unknowing and Its Consequences." In *The Bataille Reader*, edited by Fred Botting and Scott Wilson, 321–6. Oxford: Blackwell, 1997.
Bataille, Georges, and Roger Caillois. "Sacred Sociology and the Relationships between 'Society,' 'Organism' and 'Being.'" In *The College of Sociology*, edited by Denis Hollier, 73–84. Minneapolis: University of Minnesota Press, 1988.
Bayard, Caroline, and Joyce Bellows. "Editors' Introduction." *Philosophy Today* 43, no. 2 (Summer 1999): 115–20.
Bazowski, Raymond. "Contrasting Ideologies in Canada: What's Right? What's Left?" *Canadian Politics*. 3rd ed., edited by James Bickerton and Alain-G. Gagnon, 79–105. Peterborough, ON: Broadview, 1999.
Beattie, Christopher, and Stuart Crysdale, eds. *Sociology Canada: Readings*. Toronto: Butterworth, 1974.
Beer, Samuel H. *British Politics in the Collectivist Age*. New York: Alfred A. Knopf, 1965.
- "In Memoriam: Louis Hartz." *PS: Political Science and Politics* 19, no. 3 (Summer 1986): 735–7.
Bell, David V.J. *The Roots of Disunity: A Study of Canadian Political Culture*. Rev. ed. Toronto: Oxford University Press, 1992.
Bell, Shannon. *Fast Feminism: Speed Philosophy, Pornography, and Politics*. New York: Autonomedia, 2010.
Benjamin, Andrew. *Philosophy's Literature*. Manchester, UK: Clinamen, 2001.

Benjamin, Jessica. *The Bonds of Love: Psychoanalysis, Feminism, and the Problem of Domination*. New York: Pantheon Books, 1988.

Benjamin, Walter. "On Language as Such and on the Language of Man." In *Walter Benjamin: Selected Writings*. Vol. 1, *1913–1926*, edited by Marcus Bullock and Michael W. Jennings, 62–74. Cambridge: Belknap, 1996.

Berger, Carl. *The Sense of Power: Studies in the Ideas of Canadian Imperialism*. Toronto: University of Toronto Press, 1970.

– *The Writing of Canadian History: Aspects of English-Canadian Historical Writing: 1900–1970*. Toronto: Oxford University Press, 1976.

Bibby, Reginald. *Mosaic Madness*. Toronto: Stoddart, 1990.

Bissoondath, Neil. *Selling Illusions: The Cult of Multiculturalism*. Toronto: Penguin, 2002.

Bland, Salem Goldworth. *The New Christianity*. Toronto: University of Toronto Press, 1973.

Bois, Alain. *Formless: A User's Guide*. New York: Zone Books, 1997.

Bornstein, Stephen. "Gad Horowitz versus Americrap." *Varsity*, 19 January 1968.

Bourdieu, Pierre. *Homo Academicus*, translated by Peter Collier. Stanford: Stanford University Press, 1988.

Boyko, John. *Into the Hurricane: Attacking Socialism and the NDP*. Winnipeg: Shillingford, 2006.

Brien, Kevin M. *Marx, Reason and the Art of Freedom*. 2nd ed. Amherst, NY: Humanity Books, 2006.

Britzman, Deborah. *After-Education: Anna Freud, Melanie Klein, and Psychoanalytic Histories of Learning*. New York: SUNY, 2003.

Brooks, Stephen. *Canadian Democracy: An Introduction*. 4th ed. Toronto: Oxford University Press, 2004.

Brym, Robert. *From Culture to Power: The Sociology of English Canada*. Toronto: Oxford University Press, 1989.

– "Political Conservatism in Atlantic Canada." In *Underdevelopment and Social Movements in Atlantic Canada*, edited by Robert J. Brym and R. James Sacouman, 59–79. Toronto: New Hogtown, 1979.

Cairns, Alan. *Citizen's Plus: Aboriginal Peoples and the Canadian State*. Vancouver: University of British Columbia Press, 2000.

Campbell, Colin. "On Intellectual Life, Politics and Psychoanalysis: A Conversation with Gad Horowitz." ctheorynet. http://ctheory.net/articles.aspx?id=397.

Celan, Paul. "Praise of Distance." In *Selected Poems and Prose of Paul Celan*, edited and translated by J. Felstiner, 24–5. New York: W.W. Norton, 2001.

Christian, William. *George Grant: A Biography.* Toronto: University of Toronto Press, 1993.

– *Parkin: Canada's Most Famous Forgotten Man.* Toronto: Blue Butterfly, 2008.

Christian, William, and Colin Campbell. *Political Parties and Ideologies in Canada: Liberals, Conservatives, Socialists, Nationalists.* 2nd ed. Toronto: McGraw-Hill Ryerson, 1983.

Citrin, Jack, Beth Reingold, and Donald P. Green. "American Identity and the Politics of Ethnic Change." *Journal of Politics* 52, no. 4 (November 1990): 1124–54.

Clastres, Pierre. *Society against the State.* New York: Zone Books, 1983.

Cohen, Matt. *Typing: A Life in Twenty-Six Keys.* Toronto: Random House, 2000.

Coleman, Frank M. *Hobbes and America.* Toronto: University of Toronto Press, 1977.

Connor, Peter Tracy. *Georges Bataille and the Mysticism of Sin.* Baltimore: Johns Hopkins University Press, 2000.

Cook, Ramsay. Letter. *Canadian Forum* 48, no. 570 (July 1968): 81–2.

– *The Maple Leaf Forever: Essays on Nationalism and Politics in Canada.* Toronto: Macmillan, 1971.

– "A Nationalist Intellectual behind Every Maple Tree." *Saturday Night*, April 1970.

Crowe, Harry. Review of *Canadian Labour in Politics*, by Gad Horowitz. *Canadian Journal of Political Science* 2, no. 2 (June 1969): 270–1.

Davidson, Scott. "Taking Responsibilities Seriously: Levinas and Human Rights." Paper presentation, Annual Meeting of the Levinas Research Seminar, Hamilton, ON, spring 2007.

Davis, Bob. "The Death of Isaiah Berlin." *Friend* 3, no. 2 (2001): 20.

Deleuze, Gilles, and Felix Guattari. *A Thousand Plateaus: Capitalism and Schizophrenia.* Translated by Brian Massumi. Minneapolis: University of Minnesota Press, 1987.

Derrida, Jacques. "Circumfession." In *Jacques Derrida*, trans. Goeffrey Bennington. Chicago: University of Chicago Press, 1993.

– *On the Name*, edited by Thomas Dutoit, translated by David Wood, John P. Leavey Jr, and Ian McLeod. Stanford: Stanford University Press, 1995.

– *The Post Card: From Socrates to Freud and Beyond*, translated by A. Bass. Chicago: University of Chicago Press, 1987.

– "What Is a 'Relevant' Translation?" *Critical Inquiry* 27, no. 2 (Winter 2001): 174–200.

Dickerson, Mark O., Thomas Flanagan, and Neil Nevitte, eds. *Introductory Readings in Government and Politics.* Toronto: Methuen, 1983.

Diggins, John. *The Lost Soul of American Politics: Virtue, Self-Interest, and the Foundations of Liberalism*. New York: Basic Books, 1984.

Disraeli, Benjamin. *Sybil*, edited by Sheila M. Smith. New York: Oxford University Press, 1981.

Dudiak, Jeffrey. *The Intrigue of Ethics*. New York: Fordham University Press, 2001.

Dworetz, Steven M. *The Unvarnished Doctrine: Locke, Liberalism and the American Revolution*. Durham, NC: Duke University Press, 1990.

Dyck, Rand. *Canadian Politics: Critical Perspectives*. 4th ed. Scarborough, ON: Thomson Nelson, 2004.

Eisenstadt, Oona. "Anti-Utopianism Revisited," edited by Dara Hill and Rebecca Nicholson-Weir. *Shofar: An Interdisciplinary Journal of Jewish Studies* 26, no. 4 (Summer 2008): 120–38.

Engels, Fredrick. Introduction to *Socialism: Utopian and Scientific*. In *Karl Marx and Frederick Engels: Selected Works in One Volume* by Karl Marx and Frederick Engels, 379–98. New York: International Publishers, 1968.

Federation of Feminist Women's Health Centers. *A New View of a Woman's Body*. Los Angeles: Feminist Health, 1991.

Felman, Shoshana. "Psychoanalysis and Education: Teaching Terminable and Interminable." In *Yale French Studies, The Pedagogical Imperative: Teaching as a Literary Genre* 63 (1982): 21–44.

Fierlbeck, Katherine. *Political Thought in Canada: An Intellectual History*. Peterborough, ON: Broadview, 2006.

Finnigan, Bryan, and Cy Gonick, eds. *Making It: The Canadian Dream*. Toronto: McClelland and Stewart, 1972.

Flanagan, Thomas. *First Nations? Second Thoughts*. Montreal and Kingston: McGill-Queen's University Press, 1999.

Forbes, H.D. "Hartz-Horowitz at Twenty: Nationalism, Toryism and Socialism in Canada and the United States." *Canadian Journal of Political Science* 20, no. 2 (June 1987): 287–315.

– "Rejoinder to A Note on Hartz-Horowitz at Twenty: The Case of French Canada." *Canadian Journal of Political Science* 21, no. 4 (December 1988): 807–11.

Foucault, Michel. *Fearless Speech*. Edited by Joseph Pearson. New York: Semiotext(e), 2001.

– "'Society Must Be Defended': Lectures at the Collège de France 1975–1976," edited by Arnold I. Davidson, Mauro Bertani, and Alessandro Fontana, translated by David Macey. New York: Picador, 2003.

– "What Is Enlightenment?" In *The Foucault Reader*, edited by Paul Rabinow, translated by Catherine Porter, 32–50. New York: Pantheon, 1984.

Fox, Paul W., ed. *Politics: Canada*. 4th ed. Toronto: McGraw-Hill Ryerson, 1977.

Freud, Sigmund. "An Autobiographical Study." In *The Freud Reader*, edited by P. Gay, 3–41. New York: W.W. Norton, 1995.

– "A Case of Paranoia Running Counter to the Psychoanalytic Theory of the Disease." In *The Standard Edition of the Complete Psychological Works of Sigmund Freud. Vol. 14, (1914–1916): On the History of the Psycho-Analytic Movement, Papers on Metapsychology and Other Works*, edited by J. Strachey, 261–72. London: Hogarth.

– *Five Lectures on Psychoanalysis*. New York: W.W. Norton, 1977.

– "From the History of an Infantile Neurosis." In *The Standard Edition of the Complete Psychological Works of Sigmund Freud. Vol. 14, (1914–1916): On the History of the Psycho-Analytic Movement, Papers on Metapsychology and Other Works*, vol. 17. edited by J. Strachey, 1–124. London: Hogarth, 1957.

– *Group Psychology and the Analysis of the Ego*. New York: W.W. Norton, 1959.

– "Inhibitions, Symptoms and Anxiety." In *The Standard Edition of the Complete Psychological Works of Sigmund Freud. Vol. XIV, (1914–1916): On the History of the Psycho-Analytic Movement, Papers on Metapsychology and Other Works*, vol. 20. edited by J. Strachey, 75–176. London: Hogarth, 1959.

– *On Metapsychology: The Theory of Psychoanalysis*. New York: Penguin Books, 1991.

– "On the History of the Psycho-Analytic Movement." In *The Standard Edition of the Complete Psychological Works of Sigmund Freud. Vol. 14, (1914–1916): On the History of the Psycho-Analytic Movement, Papers on Metapsychology and Other Works*, edited by J. Strachey, 1–66. London: Hogarth, 1957.

– "Thoughts for the Times of War and Death." In *The Standard Edition of the Complete Psychological Works of Sigmund Freud. Vol. 14, (1914–1916): On the History of the Psycho-Analytic Movement, Papers on Metapsychology and Other Works*, edited by J. Strachey, 273–300. London: Hogarth, 1957.

– "The 'Uncanny.'" In *The German Library: Psychological Writings and Letters*, edited by Sander Gilman, 120–53. New York: Continuum, 1995.

Friedlander, Judith. "Translator's Introduction." In *The Defeat of The Mind* by Alain Finkielkraut, ix–xix. New York: Columbia University Press, 1995.

Friesen, Joe. "Let Farmers Decide about Wheat Board, Tory MP Says." *Globe and Mail*, 11 November 2006.

Galbraith, Gordon S. "British Columbia." In *The Provincial Political Systems: Comparative Essays*, edited by David J. Bellamy, Jon H. Pammett, and Donald C. Rowat, 62–75. Toronto: Methuen, 1976.

Garfield, Jay L. "Epoche and Sunyata: Skepticism East and West." *Philosophy East and West* 40, no. 3 (July 1990): 285–307.

– *The Fundamental Wisdom of the Middle Way: Nagarjuna's Mulamadhyamaka-karika*. Oxford: Oxford University Press, 1995.

Gikatilla, R. Joseph. *Gates of Light: Sha'are Orah*, translated by Avi Weinstein. Walnut Creek, CA: AltaMira, 1998.

Girard, René. *Deceit, Desire, and the Novel: Self and Other in Literary Structure*, translated by Yvonne Freccero. Baltimore: Johns Hopkins University Press, 1965.

– *I See Satan Fall like Lightning*. Translated by James G. Williams. New York: Orbis Books, 2001.

Goetzmann, William H., ed. *The American Hegelians: An Intellectual Episode in the History of Western America*. New York: Alfred A. Knopf, 1973.

Grace, Sherill. *Canada and the Idea of North*. Vancouver: University of British Columbia Press, 2003.

Granatstein, J.L., and Peter Stevens, eds. *Forum: Canadian Life and Letters, 1920–70*. Toronto: University of Toronto Press, 1972.

Grant, George. *Collected Works of George Grant*, edited by Arthur Davis and Henry Roper. Vol. 3, *1960–1969*. Toronto: University of Toronto Press, 2005.

– *Lament for a Nation: The Defeat of Canadian Nationalism*. Toronto: McClelland and Stewart, 1965.

– Letter to the editor. *Canadian Dimension*, 2 June 1965.

Gulka-Tiechko, Myron G.G. "Inter-War Ukrainian Immigration to Canada, 1919–1939." Master's thesis, University of Manitoba, 1983.

Guy, James John. *People, Politics and Government: A Canadian Perspective*. 6th ed. Toronto: Pearson, 2006.

Guy, Matthew. "'Not to Build the World Is to Destroy It': Levinas on Holy History and Messianic Politics." Paper presentation, Inaugural Meeting of the North American Levinas Society, Purdue University, May 2006.

Hall, Anthony. *The American Empire and the Fourth World*. Montreal and Kingston: McGill-Queen's University Press, 2005.

Halperin, David. *Saint Foucault: Towards a Gay Hagiography*. New York: Oxford University Press 1995.

Hamilton, William. "The Evolution of Altruistic Behavior." *American Naturalist* 97, no. 896 (September–October 1963): 354–6.

Handelman, Susan. *Fragments of Redemption*. Bloomington: Indiana University Press, 1991.

Harmon, Frances A. *The Social Philosophy of the St Louis Hegelians*. New York: Columbia University Press, 1943.

Harmon, Oren. *The Price of Altruism*. New York: W.W. Norton, 2010.

Hartz, Louis. *Economic Policy and Democratic Thought: Pennsylvania, 1776–1860*. Cambridge, MA: Harvard University Press, 1948.

–, ed. *The Founding of New Societies: Studies in the History of the United States, Latin America, South Africa, Canada, and Australia.* New York: Harcourt, Brace and World, 1964.

– "Fragmentation Patterns: Feudal, Liberal, and Radical." In Hartz, *Founding of New Societies*, 24–48.

– *The Liberal Tradition in America: An Interpretation of American Political Thought since the Revolution.* New York: Harcourt, Brace, 1955.

Heap, James L., ed. *Everybody's Canada: The Vertical Mosaic Re-examined.* Toronto: Burns and MacEachern, 1970.

Heidegger, Martin. *What Is Called Thinking?*, translated by J. Glen Gray. New York: Harper and Row, 1968.

Hershock, Peter D. *Liberating Intimacy: Enlightenment and Social Virtuosity in Ch'an Buddhism.* Albany: SUNY, 1996.

Herzog, Annabel. "Is Liberalism 'All We Need'? Levinas's Politics of Surplus." *Political Theory* 30, no. 2 (April 2002): 204–27.

Hobbes, Thomas. *Leviathan*, edited by Edwin Curley. Indianapolis, IN: Hackett, 1994.

Hodgins, Bruce W., and Robert J.D. Page, eds. *Canada since Confederation: Essays and Interpretations.* Georgetown: Irwin-Dorsey, 1972.

Holland, K. *Workers Vanguard* (Toronto), 16 December 1968.

Hollier, Denis. *Against Architecture: The Writings of Georges Bataille*, translated by Betsy Wing. Cambridge: MIT, 1989.

Honig, Bonnie. *Democracy and the Foreigner.* Princeton: Princeton University Press, 2001.

Horowitz, Aron. *Striking Roots: Reflecting on Five Decades of Jewish Life.* Oakville, ON: Mosaic, 1979.

Horowitz, Asher. *Rousseau, Nature, and History.* Toronto: University of Toronto Press, 1987.

Horowitz, Asher, and Gad Horowitz. "An Ethical Orientation for Marxism: Geras and Levinas." *Rethinking Marxism* 15, no. 2 (2003): 181–95.

–, eds. *Difficult Justice: Commentaries on Levinas and Politics.* Toronto: University of Toronto Press, 2006.

– *"Everywhere They Are in Chains": Political Theory from Rousseau to Marx.* Toronto: Nelson Canada, 1988.

– "Is Liberalism All We Need? Prelude via Fascism." In *Difficult Justice: Commentaries on Levinas and Politics*, edited by Asher Horowitz and Gad Horowitz, 12–23. Toronto: University of Toronto Press, 2006.

Horowitz, Gad. "Aporia and Messiah in Derrida and Levinas." In Horowitz and Horowitz, 307–30.

– "Bringing Bataille to Justice." *Public* 37 (2008): 138–43.

- "Canada in the Second Hundred Years." Unpublished paper, 1967.
- *Canadian Labour in Politics*. Toronto: University of Toronto Press, 1968.
- "Conservatism, Liberalism, and Socialism in Canada: An Interpretation." *Canadian Journal of Economics and Political Science* 32, no. 2 (May 1966): 143–71.
- "Conservatism, Liberalism and Socialism: An Interpretation." In *Party Politics in Canada*, edited by Hugh G. Thorburn, 146–62. Scarborough, ON: Prentice Hall Canada, 1996.
- "A Conversation on Technology and Man." *Journal of Canadian Studies* 4, no. 3 (August 1969): 3–6.
- "Creative Politics." *Canadian Dimension* 3, no. 1 (November/December 1965): 14–15, 28.
- "Creative Politics, Mosaics and Identity." In *Everybody's Canada: The Vertical Mosaic Re-examined*, ed. James L. Heap, 4–31 (Toronto: Burns and MacEachern, 1970).
- "emmanuel, Robert." In *Buddhisms and Deconstructions*, edited by Jin Y. Park, 183–96. Lanham, MD: Rowman and Littlefield, 2006.
- "emmanuel, Robert." *Journal of Contemporary Thought* 14 (Winter 2001): 183–90.
- "The Foucaultian Impasse: No Sex, No Self, No Revolution." *Political Theory* 15, no. 1 (February 1987): 61–80.
- "The Future of English Canada." *Canadian Dimension* 2, no. 5 (July/August 1965): 12–14.
- "Global Pardon: Pax Romana, Pax Americana, and Kol Nidre." *Bad Subjects* 58 (December 2001). http://bad.eserver.org/issues/2001/58/horowitz.html.
- "Groundless Democracy." In *Shadow of Spirit: Postmodernism and Religion*, edited by Philippa Berry and Andrew Wernick, 156–64. London: Routledge, 1992.
- "Horowitz and Grant Talk." *Canadian Dimension* 6, no. 6 (November/December 1969–January 1970): 18–20.
- "Ideals of Democracy and Social Reality." CBC Television. Transcript. 9 January 1966.
- "Mosaics and Identity." *Canadian Dimension* 3, no. 2 (January/February 1966): 17–19.
- "Mosaics and Identity." In *Canadian Political Thought*, edited by H.D. Forbes, 359–64. Toronto: Oxford University Press, 1985.
- "Mosaics and Identity." In *Making It: The Canadian Dream*, edited by Bryan Finnigan and Cy Gonick, 465–73. Toronto: McClelland and Stewart, 1972.

– "The 'Myth' of the Red Tory?" *Canadian Journal of Political and Social Theory* 1, no. 3 (1977): 3–6.
– "Notes on 'Conservatism, Liberalism and Socialism in Canada.'" *Canadian Journal of Political Science* 11, no. 2 (June 1978): 383–99.
– "Nouveau Partie Democratique." *Canadian Dimension* 2 (July–August 1965): 16–17.
– "On Techniques of the Self – With a Look Back at the General Semantics Movement." Public lecture, Theory, Culture, Politics Program, Trent University, Peterborough, ON, 18 November 1999.
– "On the Fear of Nationalism." *Canadian Dimension* 4, no. 4 (May/June 1967): 7–9.
– "On the Fear of Nationalism." In *Canadian Political Thought*, edited by H.D. Forbes, 364–8. Toronto: Oxford University Press, 1985.
– "On the Fear of Nationalism." In *Politics: Canada*, 4th edition, edited by Paul W. Fox, 112–15. Toronto: McGraw-Hill Ryerson, 1977.
– "On the Fear of Canadian Nationalisms: A Sermon to the Moderates." In *Comparative Political Problems: Britain, United States, and Canada*, edited by John E. Kersell and Marshall W. Conley, 255–9. Scarborough, ON: Prentice-Hall, 1968.
– "Our Cup Runneth Over." *Manitoban*, 20 September 1957.
– "Les *perils* de la *complaisance*." *Le Devoir*, 10 April 1971.
– "The Perils of 'Complaisance.'" *Canadian Forum* 51, nos. 603–4 (April/May 1971): 39–41.
– "Quebec and Canadian Nationalism: Two Views." *Canadian Forum* 50, no. 600 (January 1971): 357.
– *Repression: Basic and Surplus Repression in Psychoanalytic Theory: Freud, Reich and Marcuse*. Toronto: University of Toronto Press, 1977.
– "Le statut particulier, formule libératrice pour les deux communautés." *Le Devoir*, 30 June 1967.
– "Tories, Socialists and the Demise of Canada." In *Canada: A Guide to the Peaceable Kingdom*, edited by William Kilbourn, 254–60. Toronto: Macmillan, 1970.
– "Tories, Socialists and the Demise of Canada." *Canadian Dimension* 2, no. 4 (May/June 1965): 12–15.
– "Tories, Socialists and the Demise of Canada." In *Canadian Political Thought*, edited by H.D. Forbes. Toronto: Oxford University Press, 1985: 352–9.
– "Toward the Democratic Class Struggle." *Journal of Canadian Studies* 1, no. 3 (November 1966): 3–10.
– "The Trudeau Doctrine." *Canadian Dimension* 5, no. 5 (June/July 1969): 9–11.
– "Trudeau vs Trudeauism." *Canadian Forum* 48, no. 568 (May 1968): 29–30.

- "21 Voices Call Out for Canada." *Globe and Mail,* 5 November 1966.
- "Why René Lévesque Became a Separatist – Part III: A Symposium on René Lévesque," *Canadian Dimension* 5, nos. 2 and 3 (January–March 1968): 20–1.
Horowitz, Gad, Cy Gonick, and G. David Sheps. "An Open Letter to Canadian Nationalists." *Canadian Dimension* 4, no. 4 (May/June 1967): 1, 44.
House, J.D. *Against the Tide: Battling for Economic Renewal in Newfoundland and Labrador.* Toronto: University of Toronto Press, 1999.
Huyler, Jerome. *Locke in America: The Moral Philosophy of the Founding Era.* Lawrence, KS: University Press of Kansas, 1995.
Idel, Moshe. *Kabbalah: New Perspectives.* New Haven, CT: Yale University Press, 1988.
Ignatieff, Michael. *The Rights Revolution.* Toronto: Anansi, 2000.
- *True Patriot Love: Four Generations in Search of Canada.* Toronto: Viking, 2009.
Irigaray, Luce. *I Love to You: Sketch of a Possible Felicity in History,* translated by Alison Martin. New York: Routledge, 1996.
- *Speculum of the Other Woman,* translated by Gillian C. Gill. Ithaca, NY: Cornell University Press, 1985.
- *Thinking the Difference for a Peaceful Revolution,* translated by Karin Montin. New York: Routledge, 2001.
- *This Sex Which Is Not One,* translated by Catherine Porter. Ithaca, NY: Cornell University Press, 1985.
- "Volume without Contours," translated by David Macey. In *The Irigaray Reader,* edited by Margaret Whitford, 53–67. Oxford: Blackwell, 1995.
- "Women-Mothers: The Silent Substratum of the Social Order," translated by David Macey. In *The Irigaray Reader,* edited by Margaret Whitford, 47–52. Oxford: Blackwell, 1995.
Jabès, Edmund. *The Book of Resemblances II: Intimations; The Desert,* translated by Rosmarie Waldrop. Hanover: University Press of New England, 1991.
Jackson, Robert J., and Doreen Jackson. *Politics in Canada: Culture, Institutions, Behaviour and Public Policy.* 6th ed. Toronto: Pearson, 2006.
Johnston, Richard. "The Ideological Structure of Opinion on Policy." In *Party Democracy in Canada,* edited by George Perlin, 54–70. Scarborough, ON: Prentice-Hall, 1988.
Jones, Elwood. "The Loyalists and Canadian History." *Journal of Canadian Studies* 20, no. 3 (Autumn 1985): 149–56.
Kelebay, Yarema G. "Three Fragments of the Ukrainian Community in Montreal, 1899–1970: A Hartzian Approach." *Canadian Ethnic Studies* 12, no. 2 (1980): 74–87.
Kerney, Richard, and Mark Dooley. "Hospitality, Justice and Responsibility: Dialogue with Jacques Derrida." In *Questioning Ethics: Contemporary Debates*

in Philosophy, edited by Richard Kerney and Mark Dooley, 65–83. New York: Routledge, 1999.

Kersell, John E., and Marshall W. Conley, eds. *Comparative Political Problems: Britain, United States, and Canada.* Scarborough, ON: Prentice-Hall, 1968.

Kilbourn, William, ed. *Canada: A Guide to the Peaceable Kingdom.* Toronto: Macmillan, 1970.

King, Sallie B. *Buddha Nature.* Albany: SUNY, 1991.

Kinsman, Gary. "Trans Politics and Anti-Capitalism: An Interview with Dan Irving." *Upping the Anti: A Journal of Theory and Action* 4 (May 2007): 61–73.

Knopff, Rainer. "The Triumph of Liberalism in Canada: Laurier on Representation and Party of Government." In *Canada's Origins: Liberal Tory, or Republican?*, edited by Janet Ajzenstat and Peter J. Smith, 159–97. Ottawa: Carleton University Press, 1995.

Kornberg, Allan, Joel Smith, and David Bromley. "Some Differences in the Political Socialization Patterns of Canadian and American Party Officials: A Preliminary Report." *Canadian Journal of Political Science* 2, no. 1 (March 1969): 64–88.

Korzybski, Alfred. *Science and Sanity: An Introduction to Non-Aristotelian Systems and General Semantics.* Englewood, NJ: International Non-Aristotelian Library, 1948.

– *Science and Sanity.* 5th ed. Fort Worth, TX: Institute of General Semantics, 1994.

Kramnik, Isaac. *Republicanism and Bourgeois Radicalism.* Ithaca, NY: Cornell University Press, 1990.

Kruhlak, Orest M., Richard Schultz, and Sidney Pobihushchy, eds. *The Canadian Political Process.* Toronto: Holt, Rinehart and Winston, 1970.

kulchyski, peter. *Like the Sound of a Drum: Aboriginal Cultural Politics in Denendeh and Nunavut.* Winnipeg: University of Manitoba Press, 2005.

– *The Red Indians.* Winnipeg: Arbeiter Ring, 2008.

– Review of *Canada and the Idea of North*, by Sherrill E. Grace. *Études Inuit Studies* 28, no. 1 (2004): 197–201.

– "From Political Cultures to Cultural Politics: Indigenous Horowitz; Horowitz Dances with Wolves!" Paper presentation, Canadian Political Science Association, Congress of Humanities and Social Sciences, Vancouver, 6 June 2008.

kulchyski, peter, and Frank J. Tester. *Kiumajut (Talking Back) Game Management and Inuit Rights 1900–70.* Vancouver: University of British Columbia Press, 2007.

Land, Nick. *The Thirst for Annihilation.* London: Routledge, 1992.

Laurier, Wilfrid. "Political Liberalism." In *Canadian Political Thought*, edited by H.D. Forbes, 134–51. Toronto: Oxford University Press, 1985.

Lawlor, Mary. *Alexis de Tocqueville in the Chamber of Deputies*. Washington: Catholic University of America Press, 1959.

Lawton, Stephen. "Political Values in Educational Finance in Canada and the United States." *Journal of Educational Finance* 5 (Summer 1979): 1–18.

League for Social Reconstruction. *Social Planning for Canada*. Toronto: Thomas Nelson, 1935.

Lévesque, René. *Option Québec*. Montreal: Les editions de l'homme, 1968.

Levinas, Emmanuel. *Beyond the Verse*, translated by Gary D. Mole. Blooming-ton, IN: Indiana University Press, 1994.

– *Entre Nous: Essays on Thinking-of-the-Other*, translated by Barbara Harshav and Michael B. Smith. New York: Columbia University Press, 1998.

– *In the Time of Nations*, translated by Michael Smith. Bloomington, IN: Indi-ana University Press, 1994.

– *Nine Talmudic Readings*, translated by Annette Aronowicz. Bloomington, IN: Indiana University Press, 1994.

– *Of God Who Comes to Mind*, translated by Bettina Bergo. Stanford, CA: Stan-ford University Press, 1998.

– *Otherwise Than Being or Beyond Essence*, translated by Alphonso Lingis. Pitts-burgh: Duquesne University Press, 1998.

– *Otherwise Than Being or Beyond Essence*, translated by Alphonso Lingis. Dor-drecht: Klewer Academic, 1991.

– *Outside the Subject*, translated by Michael Smith. Stanford, CA: Stanford University Press, 1997.

– "Peace and Proximity." In *Emmanuel Levinas: Basic Philosophical Writings*, edited by Adriaan Theodoor Peperzak, Simon Critchley, and Robert Ber-nasconi, translated by Peter Atterton and Simon Critchley, 161–9. Blooming-ton, IN: Indiana University Press, 1996.

– "Reflections on the Philosophy of Hitlerism." In *Difficult Justice: Commen-taries on Levinas and Politics*, edited by Asher Horowitz and Gad Horowitz, translated by Sean Hand, 3–11. Toronto: University of Toronto Press, 2006.

– *Totality and Infinity*, translated by Alphonso Lingis. Pittsburgh: Duquesne University Press, 1969.

– "Transcendence and Evil." In *Collected Philosophical Papers*, translated by Al-phonso Lingis, 175–86. Dordrecht: Martinus Nijhoff, 1987.

Libertson, Joseph. *Proximity*. The Hague: Martinus Nijhoff, 1982.

Lipset, Seymour Martin. *Agrarian Socialism: The Cooperative Commonwealth Fed-eration in Saskatchewan; A Study in Political Sociology*. Garden City, NY: Dou-bleday Anchor, 1968.

– *The First New Nation*. New York: Basic Books, 1963.
– "Historical Traditions and National Characteristics: A Comparative Analysis of Canada and the United States." *Canadian Journal of Sociology* 11, no. 2 (Summer 1986): 113–55.
Llewelyn, John. *Appositions of Jacques Derrida and Emmanuel Levinas*. Indianapolis: University of Indiana Press, 2002.
Lloyd, Trevor, and Jack McLeod, eds. *Agenda 1970: Proposals for a Creative Politics*. Toronto: University of Toronto Press, 1968.
Locke, John. *Second Treatise of Government*, edited by C.B. MacPherson. Indianapolis, IN: Hackett, 1980.
– *Two Treatises of Government*. London: Unwin Hyman, 1987.
Loy, David. "Dead Words, Living Words and Healing Words: The Disseminations of Dogen and Eckhart." In *Healing Deconstruction: Postmodern Thought in Buddhism and Christianity*, edited by Ed Loy, 33–51. Atlanta: Scholars, 1996.
– *Nonduality: A Study in Comparative Philosophy*. Amherst, NY: Humanity Books, 1988.
Lusthaus, Dan. "Nagarjuna." Yogacara Buddhism Research Association. http://www.acmuller.net/yogacara/thinkers/nagarjuna-bio.html.
Macpherson, C.B. *Democratic Theory: Essays in Retrieval*. Oxford: Clarendon, 1973.
– *The Political Theory of Possessive Individualism*. Oxford: Oxford University Press, 1962.
Magliola, Robert. *Derrida on the Mend*. West Lafayette, IN: Purdue University Press, 1984.
– "French Deconstruction with a (Buddhist)Difference: More Cases from the *Gateless Gate [Wu-men-kuan]* and *Blue Cliff Record [Pi-yen-lu]*." *Studies in Language and Literature* 3, no. 1 (1988): 1–25.
– "In No Wise Is Healing Holistic: A Deconstructive Alternative to Masao Abe's 'Kenotic God and Dynamic Sunyata.'" In *Healing Deconstruction: Postmodern Thought in Buddhism and Deconstruction*, edited by David Loy, 99–117. Atlanta: Scholars, 1996.
– *On Deconstructing Life Worlds: Buddhism, Christianity, Culture*. Atlanta: Scholars, 1997.
Mahoney, Jill. "No 'Firewall' Needed around Alberta, Says Klein." *Globe and Mail*, 8 February 2001.
Mallory, J.R. *The Structure of Canadian Government*. Rev. ed. Toronto: Gage, 1984.
Mancke, Elizabeth. "Early Modern Imperial Governance and the Origins of Canadian Political Culture." *Canadian Journal of Political Science* 32, no. 1 (March 1999): 3–20.

Mann, W.E., ed. *Canada: A Sociological Profile.* Toronto: Copp-Clark, 1971.

Marcuse, Herbert. *Counterrevolution and Revolt.* Boston: Beacon, 1972.

– *Eros and Civilization.* Boston: Beacon, 1955.

– *An Essay on Liberation.* Boston: Beacon, 1969.

– *One-Dimensional Man.* Boston: Beacon, 1964.

Marx, Karl. *Capital.* Vol. 1, translated by Ben Fowkes. London: Penguin, 1976.

– *The Eighteenth Brumaire of Louis Bonaparte,* translated by C.P. Dutt. New York: International, 1963.

– "Manifesto of the Communist Party." In *The Marx-Engels Reader.* 2nd ed., edited by Robert C. Tucker, 469–500. New York: Norton, 1978.

– *"Introduction* to the *Grundrisse."* In *Karl Marx: Texts on Method,* edited and translated by Terrell Carver, 46–87. Oxford: Blackwell.

– "On the Jewish Question." In *Selected Writings.* 2nd ed., edited and translated by David McLellan, 46–70. Oxford: Oxford University Press, 2000.

McCormick, A. Ross. *Reformers, Rebels, and Revolutionaries: The Western Canadian Radical Movement, 1899–1919.* Toronto: University of Toronto Press, 1977.

McDaniel, Jay. "Mahayana Enlightenment in Process Perspective." In *Buddhism and American Thinkers,* edited by Kenneth K. Inada and Nolan P. Jacobsen, 50–60. Albany, NY: SUNY, 1984.

McIvor, Heather. *Parameters of Power: Canada's Political Institutions.* 4th ed. Toronto: Thomson Nelson, 2006.

McLeod, J.T., and R.S. Blair, eds. *The Canadian Political Tradition.* Toronto: Methuen, 1987.

McMenemy, John. *The Language of Canadian Politics: A Guide to Important Terms and Concepts.* Toronto: John Wiley, 1980.

McNaught, Kenneth. "Comment." In *Failure of a Dream? Essays in the History of American Socialism,* edited by John H.M. Laslett and Seymour Martin Lipset, 409–20. New York: Doubleday, 1974.

– "Comment." In *Failure of a Dream? Essays in the History of American Socialism.* Rev. ed., edited by John H.M. Laslett and Seymour Martin Lipset, 345–56. Berkeley, CA: University of California Press, 1984.

– "The NDP's Special Status Kick." *Saturday Night,* October 1967.

McRae, Kenneth D. "Louis Hartz's Impact on Political Thought in Canada." Paper presentation, Symposium on Louis Hartz, Harvard University, 23 January 1987.

– "The Structure of Canadian History." In *The Founding of New Societies,* edited by Louis Hartz, 219–74. New York: Harcourt, Brace and World, 1964.

Mendelson, Alan. *Exiles from Nowhere: The Jews and the Canadian Elite.* Montreal: R. Brass Studio, 2008.

Milligan, Frank. *Eugene A. Forsey: An Intellectual Biography*. Calgary: University of Calgary Press, 2004.

Mills, C. Wright. *The Power Elite*. New York: Oxford University Press, 1959.

Montag, Warren. "The Late Althusser: Materialism of the Encounter or Philosophy of the Void?" Paper presentation, Rileggere Il Capitale: La Lezione di Louis Althusser, Venice, Italy, 10 November 2006.

Morton, W.L. *The Progressive Party in Canada*. Toronto: University of Toronto Press, 1950.

– "The Social Philosophy of Henry Wise Wood, the Canadian Agrarian Leader." *Agricultural History* 22, no. 2 (April 1948): 114–23.

Murti, T.R.V. *The Central Philosophy of Buddhism: A Study of Madhyamika System*. New Delhi: Munshiram Manoharlal, 2006.

Nagarjuna. "Mulamadhyamikakarikas." In *The Fundamental Wisdom of the Middle Way: Nagarjuna's Mulamadhyamikakarikas*, translated by Jay L. Garfield, 1–83. New York: Oxford University Press, 1995.

Nayak, G.C. "The Madhyamika Attack on Essentialism: A Critical Appraisal." *Philosophy East and West* 29, no. 4 (October 1979): 477–90.

Naylor, R.T. "The Rise and Fall of the Third Commercial Empire of the St Lawrence." In *Capitalism and the National Question in Canada*, edited by Gary Teeple, 1–42. Toronto: University of Toronto Press, 1972.

Neville, Robert C. "Buddhism and Process Philosophy." In *Buddhism and American Thinkers*, edited by Kenneth K. Inada and Nolan Pliny Jacobsen, 120–42. Albany, NY: SUNY, 1984.

Nishitani, Keiji. *Religion and Nothingness*, translated by Jan Van Bragt. Berkeley, CA: University of California Press, 1982.

Noel, Sid. "The Ontario Political Culture: An Interpretation." In *The Government and Politics of Ontario*. 5th ed., edited by Graham White, 49–68. Toronto: University of Toronto Press, 1997.

Noel, S.J.R. *Politics in Newfoundland*. Toronto: University of Toronto Press, 1971.

Oliver, Michael, ed. *Social Purpose for Canada*. Toronto: University of Toronto Press, 1961.

Palmer, Howard. *Patterns of Prejudice: A History of Nativism in Alberta*. Toronto: McClelland and Stewart, 1982.

Palmer, Howard, and Tamara Palmer. *Alberta: A New History*. Edmonton: Hurtig, 1990.

Pawley, H. "The Two Party System." *Manitoban*, 20 September 1957.

Peperzak, Adrian. "From Intentionality to Responsibility." In *The Question of the Other: Essays in Contemporary Continental Philosophy*, edited by Arleen B. Dallery and Charles Scott, 3–22. Albany, NY: SUNY, 1989.

346   Bibliography

– Review of *Beyond Being* by Emmanuel Levinas. *Research in Phenomenology* 8 (1976): 239–61.

Pocock, J.G.A. *The Machiavellian Moment: Florentine Political Thought and the Atlantic Republican Tradition*. Princeton: Princeton University Press, 1975.

Posner, Zalman. *Think Jewish: A Contemporary View of Judaism; A Jewish View of Today's World*. Boston: Spring, 1997.

Preece, Rod. "The Anglo-Saxon Conservative Tradition." *Canadian Journal of Political Science* 13, no. 1 (March 1980): 3–32.

– "The Myth of the Red Tory." *Canadian Journal of Social and Political Theory* 1, no. 2 (1977): 3–30.

Quebec. *Québéc-Canada: A New Deal*. White paper on sovereignty association. Quebec, 1979.

Rayner, Jeremy. "The Very Idea of Canadian Political Thought: In Defence of Historicism." *Journal of Canadian Studies* 26, no. 2 (Summer 1991): 7–24.

Resnick, Philip. *The European Roots of Canadian Identity*. Peterborough, ON: Broadview, 2005.

– *Toward a Canada-Quebec Union*. Montreal and Kingston: McGill-Queen's University Press, 1991.

Rioux, Marcel. *Quebec in Question*, translated by James Boake. Toronto: James Lorimer, 1978.

Roazen, Paul, ed. Introduction to *The Necessity of Choice* by Louis Hartz, 1–24. London: Transaction Publishers, 1990.

– "Louis Hartz's Teaching." *Virginia Quarterly Review* 64, no. 1 (Winter 1988): 108–25.

Robin, Martin. *Pillars of Profit, 1934–72*. Toronto: McClelland and Stewart, 1973.

– *Radical Politics and Canadian Labour, 1880–1930*. Kingston: Industrial Relations Centre, Queen's University, 1968.

– *The Rush for Spoils: The Company Province, 1871–1933*. Toronto: McClelland and Stewart, 1972.

Rousseau, Jean-Jacques. "On the Social Contract." In *Jean-Jacques Rousseau: Basic Political Writings*, translated by Donald A. Cress, 141–227. Indianapolis, IN: Hackett, 1987.

Safarian, A.E. *Foreign Ownership of Canadian Industry*. Toronto: University of Toronto Press, 1973.

Salée, Daniel. "Quebec's Changing Political Culture and the Future of Federal–Provincial Relations in Canada." In *Canada: The State of the Federation 2001; Canadian Political Culture(s) in Transition*, edited by Hamish Telford and Harvey Lazar, 163–97. Montreal and Kingston: McGill-Queen's University Press, 2002.

Saul, John Ralston. *Reflections of a Siamese Twin: Canada at the End of the Twentieth Century*. Toronto: Penguin, 1998.

Schreyer, Ed. "Interview." *Winnipeg Tribune*, 5 July 1969.

Schwartz, Mildred. Review of *Canadian Labour in Politics* by Gad Horowitz. *Political Science Quarterly* 85, no. 4 (December 1970): 692–94.

Shain, Barry Alan. *The Myth of American Individualism: The Protestant Origins of American Political Thought*. Princeton: Princeton University Press, " 1994.

Shestov, Lev. *Athens and Jerusalem*. Athens: Ohio University Press, 1966.

Sissons, Jack. *Judge of the Far North: The Memoirs of Jack Sissons*. Toronto: McClelland and Stewart, 1968.

Smiley, Donald. "Essay in Bibliography and Criticism: Contributions to Canadian Political Science since the Second World War." *Canadian Journal of Economics and Political Science* 33, no. 4 (November 1967): 569–80.

– "Canada's Poujadists: A New Look at Social Credit." *Canadian Forum* 42, no. 500 (September 1962): 121–3.

Smith, Denis. *Ignatieff's World*. Toronto: James Lorimer, 2006.

Sniderman, Paul, Joseph F. Fletcher, Peter Russell, and Philip E. Tetlock. *A Clash of Rights: Liberty, Equality, and Legitimacy in Pluralist Democracies*. New Haven, CT: Yale University Press, 1996.

Sober, Elliott. "Evolutionary Altruism, Psychological Egoism, and Morality: Disentangling the Phenotypes." In *Evolutionary Ethics*, edited by Matthew H. Nitecki and Doris V. Nitecki, 199–216. Albany, NY: SUNY, 1993.

Sohn-Rethel, Alfred. *Intellectual and Manual Labour: A Critique of Epistemology*, translated by Martin Sohn-Rethel. London: McMillan, 1978.

Songy, Gaston. "Alexis de Tocqueville and Slavery: Judgments and Predictions." PhD dissertation, St Louis University, 1969.

Spivak, Gayatri C. *A Critique of Postcolonial Reason: Toward a History of the Vanishing Present*. Cambridge, MA: Harvard University Press, 1999.

– "Scattered Speculations on the Question of Value." In *The Spivak Reader: Selected Works of Gayatri Chakravorty Spivak*, edited by Danna Landry and Gerald Maclean, 107–40. New York: Routledge, 1996.

Swainson, Donald. "Ethnic Revolt: Manitoba's Election." *Canadian Forum* 583, no. 49 (August 1969): 98–9.

Taylor, Charles. *Philosophical Arguments*. Cambridge, MA: Harvard University Press, 1995.

– *The Pattern of Politics*. Toronto: McClelland and Stewart, 1970.

– *Reconciling the Solitudes*. Montreal and Kingston: McGill-Queen's University Press, 1993.

– Review of *Agenda 1970: Proposals for a Creative Politics* by Trevor Lloyd. *Canadian Journal of Political Science* 2, no. 3 (September 1969): 385–6.

Taylor, Charles. *Radical Tories*. Toronto: House of Anansi, 1982.

Telford, Hamish. "The Reform Party / Canadian Alliance and Canada's Flirtation with Republicanism." In *Canada: The State of the Federation 2001; Canadian Political Culture(s) in Transition*, edited by Hamish Telford and Harvey Lazar, 111–40. Montreal and Kingston: McGill-Queen's University Press, 2002.

Thomas, L.G. *The Liberal Party in Alberta, 1905–1921*. Toronto: University of Toronto Press, 1959.

Thorburn, H.G., and Alan Whitehorn, eds. *Party Politics in Canada*. 8th ed. Toronto: Prentice-Hall, 2001.

Tomlinson, Hugh, and Barbara Habberjam, trans. "Translators' Introduction." In *Bergsonism* by Gilles Deleuze, 7–10. New York: Zone Books, 1991.

Truman, Tom. "A Scale for Measuring a Tory Streak in Canada and the United States." *Canadian Journal of Political Science* 10, no. 3 (September 1977): 597–614.

Tully, James. "The Possessive Individualism Thesis: A Reconsideration in Light of Recent Scholarship." In *Democracy and Possessive Individualism: The Intellectual Legacy of C.B. Macpherson*, edited by Joseph Carens, 19–44. Albany, NY: SUNY, 1993.

Turner, Frederick Jackson. *The Significance of Sections in American History*. New York: Henry Holt, 1932.

Underhill, Frank, ed. *The Race Question in Canada*. Toronto: McClelland and Stewart, 1966.

Van Loon, Richard J., and Michael S. Whittington. *The Canadian Political System: Environment, Structure and Process*. Toronto: McGraw-Hill, 1971.

Vaneigem, Raoul. *The Revolution of Everyday Life*. 2nd ed., translated by Donald Nicholson Smith. London: Rebel, 1994.

Verter, Mitchell. "Levinas: For the Kids!" Paper presentation, second annual meeting of the North American Levinas Society, Purdue University, 11 June 2007.

Walton, Dawn, and Katherine Harding. "Can Alberta's Moderate Tories Take to 'Premier Ted Morton'?" *Globe and Mail*, 27 November 2006, A.

Whitaker, Reg. "Images of the State." In *The Canadian State: Political Economy and Political Power*, edited by Leo Panitch, 28–68. Toronto: University of Toronto Press, 1977.

Whitaker, Reginald. *The Government Party: Organizing and Financing the Liberal Party of Canada, 1930–58*. Toronto: University of Toronto Press, 1977.

Whittington, Michael S., and Richard J. Van Loon. *Canadian Government and Politics: Institutions and Processes*. Toronto: McGraw-Hill Ryerson, 1996.

Williams, George. "Mother Nature Is an Evil Old Witch." In *Evolutionary Ethics*, edited by Matthew H. Nitecki and Doris V. Nitecki, 217–32. Albany, NY: SUNY Press, 1993.

Wilson, John. "The Red Tory Province: Reflections on the Character of Ontario Political Culture." In *The Government and Politics of Ontario*, 2nd ed., edited by Donald C. MacDonald, 210–33. Toronto: Van Nostrand Reinhold, 1980.

Wiseman, Nelson. "A Note on 'Hartz-Horowitz at Twenty': The Case of French Canada." *Canadian Journal of Political Science* 21, no. 4 (December 1988): 795–806.

– "The Pattern of Prairie Politics." *Queen's Quarterly* 88, no. 2 (1981): 298–315.

– "Provincial Political Cultures." In *Provinces: Canadian Provincial Politics*, edited by Christopher Dunn, 21–62. Peterborough, ON: Broadview, 1996.

– *Social Democracy in Manitoba: A History of the CCF-NDP.* Winnipeg: University of Manitoba Press, 1983.

Wright, Robert. *The Moral Animal: Evolutionary Psychology and Everyday Life*. New York: Pantheon, 1994.

Young, Walter. Review of *Canadian Labour in Politics* by Gad Horowitz. *Canadian Historical Review* 50, no. 4 (1969): 86–7.

Zinn, Howard. "The New World: Fragments of the Old." *Nation*, 25 May 1965.

Žižek, Slavoj. *The Sublime Object of Ideology*. London: Verso, 1989.

Contributors

Edward G. Andrew is a professor emeritus in the Department of Political Science at the University of Toronto.

Ian Angus is a professor in the Department of Humanities and director of the Centre for Canadian Studies at Simon Fraser University.

Shannon Bell is a professor in the Department of Political Science at York University.

Colin J. Campbell is an instructor in the Department of Political Science at York University.

Oona Eisenstadt is Fred Krinsky Professor of Jewish Studies and an associate professor of religious studies at Pomona College.

Asher Horowitz is a professor in the Department of Political Science at York University.

Gad Horowitz is a professor emeritus in the Department of Political Science at the University of Toronto.

peter kulchyski is a professor in the Department of Native Studies at the University of Manitoba.

Michael Marder is Ickerbasque Research Professor of Philosophy at the University of the Basque Country, Vitoria-Gasteiz.

Robert Meynell is an independent scholar based in Toronto.

Jason Rovito is a doctoral candidate in the Joint Program in Communication and Culture at York and Ryerson Universities.

Sean Saraka is an independent scholar based in Boston.

Victoria Tahmasebi is an assistant professor in Women and Gender Studies at the University of Toronto Mississauga.

Nelson Wiseman is an associate professor in the Department of Political Science at the University of Toronto.